NEW YORK REVIEW BOOKS
CLASSICS

THE LIFE OF HENRY BRULARD

STENDHAL (1783–1842), the pen name of Henri Marie Beyle, was born into a prosperous family in Grenoble. At sixteen he set out for Paris, intending to pursue a career as an engineer, but instead enlisted in Napoleon's Army. Stendhal took part in campaigns in Italy, Germany, Russia, and Austria, and then, after Napoleon's fall from power, settled in Milan, where he wrote books on art and music. Expelled from Italy for political reasons in 1821, he returned to Paris; following the 1830 revolution, he secured the position, which he was to hold for the rest of his life, of French Consul to Civitavecchia. Stendhal's great novels *The Red and the Black* (1830) and *The Charterhouse of Parma* (1839) were largely ignored during his lifetime, and many of his works remained unfinished and were published only posthumously. Among his most important books are *On Love*, *Lucien Leuwen*, *The Memoirs of an Egotist*, and *The Life of Henry Brulard*.

LYDIA DAVIS is the author of several works of fiction, including *Break It Down*, *The End of the Story*, and, most recently, *Samuel Johnson is Indignant: Stories*.

THE LIFE OF
HENRY BRULARD

STENDHAL

Translated and with an Introduction by
JOHN STURROCK

Preface by
LYDIA DAVIS

NEW YORK REVIEW BOOKS

New York

This is a New York Review Book
Published by The New York Review of Books
1755 Broadway, New York, NY 10019

Library of Congress Cataloging-in-Publication Data

Stendhal, 1783–1842.
  [Vie de Henry Brulard. English]
  The life of Henry Brulard / Stendhal ; translated and with an
introduction by John Sturrock ; preface by Lydia Davis.
      p. cm.
  ISBN 0-940322-89-7 (alk. paper)
  1. Stendhal, 1783–1842. 2. Novelists, French—19th
century—Biography. I. Sturrock, John. II. Title.
  PQ2436.A2 V43 2002
  843'.7—dc21   2001006230

ISBN 0-940322-89-7

Book design by Lizzie Scott
Printed in the United States of America on acid-free paper.
10 9 8 7 6 5 4 3 2 1

January 2002
www.nybooks.com

CONTENTS

PREFACE

The other day I was listening to a program about astronomy on the radio, and in the space of about half an hour I learned at least five or six startling things, among them: that most meteors are no larger than a raisin; that a meteor the size of a grape would light up the entire sky as it descended; that if we could see him, a person poised on the edge of a black hole would appear, from the vantage point of the earth, to hover there indefinitely, frozen in time, whereas from the vantage point of the black hole itself he would be swallowed up instantly. Some of this was hard for me to understand, and while I was still agog with it, along came the next and most disturbing comment, one concerning the nature of time: there is, they said, a good deal of evidence suggesting that at the deepest level of reality, time as we are accustomed to imagine it does not actually exist, that we live in an eternal present.

If I can comprehend it at all, this idea is not a very comfortable one. I would prefer to think of objective time as an unbroken stream of equal intervals stretching infinitely far back and far forward; then I may peaceably watch subjective time as it defies measurement by behaving in its usual capricious, elastic, elusive manner, shrinking and expanding unexpectedly or collapsing in on itself. And this was my habit of thought before I heard the radio program and while I was engrossed in reading Stendhal's *Life of Henry Brulard*. For time is very much one of the subjects of this *Life*, which remarkably transfigures or transcends it, as Stendhal looks back at his past and speaks forward in time to his readers of the future, but also, by his manner of writing, brings those readers into what now seems to me, after the radio program, to be an eternal present.

Stendhal wrote this strangely fragmented, digressive, and yet beautifully structured pseudonymous memoir in four quick months over the winter of 1835–1836. He had written *The Red and the Black* five years earlier, in 1830; and he was to write *The Charterhouse of Parma* (another quick book, occupying the seven weeks from early November to late December) less than two years later, in 1838. At the age of fifty-three, he is looking back at the first seventeen years of his life, at the events of what we would call—and what he would recognize as—his "formative" years and subjecting them to a close examination and analysis "so as to work out what sort of man I have been."

Yet he is also looking ahead, contemplating and occasionally addressing the readers who will pick up his book in 1880, readers who, he thinks, may be more sympathetic to him than his contemporaries—though just as often, he frets that they will be intolerably bored by the minutiae of his life. "I have no doubt had great pleasure from writing this past hour, and from trying to describe my feelings of the time *exactly as they were*," he says, "but who on earth will be brave enough to go deeply into it, to read this excessive heap of *I*s and *me*s?"

He occasionally, even, looks beyond the readers of 1880 to those of 1900, 1935, and, surprisingly, our own 2000. He is not sure, he says, if the reader of the future will still be familiar with *Les Liaisons dangereuses* by Choderlos de Laclos—yes, we still know it, we would like to answer him. He believes the reader of 1900 and one hundred years later will certainly have a more enlightened understanding of Racine. Well, there we would probably disappoint him.

Whenever we read a book, of course, time, in a sense, collapses: we feel we are reading in the same moment the writer is writing, or that we cause him to speak, and as he speaks we hear him—there is no interval; and the converse, that we have only to stop reading for a moment, and he stops speaking. What immediate authority the handwritten message of a dead parent still has! And it is true that a reader is the necessary completion of the act of writing. Yet Stendhal's *Life*, more than most, jumps beyond the bounds of its time and tradition, speaks across nearly two centuries in an intensely personal voice.

How does it achieve such immediacy? And why is this minutely detailed tabulation by this irascible grumbler so appealing?

Certainly it shares some of the qualities of other eccentric autobiographical works that continue to strike us as fresh and new despite the passage of time (if time does indeed pass): Kafka's *Letter to His Father*, Cyril Connolly's *The Unquiet Grave*, J. R. Ackerley's *Hindoo Holiday*, Gertrude Stein's *Autobiography of Alice B. Toklas*, *Roland Barthes by Roland Barthes*, Rousseau's *Confessions*, Theresa Hak Kyung Cha's *Dictée*, Michel Leiris's *Rules of the Game*. For one thing, the style of *The Life of Henry Brulard* is plain and straightforward, conversational and direct. For another, it is full of keenly observed and striking detail—a room so cold the ink freezes on the tip of the pen, a dying man carried home on a ladder, clothes "smelling of the makers."

It is written with passion. Stendhal, like the narrator of a Thomas Bernhard novel, is terribly attached to his every feeling. He is just as furious today (at the time of his writing and our reading) as he was at age fourteen, when his greatest love was mathematics ("I fancy I said to myself: '*true or false, mathematics will get me out of Grenoble*, out of this mire that turns my stomach'") and he was endlessly frustrated by the complacency and hypocrisy of his teachers: what a shock, he says, "when I realized that no one could explain to me how it is that a minus times a minus equals a plus $(- \times - = +)$!" Further rage when no one will resolve another puzzle: is it or is it not true that parallel lines, when produced to infinity, will eventually meet?

Clear-eyed about his good points and bad, Stendhal aims for accuracy ("I am witty no more than once a week and then only for five minutes," he tells us), and what a complex and interesting person emerges from this self-examination. Stubborn, opinionated, cantankerous, yet brilliant, minutely observant, and appealingly fallible. Not an easy friend; someone in whose company one would be always on edge—he would be sure to pounce on any sign of fatuousness or mental sloth. Intellectually ambitious, and not merely concerning literature and politics: he still thinks he ought to study worms and beetles—"which nauseate me"—as he had intended to do while he was a soldier fighting under Napoleon.

He has much to say about memory because he is relying entirely on that unreliable faculty in his re-creation of his early years. There is a great deal, he tells us, that he had forgotten until the present moment of writing: things come back to him that he has not thought of for decades. He often says that a certain memory is obscured because of the great emotion he experienced at the time: the emotion wiped out the memory. He points out, further, that if he remembers this much of an event, he has also forgotten a great deal more, but that if he were to begin supplementing the truth with his imagination, he would be writing a novel and not a memoir. "I protest once again that I don't claim to be describing things in themselves, but only their effect on me."

Yet *The Life of Henry Brulard* has several even more unusual features. For one thing, there are the *aide-memoire* sketches, nearly two hundred of them, thin, spidery diagrams with scribbled explanations showing where young Stendhal was positioned in relation to others, in a room or on a mountainside, in a street or a square ("I clouted him with all my might at O"), and these sketches, minimal, crabbed, and repetitious as they are, oddly enough make his memories more real to us too.

For another, there is his abiding and multilayered pretense at self-concealment. He not only refers to himself at points as a certain overly loquacious "Dominique," but more significantly titles the book (on the title-pages of several sections of the manuscript) as *Life of Henry Brulard written by himself* and then describes it, for the benefit of "Messrs of the police," not as an autobiography but as a novel in imitation of the very bland and innocent *Vicar of Wakefield*. Now, all the layers of the self-concealment are quite transparent: he is not Henry Brulard, he is not writing a novel, and this book does not in any obvious way resemble Goldsmith's tale. It seems unlikely that he is making a serious effort to protect himself, or even that this is merely a sustained joke. It seems more likely that the man we obligingly refer to as Stendhal, but who was of course actually Henri Beyle, and who made a habit of adopting a variety of pseudonyms in his published writings, must have been more comfortable erecting a screen of fiction behind which he could give himself permission to write with utter sincerity. There is in fact a wonderful moment well into the book where the real and the fictional names are forcibly melded in an act of sheer impudence, when Stendhal refers to "the five letters: B,R,U,L,A,R,D, that form my name."

And then, the book appears to be unfinished. Certainly it is unusually rough. Passages of expansive, fully developed narrative will be followed by a succession of terse one-sentence paragraphs, fleeting afterthoughts, qualifications, or digressions inspired by his narration—and perhaps such brief paragraphs are a perfect representation of the disconnected way in which our thoughts sometimes move. Stendhal has left blank spaces in the text where he has forgotten a name or can't think of the right adjective. He has abbreviated words freely, motivated sometimes by haste and sometimes by (he says) a fear of censorship. He includes occasional cryptic private references and secret codes. He inserts reminders to himself throughout the text, usually in the margins, or corrects errors as he goes along (below a diagram: "Entrance steps or rather no entrance steps"). He repeats himself, twice asserting, for instance, that the only passions that have remained with him throughout his life (besides the desire to write and to live in Paris) are his love of Saint-Simon and of spinach. Other marginal notes describe his present state as he writes: "18 December 1835. At 4.50, not enough daylight. I stop.... From 2 to half-past 4, twenty-four pages. I am so absorbed by the memories unveiling themselves to my gaze I can scarcely form my letters."

And so it is a curiosity, an anomaly: the book appears rough, unfinished, and yet there are suggestions throughout that this may be just what its author intended. I would like to know—because if Stendhal meant to leave it as it is, he has in effect written a surprisingly modern book. Did he or didn't he plan to fill in the blank spaces, write out the abbreviated words, delete the notes to himself, and in general revise and rewrite to "smooth it out"? Reading with this question in mind, I came to a clue in a marginal note: "Idea. If I don't correct this first draft, perhaps I shall manage not to tell lies out of vanity." It would seem that this thought came to him only as he was writing. Not far away another clue appeared: "I'm well aware that all of this is too long, but I get amusement from finding these early if unhappy times reappear, and I ask M. Levavasseur to shorten it should he publish. H. Beyle." Apparently, at this point, he did not intend to go back and shorten it himself. Toward the end of the book, I came to another: "I shall perhaps have to reread and emend this passage, contrary to my intentions...." (The book ends with seven drafts of "Testaments" bequeathing the manuscript to a host of possible publishers, including the bookseller Levavasseur, with instructions to publish it fifteen years after Stendhal's death with all the women's names changed and none of the men's.)

Why is the fragmented, the rough, sometimes so much more inviting than the seamless, the polished? Because we are closer to the moment of creation? ("Handwriting," he notes in a margin. "This is how I write when my thoughts are treading on my heels. . . .") Because we are intimate witnesses to the formulation of the thought? Inside the experience of the writer instead of outside? Because we are closer to the evolution by which an event of the past, long forgotten —though evidently somewhere present in the brain cells of the writer—is reawakened, reimagined, re-presented, put into words? ("My heart is pounding still as I write this thirty-six years later. I abandon my paper, I wander round my room and I come back to writing.") As though we were taking part ourselves, involved in and identifying with the action, the action being in this case the re-creation and understanding of a life?

Perhaps, too, a work that comes to us so fresh, so raw, from the writer's mind is more exciting because we see how precarious is the writer's control—the material is almost more powerful than he is. As Stendhal himself says, it was the material—his ideas, his memories—that commanded him, not some "literary ideal." And so it is a work that changes as he writes it, that is full of his own discovery as he goes along; and for his own purposes, and to our delight, he notes the elaboration of this memoir even as he writes it.

At one point in his narration Stendhal refers casually to a moment later in his life when he was in mortal danger: alone in a Silesian field, he saw coming towards him a company of Cossacks. He does not go on to tell us what happened next. I wondered, as I continued reading, whether he was merely being artful and would satisfy my curiosity before the book ended. I suspected he would not, and he did not. His intention in the book, after all, is not to tell a dramatic story. Yet a different, and greater, drama unfolds as we read, because of the constant double surprise: being alongside him as he works, rather than being handed the result of a later revision, we surprise him in the very act of writing even as he surprises himself in the act of remembering and understanding. And so we are privileged to watch what is really the very dramatic moment, enacted again and again, of the unremembered or half-remembered being fully brought to mind, the unformed being formed, the internal becoming external, the private becoming public.

—LYDIA DAVIS

INTRODUCTION

In *The Life of Henry Brulard* one of France's greatest novelists looks ruthlessly back at his experience of childhood and adolescence: at seventeen years which he would have us know were ones for him of solid unhappiness. Stendhal's is the most unforgiving of autobiographies, long on resentment against his family, his hometown and his fellow-countrymen, and exceedingly short on charity; but it is also one of the most readable: throwaway in manner, full of droll asides and caustic judgments, and brilliantly lucid when reaching into the psychological depths of both its author and those around him. *Henry Brulard* has no truck with the gravity or good manners of so much nineteenth-century writing; indeed, it is hard to credit that it is a product of the 1830s.

But then it is the work of a man who was born in one century, who did his writing in another, but who thought he might find readers capable of appreciating him only in a third, and that our own century. Even more than most autobiographies, *Henry Brulard* was a book offered to futurity, to be published if at all only once its much misunderstood author was safely dead and out of reach of those he had wanted to malign. It may stand as a posthumous act of score-settling. Stendhal's literary executor was too taken aback by it to let it be published, and it appeared for the first time only in 1890, forty-eight years after its author's sudden death, of apoplexy, in a Paris street. Even then a nervous editor thought that the work's graceless style, if not its apparent nihilism, would be too much for sensitive readers, and groomed the manuscript accordingly.

Stendhal's idea that the future might take to him as a writer, even if the present did not, was prophetic: the future has taken to him. The iconoclastic philosophy and abrupt literary manner that were found either puzzling or rebarbative by his contemporaries will seem certainly familiar and perhaps congenial by someone reading *Henry Brulard* today. In this autobiography Stendhal makes the case for himself as a defiant anachronism, a man forced to live in, without in any sense belonging to, the 1830s. For someone of his passionate tastes the times were all wrong, they were venal, complacent, hypocritical: in a word, *bourgeois* (a term of condemnation Stendhal uses with all the venom of a Jean-Paul Sartre or other rumbustious left-winger of the 1950s and 1960s). As such, they allowed no scope for that glorious impetuosity in thought and deed which Stendhal held to as his ideal in life and to which in his young days he had been exposed in reality. For this now middle-aged autobiographer had been a child, first of the French Revolution and then of the Empire. Born in 1783, he had in his late teens and all through his twenties been a part of the great Napoleonic adventure. He had served the Emperor as a soldier and administrator, had known him personally, and had had dramatic, hazardous experiences of war, in Italy, in Germany and in Russia.

But all that ended in 1814: "I fell with Napoleon," he writes in *Henry Brulard*, meaning not only that with the Empire at an end he was suddenly unemployed, but that history at that moment had turned fatally against him. His uncompromising republicanism and cult of a heroic spontaneity were bound from now on to alienate him from the canny time-servers and careerists among whom he would have to live. To find, after 1815, a Bourbon king back on the throne of France, the reactionary Austrians occupying so much of his beloved northern Italy, and the bourgeoisie he had grown up hating in Grenoble everywhere imposing its contemptible values, this was too much for Stendhal, and his sense of being a stranger in his own country and his own time is a persistent motif of *Henry Brulard*. This is anything but a solemn book but it is a genuinely bitter one, being the partial life-story of someone at once proud and yet disturbed at feeling that he had been born and raised to be a man apart.

Henry Brulard was written in the winter of 1835–6, in haste; not because Stendhal lacked the time to take more trouble over it, but because as a writer he cultivated haste. It is an engagingly youthful book in reaffirming the insolent political and other opinions he had first adopted as a boy, but it was written by a man unhappily aware of being well advanced into middle age. "Is it really possible? Fifty! I am coming up to fifty...": this is Stendhal in the preamble, as if the thought of that dire anniversary had just now struck him, and was the inspiration he needed in order to begin. But *Henry Brulard* was not begun on the day when he claims that it was (a day when, as it happens, he wasn't even where he claims to have been, but travelling in the Abruzzi mountains). He started on it in truth three years later. By 1835, he was no longer coming up to fifty, he was past it; he, long ago the star mathematician of the Ecole Centrale in Grenoble, can work it out: born 1783, three from five leaves two, eight from three five, he is fifty-two and, committed hedonist that he is, gloomy at knowing that the years of pleasure are behind him.

Why then pretend, as he does in a speciously exact opening sentence, that it is still 1832 and that this very morning, October 16, he was enjoying the sunshine and the beautiful view from the Janiculum Hill in Rome? Partly to display what could best be called a studied negligence in respect of dates, which is very much part of *Henry Brulard*. Were he to give no dates at all he might be accused of "vagueness," a bourgeois failing that he links with hypocrisy, as a pet aversion. It is by developing a passion for mathematics and numbers that he has escaped from bourgeois Grenoble, and his autobiography is full of these gestures towards a mathematical precision. He gives dates, in plenty, but seldom with any assurance that they are the right ones. When was it exactly that his father died? Was it in 1819? That's what "they" say. Or the grandfather of whom he was fond and who comes so uncommonly well out of the story? Did he die in 1806, or was it 1813? It is beneath Stendhal to know boring details of this kind for certain. If it is Stendhal the hypocrisy-hating student of mathematics who inserts so many days, months and years into the text, it is Stendhal the impenitent dreamer, the student of *rêverie*, who wants us to know that such footling mundanities are not for him.

There is a second reason too I think why he should have begun *Henry Brulard* when and where he does, having to do with the place and not the date. The Janiculum Hill in Rome is a site entirely propitious to the kind of autobiography on which he is embarking. *Henry Brulard* is the most explicitly visual of all autobiographies (rivalled, if at all, only by Vladimir Nabokov's entrancing *Speak, Memory*). In it Stendhal "sees" his past, which returns to him in the form of "images" or, as I have sometimes translated them, "mental pictures." This graphic record is not open to contradiction: the pictures it contains are private and deemed to be utterly reliable. As Stendhal writes the "images" come crowding back, in such numbers and with such rapidity that he is hard put to keep up with them.

But a succession of "images" on its own cannot be the whole of the book: if the pictures represent the past, what of the present, the moment in time from which they are being seen? The present is the writer's opportunity to provide as it were the captions to the pictures, or to attempt from the vantage point of his maturity to explain scenes that have occurred many years before and which he would not have been able to explain at the time. *Henry Brulard* is peculiarly modern in trading as it does on the discontinuity in the writer's record of his past, which Stendhal likens to a fresco painted on plaster, portions of which have fallen away, exposing the bare brickwork. He is much too scrupulous to claim to be restoring this mural; all he will do is to try and "place" and comment on the surviving fragments of it, and in doing so to draw attention to the time which has elapsed between then and now. Always he stresses that his mental pictures *qua* pictures are not in doubt, whereas his attempts at their explanation may, for all he knows, be wide of the mark. This perhaps is his version of the old adage: "Trust the tale and not the teller."

But talk of "frescos" or of mental "images" is of necessity only talk: mental "pictures" are drawn metaphorically, with words, they are not real pictures. Stendhal, however, supports them in *Henry Brulard* with real images, in the form of the sketch-maps and diagrams that are scattered through the text and which depict the layout of the principal settings of his early life, both indoors and out.[1] There are more than 170 of them, quite crudely drawn and captioned as one would expect, but far from merely incidental to the verbal text in establishing the writer's private cartography. Some Stendhal drew in the margins of his manuscript, where he was much given to annotation, others on the reverse side of his paper. They have rightly become, as in this edition, an integral part of the finished work (the earliest editors of *Henry Brulard* were very wrong to leave them out), even if it isn't possible to reproduce them full-size or so as to make them properly legible.[2] If nothing else, the drawings should be valued as tokens

1. Into the Ms of *Henry Brulard* he also had bound reproductions of some twenty engravings made from works of art from the Italian Renaissance. These have no direct bearing on the text and have been omitted from the present edition.

2. The most thoughtful and informative study of these drawings is in Martine Reid's *Stendhal en images: Stendhal, l'autobiographie et "La Vie de Henry Brulard"* (Geneva: Droz, 1991). I am extremely grateful to Ms Reid for sending me a copy of her book, whose information and insights I have drawn on here.

of Stendhal's wish to display the objective *facts* in reconstructing his childhood and adolescence, a time of life famously open to distortion when looked back on and nowhere more so than in its remembered topography. Stendhal's scrawled maps are for him an *aide-mémoire* and for ourselves genuinely poignant in their particularity.

Where better then for the text of *Henry Brulard* to be made to originate than on the Janiculum Hill, a Roman viewpoint which does duty in space for the unwelcome eminence that Stendhal has now reached in time? For what he sees from the Janiculum is no common prospect: "This," he reflects, "is a place like no other in the world," for nowhere else can such grand remains of the ancient world be found forming a whole with the constructions of the modern world, "from the Appian Way with the ruins of its tombs and aqueducts to the magnificent garden of the Pincio built by the French." The historical and the contemporary, the Italian and the French: in this staged panorama Stendhal has sketched in the twin axes of his forthcoming subject-matter, as he juxtaposes his ancient self with his modern self of 1835, and his fidelity to Italy with his deep sense of alienation from his native France. As a narrative indeed, and despite all its many impulsive dartings forward in time, *Henry Brulard* may be said to tell the story of Stendhal's wilful exiling of himself, as he proceeds on his way from his birth in Grenoble in 1783 to his rapturous introduction to Italy in 1800, an event which comes freighted with the happiness he was to enjoy in Milan many years later, after 1814.

Strictly speaking, 1832 may be three years out as the date when Stendhal began to write *Henry Brulard*, but it wasn't a year chosen by him at random. For that indeed was when his thoughts had originally turned in a practical way towards autobiography. In the summer of 1832 he wrote his *Souvenirs d'égotisme* or "Egotistical Memories," as a first, less than orderly attempt at what he called an "examen de conscience," or inquiry into what manner of man he appeared to be on the strength of all that he had been through in his life so far. Unlike most autobiographers, he wanted in writing not to display self-knowledge but to acquire it and by determining, if he could, his own nature, to progress in the knowledge of humanity in general; he was launched on the definitive quest which was to be renewed three years later in *Henry Brulard*.

The *Souvenirs d'égotisme* are an agreeable but wandering mixture of the analysis of character, both his own and other people's, and anecdote, as he discharges his bile against the stupidity and illiberalism of the times. Nominally, they are a record of his life as a writer, literary journalist and dandified man about town in Paris during the decade of the 1820s. Stendhal had returned to Paris in 1821, following what he was ever afterwards to celebrate as six idyllic years spent living, writing and falling in love in Milan. This was the idealized North Italian city into which his first innocent entry as a seventeen-year-old recruit to Napoleon's army forms the culmination of *Henry Brulard* and to which he went expectantly back in 1814, after the fall of Napoleon and the restoration of King Louis XVIII had made Paris seem an irredeemably inhospitable home for him. (He didn't return during the Hundred Days, participation in which he left to his boyish surrogate Fabrice del Dongo, who in *The Charterhouse of Parma* sets instinctively off from Italy to fight for his hero Napoleon and then, in a celebrated episode of the novel, has to endure the confusion and eventual disaster of the battle of Waterloo.)

In Milan, Stendhal developed a love of Italian opera, Italian women and Italian art. And in the years during which he was based there he also became an author, publishing lives of the composers, Haydn, Mozart and Metastasio, his *Histoire de la peinture en Italie*, and an opinionated account of his travels elsewhere in Italy, *Rome, Naples et Florence*. But he left the city in 1821 in despair, having failed to consummate what he at the time regarded as the great love affair of his life, with the invincibly high-minded Métilde Dembowski, the estranged wife of a Polish general—in *Henry Brulard* she has to compete with three others for the position of the "greatest passion" of his life. But his defeat at the hands of Métilde was not wasted: it gave autobiographical substance to his famous treatise *On Love*, which was first published in 1822.

His last, melancholy leave-taking of her is nevertheless the inaugural event of the *Souvenirs d'égotisme*, in which Stendhal claims to have returned to Paris with a total capital of 3,500 francs and a determination to "blow my brains out" when that had been spent. But if he fancied the idea of suicide, the reality put him off; he decided to stay alive in Paris, partly out of "political curiosity" and partly out of a fear that suicide might actually hurt. He survived the 1820s well enough, full of contempt for the politics that were the object of his curiosity but a tireless frequenter of the Paris salons, in which he had learnt to excel, as a conversationalist known and quoted for his unusual opinions. The Stendhal of these years was by all accounts enjoyed by others for the unpredictability and sharpness of his tongue but not much liked by them: his foremost biographer, Michel Crouzet, describes his reputation in 1820s Paris as that of "an amusing mystery, a witty man who dazzled and alarmed, a being apart haloed in scandal, in outrage, in paradox: *someone* whom nothing could *contain*."

Stendhal the socialite himself believed that at a given moment in 1826 (or was it 1827? he is inclined as ever to vary the date), he became an *homme d'esprit* or "wit." However fanciful it may be to date it so precisely, this for him was an important rite of passage. What it meant was that he had finally, at the age of forty-three, found the *sang-froid* to improvise successfully when talking in the company of strangers, to be himself that is, and thus to cut a very different figure from the gauche and tongue-tied provincial he recalls himself in *Henry Brulard* as having been on his Parisian début a quarter of a century before. To be an *homme d'esprit* for Stendhal was to belong to the most estimable social caste of all, to the aristocracy of the quick of mind and tongue. To have "wit" is a good, regardless of whether you be well-born or as socially inferior as the local shoemaker's wife. Those who lack it form the vast and negligible class of wit-less dullards.[3]

Devoid of chronological impulsion as they are, the *Souvenirs d'égotisme* drift rather than progress through the Parisian decade which is their ostensible subject. They stop without warning, concluding in a typical marginal note by Stendhal to the effect that "the heat has taken away my thoughts at half-past one." The text runs to some 40,000 words and took him just fourteen days to write. *Henry Brulard*, which is three times as long, was begun on 23 November 1835, and brought to an end, or else allowed to lapse, very much in the style of the earlier manuscript, on 26 March of the following year, the marginal note this time recording that his *congé* has just been granted so that he can return to Paris: "The imagination flies off elsewhere: this work is broken off." In point of fact, it was several more weeks before he left Italy for Paris; but then why go on when he had just reached the high point of his first arrival in Milan? Broken off or not, *Henry Brulard* has a certain completeness, even though it touches only erratically on the experiences of its author's life after 1800.

I have said that Stendhal liked to write quickly. His first novel, *Armance*, which was published anonymously and to almost no acclaim in 1826, took him some nine days in

3. The terms *esprit* and *homme d'esprit* set problems for the translator of Stendhal. In his usage *esprit* seems to be as much "cleverness" as "wit," and the *homme d'esprit* as often a "clever man" as a "wit" in the Oscar Wilde sense, of a coiner of memorable aphorisms and quotable repartee. But I have preserved the word "wit" in the English wherever possible, in order to try and reflect the high status the term *esprit* has for Stendhal.

the original drafting; his masterpiece, *The Charterhouse of Parma*, by no means a short book, occupied him for fifty-three days in the winter of 1838–9. In the case of *Henry Brulard* he drew attention to the sustained urgency of its composition by keeping a record of the date as he went in the margins of the manuscript or by referring in the text itself to the number of sheets of paper he had just covered at one sitting. (Most of these marginal datings do not appear in the present edition, where they would make for too many footnotes; it is enough to know without having to be reminded that Stendhal liked to pace himself in this fashion.)

It was important to Stendhal not only to write quickly but for it to be known that he did so; it behoved a resolutely insouciant man such as himself not to be thought of as labouring over his writing. Hard work was not his thing; the creeping "industrialism" of the early nineteenth century he despised. Indeed, he complained of the English after a visit to this country that they worked too hard, and so offered a discreditable contrast to the Italians who, sensual southerners that they were, worked only as much as they absolutely needed to before reverting to their pleasures. Stendhal may have admired England for its liberal constitution and, most unusually for a Frenchman of his time, have admired Shakespeare as a dramatist infinitely freer in his language and staging than had been permitted to Racine, but he was a man temperamentally of the Catholic south, not of the cold, Protestant north, whose work ethic he found both unnatural and repellent.

"Style" in writing he had, literally, no time for; it was the product of a conscious effort and, as such, falsely ingratiating. Those who practise it—Chateaubriand is the most notable of the writers pilloried in *Henry Brulard*—are no better than hypocrites, because they mask their immediate feelings and impressions beneath the expensive tailoring of their prose. In reaction against what he saw as the hollow grandiloquence of Chateaubriand and his kind, Stendhal claimed to have modelled his own aggressively functional way of writing on the Code Civil, a corpus of legal statutes which makes no obvious concessions to grace or artistry. The prose of *Henry Brulard* is *echt*-Stendhal, bald and to the point, produced quickly and without benefit of second thoughts. To be true to oneself in writing, and to convey as exactly as possible the contents of one's mind, means, so far as Stendhal is concerned, avoiding all the habitual embellishments of literature and aiming to achieve the stylistic neutrality of what is sometimes referred to by French critics as *l'écriture blanche* or "blank writing." Than which, needless to say, no literary style could be more distinctive.

If "style" for Stendhal was something to avoid in writing, it came necessarily into living, because life as most of us are compelled to live it is seldom favourable to spontaneity. Stendhal was no hermit, he always meant to succeed in the world, starting as an ambitious schoolboy in provincial Grenoble who was determined to get himself to the capital. But whoever wants to succeed socially or politically or even artistically can hardly do so without having learnt a certain duplicity, whereby a calculating public self may be trained to provide a mask for the spontaneous private one. Stendhal may affect in *Henry Brulard* to despise worldly success as being available only to those who have sold their souls, but he had made his own way shrewdly enough in the world at times without too grievous a sacrifice of his integrity. He had learnt to play a part. Literally so, inasmuch as when he was a young man in Paris, on the make sexually if not socially, he had taken acting lessons, in order to overcome his timidity and acquire the technique of appearing "natural"! Against the misanthropic purist of *Henry Brulard*, who sees arrant hypocrisy wherever he looks, we need to set the heroes of his three great novels, Julien Sorel in *The Red and the Black*, Fabrice del Dongo, and Lucien Leuwen in the unfinished novel of that name, who for all their nobility of sentiment are well able to take on society at its own corrupt games and play the *arriviste*. These fictional heroes are embodiments of the *espagnolisme* that Stendhal ascribes in *Henry Brulard* to his great-aunt Elisabeth, a quality she has passed on to him. But what is a good in fiction has proved less so in life: it has, he says, taken him many years to stop dreaming extravagant dreams *à la* Don Quixote and to learn to endure the world as it really, ignobly is. But to endure it scornfully and without caring: that is the stoical creed of "beylisme," the philosophy of the man who took for a motto the acronym SFCDT, the initial letters of the words "se foutre carrément de tout," or "not to give a twopenny damn for anything."

In order to write, an autobiographer may abdicate temporarily from society and from the duplicitous rules it imposes on its members. Whether at work or at one's pleasures, it is not possible in company to be unfailingly oneself, even for a Stendhal, whose reputation was of a man revelling in his idiosyncrasy. In a social setting an absolute sincerity would be both freakish and unwelcome. Not so, however, in the seclusion into which the autobiographer has withdrawn. Sincerity indeed is the one justification which the sociable Stendhal can find for writing at such unsociable length about himself. How, other than by a promise to be utterly truthful, can he lift the curse from writing exclusively in the first person and of his own past life? The question is one he returns to several times in the course of *Henry Brulard*, but which he had already raised and answered at the start of the *Souvenirs d'égotisme*: "I am profoundly convinced that the one antidote that can make the reader forget the everlasting *I*s the author is about to write, is a perfect sincerity."

Like the *Souvenirs* before it, *Henry Brulard* begins not in confidence but in doubt, as if its author were engaged on a genuine and not a merely conventional quest for self-knowledge. In the opening pages Stendhal puts for a second time the leading questions appropriate to the kind of autobiographer he means to be: "What have I been? What am I?" Many autobiographers write as if they already knew the answers to these questions; they are sure they know both what they have been and what they are, and now they will tell us. For them the autobiographical quest is implicitly over even before it has begun. But Stendhal belongs to another, more sceptical and more sympathetic tradition of writing, the tradition of Montaigne, and of those who write about themselves, not because they are sure they know already what kind of person they are, but because they hope they may find out in the course of writing. This is the insistent refrain of *Henry Brulard*: I am discovering these things as I write. The memory which the writer prompts each new time he sits down at his table, and the gloss he provides for the "images" it delivers, will together remake a "life."

"What have I been? What am I?": taken together, these two questions impose a certain form on *Henry Brulard*. Stendhal wants to learn whether he is the same person now as he has always been, or whether great changes have taken place in his character since he was a boy in Grenoble. It is hardly surprising that he should quickly fall to declaring the constancy of his character, and not its fickleness, when the whole purpose of autobiography must be to consolidate, not to undermine whatever view the author may gather of himself. The middle-aged Stendhal delights in assuring us that he is unchanged, that "I am *encore* in 1835 the man of 1794" (the sentence is in English, for reasons I shall come to), or that he can now see that at the age of ten "I was in pursuit of happiness exactly as I am today: in other more common terms: my character was absolutely the same as today." The vivid memory which has given rise to this jubilant conclusion is of the joy he had felt on hearing the news of the execution of King Louis XVI in 1793. Forty-two years on from that event, which had so appalled his immediate family,[4] he is writing as a gloatingly unrepentant regicide, so turning the scrupulous gap which he observes throughout *Henry Brulard* between past and present to further advantage by flaunting cruel and radical opinions which are shocking now for the rather different reason that he knows he will be thought too *old* to be holding them. But other men, his contemporaries, his former schoolfriends, have mellowed and matured, that is, they have sold out, have lost their idealism, have become drearily prosperous bourgeois; Stendhal alone has not sold out, is as unbiddable as ever he was, is the *enfant terrible* who refuses to learn (and to earn).

In the 1830s, it was far from orthodox to suppose that the experiences of childhood and adolescence might be determining of the course of our later lives. The fatalistic doctrines of Sigmund Freud were half a century or more into the future. But then Stendhal was writing for the future, for the readers that he whimsically predicted he might find in 1880 or 1900 or even 1935, when the hostility or bafflement shown towards him by his contemporaries might have died with them. *Henry Brulard* fits extraordinarily well into the post-Freudian age, concentrating as it does on the early part of Stendhal's life, and on his relationships with the other members of the household, his father, his aunt, his grandfather, his great-aunt, his two sisters. There are numerous proleptic references to much more dramatic and imposing episodes in his life, notably during the Napoleonic wars, but it is the introverted setting of family and home which dominates *Henry Brulard* and makes of it a book more of our than of its own time.

It is the most suggestively Oedipal of all pre-Freudian autobiographies, a case-study almost of the now standard, if

4. One would hardly guess, from reading *Henry Brulard*, that Stendhal's native Grenoble was politically an unusually progressive place at the time of the French Revolution. For a less prejudiced view of it than his, see the pages on Grenoble in Simon Schama's virtuoso account of the Revolution, *Citizens* (Knopf, 1989), pp. 272–80.

questionable notion that the male infant must early on in his development turn blindly against the father as a hated rival for his mother's love. Stendhal's mother had died when he was seven years old, and this he looks on as the great, the formative disaster of his life, the precipitant of his sense of alienation within his family and later within the world as a whole. He doesn't hesitate to say that he had loved his mother and *Henry Brulard* reads as if it were in some sense a love-offering that he is making to her: interestingly, Stendhal began writing it on the November anniversary of her death. His love for his mother, which he remembers as having taken a very physical form, is opposed starkly to his dislike of his father and of his mother's sister, the Aunt Séraphie who plays so baleful a part in his childhood and with whom he suspects his widowed father of having fallen in love. Socially, the death of his mother has brought about a crippling isolation, because in their grief, his relations have broken off all ties with Grenoble society. The boy Stendhal is housebound, without friends of his own age, and is the victim of a domestic tyranny until such time as he is allowed to go to school. He paints a truly dark and deprived picture of these early years.

In fact, however, the darkness may have something to do with what had transpired between Stendhal and his father in the years after he left Grenoble. Chérubin Beyle did well financially during the Empire, but then ruined himself in foolish speculations, thus depriving his only son of the inheritance on which he had been banking. The contempt for money that Stendhal displays in *Henry Brulard* is far from disinterested: he could himself have done with more of it, especially by the time he came to write his autobiography, when he had been forced to take a job in the French consular service, only to find that he was being paid at the bottom rate despite his relatively advanced age. He had reason to begrudge his father's improvidence.

Oedipus complexes aside, Stendhal also presents himself

in *Henry Brulard* as party to a Freudian Family Romance, by tinkering with his ancestry so as to make it fit better with his needs. He doesn't go so far as to suggest that he wasn't really the son of Chérubin Beyle at all but of some more distinguished sire, but he plays down his father's side of the family so as to associate himself more closely with his beloved mother's side. The Beyles are presented as irredeemably French, resident in the Dauphiné since the Middle Ages. Stendhal has no love for the Dauphiné (apart from its mountains), the character of whose people he tells us a number of times is narrow, petty and calculating, the very opposite of generous or spontaneous.

The Beyles are not suitable to have intermarried with the Gagnons, that is, with his mother's family. This is a name Stendhal likes to imagine as deriving from the Italian Guadagni or Guadaniamo or Gagnoni, and to have been gallicized after an earlier bearer of it had fled to France following "some unimportant murder in Italy." It appeals to him to trace his origins back not just to an Italian but to a man sufficiently wild and lawless to have committed a murder—the "unimportant" is the only concession Stendhal is prepared to make to a conventional squeamishness in these matters. And in case there be any doubt that good, thick Italian blood flows in his veins, he finds Italianate features in the heads and faces of his Gagnon relatives (though his shrewish aunt Séraphie can only be seen as a disgrace to her family name). There is, sadly, no genealogical evidence that would confirm that the Gagnons once came from Italy; they seem to have been Provençal.

It is an unhappy fact that, Italophile or not, Stendhal was living in Italy when he wrote *Henry Brulard* and not enjoying it. Whenever he reverts in the book to his present situation, it is to complain about it. By 1835, he had been for five years the French consul in the small seaside town of Civitavecchia, to the north of Rome; a less than dedicated employee of the French foreign service, but an employee none the less. He had been obliged to take a regular job at the end of the 1820s, because he could no longer afford to live without one. He had a pension from his years of army and bureaucratic service under the Empire and he had made some, though not very much, money from his writing, both as a contributor to literary journals in Paris and London and as the author of books. But his books did not sell: *De l'amour* may today be treasured as a classic essay in the psychology of love, but in the first two years of its existence it sold a total of forty copies. By 1830, Stendhal's income as an author was negligible—indeed, over his whole lifetime, it is calculated that he earned less than 6,000 francs from his publications.

1830 was a year of crisis, in the political affairs of France as in Stendhal's fortunes. In the early part of that year he had been working on the first of his major novels, *The Red and the Black*, the story of the passionate but timid Julien Sorel, a country boy who is determined to find a social destiny that will match his dreams rather than the inglorious circumstances of his birth. Stendhal had also met Giulia Ranieri, a patrician young woman from Siena whom he might well have ended by marrying, had her guardian not objected to him as a suitor: she was the one woman to whom he is known to have proposed, an indication no doubt that the ageing aficionado of love was beginning to fear loneliness. But then, at the end of July 1830, as he was in the middle of correcting the proofs of his novel, there occurred the July Revolution, the three days of quite modest yet momentous disturbance in the streets of Paris which brought to an end the reign of the last Bourbon king, Charles X, and installed in his place the Constitutional Monarchy of King Louis-Philippe. In *Henry Brulard* Stendhal refers to his own role of interested spectator in Paris as shooting started in the Palais-Royal. As an unregenerate republican (or anarchist), he of course would have preferred no king at all, but was realist enough to see that the new regime would be friendlier in its patronage of liberals like himself than the one that had ended. He lost no time in approaching it for a post. He was hoping he might be given a prefecture in France itself, perhaps in Brittany. Instead, he was offered the consulship in Trieste.

Trieste was at that time in the possession of Austria, and the Austrians had no more liking for Stendhal than he for them. He had fallen foul of them in Milan, also then an Austrian city, where he had finally been declared *persona non grata* in 1827, on the grounds that he was a well-known liberal, which was true, and a dangerous political agitator, which was not. He had associated there with enemies of the Habsburg regime, notably the intrepid Métilde Dembowski, but there is no record of his having been an activist. But the Austrian authorities now objected to his coming to Trieste as consul, and after only a very few months there Stendhal was posted south to Civitavecchia, where he was to remain on and off until the end of his life, eleven years later. Politically speaking, Civitavecchia was no more congenial to him than Trieste; it belonged not to Austria but to the Papal States, and the Vatican was none too pleased that the new French consul should be this determined libertine, republican sympathizer and religious unbeliever.

Stendhal survived there, though it may well be that he would have preferred a flattering expulsion as a political undesirable to the boredom and solitude by which he was afflicted in a small town that had none of the comforts he had enjoyed of old in Milan. He took to neither the work he was expected to do nor the company he was forced to keep, and had no greater enemy than the chancellor in the consulate, with whom he was constantly at loggerheads. Readers of *Henry Brulard* can be in no doubt as to his detestation of Civitavecchia. What is less clear from the book is how frequently Stendhal managed to be absent from his consulate, either in Rome, where he found himself a *pied-à-terre* and where music and more intelligent company were to be had, or travelling elsewhere in Italy. In all, he was absent from Civitavecchia for four and a half years out of the eleven that he should by rights have spent there—between 1836 and 1839 he used his influence in high places in Paris to secure an extraordinary paid leave of three years, a generous break he took advantage of as it was coming to an end to write and to publish *The Charterhouse of Parma*.

It is a painful thought that the mind capable of elaborating in a month and a half the social, political and psychological ingenuities of that wonderful novel should then have had to sink back into the bureaucratic nothingness and tedium of Civitavecchia, which from now on Stendhal was to find it harder to escape. The man capable of writing the *Charterhouse*, or *Henry Brulard*, was assuredly not cut out for the dim routine of an office, nor for the bland evasions called for from a diplomat. What he craved in the desert of Civitavecchia was the stimulus of the salon, or some urbane milieu in which he could practise his wit and his love of paradox. What wonder then that he should there have turned to autobiography, for the autobiographer is a writer who works in solitude at the presentation of himself to an imaginary society—and no autobiographer was ever more anxious than Stendhal in *Henry Brulard* to address his readers directly, as if he were speaking to them face to face rather than writing.

The experience of Civitavecchia didn't cure him of his passion for Italy. Even the title he gave to his autobiography pays an oblique homage to the country, or to the anachronistic idea that Stendhal held of it. Each section of the manuscript has its own rather different title-page (see p. xxxix of this edition), but common to all three of them is the title: *The Life of Henry Brulard written by himself*. This surely was meant to echo the title found for the memoirs of the great Renaissance sculptor and silversmith, Benvenuto

Cellini, *The Life of Benvenuto Cellini written by himself.* For Stendhal, Cellini was an ideal figure, someone who had been an artist but also a fearless, outrageously egotistical man of action, for whom the odd "small murder" would have been nothing. He was ideal too in a less obvious way, as an autobiographer: Cellini's *Life* was written in the middle of the sixteenth century but not published for the first time until near the end of the eighteenth; in Stendhal's time it was very much a new book. The delay of more than two centuries between its writing and its publication Stendhal takes for an assurance that his autobiography too may survive unpublished for many years and then be launched dramatically into public view. The series of comical "Testaments" that he left with the manuscript (see p. 489), containing his instructions for whoever might one day decide to publish *Henry Brulard,* are delightful, but they are more than just a joke: they are Stendhal's typically unconcerned way of letting us know that he is much concerned with futurity.

The question must arise: how can a book bearing the title *The Life of Henry Brulard written by himself* be offered as his autobiography by an author whose name is not Henry Brulard? This goes against the rules, because an autobiographer above all has no business publishing under an alias. Nor is the pretence that *Henry Brulard* is the life-story of someone of that name kept up for long in the text itself. Stendhal appears there a few times as Henry Brulard but more often under his true family name of Henri Beyle (not forgetting one or two textual appearances as the mysterious "Dominique"). This patronymic he found so unattractive he never once published under it, preferring instead to write under an extraordinary and mystifying variety of pseudonyms. To understand the lengths to which this compulsive taste for authorial disguise went, you need only look up the entry for Beyle (Henri) in the index of names in the scholarly Pléiade edition of his autobiographical writings, where you are faced with this copious list:

See the pseudonyms: BANTI (Henri-Clarence), FAIR-MONTFORT (Octavien-Henri), LEIMERY, SEYMOURS, LE BOURLIER, DOMINIQUE, MYSELF, L. (colonel), CERANUTO, d'AVERNEY, LERY (M. de), CHARLIER (Is. Ich.), COSTE, BOMBET (Louis-César-Alexandre), BARETT, AUBERTIN, l'ANIMAL, l'évêque d'EGRAH, STENDHAL, BLIARCE, JACQUES, BRULARD (Henry), DARLINCOURT.

And even this pales compared with the number of aliases Stendhal appears under in his correspondence, experts on which now claim to have located some 350 of them. The horror he expresses in *Henry Brulard* of the first-person pronouns was clearly a rare source of invention for him.

The false name of Henry Brulard is not arbitrary, any more than the false date at which he claimed to have begun writing the book. It is an alias doubly indicative of his wish not to be who he in point of fact was. The spelling of Henry with a *y* instead of an *i* makes him appear a little bit English, a *gentleman* if not quite a *milord*. The substitution of the name Brulard for Beyle places him firmly on his mother's side of the family, where there had, earlier in the eighteenth century, been a Father Brulard, an "astute," sybaritic monk. The physical resemblance between the infant Henri Beyle and this "uncle or great-uncle" has been remarked upon by his grandfather, according to Stendhal, who uses it to prove his own innate allegiance to the Gagnon side of things and dissociation from the Beyles. And to a French ear or eye the name Brulard will seem to derive from the verb *brûler*—"to burn" —and to have ardent connotations entirely in keeping with the character that Stendhal ascribes to himself of a fiery young dreamer born to quite the wrong father.

The spelling of the name Henry is only the first of a number of resorts made by him in *Henry Brulard* to the English language. There is a scattering of English phrases in the text and now and again a whole sentence in English. Stendhal's is a fractured English, seldom if ever grammatically correct, and resorted to for very Stendhalian reasons. He does not use it because he believes that for certain thoughts English is more precise or expressive than French; on the contrary: he uses it most often in order to achieve a playful disguise for a thought which he wants us to suppose would be too brazen, or politically risky, were he to write it in French. He is playing a game with the censorship, even if there is no likelihood of a censor ever reading what he is writing. The use of English goes with his suggestion on his proposed title-page that *Henry Brulard* is not an autobiography but a "novel imitated from *The Vicar of Wakefield*," a charmingly unlikely suggestion aimed at throwing "Messrs of the police" off the scent. Stendhal seems never to have outgrown this love of conspiracy and of codes, though when it came to the real thing he proved spectacularly incompetent—as a diplomat in Civitavecchia he contrived to enclose the key along with his coded despatches when he sent them back to his superiors in Paris.

And so it is in *Henry Brulard*, where the disloyal remarks he makes in English about the current regime in France would hardly be found impenetrable by a French censor. Stendhal's mystifications are intended to amuse, not to defeat his readers. "I am *encore* in 1835 the man of 1794": in this less than coded sentence a portly, ageing, melancholy Frenchman in Italy declares his undying loyalty to the most ferocious principles of the 1789 Revolution, and does so in a form that underlines how very different he believes himself to be from all other Frenchmen, whose language at this point he disdains to share. There indeed speaks Henri Beyle, an autobiographer who has no time for the fallen bourgeois world, who despises his compatriots, but who digs deep into himself and his past in order to try and discover why this should be so—to our own vast benefit and pleasure as his future readers.

—JOHN STURROCK

A NOTE ON THE TRANSLATION

The French text used here is that of the definitive 1982 Pléiade edition of *Henry Brulard*, edited by Professor V. Del Litto, of whose magnificently full notes in that edition I have also made use. Those words and phrases which appear in the original in Stendhal's English appear in this translation in small capitals, THUS. Stendhal's own footnotes or additions to the main text are marked with symbols; my own explanatory footnotes are marked with arabic numerals, or occasionally inserted within Stendhal's notes in brackets and introduced by the word *trans*. The words or bits of words appearing in square brackets reproduce the editorial interpolations of the Pléiade edition; I have kept some though not all of these, in order to preserve the impression of haste and nonchalance so characteristic of Stendhal's prose.

I am grateful for items of help given to me in making this translation by Alison Finch, Douglas Johnson and Richard Holmes.

—J.S.

TITLES[1]

LIFE OF H[ENR]Y BRUL[ARD]
written by himself.
LIFE. Nov[ember 18]35.

———

LIFE OF HENRY BRULARD
written by himself. Novel imitated from
The Vicar of Wakefield.

To Messrs of the Police.
This is a novel imitated from the *Vicar of Wakefield.*
The hero, Henry Brulard, writes his life, at the age of fifty-two,
after the death of his wife, the celebrated Charlotte Corday.[2]
Beginning of the work volume I. I, Henry Brulard wrote what
follows in Rome between 1832 and 1836.

———

1. These are the various title-pages for the first three "volumes" of his autobiography, as included by Stendhal in the Ms.

2. The celebrated assassin of the French Revolutionary leader, Marat; she was guillotined in 1793. The implication of this sardonic claim to kinship by Stendhal is that he is perfectly respectable politically as having been the husband of so heroic a reactionary.

VOLUME II
LIFE OF HENRY BRULARD
written by himself, a moral novel.

To Messrs of the Police, nothing political. The hero of this
novel ends by becoming a priest like Jocelyn.[3]

LIFE OF HENRY BRULARD
written by himself, volume two.

Novel imitated from the *Vicar of Wakefield*
above all in the purity of its sentiments.

LIFE OF H[ENR]Y BRULARD
VOLUME III.

Third volume begun 20 January 1836 at page 501,
finished 10 March 1836 at Civita-Vecchia at 796.
Life of Henry Brulard, written by himself. Novel of
details, imitated from the *Vicar of Wakefield*.

To *Messieurs* of the Police.
Nothing political in this novel. The scheme is a hothead of
every kind who grows weary and slowly sees the light and ends
by devoting himself to the cult of luxurious town-houses.

---

3. The priest-hero of a long poem by Alphonse de Lamartine, published in 1836. The
religiose and sentimental Lamartine was not a writer admired by Stendhal.

THE LIFE OF
HENRY BRULARD

CHAPTER 1

This morning, 16 October 1832, I found myself at San Pietro in Montorio, on the Janiculum Hill in Rome; it was gloriously sunny.[1] A light, barely perceptible sirocco was causing a few small white clouds to float above Monte Albano, the air was filled with a delightful warmth; I was happy to be alive. I could make out Frascati and Castel Gondolfo perfectly, four leagues off, and the Villa Aldobrandini which has Domenichino's sublime fresco of Judith. I can see perfectly the white wall marking the most recent restorations made by Prince F[rançois] Borghese, the very same whom I saw at Wagram as a colonel in the cuirassiers on the day my friend, M. de Noue, had his leg* taken off.[†] In the far distance, I can see the rock of Palestrina and the white house of Castel San Pietro which was once its fortress. Below the wall against which I'm leaning are the big orange-trees in the orchard of the Capuchins, then the Tiber and the Priory of Malta, a bit further on on the right the tomb of Cecilia Metella, San Paolo and the Pyramid of Cestius. Facing me I see Santa Maria Maggiore and the long

1. These words were in fact written in 1835; on the date in question Stendhal was not even in Rome. It was the *idea* of writing his "Memoirs" which seems to have come to him in 1832.

*To be fitted in.

  1790. Federation of the Champ-de-Mars. Seen in Gr[enoble] from the p[lace Grenette].

  1791. Anxiety of the family. Flight to Varennes.

[†] *Book* begun 23 November 1835.

  Table of contents to guide myself a little (analysis of the chapters shown opposite).

  Chapter 1. I, Henry Brulard, wrote what follows in [Rome] from 1832 to 36.

lines of the palace of Monte-Cavallo. The whole of Rome, ancient and modern, from the ancient Appian Way with the ruins of its tombs and aqueducts to the magnificent garden of the Pincio built by the French, is spread out in front of me.

This is a place like no other in the world, I mused to myself, and in spite of myself ancient Rome won over modern Rome, my memories of Livy all coming crowding back. On Monte Albano to the left of the monastery I could see the fields of Hannibal.

What a magnificent view! It is here then that Raphael's "Transfiguration" was admired for two and a half centuries.* How different from the miserable grey marble gallery where it is interred today in the depths of the Vatican! So, for two hundred and fifty years that masterpiece has been here: two hundred and fifty years! In three months I shall be fifty; is that really possible? 1783, 93, 1803; I'm counting it out on my fingers. And 1833: fifty. Is that really possible? Fifty! I'm going to be fifty, and I was singing the aria from Grétry: "Quand on a la cinquantaine."[2]

This unforeseen discovery didn't in the least annoy me, my mind had been on Hannibal and the Romans. Greater men than I have died indeed! After all, I told myself, I haven't made such bad use of my life. *Use!* Ha! That's to say, chance hasn't dealt me too many misfortunes, for, truth to tell, have I even begun to direct my life?

To go and fall in love with Mlle de Griesheim! What had I to hope for from a high-born young lady, the daughter of a general in favour two months earlier, before the battle of Jena? Brichard was quite right when he told me with

---

*To be checked.

2. "When one gets to be fifty": the aria is from a comic opera called *La Fausse Magie*, with music by André Modeste Grétry (1741–1813). In fact, "fifty" should be "sixty," the aria starting "Quand on a la soixantaine."

his usual malice: "When you love a woman, you say to yourself: 'What do I want from her?'"

I sat down on the steps of San Pietro and there I mused on this idea for an hour or two. I'm going to be fifty, it's high time I knew myself. What have I been? What am I? The truth is, I'd be very hard put to say.

I pass for a man of much wit, very unfeeling, a roué even, and I find I have been constantly preoccupied with unhappy love affairs. I loved Mme Kubly, Mlle de Griesheim, Mme de Dipholtz, Métilde, to distraction, but I didn't possess them, and several of these amours lasted three or four years. Métilde took over my life totally from 1818 to 1824. And I'm not cured yet, I added, after having mused on her alone for a full quarter of an hour perhaps. Did she love me?

I was moved and [*several illegible words*]. And Menti, into what grief did she not plunge me when she left me! Thereupon I shuddered at the thought of 15 September 1826, in Saint-Omer, on my return from England. What a year I spent from 15 Sep 1826 to 15 Sep 1827! On the day of that fearful anniversary I was on the island of Ischia; and I observed a perceptible improvement: instead of pondering my misfortune directly, like a few months earlier, I now pondered only the *memory* of the unhappy state into which I had been plunged in October 1826, for example. This observation consoled me greatly.

What then have I been? I can't know. Of which friend can I ask that, however enlightened? M. Di Fiori himself couldn't give me an opinion. To which friend have I ever said a word about my disappointments in love?

And what is singular and very unfortunate, I was telling myself this morning, is that my *victories* (as I called them at the time, my head being filled with military matters) didn't cause me a pleasure one half as great as the profound unhappiness my defeats caused me.

My astonishing victory over Menti didn't cause me a

pleasure comparable to the hundredth part of the pain she caused me by leaving me for M. de Rospiec.

Was I sad by nature then? . . . Whereupon, not knowing what to say, I began unthinkingly to admire once more the sublime sight of the ruins of Rome and of its modern grandeur: the Coliseum facing me and beneath my feet the Farnese Palace with the arches of Carlo Maderno's* lovely open gallery, the Corsini Palace beneath my feet.

Have I been a witty man? Did I have a talent for anything? M. Daru used to say I was as ignorant as a carp; yes, but it was Besan[çon] who reported that to me and the cheerfulness of my character made that morose former secretary-general very jealous. But was I cheerful by nature?

Finally, I only descended from the Janiculum when the light evening mist arrived to warn me I would soon be seized by the sudden and very disagreeable and unhealthy cold which in these parts immediately follows the setting of the sun. I hurried to get back to the *palazzo* Conti (*piazza Minerva*); I felt exhausted. I was in trousers of white English [*a blank*]; inside the waistband I wrote: "16 Octobre 1832. Je vais avoir la cinquantaine," abbreviated thus so as not to be understood: "J. vaisa voirla 5c."[3]

In the evening, returning somewhat bored from the ambassador's soirée, I said to myself: "I ought to write my life, perhaps in the end, when it is finished in two or three years' time, I shall know what I've been, cheerful or sad, a witty man or a fool, a man of courage or fearful, in sum happy or unhappy in fact, I can get M. Di Fiore to read the manuscript."

The idea appealed to me. Yes, but the terrible quantity of *I*s and *Me*s! That would be enough to put the most well-

---

*To be checked. [*trans.* In fact, it is uncertain whether the architect Carlo Moderna (1556–1629) had anything to do with building the Farnese Palace.]

3. This is one of Stendhal's simplistic codes for disguising what he wanted to say, involving altering the normal word divisions.

disposed reader's back up. *I* and *Me*, talent aside, that would be like M. de Chateaubriand, that king of the *egotists*.[4]

De *je* mis avec *moi* tu fais la récidive . . .[5]

I say this line to myself every time I read a passage by him.

It is true one might write using the third person: *he* went, *he* said. Yes, but how to take account of the inner movements of the soul? It's on this above all that I would like to consult Di Fiore.

Only now, 23 November 1835, do I continue. The same notion of writing MY LIFE came to me lately on my journey to Ravenna; truth to tell, I've had it many times since 1832, but I have always been put off by the awful problem of the *I*s and *Me*s, which would turn people against the author, I don't feel I have the talent to get round it. Truth to tell, I am very far from certain that I have the talent to get myself read. I sometimes find great pleasure in writing, and that's all.*

4. François René de Chateaubriand (1768–1848) was in turn soldier, explorer, diplomat, politician and above all author, especially of the magnificent *Mémoires d'Outre-tombe*, published after his death. Stendhal despised him for being a Christian, a reactionary and a particularly fulsome stylist—see his scornful remarks a little further on concerning Chateaubriand's *Génie du christianisme*.

5. Literally, "Of *I* put with *me* you are guilty again . . ." This is an adaptation of a line from Molière which actually reads: "De pas mis avec rien tu fais la récidive."

*Instead of all this chitchat, perhaps this will suffice: Brulard (Marie-Henry), born in Grenoble in 1786, into a good bourgeois family with claims to nobility, there were no prouder aristocrats nine years later in 1792. He was witness early on to the spite and hypocrisy of certain people, whence his instinctive hatred for [rel]ig[ion]. His childhood was happy up until the death of his mother, whom he lost at the age of seven, then the pr[iests] made it into a hell. To escape he studied mathematics passionately and in 1797 or 98 carried off the first prize, while five pupils, who two months later passed into the Ecole Polytechnique, didn't get the second. He arrived in Paris the day following the 18 Brumaire (Nov 9 1799), but took good care not to sit the examination for the Ecole Polytechnique. He left with the army of reserve for the love of it and crossed the Saint-Bernard two days after the First Consul. On his arrival in Milan, M. Daru, his cousin, at that time an *inspecteur aux revues* in the army, got him into the Sixth Dragoons as a serg[eant] and soon as a sub[altern], of which M. Le Baron, his friend, was the colonel. In his regiment B., who had an allowance of 150fr a month and claimed to be rich, he was seventeen years old, was envied and not very

If there is another world, I shan't fail to go and call on Montesquieu,[6] if he says to me: "My poor friend, you had no talent whatsoever," I shall be angry but in no way surprised. I often feel this, what eye can see itself? It's not three years since I discovered the *reason why*.

I can see clearly that many writers who enjoy great renown are detestable. What it would be blasphemy to say today about M. de Ch[ateau]briand (a sort of Balzac[7]) will be a TRUISM in 1880. My opinion of this Balzac has never altered; on its appearance around 1803, I found the *Génie du ch[ristianisme]* ridiculous. Crozet was seduced on the Mont-Cenis with M. Darrien. But is it to have talent to be aware of the defects of others? I see the worst painters seeing one another's defects very clearly: M. Ingres is quite right against M. Gros, and M. Gros against M. Ingres. (I choose those who will still be being talked about perhaps in 1935.)

Here is the reasoning which has reassured me with respect to these memoirs. Supposing I go on with this manuscript and that, once written, I don't burn it; I shall bequeath it not to a friend who may get religion or sell out to a party like that

well received; however he got a fine certificate from the army council. One year later, he was aide-de-camp to the brave Lt Gen. Michaud, took part in the Mincio campaign against Gen. Bellegarde, passed judgment on the folly of Gen. Brune and had delightful spells of garrison duty in Brescia and Bergamo. Obliged to leave General Michaud, because you needed to be at least a lieutenant to carry out the functions of an aide-de-camp, he rejoined the Sixth Dragoons at Alba and Savigliano (Piedmont), contracted a fatal illness in Saluces; bled fourteen times, ridiculous escapade with a great lady.

Bored by his comrades, in suede breeches, B. went to Gr[enoble], fell in love with Mlle Victorine M[ounier], and took advantage of the brief peace to resign his commission and go to Paris, where he spent two years of solitude, thinking only of amusing himself by reading the *Lettres Persanes*, Montaigne, Cabanis, Tracy, and in point of fact completing his education.

6. Charles de Secondat, Baron de la Brède et de Montesquieu (1689–1755), celebrated chiefly as a political scientist and as the author of *L'Esprit des lois*, in which he argued for the separation of the powers and a liberal constitution.

7. The Balzac in question is Guez de Balzac (1597–1654), for Stendhal the archetype of an over-ornate and affected writer.

jean-sucre[8] Thomas Moore; I shall bequeath it to a bookseller, to M. Levavasseur for example (Place Vendôme, Paris).

There is a bookseller then who, once I am gone, receives a fat bound volume in this detestable handwriting. He will get some small part of it copied and will read it; if he finds the thing tedious, if no one is talking about M. de S[tendh]al any longer, he will abandon the whole jumble of papers to be rediscovered perhaps two hundred years later like the *Memoirs* of Benvenuto Cellini.

If he prints and the thing is found tedious, it will be talked of after thirty years the way we talk today of *La Navigation*, the poem by the spy d'Esménard about whom there was so much discussion at M. Daru's lunch-table in 1802. And yet this spy was, I fancy, the censor or editor of all the newspapers which *poffed* him (from TO PUFF) to excess each week. He was the Salvandy of those days, even more impudent if that is possible, but with many more ideas.[9]

My confessions won't exist therefore thirty years after they are printed, if readers find the *I*s and *Me*s too tiresome; all the same I shall have had the pleasure of writing them and of conducting a thorough examination of my conscience. Moreover, if they are a success, I run the chance of being read in 1900 by the souls I love, the Mme Rolands,[10] the Mélanie Guilberts,[11] the [*a blank*].

8. This is a coining of Stendhal's own, of uncertain force. It is presumably his version of *jean-foutre*, a contemptuous vulgarism equivalent to "moron" or "stupid bugger." But the *sucre* ("sugar") introduces a suggestion also of hypocrisy, that first of all Stendhalian vices.

9. Count Narcisse-Achille de Salvandy (1795–1856), author and politician and for Stendhal the typical literary intriguer and *arriviste*.

10. Mme Roland de la Platière (1754–1793), who before the Revolution had had a politically influential salon in Paris and who died very courageously on the scaffold during the Terror.

11. Mélanie Guilbert (1780–1828), an actress whom Stendhal followed to Marseille and lived with there in 1805–6.

For example, today, 24 November 1835, I have come from the Sistine Chapel where I derived no pleasure at all, though equipped with a good glass for looking at the ceiling and Michelangelo's *Last Judgment*; but an excess of coffee committed the day before yesterday at the Caetanis, to be blamed on a machine brought back from London by Mi[chel]angelo [Caetani], led to an attack of neuralgia. The machine was too good. The coffee was too excellent, a bill of exchange drawn on my future well-being for the sake of the present moment, and brought my old neuralgia on again, and in the Sistine Chapel I was like a sheep, *id est* without pleasure, my imagination was unable to take wing. I admired the gold brocade drapery, painted al fresco, next to the throne, i.e. the Pope's large walnut-wood armchair. This drapery bears the name of Sixtus IV, Pope (*Sixtus IIII Papa*), you can touch it with your hand; it's two feet away from your eye but still creates an illusion after three hundred and fifty-four years.

Being no good for anything, not even for writing the official letters of my trade, I've had a fire lit and I'm writing this, without being untruthful I hope, without harbouring any illusions, with pleasure like a letter to a friend. What will that friend's ideas be in 1880? Very different from our own! Today, these two ideas are highly indiscreet, an outrage for three-quarters of my acquaintance: the "most scoundrelly of Kings," "the hypocritical Tartar," applied to two names I don't dare write[12]; in 1880 these verdicts will be TRUISMS that even the Kératrys[13] of the day will no longer dare repeat. This is new for me: to speak to people of whose cast of mind, whose style of education, whose prejudices and religion I am wholly ignorant! What an encouragement to be *truthful* and nothing but *truthful*, that's all that counts. Benvenuto was *truthful*

12. The two names are those of the current French king, Louis-Philippe, and the tsar of Russia, Nicholas II.

13. Auguste-Hilarion de Kératry (1769–1859), novelist and politician and, for Stendhal, another contemptible literary intriguer.

and we follow him with pleasure, as if it had been written yesterday, whereas we skip the pages of that jesuit Marmontel, who like a true academician yet takes all possible precautions not to give offence.[14] I refused to buy his *Memoirs* in Leghorn at twenty *sous* the volume, even though I adore writings of that kind.

But how many precautions does one not need to take to avoid being untruthful!

For example, at the start of the first chapter, there is something which may seem like bragging: no, reader, I was not a soldier at Wagram in 1809.

You must know that forty-five years before your time, it was fashionable to have been a soldier under Napoleon. So today, in 1835, it is a falsehood altogether deserving of being written to let it be understood indirectly and without absolute untruthfulness (*jesuitico more*) that one was a soldier at Wagram.

The fact is that I was a sergeant and a subaltern in the 6th Dragoons when that regiment arrived in Italy in May 1800, I believe, and that I resigned my commission at the time of the brief peace in 1803. I was bored in the extreme by my comrades, and thought nothing could be sweeter than to live in Paris, as a *philosophe*, that was the word I then used with myself, on the 150fr a month which my father gave me. I supposed that with him gone I should have double or twice double; with my burning zeal for knowledge at that time, it was far too much.

I didn't become a colonel, as I would have done with the powerful protection of M. le Comte Daru, my cousin, but I think I was much happier. Soon I no longer thought of studying M. de Turenne and of imitating him, the idea that had been my fixed goal during the three years when I was a dragoon.[15]

14. Jean-François Marmontel (1723–1799), a follower of Voltaire and author of some celebrated *Mémoires*.

15. The Vicomte de Turenne (1611–1675) was France's most celebrated and successful strategist in the civil and external wars of the seventeenth century.

At times this conflicted with another idea: to write comedies like Molière and live with an actress. I already had at that time a mortal distaste for respectable women and the hypocrisy indispensable to them. My vast laziness won the day; once in Paris I went six whole months without visiting my family (Messrs Daru, Mmes Le Brun, M. and Mme de Baure), I kept telling myself *tomorrow*; I spent two years in this way, on the fifth floor in the Rue d'Angivilliers with a beautiful view of the colonnade of the Louvre, and reading La Bruyère, Montaigne and J.-J. Rousseau, whose bombastic language soon put me off. There my character was formed. I also read many of the tragedies of Alfieri, striving to get pleasure from them; I venerated Cabanis,[16] Tracy[17] and J.-B. Say[18]; I often read Cabanis, whose vague style distressed me. I lived solitary and crazy like a Spaniard, a thousand leagues from real life. Good Father Jeki, an Irishman, gave me English lessons, but I made no progress; I was mad on *Hamlet*.

But I'm letting myself get carried away, I am digressing, I shall be unintelligible if I don't stick to the order of events, and moreover the circumstances won't come back to me so well.

At Wagram in 1809, then, I wasn't in the army, but on the contrary an assistant in the War Commissariat, a position into which my cousin M. Daru had put me "to keep me from vice," as my family would have said. For my solitude in the Rue d'Angivilliers had ended with my living for a year in Marseille with a charming actress who had the loftiest sentiments and to whom I never gave a *sou*. First of all for the most excellent reason that my father was still giving me

16. Georges Cabanis (1757–1808), doctor and *philosophe*, and a leading member of the group of Ideologues.

17. Antoine Destutt de Tracy (1754–1836), *philosophe* and acknowledged leader of the Ideologues.

18. Jean-Baptiste Say (1767–1832), the greatest of the early French economists, and a disciple of Adam Smith.

150frs a month on which I had to live and this allowance wasn't paid regularly in Marseille in 1805.

But I'm digressing again. In October 1806, after Jena, I was an assistant in the War Commis[sariat], a post reviled by the soldiers; in 1810, on 3 August, commissioner to the Council of State, inspector-general of Crown Furnishings and Buildings a few days later. I was in favour, not with the master, Nap[oleon] didn't speak to madmen of my sort, but well regarded by the best of men, M. le Duc de Frioul (Duroc). But I'm digressing.

CHAPTER 2

I fell with Nap[oleon] in April 1814. I came to Italy to live as in the Rue d'Angivilliers. In 1821, I left Milan, despair in my soul because of Métilde and with a good mind to blow my brains out. At first everything bored me in Paris; later, I wrote in order to distract myself; Métilde died, no point therefore in returning to Milan. I had become perfectly happy; which is overstating it, but very passably happy, in 1830, when I wrote *Le Rouge et le noir*.

I was delighted by the July Days[1]; I saw the shooting beneath the columns of the Théâtre Français; very little danger on my part. I shall never forget that lovely sunshine and the first sight of the tricolour, on the 29 or 30, around eight o'clock, after sleeping at Commander Pinto's, whose niece was frightened. On 25 September I was appointed c[onsul] in Trieste by M. Molé, whom I had never met. From Trieste I came in 1831 to C[ivit]a-V[ecchi]a and Rome, where I still am and where I'm bored for want of being able to exchange ideas. I need from time to time to converse in the evenings with clever people otherwise I feel as if I'm being asphyxiated.

Here then are the major divisions of my tale: born in 1783, a dragoon in 1800, a student from 1803 to 1806. In 1806, assistant to the War Com[miss]ariat, an intendant in Brunswick. In 1809, gathering up the wounded at Essling or at Wagram, carrying out missions along the Danube on banks covered in

1. The "Revolution" in Paris of July 1830, which saw the removal of the last Bourbon king, Charles X, and the succession of Louis-Philippe.

snow, at Linz and Passau, in love with Mme la Comtesse Petit, asking to go to Spain in order to see her again. On 3 August 1810, appointed by her more or less as commissioner to the Council of State. This life of high favour and expenditure led me to Moscow, made me an intendant at Sagan in Silesia, and finally to fall in April 1815. Who would have believed it! Speaking for myself, the fall pleased me.

After the fall, student, writer, madly in love, getting *L'Histoire de la p[einture] en Italie* published in 1817; my father had become an ultra,[2] was ruined and died in 1819, I think it was; I came back to Paris in June 1821. I was in despair because of Métilde; she died; I loved her better dead than unfaithful; I wrote, I was consoled, I was happy. In 1830, in the month of September, I reentered the administrative rut in which I still am, nostalgic for my life as a writer on the third floor of the Hôtel de Valois, 71 Rue de Richelieu.

I have been a man of wit since the winter of 1826. Before, I kept silent out of laziness. I pass, I believe, for the most cheerful and unfeeling of men; it's true I have never said a single word about the women I have loved. In that respect I have experienced totally all the symptoms of the melancholic temperament as described by Cabanis. I have had very little success.

But the other day, musing on life on the lonely road above Lake Albano, I decided my life could be summed up in these names, whose initial letters I wrote in the dust, like Zadig,[3] with my stick, sitting on the little seat behind the Stations of the Cross in the *Minori Osservanti* built by Urban VIII's brother, Barberini, near those two beautiful trees enclosed by a little circular wall:

Virginie (Kubly),
Angela (Pietragrua),

2. I.e. an extreme Catholic and monarchist; for the republican unbeliever Stendhal this is a term of high abuse.

3. The wise and virtuous hero of Voltaire's philosophical novella of that name. It is Zadig's lover, Astarté, who in fact traces the letters of his name in the dust.

Adèle (Rebuffel),
Mélanie (Guilbert),
Mina (de Griesheim),
Alexandrine (Petit),
Angéline, whom I never loved (Bereyter),
Angela (Pietragrua),
Métilde (Dembowski),
Clémentine,
Giulia,

and lastly, for a month at the most, Mme Azur whose Christian name I've forgotten,

and unwisely, yesterday, Amalia (B[ettini]).

Convent.—Road leading to Albano.—Zadig.—Astarté.—Lake Alba[no].

The majority of these charming creatures didn't honour me with their favours; but they have literally occupied the whole of my life. To them there succeeded my books. In reality, I have never been ambitious, but in 1811, I thought I was ambitious.

My habitual state in life has been that of an unhappy lover, loving music and painting, that is to say enjoying the products of those arts, not practising them clumsily. I have sought out views of beautiful landscapes with an exquisite sensibility; it is for that alone that I have travelled. Landscapes were like a *violin bow* playing on my soul, and prospects which no one mentioned (the line of rocks as you approach Arbois, I believe, and coming from Dôle along the main road, was for me an obvious and perceptible image of Métilde's soul). I can see that rêverie has been what I preferred to anything else, even to passing for a wit. I only took the trouble, I only acquired the rank of an improviser in dialogue, for the benefit of the company in which I found myself, in 1826, because of the despair in which I spent the early months of that fateful year.

I found out lately from reading it in a book (the letters of Victor Jacquemont,[4] the Indian) that someone managed to think me brilliant. A few years ago, I saw the same thing more or less in a then fashionable book by Lady Morgan.[5] I had forgotten this fine quality which has made me so many enemies. Perhaps it was a quality only in appearance, and my enemies are creatures too vulgar to be judges of brilliance; how can a Comte d'Argout be any judge of *brilliance*, for example? A man for whom happiness is reading two or three duodecimo volumes a day of novels written for chambermaids! How could M. de Lamartine[6] be any judge of wit? In the first place he has none and in the second he too devours two volumes a day of the most worthless books (met in Florence in 1824 or 1826).

4. Victor Jacquemont (1801–1832), naturalist and traveller, principally in India and Tibet.

5. Authoress of a book called *France in 1829 and 1830*, in which she wrote of "the brilliant Beyle" and of the pungency of his conversation.

6. Alphonse de Lamartine (1790–1869), Romantic poet and later diplomat and liberal politician, who stood unsuccessfully for the presidency of the Republic in 1848.

The great DRAW-BACK of being witty is that you have to keep your eyes fixed on the semi-idiots around you, and *absorb their worthless sensations*. My failing is to attach myself to the least slow in imagination and to become unintelligible for the remainder who are perhaps all the better pleased.

Since I have been in Rome I am witty no more than once a week and then only for five minutes; I prefer to daydream. The people here have insufficient grasp of the subtleties of the French language to sense the subtlety of my remarks; they need some of the coarse wit of the commercial traveller, like Mélodrame,[7] who enchants them (example: M[ichel]angelo Caetani) and is their veritable daily bread. The sight of such a success chills me; I no longer deign to speak to people who have applauded Mélodrame. I can see the utter nothingness of vanity.

Two months ago then, in September 1835, thinking about writing these *Memoirs*, on the shore of Lake Albano (two hundred feet above the level of the lake), I wrote these initials in the dust like Zadig:

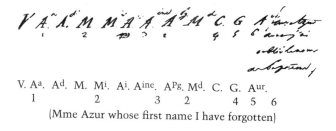

V. A^a. A^d. M. M^i. A^i. A^{ine}. A^{Pg}. M^d. C. G. A^{ur}.
 1   2   3   2   4   5   6
(Mme Azur whose first name I have forgotten)

I pondered deeply on these names, and on the astonishing follies and stupidities they made me do (I say astonishing for me, not for the reader, and anyway I don't repent of them).

In actual fact, I possessed only six of these women that I loved.

---

7. The pseudonym of a French diplomat met by Stendhal in Rome.

The greatest passion lies between Mélanie 2, Alexandrine, Métilde and Clémentine 4.

Clémentine is the one who caused me the most grief by leaving me. But was this grief comparable with that caused by Métilde who refused to tell me she loved me?

With all of them, and with several others, I was always the child; so I had very little success. But in return, they were my passionate preoccupation, and have left behind memories that enchant me (some after twenty-four years, like the memory of the Madonna del Monte in Varese, in 1811). I was not promiscuous, not enough so; I was preoccupied only by the woman I loved, and when I wasn't in love I pondered the spectacle of human affairs or read with delight Montesquieu or Walter Scott.

And so, as children say, I am so far from being blasé about their wiles and small graces that at my age, fifty-two, and writing this, I am still quite under the spell of a long *chiacchierata*[8] which Amalia had with me yesterday evening at the Valle Th[eatre].

In order to consider them as philosophically as possible and thereby try to strip them of the halo which *makes my eyes go funny*, which dazzles me and removes the ability to see clearly, I shall *arrange* these ladies *in order* (the language of mathematics) according to their various qualities. I shall say then, to begin with their habitual passion: vanity, that two of them were countesses and one a baroness.

The richest was Alexandrine Petit, her husband and she especially spent a good 80,000 francs a year. The poorest was Mina de Griesheim, the younger daughter of a general who had no fortune at all and was the favourite of a fallen prince, whose sa[lar]y supported the family, or Mlle Bereyter, an actress at the *Opera Buffa*.

I am seeking to destroy the attraction, the DAZLING [*sic*] of events, by looking at them in this military way. It is

8. "Gossip."

20

my one expedient, if I am to arrive at the truth on a subject I have no one I can talk to about. The melancholic temperament (Cabanis) being reticent, I have always been foolishly, unbelievably discreet about such matters. As for wit, Clémentine outdid all the others. Métilde outdid them in her high-minded, Spanish sentiments; Giulia, I fancy, in strength of character, though at the start she had seemed the weakest; Angela P[ietragrua] was a sublime Italian-style tart, *à la* Lucrezia Borgia, and Mme Azur an unsublime tart, *à la* du Barry.[9]

Money declared war on me twice only: at the end of 1805, and in 1806 up until August, when my father no longer sent me any money, and without *warning me*, that was the bad part. He went five months one time without paying me my allowance of 150fr. Days of great hardship with the viscount, he receiving his allowance on time but regularly gambling it all away the day he got it.[10]

In 1829 and 30, I got into difficulties more out of not taking care and insouciance than out of a genuine absence of means, since between 1821 and 1830 I made three or four journeys to Italy, England and Barcelona, and at the end of that time I only owed 400fr.

My greatest lack of money led me to take the unpleasant step of borrowing 100fr or sometimes 200 from M. Besan[çon]. I gave them back after one or two months; and finally, in September 1830, I owed 400fr to my tailor Michel. Those acquainted with the way of life of young people of my generation will find that very modest. From 1800 to 1830 I never owed my tailor Léger a *sou*, nor his successor Michel (22, Rue Vivienne).

My friends of those days, 1830, Messrs de Mareste,

9. Jeanne Bécu, Comtesse du Barry (1743–1793), the favourite of King Louis XV, guillotined during the Terror.

10. The "viscount" was Stendhal's close friend, Louis de Barral, who will be referred to more fully later.

Colomb, were friends of a peculiar kind: they would no doubt have taken active steps to rescue me from a serious danger, but when I went out in a new coat they would have given 20fr, the first of them especially, for someone to throw a glass of dirty water over me. (Except for the Vicomte de Barral and Bigillion [of Saint-Ismier], well nigh all my friends, all through my life, have been of this kind.)

They were good, very provident folk who by assiduous hard work or assiduous cleverness had amassed a salary or investment income of 12 or 15,000 [francs], and who could not bear to see me blithe, without cares, happy with an exercise-book of blank paper and a pen, and living on no more than 4 or 5,000fr. They would have liked me a hundred times better if they had seen me wretched and cast down at having only half or a third of their income, I who in the old days had perhaps rather shocked them when I had a coachman, two horses, a barouche and a gig, for that was how high my luxuriousness had mounted in the days of the Emperor. Then I was or believed I was ambitious; what worried me about that supposition was that I didn't know what to hope for. I was ashamed of being in love with the Comtesse A[lexandrine] Petit; I kept a mistress, Mlle A. Bereyter, an actress at the *Opera Buffa*; I ate at the Café Hardy; I was unbelievably energetic. I would come back from St-Cloud to Paris on purpose to attend one act of the *Matrimonio Segreto* at the Odeon (Mme Barilli, Barilli, Tacchinardi, Mme Festa, Mlle Bereyter). My gig was waiting at the door of the Café Hardy: that's what my brother-in-law has never forgiven me for.

All this might have been thought conceited, yet it wasn't. I was looking to enjoy myself and to be energetic, but not to appear to be having more enjoyment or to be more energetic than was actually the case. M. Prunelle, a doctor, a witty man, whom I liked for being so rational, horribly ugly, celebrated since as the venal deputy and mayor of Lyon around 1833, with whom I was acquainted in those days, said of me: "He's mighty pleased with himself."

That verdict reverberated among my acquaintance. Maybe they were right, at that.

My excellent brother-in-law, a true bourgeois, M. Périer-Lagrange (a former merchant who ruined himself unwittingly practising agriculture near La Tour-du-Pin), dining with me at the Café Hardy and, seeing me order the waiters firmly about, because all the duties I had to perform meant I was often in a hurry, was overjoyed because the waiters made some joke among themselves to the effect that I was conceited, which in no way put me out. I have always and as if instinctively profoundly despised the bourgeoisie (so well borne out since by the Chambers[11]).

At the same time I could just about see also that only among the bourgeoisie were there to be found energetic men like my cousin Rebuffel (a merchant in the Rue St-Denis), Father Ducros, the town librarian in Grenoble, the incomparable Gros (of the Rue St-Laurent), a geometer of the highest class and my mentor, unbeknownst to my masculine relations, for he was a Jacobin and my entire family bigoted reactionaries. These three men possessed my whole esteem and my whole heart, insofar as respect and the difference in age allowed of the intercourse through which we come to love someone. Even with them, as later with the individuals I loved too much, I was dumb, immobile, stupid, unfriendly and sometimes offensive by dint of my devotion and absence *of self*. My *amour-propre*, my self-interest, my ego had vanished in the presence of the person I loved, I was transformed into them. What when this person was a slut like Mme Pietragrua? But I am anticipating again. Shall I have the courage to write these *Confessions* in an intelligible manner? One needs to tell a story, and I am recording *observations* on tiny events, which need to be recounted very distinctly, precisely because of their microscopic size. What patience you will require, oh my reader!

11. I.e. the Chambre des Députés, now the Assemblée Nationale, and the Chambre des Pairs, or upper house, which existed from 1814 to 1848.

According to me then, *energy* was only to be found even to my way of thinking (in 1811) among the class which battles against real need.

My high-born friends, Messrs Raymond de Bérenger (killed at Lutzen), de St-Ferréol, de Sinard (devout died young), Gabriel du Bouchage (a sort of swindler or not very scrupulous borrower of money, today a peer of France and a verbose ultra), Messrs de Monval, had always struck me as having something odd about them, a terrible respect for the *proprieties* (Sinard, for example). They were always trying to be *fashionable* or *comme il faut*, as they used to say in Grenoble in 1793. But I was far from seeing this idea clearly. It is no more than a year since my idea about *nobility* was finally completed. My moral life has been instinctively spent paying close attention to five or six main ideas, and attempting to see the truth about them.

Raymond de Bérenger was excellent and a genuine example of the maxim, *noblesse oblige*, whereas Monval (who died a colonel, and generally despised, around 1829 in Grenoble) was the ideal of a centrist deputy. All this was already perfectly visible when these gentlemen were fifteen years old around 1798.

I can see the truth about most of these things clearly only as I write them in 1835, so shrouded have they been up until now in the halo of youth, deriving from the extreme vivacity of my sensations.

By dint of employing the methods of philosophy, by classifying the friends of my youth for example by *kinds*, as M. Adrien de Jussieu does with his plants (in botany), I am seeking to attain to the truth that eludes me. I realize that what I took for high mountains, in 1800, were for the most part only *molehills*; but that is a discovery I have only made very belatedly.

I can see that I was like a highly strung horse and it is to a remark made to me by M. de Tracy (the illustrious Count

Destutt de Tracy, peer of France, member of the Académie Française and, far better, author of the law of the 3 Germinal concerning the Ecoles Centrales), it is to a remark made to me by M. de Tracy that I owe this discovery.

I need an example. For a trifle, a door left half open at night for example, I used to imagine two armed men waiting to stop me getting to a window overlooking a gallery where I could see my mistress. That was an illusion that a sensible man like my friend, Abraham Constantin, would not have had. But after a few seconds (four or five at the most) the sacrifice of my life had been made and was perfect, and I would dash forward like a hero to meet with my two enemies who turned into a half-closed door.

Not more than two months since, something of this sort, morally speaking anyway, happened to me again. The sacrifice had been made and all the necessary courage was present, when after twenty hours I realized, rereading a letter I had misread (from M. Hérard), that it was an illusion. I always read anything I find painful very quickly.

So, classifying my life like a collection of plants. I shall find:

Childhood and early education, from 1786 to 1800	15 years
Military service from 1800 to 1803	3 years
Second education, absurd amours with Mlle Adèle Clozel and with her mother who treated herself to her daughter's lover; life in the Rue d'Angivilliers; lastly, delightful stay in Marseille with Mélanie, from 1803 to 1805	2 years
Return to Paris, end of education	1 year
Service under Napoleon, from 1806 to the end of 1814 (from October 1806 to the abdication in 1814)	7 years

April, my adhesion in the same issue of
the *Moniteur* as Napoleon's abdication.[12]
Travels, great and terrible amours;
consolation from writing books, from
1814 to 1830   15 years
Second service, consul from September 15,
1830 to the present quarter of an hour   5 years

I began in society through the salon of Mme de Valserre, a pious woman with an odd, chinless face, the daughter of M. le Baron des Adrets and a friend of my mother's. That was probably around 1794. I had a fiery temperament and the timidity described by Cabanis.* I was excessively affected, I believe, by the beauty of Mlle Bonne de St-Vallier's arm; I can see her face and her beautiful arms, but the name is uncertain; perhaps it was Mlle de Lavalette. M. de Saint-Ferréol, whom I have never heard speak of since, was my enemy and rival, M. de Sinard a mutual friend calmed us down. All this took place in a magnificent ground-floor room giving on to the garden of the Adrets' mansion, now pulled down and turned into a bourgeois house, in the Rue Neuve in Grenoble. At the same period there began my passionate admiration for Father Ducros (a secularized Franciscan friar, and a man of the highest ability, or so it seems to me). For a bosom friend I had my grandfather, M. Henri Gagnon, a doctor.

After all these general reflections, I am about to be born.

---

12. His adhesion as a member of the Council of State to the new regime, of the restored King Louis XVIII.

*Written as night falls.

CHAPTER 3

My earliest memory is of having bitten the cheek or forehead of Mme Pison du Galland, my cousin, wife of the witty man who was a deputy in the Constituent Assembly.[1] I can see her still, a woman of twenty-five, stout and with a lot of rouge. It was this rouge seemingly which nettled me. Sitting in the middle of the field known as the *glacis* of the Porte de Bonne, her cheek was at exactly my height.

"Give me a kiss, Henri," she said to me.

I wouldn't. She became angry. I bit hard. I can see the scene, but no doubt because it was instantly made into a crime and was forever being brought up against me. The *glacis* of the Porte de Bonne was covered in marguerites. This is a pretty little flower which I used to make into bouquets. That meadow of 1786 is today no doubt in the middle of the town, to the south of the college church. My aunt Séraphie declared I was a monster and that I had an atrocious character. This aunt Séraphie had all the sourness of a pious spinster who hadn't managed to find a husband. What had happened to her? I have never found out, we never do find out the scandalous chronicle of our relations, and I left the town for good at sixteen, after three years of the most intense passion which had relegated me to a complete solitude.

My second characteristic act was blacker by far.

I had made a collection of rushes again from the *glacis* of the Porte de Bonne (Bonne de Lesdiguières). Ask what the

---

1. The title taken by the States-General in July 1789, which enacted the first laws of the Revolutionary period.

botanical name of the rush is, a grass cylindrical in shape like a chicken feather and a foot long.

I had been brought back to the house, one first-floor window of which looked out on to the Grande-Rue at the corner of the Place Grenette. I was making a garden by cutting these rushes into sections two inches long, which I set into the gap between the balcony and the *drip-stone* of the window. The kitchen knife I was using slipped from me and fell into the street, a dozen feet that is to say, near a Mme Chenevaz or onto that lady. She was the most spiteful woman in the whole town (the mother of Candide Chenevaz, who adored Richardson's *Clarissa Harlowe* when he was young, later one of M. de Villèle's three hundred[2] and rewarded with the post of first president in the King's court in Grenoble, died in Lyon without having been called).

My aunt Séraphie said I had wanted to kill Mme Chenevaz; I was declared to be possessed of an atrocious character, told off by my excellent grandfather, M. Gagnon, who was afraid of his daughter Séraphie, whose piety was a by-word in the town, told off even by that exalted, Spanish character, my excellent great-aunt Mlle Elisabeth Gagnon.

I rebelled, I may have been four years old: my horror of religion dates from that time, a horror which my reason has had the greatest difficulty in reducing to its rightful dimensions, and then only quite recently, not six years since. At almost the same time, my instinctive filial love for the Republic, fanatical in those days, was first born.

I was no more than five years old.*

2. Jean-Baptiste Guillaume Joseph, Comte de Villèle (1773–1854), an ultraist politician, powerful in the 1820s. The "three hundred" must refer to the 300 francs stipulated in a law proposed by Villèle, but never enacted, as the sum qualifying those who possessed it to leave all their property to their eldest son.

*M. Gagnon buys the house next door from the Mmes de Marnais; we change apartments; I wrote everywhere on the plaster *cramps* "Henri Beyle 1789." I can still see this beautiful inscription which amazed my worthy grandfather. Therefore, my attempt on the life of Mme Chenevaz was prior to 1789.

This aunt Séraphie was my evil genius all through my childhood; she was loathed, but was held in high repute within the family. I presume that subsequently my father was in love with her; at any rate there were long walks to the Granges, in a marsh underneath the town walls, on which I made an *unwanted third* and on which I was very bored. I used to hide when the moment came to go on these walks. This was when the scant friendship I had for my father foundered.

In point of fact I was brought up exclusively by my excellent grandfather, M. Henri Gagnon. This extraordinary man had made a pilgrimage to Ferney to visit Voltaire and been received by him with distinction.[3] He had a small bust of Voltaire, hardly bigger than a fist, mounted on an ebony stand six inches high. (This was in strange taste, but the fine arts were not Voltaire's strong suit nor that of my excellent grandfather.)

This bust stood in front of the desk on which he wrote, his study was at the far end of a vast apartment looking out on to an elegant terrace decked with flowers. For me it was a rare favour to be allowed in there, and a rarer one to see and to touch the bust of Voltaire.

But for all that, for as far back as I can remember, Voltaire's writings have always seemed to me supremely disagreeable, I found them childish. I can say that I have never liked anything by that great man. I couldn't then see that he was the law-giver and apostle of France, its Martin Luther.

M. Henri Gagnon wore a powdered round wig with three rows of curls because he was a doctor of medicine, and a doctor in vogue among the ladies, even accused of having been the lover of several, of a Teisseire among others, one of the prettiest in the town, whom I don't recall ever having seen, because at that time they had fallen out, but who gave me so to understand later in a curious manner. Because of his

3. Voltaire lived at Ferney outside Geneva from 1760 to 1778.

wig, my excellent grandfather has always seemed to me to have been eighty years old. He suffered from the vapours (like myself, poor devil), from rheumatism, and had difficulty walking, but on principle he never got into a carriage and never put on his hat: a small triangular hat for putting under his

arm and which was my delight, when I was able to get hold of it and put it on my head, which the whole family thought showed a lack of respect, and in the end, out of respect, I ceased to concern myself with the triangular hat and his small cane with its boxroot knob and tortoiseshell surround. My grandfather adored the apocryphal correspondence of Hippocrates, which he read in Latin (though he knew some Greek), and Horace in the edition of Johannes Bond, printed in horribly minuscule characters. He passed these two enthusiasms on to me and indeed nearly all his tastes, though not in the way he would have liked, as I shall explain later.

If ever I go back to Grenoble, I must have a search made for the birth and death certificates of that excellent man who adored me and had no love for his son, M. [Romain] Gagnon, the father of M. Oronce Gagnon, a squadron commander in the dragoons, who killed his man in a duel three years ago, for which I am grateful to him; he is probably no fool. It is thirty-three years since I last saw him, he might be thirty-five.

I lost my grandfather while I was in Germany. Was it in 1807 or 1813? I have no clear recollection. I remember I travelled to Grenoble to see him again; I found him very downcast; that very amiable man, who had been the life and soul of the *evenings* he went to, hardly spoke any more. He said to me: "This is a farewell visit."

And then changed the subject; he had a horror of the stupid sentimentality of families.

A memory comes back to me. Around 1807, I had myself painted, in order to persuade Mme Alex[andrine] Petit to have herself painted also, and because she objected to the number of sittings, I took her to a painter opposite the fountain of the Diorama who painted you in oils at a single sitting, for 120 francs. My worthy grandfather saw this portrait which I had sent to my sister, I fancy, in order to get rid of it; his mind was already far gone, he said on seeing the portrait: "This is the real one."

And then relapsed into sadness and prostration. He died soon afterwards, I fancy, at the age of eighty-two, I believe.

If that date is accurate, he must have been sixty-one in 1789 and been born around 1728. He sometimes used to recount to us the battle of l'Assiette, an attack in the Alps vainly attempted by the Ch[evali]er de Belle-Isle in 1742, I believe.[4] His father, a decisive man, full of energy and of honour, had sent him there as an army surgeon, in order to form his character. My grandfather had begun his medical studies and may have been eighteen or twenty years old, which again points to 1724 as the period of his birth.

He owned an old house situated in the best position in the town, on the Place Grenette, at the corner of the Grande-Rue, facing due south, with in front of it the town's most beautiful square, the two rival cafés and the centre of fashionable society. There, in a first-floor apartment, very low-ceilinged but admirably cheerful, my grandfather lived up until 1789.

He must have been rich at that time because he bought a superb house situated behind his own which belonged to the de Marnais ladies. He occupied the second floor of his house, on the Place Grenette, and the whole of the corresponding floor in the de Marnais house, and made for himself the finest

4. In fact in 1747, when the French army of Italy met the troops of the Duke of Savoy and, contrary to what Stendhal says, defeated them.

living quarters in the town. There was a staircase which was magnificent for those days and a drawing-room which might have been thirty-five feet by twenty-eight.

Alterations were made to the two bedrooms of the ap[artment] overlooking the Place Grenette, and among other things, a *gippe* (a partition made out of plaster and bricks

1. My mattress.—2. Me.—3. Henriette's bed.—4. Fireplace.— 5. Dark clothes closet.—6. Dressing-room.—7. Big window overlooking the Rue des Vieux-Jésuites.—7'. Small window.—8. Door to the drawing-room.—9. Private exit.

set edge-wise one on top of the other) in order to divide the bedroom of my terrible aunt Séraphie, M. Gagnon's daughter, from that of my great-aunt Elisabeth, his sister. Iron *cramps* were set into this partition and on the plaster over each of these cramps I wrote "Henri Beyle 1789." I can still see those beautiful inscriptions, at which my grandfather marvelled. "Since you can write so well," he told me, "you're worthy of starting Latin."

This remark filled me with a kind of terror and a pedant

fearful to behold, M. Joubert, tall, pale and thin, and supporting himself on a *thorn-stick*, came to show me, to teach me *mura*, the mulberry. We went to buy a primer from M. Giroud, the bookseller, at the far end of a courtyard opening on to the Place aux Herbes. I hardly realized at the time what an instrument of destruction I was being bought.

This was the start of my misfortunes.

But for a long time now I have been putting off telling a crucial story, one of those perhaps which will lead me to throw these memoirs onto the fire.

My mother, Mme Henriette Gagnon, was a charming woman, and I was in love with my mother.

I hasten to add that I lost her when I was seven years old.

In loving her at the age of six perhaps, in 1789, I had absolutely the same character as in 1828, when I was furiously in love with Alberthe de Rubempré. My manner of going in pursuit of happiness had not changed at all in essence[5]; with this one exception: that where the physics of love is concerned, I was like Caesar would be were he to return to a world employing cannon and small arms. I would soon have learnt it and it would have changed nothing fundamentally in my tactics.

I wanted to cover my mother in kisses and for there not to be any clothes. She loved me passionately and kissed me often, I returned her kisses with such ardour she was as if compelled to move away. I loathed my father when he came and interrupted our kissing. I always wanted to give her them on her bosom. Kindly condescend to remember that I lost her in childbirth when I was scarcely seven years old.

She was plump, and in the bloom of life; she was very pretty, and only not sufficiently tall, I fancy. Her features were noble and of an ideal serenity; very lively, preferring to run and do things herself rather than give orders to her

5. This is the first mention of the celebrated *chasse au bonheur*, or "pursuit of happiness" which Stendhal declared to be the one aim of his existence.

33

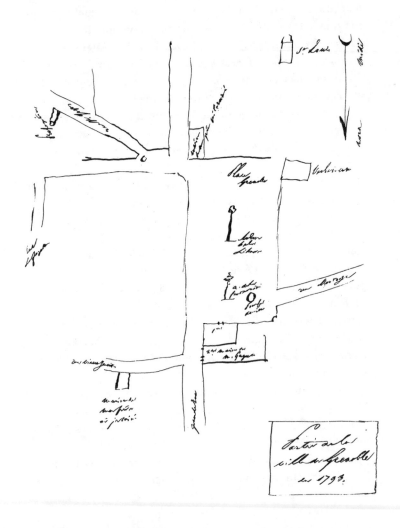

Part of the town of Grenoble in 1793.

Propagation.—Rue St-Jacques.—My father's house which ruined him.—St-Louis.—South.—North.—Rue La Fayette.—Place Grenette.—Verbe Incarné.—Tree of Liberty.—Tree of Fraternity.—Old pump.—Rue Montorge.—Rue [des] Vieux-Jésuites.—My father's house where I was born.—First. Second house belonging to M. Gagnon.—Grande-Rue.

three maidservants and lastly often reading Dante's *Divine Comedy* in the original, of which much later on I found five or six copies in different editions in her rooms, which had remained locked since her death.

She perished in the flower of her youth and beauty in 1790; she may have been twenty-eight or thirty years old.

This was the start of my moral life. My aunt Séraphie dared to reproach me for not weeping enough. Judge of my grief and of what I felt! But it seemed to me that I would see her again the next day, I didn't understand death. Thus it is forty-five years since I lost what I loved best in the world.

She can't be offended by the liberty I am taking with her by revealing that I loved her; if ever I meet with her again I shall tell her so once more. In any case she had no part in this love. She didn't behave as they do in Venice, like Mme Benzoni with the author of *Nella*.[6] As for myself I was as criminal as could be, I was furiously in love with her physical charms.

One evening, when by some chance I had been put to sleep in her bedroom on the floor, on a mattress, that woman who was as quick and agile as a hind jumped over my mattress so as to save time getting to her bed.

Her bedroom remained locked for ten years after her death. My father reluctantly gave me permission to set up an oilcloth blackboard and work at my mathematics in there in 1789. But none of the servants went in, they would have been severely reprimanded; I alone had the key. This sentiment of my father's does him great honour in my eyes now that I reflect on it.

She died then in that bedroom, in the Rue des Vieux-Jésuites, the fifth or sixth house on the left coming from the Grande-Rue, facing the house of M. Teisseire.

6. The Countess Benzoni (1757–1839) was a Venetian noblewoman whose son Vittorio was the author of a long poem entitled *Nella*. There is no evidence to suggest an incestuous relationship between them.

There I was born; this house belonged to my father, who sold it when he started building his new street and committing follies. The street that ruined him he named the Rue Dauphin (my father was an extreme *ultra*, on the side of the pr[iests] and nobles), and is nowadays called, I believe, the *Rue La Fayette*.

I spent my life at my grandfather's, whose house was hardly more than a hundred paces from our own.

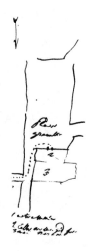

Place Grenette—1. Our house.—2. My grandfather's house.— 3. Marnais house.

CHAPTER 4

I could write a volume on the circumstances of the death of someone so dear.

That's to say, I know nothing whatsoever of the details. She died giving birth seemingly through the clumsiness of a surgeon called Hérault, a fool seemingly chosen out of pique against another accoucheur, a man of wit and ability; this is more or less how Mme Petit died in 1814. I can describe at length only my feelings which would probably seem exaggerated or incredible to the spectator accustomed to human nature as falsified in novels (I don't mean Fielding [*a blank*]) or as etiolated in novels constructed from the emotions of Paris.

I must inform the reader that the Dauphiné has its own way of feeling, intense, obstinate, argumentative, which I have met with in no other region. To the clear-seeing eye, music, the countryside and novels ought to change with every three degrees of latitude. For example, at Valence on the Rhône the Provençal character ends, the Burgundian character starts at Valence and gives way, between Dijon and Troyes, to the Parisian character—polished, witty, without depth, very aware of what others are thinking, in fact.

The Dauphinois character has a tenacity, a depth, a wit, a finesse that you would look for in vain in the civilization of Provence or Burgundy, its neighbours. Where the Provençal breathes out dreadful insults, the Dauphinois is thoughtful and communes with his own heart.

Everyone knows that the Dauphiné was a State separate

from France and half Italian in its politics up until the year 1 [*a blank*]. Then Louis XI, the dauphin, who had quarrelled with his father, administered the region for [*a blank*] years, and I am ready to believe that it was this profound and profoundly timid spirit, hostile to all impulsiveness, who put his stamp on the Dauphinois character. Even in my own time, it was the belief of my grandfather and my great-aunt Elisabeth, who had a typically energetic and generous sense of family, that Paris was not a model, it was a far-off, hostile town whose influence was to be feared.

Now that I have wooed my unfeeling readers with this digression, I shall relate that the day preceding my mother's death, my sister Pauline and I were taken for a walk in the Rue Montorge; we came back past the houses on the left-hand side of that street (to the north). We had been installed at my grandfather's, in the house on the Place Grenette. I was asleep on the floor, on a mattress between the window and the fireplace, when around two in the morning the whole family returned, uttering sobs.

"But why didn't the doctors find a cure?" I said to old Marion (a servant straight out of Molière, a friend of her employers, but who certainly spoke her mind to them, who had met my mother when very young, had seen her married ten years earlier (in 1780), and who loved me dearly).

Marie Thomasset, from Vinay, a typical Dauphinois character, called by the diminutive *Marion*, spent the night sitting beside my mattress, shedding hot tears and having seemingly been charged with restraining me. I was far more surprised than distraught; I didn't understand death, I hardly believed in it.

"What!" I said to Marion, "I shall never see her again?"

"How do you expect to see her again, if they be taking her to the cemetery?"

"And where is the cemetery?"

"In the Rue des Mûriers, the one for Notre-Dame parish."

The whole of that night's dialogue is still with me, and it would only be up to me to transcribe it here. Here was when my moral life truly began: I must have been six and a half. Anyway these dates can easily be verified from the official registers.

I feel asleep, the next day when I woke up Marion said to me: "You must go and kiss your father."

"What, my little mamma is dead! What, shan't I see her again?"

"Will you be quiet. Your father can hear you, he's there in your great-aunt's bed."

I went reluctantly up beside the bed, which was dark because the curtains were drawn. I felt an antipathy towards my father and was loth to embrace him.

A moment later the *abbé* Rey arrived, a very tall, very cold man, *pitted* with smallpox, with a kindly but unintelligent look, talking through his nose, who shortly afterwards became vicar-general. He was a friend of the family.

Will it be believed? Because of his pr[iestly] state I felt an antipathy towards him.

M. *l'abbé* Rey took up his position by the window; my father got up, put on his dressing-gown, came out of the alcove which was enclosed behind green serge curtains. There were two beautiful curtains of pink taffeta, with white brocade, which hid the others during the day.

The *abbé* Rey embraced my father in silence. I found my father very ugly. His eyes were puffed and he kept giving way to tears. I had remained in the unlit alcove and had a very good view.

"My friend, this comes from God," the *abbé* said at last; and this remark, spoken by a man whom I hated to another whom I hardly liked, gave me profoundly to think.

I shall be thought hard-hearted: as yet I was only surprised by my mother's death. I didn't understand the word. Shall I dare to write what Marion often repeated to me afterwards by way of a reproach? I began to speak ill of G O D.

Anyway, suppose I am lying about these *spears* of intelligence breaking through the soil; I am certainly not lying about everything else. If I am tempted to lie, it will be when it comes to telling of my very serious failings much later on. I have no faith in the idea that intelligence in a child promises superiority in the man. In a genre less subject to illusion, because after all its monuments survive, all the bad painters I have known have done astonishing things around the age of eight or ten *giving promise of genius.*

Alas, nothing gives promise of genius, perhaps obstinacy is a sign of it.

The next day, there was the matter of the funeral. My father, whose face was in truth completely altered, clad me in a sort of black cloak of black wool which he tied round me at the neck. The scene took place in my father's study in the Rue des Vieux-Jésuites; my father was mournful and the whole study was lined with funereal folios, ghastly to behold. D'Alembert and Diderot's E N C Y C L O P E D I A, in its blue binding, was the one exception to the general ugliness.

This lawyer's den had belonged to M. de Brenier, the husband of Mme de Valserre and a c[ounsel]ler in the Parlement. Once widowed, Mme de Valserre had inherited from him and had changed her name, Valserre being better and more aristocratic than de Brenier. She had since become a canoness.

All the friends and relations gathered in my father's study.

Clad in my black cloak, I was between my father's knees [at] 1. M. Pison senior, our cousin, a serious-minded man, but serious in the way men of the law-courts are, and highly respected in the family as the very spirit of propriety (he was thin, fifty-five years old and most distinguished in appearance), entered and placed himself at 3.

Instead of weeping and being sad, he started making conversation as normal and talking about the court. (Perhaps it was the court of the Parlement, that is very likely.) I thought he was talking about foreign courts, and was deeply shocked by his unfeelingness.

A moment later my uncle entered, my mother's brother, a young man as well set-up and as attractive as could be and dressed in the height of fashion. He was the town philanderer;

Rue [des] Vieux-Jésuites.—My mother's bedroom.—Reception room.—1. My father in his armchair.—2. Fireplace.—3. M. Pison. —4. My uncle.—Small room.—Chambermaid's room.—Vestibule to the drawing-room.—Bed.—Kitchen.—Dining-room.—Ante-room.—Kitchen garden.—Range.—Passageway.—Front door. —Courtyard.—Staircase.—Lamouroux garden.—Lime-trees.— Main part of building where I was put with my tutor, M. *l'abbé* Raillane.

he too began making conversation as normal with M. Pison; he placed himself at 4. I was violently indignant and I remembered that my father had called him a frivolous man. However, I noticed that his eyes were very red, and he had the prettiest of faces; that calmed me down a little.

His hair was dressed in the height of fashion and with a perfumed powder; his coiffure consisted of a square pouch of black taffeta with two large dog's ears (that was the term for them six years later), such as M. le Pr[inc]e de Talleyrand[1] wears today.

A loud noise was heard, it was my poor mother's coffin being carried into the drawing-room to be taken out.

"Ah, I don't know the order of these ceremonies," said M. Pison with an indifferent air as he stood up, which shocked me greatly; that was my last *social* sensation.

On entering the drawing-room and seeing the coffin draped in a black cloth *where my mother was* I was gripped by the most violent despair: I finally understood what death was.

My aunt Séraphie had already accused me of being unfeeling.

St-Hugues.—Cath[edral].—Place Notre-Dame.

I shall spare my reader the account of all the phases of my despair in the parish church of St-Hugues. I was suffocating; I believe they were forced to take me out because my grief was making too much noise. I have never been able to look unmoved at that church of St-Hugues and the cathedral ad-

1. Charles-Maurice de Talleyrand-Périgord (1754–1838), first a churchman, then a diplomat and politician, and a consummate and prominent survivor under the Revolution, Napoleon and all subsequent regimes.

joining it. The mere sound of the cathedral bells, even in 1828, when I went back to revisit Grenoble, brought on a dry, dismal sadness, unpitying, the sadness that is close to anger.

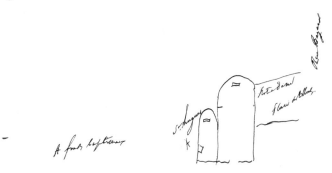

St-Hugues.—Notre-Dame.—Place des Tilleuls.—Rue Bayard.— A. Baptismal fonts.

On reaching the cemetery which was in a bastion near the Rue des Mûriers (today, in 1828 at least, occupied by a large building, the magazine of the Engineering corps), I lost my head as Marion told me afterwards. It seems I didn't want them to throw earth on my mother's coffin, claiming it would hurt her. But:

> Sur les noires couleurs d'un si triste tableau
> Il faut passer l'éponge ou tirer le rideau.[2]

As a consequence of the complex interplay of characters in my family, it came about that all the joys of childhood ended with my mother.*

2. The lines come from Corneille's little known play *Rodogune,* and might be translated literally as "Over the black colours of so sad a picture/We must pass the sponge or draw the curtain."

*Where I am concerned, the blackest malice succeeds to kindness and gaiety.

CHAPTER 4a

MEMORIES

Here are the memories which remain to me after forty-six years of the happy days spent in the time of my mother. Drawing-rooms, suppers, the [*illegible*], the *abbé* Chelan. I'm in revort.[1] Departure for Romans, Barthélemy d'Orbane, who [*word crossed out*] M. B[arthélemy d'Orbane] teaches me to pull faces.

1. This refers to an episode to be recounted in Chapter 5.

CHAPTER 5

SMALL MEMORIES OF MY EARLY CHILDHOOD *

While we occupied the first floor overlooking the Place Grenette, before 1790 or more accurately up until the middle of
1789, my uncle, a young lawyer, had a pretty little apartment
on the second floor, on the corner of the Place Grenette and
the Grande-Rue. He used to laugh with me, and let me watch
him strip off his fine clothes and put on his dressing-gown, in
the evenings at nine o'clock before supper. For me this was a
delightful moment, and I used to come back down to the first
floor happy as could be bearing the silver candlestick in front
of him. My aristocratic family would have thought itself
dishonoured had the candlestick not been of silver. True it
didn't contain the noble wax candle, the custom then was to
use tallow. But we had this tallow brought with great care in
a box from the vicinity of Briançon; it had to be made from
goat's fat, and when the time came a friend we had in the
mountains there was written to to that effect. I can still
see myself watching the tallow being unpacked and eating
bread and milk out of a silver bowl; the rubbing of the spoon
against the wet milk on the bottom of the bowl struck me as
odd. Our relationship with this friend in Briançon was almost

---

* 17–22 December. To be dictated and written out in its place, page 75 of the first volume. Bind this ms to the end of the second.

To be placed first volume.

Small memories to be placed AFTER THE account OF MY MOTHER'S
DEATH. Barthélemy d'Orban[e]. Departure for Romans, great snowstorm. Departure for Vizille. Hatred of Séraphie for the Barnave young ladies in front of whose
campagne (country house) we were passing at St-Robert.

The Bastille fortified between 1828 and 1836 by Gen[eral] Haxo (tireless braggart).—Mountain.—Ste-Marie-d'en-Haut.—Isère.— Wooden bridge.—Theatre.—Hôtel de Bonne.—Prison.—A. Tickets. —Place St-André. Tower of the Prefecture.—Passageway to the Concert Hall.—Former palace of the Constable of Lesdiguières, I believe.

one of *mutual hospitality* such as you find in Homer, a natural consequence of the general mistrust* and barbarism.

My uncle, young, brilliant, frivolous, was held to be the most attractive man in the town, to the point where, many years later, Mme Delaunay, seeking to prove her virtue, who had, however, strayed a good many times: "And yet," she said, "I never gave in to the younger M. Gagnon."

My uncle, as I say, made mock of the solemnity of his father, who, meeting him one day in company in expensive clothes which he hadn't paid for, was much astonished.

"I very quickly made myself scarce," added my uncle, recounting this episode to me.

One evening, in spite of everyone (but who then was the opposition prior to 1790?), he took me to the theatre. They were doing *Le Cid*. "But that child is crazy," said my excellent grandfather when I got back.

His love of literature had stopped him offering any very serious opposition to my outing to the theatre. So I saw *Le Cid* performed, but, I fancy, in a suit of sky-blue satin with white satin shoes.

In speaking his verses, or at some other point, brandishing his sword over-zealously, the Cid injured himself in the right eye.

"He all but put his eye out," it was said around me.

I was in the first tier of boxes, the second on the right.

Another time my uncle was indulgent enough to take me to *La Caravane du Caire.*[1] (I impeded him in his manœuvres with the ladies. I could see that very easily.) The camels drove me absolutely frantic. I went wild with delight over

---

*Style. Order of ideas. Prepare the attention by a few words in passing: 1. about Lambert; 2. about my uncle, in the early chapters.

Style. Relation of words to ideas. Dict[ionary] of the Academy, article St-Marc-Girardin, knight of König von Jean-f[outre]. *Débats* [*trans.* The reference is to an article by the journalist Emile de Girardin (1806–81) in the *Journal des Débats* concerning slang and how slang terms enter the official language.]

1. An opera by Grétry, first sung in 1783.

L'Infante de Zamora,[2] in which a poltroon, or else a cook, sang an arietta wearing a helmet with a rat for its crest. This for me was true comedy.

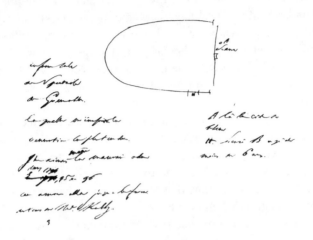

A. Stage.
    A. The Cid injures himself.—H. Henri B, not yet six years old. Vile auditorium in Grenoble which filled me with the fondest veneration. I even loved its nasty smell around 1794, 95 and 96. This love became frantic in the days of Mlle Kubly.

I said to myself, very obscurely no doubt and not as clearly as I write it here: "Each moment of my uncle's life is as delightful as the ones whose pleasure I share at the theatre. The finest thing in the world therefore is to be an attractive man, like my uncle." It didn't enter my five-year-old head that my uncle wasn't as happy as I was watching the camels of the caravan file past.

But I went too far: instead of being a philanderer, I became passionate with the women whom I loved, and almost indifferent and above all without vanity towards the others; hence my lack of success and my *fiascos*. Perhaps no man

2. A popular comic opera of the time by Framéry, first put on in 1780.

in the Emperor's court possessed fewer women than I did, who was believed to be the lover of the wife of the First Minister.[3]

The theatre, or the sound of a beautiful bass bell (as at the church of [*a blank*], above Rolle, in May 1800, on my way to the Saint-Bernard) have and always have had a profound effect on my emotions. The m[ass] even, that I be[liev]ed in so little, filled me with seriousness. When still very young, and certainly before I was ten and the *abbé* Gardon's note, I believed that G O D despised these play-actors. (After forty-two years of thinking about it I still believe this mystification to be too useful to those who practise it not to find people to carry it on. Story of the medal, told yesterday by [*illegible*], Dec[ember] 1835.)

I have the clearest, sharpest memory of my grandfather's round, powdered wig, it had three rows of curls. He never wore a hat.

This costume had helped, I fancy, to make him known and respected by the common people from whom he never accepted any money for his doctor's services. He was the doctor and the friend of most of the noble houses. M. de Chaléon, the sound of whose passing bell I can still recall ringing from St-Louis at the time of his death; M. de Lacoste, who died of apoplexy in the Terres-Froides, at La Frette; M. de Langon, from the high nobility, so the records said; M. de Raxis, who had scurvy and threw his coat down on the floor in my grandfather's room, who told me off very restrainedly because, after speaking of this episode, I pronounced the name of M. de Raxis; M. and Mme des Adrets, Mme de Valserre their daughter, in whose drawing-room I *met company* for the first time. Her sister, Mme de Mareste, struck me as very pretty and was said to be promiscuous.

He was and had been for the last twenty-five years, at the time when I knew him, the instigator of every useful enterprise

3. This was Pierre Daru, with whose wife Alexandrine Stendhal fell in love.

(which, given how childish politics were in those far-off [1760] days, one might call liberal). The library they owed to him. This was no small undertaking. It first had to be bought, then a site found, then a librarian endowed. He defended any young person who showed a liking for study, first of all

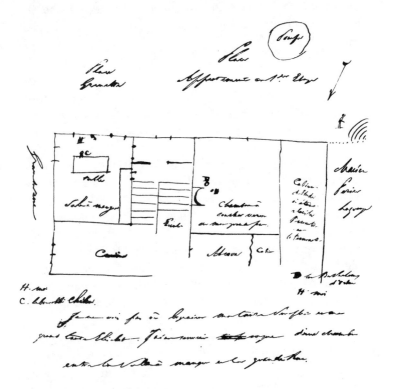

Plan first-floor apartment.

Place Grenette.—Pump.—Grande-Rue.—Table.—Dining-room. —Staircase.—My grandfather's green bedroom.—Study where the barometer and thermometer were placed.—Périer-Lagrange house. —Kitchen.—Alcove.—Cabinet.—H. Me.—The worthy *abbé* Chelan. —D. M. Barthélemy d'Orbane.—H. Me.

I can't see where my aunt Séraphie and my great-aunt Elisabeth were lodged. I have a vague memory of a room between the dining-room and the Grande-Rue.

against their parents and then more practically. To recalcitrant parents he would cite the example of Vaucanson.[4]

When my grandfather returned from Montpellier to Grenoble (doctor of medicine), he had a fine head of hair, but the public opinion of 1760 declared imperiously that if he didn't acquire a wig no one would have faith in him. An old cousin, Didier, who made him her heir along with my aunt Elisabeth and died around 1788, had been of that opinion. This worthy cousin used to make me eat yellow bread (with saffron) when I went to visit her on St Laurent's day. She lived in the street

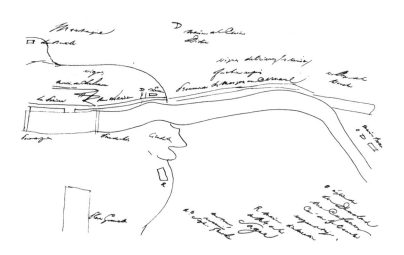

Mountain.—The Bastille.—D. Cousin Didier's house.—Vineyards.
—Slope up to Chalemont.—La Perrière.—Rue St-Laurent.—
St-Laurent.—Delightful (and well-worked) vineyards very well
situated.—Promenades of carnival maskers.—Village of La Tronche.
—Barral house.—Stone bridge.—Wooden bridge.—Citadel.—Place
Grenette.—O. Church of M. Dumolard, my confessor, *curé* of La
Tronche and a great *tejé* [jesuit].—Mlle de la Saigne's private school.
My sister, her friend, Mlle Sophie Gautier.

4. Jacques de Vaucanson (1709–1782) became famous as the inventor of automata. He was born in Grenoble.

and near the church of St Laurent; in the same street, my former nursemaid Françoise, whom I still adored, had a grocery shop; she had left my mother to get married. She was replaced by the beautiful Geneviève, her sister, whom my father played the gallant with, so it was said.

My grandfather's room, on the first floor overlooking the Grenette, was painted a crude green and from that time on my father used to say to me: "Grandpa may be very clever but he has no artistic taste."

The timid nature of the Frenchman means that he seldom uses bold colours: green, red, blue, bright yellow; he prefers uncertain shades. This apart, I can't see why my grandfather's choice was blameworthy. His bedroom faced due south; he read hugely, he wanted to spare his eyes, of which he sometimes complained.

But my reader, should these fripperies ever find one, will see easily enough that all my *reasons why*, all my explanations may be quite mistaken. I only have very clear mental pictures, that's all; all my explanations come as I write this, forty-five years after the events.

My excellent grandfather, who was in point of fact my true father and my close friend up until my decision, around 1796, to extricate myself from Grenoble through mathematics, often told of a wonderful thing.

My mother having had me carried into his (green) room, on the day I became one year old, 23 January 1784, was holding me upright near the window; my grandfather was over by the bed, he called me, I resolved to walk and got to him.

At that time I was talking a little and for a greeting would say *hateur*. My uncle used to tease his sister Henriette (my mother) about how ugly I was. It seems I had an enormous head, without any hair, and that I resembled Father Brulard, an astute monk, a bon viveur and very influential in his monastery, an uncle or great-uncle dead before I appeared.

I was very adventurous, whence two accidents recounted with terror and regret by my grandfather. Near the rocks by

Detail 23 January 1788 – 5 [1783].

Place Grenette.—Me.—Study.—My grandfather.—Alcove and
bed.—Place Grenette.—Pump.—Bedroom (uncertain).—Dining-
room.—Passageway.—My grandfather's green room. Cabinet.
A'. The top of this partition was glass to give light to the staircase. There was a door at V.

the Porte de France, I pricked a mule with a faggot sharpened into a point with a knife. It planted both hooves in my chest and knocked me down. "He could easily have been killed," said my grandfather.

I can picture the event, but probably this isn't a direct memory, it is only the memory of the mental image I formed of the affair a long way back at the time of the first accounts I was given of it.

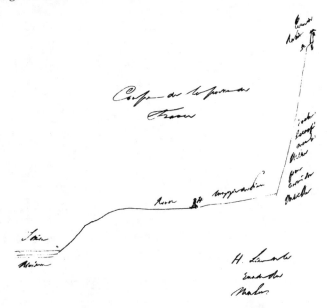

Cross-section of the Porte de France.
Rabot tower.—Isère, river.—Road.—Stone depot.—Steep rocks with quarry for getting rubble.—H. Place where the mule lashed out.

The second tragic event was that, in between my mother and my grandfather, I broke two front teeth falling onto the corner of a chair. My good grandfather couldn't get over his astonishment: "Between his mother and me!" he would repeat, as if lamenting the power of fatality.

The main characteristic of the first-floor ap[artmen]t as I

saw it was that I could hear the rumble of the iron bar which they did the pumping with; I got much pleasure from its long drawn-out, not at all grating lament.

Dauphinois good sense was more or less in revolt against the court. I can remember very well my grandfather setting off for the States in Romans[5]; at that time he was a patriot, highly regarded, but among the more moderate; picture to yourself Fontenelle as a tribune of the people.[6]

On the day of his departure, it was freezing hard (it was [*to be checked*] the great winter of 1789 to 1790), there was a foot of snow on the Place Grenette.

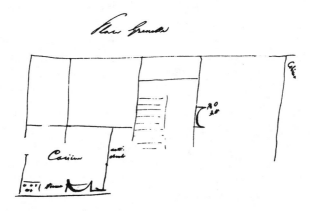

Place Grenette.—Cabinet.—Kitchen.—Anteroom.—Range.

There was a huge fire in the fireplace in my grandfather's room. The room was full of friends who had come to see him get into his carriage. M. Barthélemy d'Orbane, a close friend of the family, the most celebrated legal consultant in

5. I.e. the local political assembly, for the Dauphiné.

6. Bernard Le Bovier de Fontenelle (1657–1757), author and *philosophe*, renowned for his even temper and generosity of spirit.

the town, an oracle in questions of law, a fine position in a town with a parlement,[7] was at O and myself at H, in front of the crackling fire. I was the hero of the hour, for I'm convinced my grandfather missed only me in Grenoble and loved only me.

In this position, M. Barthélemy d'Orbane taught me to pull faces. I can see him now and myself too. It was an art in which I made the most rapid progress; I laughed myself at the expressions I put on in order to make others laugh. They soon objected to this growing liking for pulling faces but to no avail; it still survives, I often laugh at the expressions I put on when I'm alone.

A conceited fop goes past in the street wearing an affected expression (M. Lysi[maque], for example, or M. le Comte [*a blank*], the lover of Mme Del Monte), I imitate his expression and I laugh. My instinct is to imitate the movements or rather the affected positions of the face rather than those of the body.

In the Council of State, I used to imitate unwittingly and very riskily the self-important air of the famous Comte Regnault de St-Jean-d'Angély, who was sitting three yards away. Especially when, the better to hear the choleric *abbé* Louis, who was on the other side of the chamber facing him, he turned down the inordinately long collars of his shirt.

This instinct, or this art, for which I'm indebted to M. d'Orbane, has made me many enemies. Currently, the sensible Di Fiore upbraids me for my concealed irony, or rather ill-concealed irony which I can't help revealing in the right-hand corner of my mouth.

At Romans, my grandfather came within only five votes of being made a deputy.

"I'd have died there," he often repeated later, congratulating himself on having refused the votes of several rural bour-

7. Under the Ancien Régime, the provincial *parlements* were judicial rather than political bodies.

geois who had confidence in him and came to the house in the mornings to consult him.

His Fontenelle-like cautiousness stopped him having serious ambitions; he was very fond however of delivering speeches before a selected audience, at the Library for example. I can see myself there still, listening to him in the main auditorium filled with people, immense to my eyes. But why the crowd? What was the occasion? That's what the mental image doesn't say. It's only an image.

My grandfather often used to tell us of how in Romans his ink, which stood on his well heated mantelpiece, froze on the tip of his pen. He was not appointed, but got one or two deputies appointed whose names I have forgotten, but he never forgot the service he had rendered them and kept his eye on them in the assembly where he faulted them for their energy.

I was very fond of M. d'Orbane as well as the fat canon his brother; I used to go and call on them in the Place des Tilleuls or underneath the archway leading from the Place Notre-Dame into the Place des Tilleuls, only a step or two from Notre-Dame where the canon was a precentor. My father or grandfather used to send the celebrated advocate plump turkeys on the occasion of Christmas.

I was very fond too of Father Ducros, the defrocked Franciscan (from the monastery situated between the Jardin de Ville and the Franquières mansion, which I remember as being in the style of the Renaissance).

I was fond also of the amiable *abbé* Chelan, the *curé* of Risset near Claix, a small, lean man, all nerves and fieriness, of a sparkling wit, already middle-aged, appearing old to me, but who was perhaps only forty or forty-five, and whose arguments at table amused me vastly. He never failed to come and dine at my grandfather's when he came to Grenoble, and dinner was much more cheerful than usual.

One day, at supper, he had been talking for three-quarters of an hour holding a spoonful of strawberries in his hand. As he was about to eat the strawberries: "*Abbé*, you won't be saying your mass tomorrow," said my grandfather.

"Excuse me, I shall say it tomorrow, but not today, because it's past midnight."

This exchange kept me happy for a whole month, it seemed to me to be sparkling with wit. Such is wit for a young nation or a young man, the emotion is in them; witness the witty ripostes admired by Boccaccio or Vasari.

In those happy days, my grandfather took reli[gion] very unseriously, and these gentlemen were of his way of thinking; he only became sad and somewhat religious after my mother died (in 1790) and then, I believe, in the uncertain hope of finding her again in the next world. (Like M. de Broglie, who said of his attractive daughter, who died aged thirteen: "To me it's as if my daughter were in America.")

I fancy that M. *l'abbé* Chelan was dining at the house on the "Day of Tiles." This was the day when I saw the first blood spilt by the French Revolution. It was an unfortunate journeyman hatter S, fatally wounded by a bayonet S' in the small of his back.

We left the table in the middle of dinner T. I was at H and the *curé* Chelan at C.

I shall look up the date in some calendar of events. The mental image couldn't be sharper, it dates back forty-three years perhaps.

A M. de Clermont-Tonnerre, who was in command in the Dauphiné and occupied the government residence, an isolated house overlooking the ramparts (with a superb view over the slopes of Eybens, a beautiful, tranquil view, worthy of Claude Lorrain), entered through a beautiful courtyard in the Rue Neuve, near the Rue des Mûriers, wanted, I fancy, to disperse a gathering; he had two regiments, against which the populace defended itself by hurling down tiles from on top of the houses: hence the name, the "Day of Tiles."*

*I left a watercolour of this uprising done by M. Le Roy behind in Grenoble.

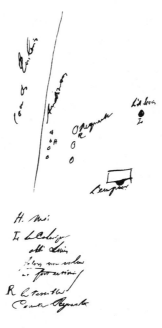

Courtyard of the Tuileries.—Commissioners.—Regnault.—The ab[bé] Louis. The Emperor.

H. Me.—L. The choleric abbé Louis (*at that time* not a thief but highly esteemed).—R. The terrible Comte Regnault.

One of the warrant officers in these regiments was Bernadotte, the present King of Sweden, as noble a soul as that of Murat, the King of Naples, though far more astute. Lefèvre, the wigmaker and a friend of my father's, often recounted to us how he had saved the life of General Bernadotte (as he used to say in 1804), who was cornered at the end of an alleyway. Lefèvre was a handsome, very brave fellow, and M[arsha]l Bernadotte had sent him a present.

But all this is history, recounted by eye-witnesses it's true, but which I didn't see. In future, in Russia and elsewhere, I only want to tell what *I have seen.*

---

*Is this learned tailpiece a good idea?

My relations having left the dinner-table before the end and finding myself alone at the dining-room window, or rather at the window of a room overlooking the Grande-Rue, I saw an old woman holding her old shoes in her hand and shouting at the top of her voice: "I'm in *revort*! I'm in *revort*!"

She was going from the Place Grenette into the Grande-Rue. I saw her at R coming from R'.

The absurdity of this revolt struck me forcibly. One old woman against a regiment! That same evening, my grandfather told me the story of the death of Pyrrhus.[8]

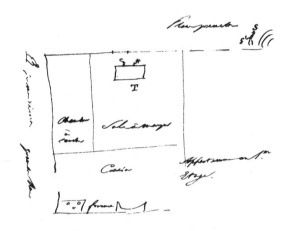

Place Grenette.—I'm in revort.—Grande-Rue.—Bedroom.—Dining-room.—Kitchen.—First-floor apartment.—Range.

My thoughts were still on the old woman when I was distracted by a tragic spectacle at O. A journeyman hatter, wounded in the back by a bayonet, so it was said, was walking with great difficulty, supported by two men round whose shoulders he had passed his arms. He had no coat; his shirt and nankeen or white trousers were soaked in blood, I can see him still, the wound from which the blood was flowing in

8. The Greek king who was killed by a tile thrown from a roof.

abundance was in the small of his back, roughly opposite his navel.

They were making him walk with difficulty to get him to his room, situated on the sixth floor of the Périer house, and when he got there he died.

Place Grenette.

My parents reprimanded me and removed me from the window of my grandfather's room so that I shouldn't see this horrible spectacle, but I kept returning. The window belonged to a first-floor room with very low ceilings.

I could see that poor devil again on each floor of the staircase in the Périer house, a staircase lit from tall windows overlooking the square.

Naturally enough, this is the clearest memory remaining to me from that time.

By contrast, I struggle to recapture a few vestiges of the memory of a public bonfire in Le Fontanil (road from Grenoble to Voreppe) where they had just burned *Lamoignon*.[9] I greatly regretted not seeing a large straw figure with clothes on. The fact is that my relations, *right-thinking* and much put out by any departure from *good order* ("Order prevails

---

9. Chrétien-François II de Lamoignon (1735–1789), a Chancellor whose tax policies were unpopular and who was burnt in effigy at Grenoble in 1788.

in Warsaw," said M. le G[enera]l Seb[astiani] around 1832[10]), didn't want me to be impressed by this evidence of the anger and vitality of the common people. Even at that age, I was of the opposite opinion; or perhaps my eight-year-old opinion is concealed by the very decided opinion which I held aged ten.

One time, Messrs Barthélemy d'Orbane, Canon Barthélemy, M. *l'abbé* Rey, M. Bouvier, everyone, were talking at my grandfather's about the imminent arrival of M. le M[arécha]l de Vaux.[11] "He'll make his entrance here like in a ballet," said my grandfather.

I thought hard about this bon mot which I didn't understand. What could an old marshal and a broom have in common, I said to myself?[12]

He died, I was deeply moved by the majestic sound of the bells. I was taken to see the *chapelle ardente* (in the army commander's residence, I fancy, near the Rue des Mûriers, a memory that is almost erased); I was struck by the spectacle of that black tomb lit in broad daylight by a large number of wax candles, the windows being closed. It was the idea of death appearing for the first time. I was taken by Lambert, my grandfather's manservant (*valet de chambre*) and my close friend. He was a handsome young man, very wide-awake.

One of his friends came and said to him: "The ma[rsh]al's daughter is nothing but a miser; the black cloth she's given the drummers to drape their drums with isn't enough to make a pair of breeches. The drummers are complaining bitterly, the custom is to give what it takes to make a pair of breeches."

Back at the house, I discovered that my relations also were talking about the marshal's daughter's miserliness.

10. Sebastiani was then French foreign minister and made this comment when Russian troops entered Warsaw in 1831.

11. Noël de Jourda, Comte de Vaux (1705–1788), appointed army commander in the Dauphiné after the "Day of Tiles."

12. The French for a broom is *balai*, hence the confusion with the word *ballet*.

The day after was a day of battle for me, I had great difficulty, I fancy, persuading them to let Lambert take me to see the cortège go past. There was a vast crowd. I can see myself at point H, between the main road and the Isère, near the lime kiln, two hundred paces this side and to the east of the Porte de France.

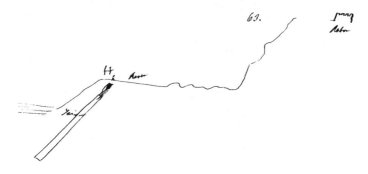

Rabot.—Road.—Isère.

The sound of the drums draped in the small swatches of black cloth insufficient to make a pair of breeches stirred me deeply. But here's something very different: I found myself at point H, at the far left-hand end of a battalion of the Austrasian regiment, I believe, white coats with black facings, L is Lambert giving me H his hand. I was six inches away from the last soldier of the regiment S.

Isère.—Battalion facing the rocks.

He suddenly said to me: "Move away a bit so I don't hurt you when I *fire*."

So they were going to fire! All these soldiers! They had reversed their arms.

I was scared to death; out of the corner of my eye I watched the black carriage in the distance slowly advancing across the stone bridge, drawn by six or eight horses. I waited trembling for the volley. The officer finally gave a shout, followed at once by the volley: gunfire. A great weight was lifted from me. At that moment the crowd dashed towards the draped carriage which I was delighted to see, I fancy there were wax candles.

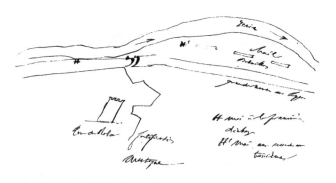

Isère.—Mall.—Battalions.—Main road to Lyon.—Rabot tower.—Fortifications.—Mountain.—H. Me at the first volley.—H'. Me at the second and third.

They let off a second, perhaps a third volley, outside the Porte de France, but I had had my baptism of fire.

I fancy I can also remember something of the departure for Vizille (the provincial States, held at the Château of Vizille, built by the Constable of Lesdiguières). My grandfather adored old things and evoked a sublime mental picture of this château for me by the way he talked about it. I was beginning to develop a veneration for the nobility, but my friends, Messrs de Saint-Ferréol and de Sinard, soon cured me.

They took mattresses, tied on behind the (two-wheeled) post-chaises.

"Young Mounier," as my grandfather used to say, came to

the house. It was as the result of an abrupt separation that his daughter and I didn't subsequently develop a violent passion for one another, a half-hour I spent underneath a carriage entrance in the Rue Montmartre, near the boulevard, during a downpour, in 1803 or 1804, when M. Mounier went to perform the duties of a prefect in Rennes. My letters to his son Edouard; letter from Victorine, addressed to me. The best of it is that Edouard, I fancy, believes I went to Rennes.

The small, stiff, badly painted portrait to be seen in a room adjoining the Public Library in Grenoble, showing M. Mounier in his prefect's uniform, unless I'm mistaken, is a good likeness. The face shows firmness but a limited intelligence. His son, whom I knew well in 1803 and in Russia in 1812 (Viazma-on-guts[13]), is a dullard, astute, sly, a true Dauphinois just like Casimir Périer, the minister,[14] but the latter has met someone even more of a Dauphinois than himself. Edouard Mounier has the Dauphinois drawl even though brought up in Weimar, he is a peer of France and a baron, and sits bravely in judgment in the Court of Peers (1835, December).[15]

Will the reader believe me if I dare to add that I wouldn't want to change places with Messrs Félix Faure and Mounier, peers of France and once my friends?

My grandfather, a fond and zealous friend to any young person who liked hard work, lent M. Mounier books and supported him against his father's criticisms. Going down the Grande-Rue, he would sometimes go into the latter's shop and talk to him about his son. The old draper, who had a lot of children and could think only in utilitarian terms, was mortally aggrieved to see this son wasting his time reading.

M. Mounier junior's strong point was his character, but his

13. The Viazma is a river near Smolensk and was the scene of a bloody battle in 1812, during Napoleon's Russian campaign.

14. Casimir-Pierre Périer (1777–1832), became president of the Chamber of Deputies in 1830 and subsequently minister of the interior. He was a native of Grenoble.

15. This is the first of several references to the case of the "April conspirators," who in 1834 had been arrested for plotting against the monarchy.

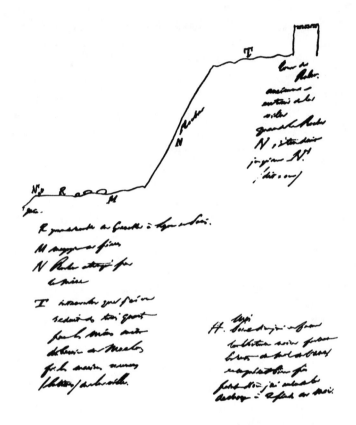

Rabot tower. Old entrance to the town when the rocks N extended as far as N' (so they say).—Rocks.—Isère.—R. Main road from Grenoble to Lyon and Paris.—M. Stone depot.—N. Rocks eaten into by the quarry.—T. Gap I saw reduced by three quarters by quarrying as a result of the need for stone for the new houses (masonry) in the town.—H. Me. Point from which I saw the black carriage pass bearing the remains of the M[aréch]al de Vaux, and what's worse, point from which I heard the guns go off two feet away from me.

understanding didn't match his steadiness. My grandfather used to laugh when telling us, a few years later, of how when Mme Borel, who was to become M. Mounier's mother-in-law, came in to buy some cloth, M. Mounier, as his father's assistant, laid out the bolt, felt the cloth and added: "This cloth sells at twenty-seven *livres* the ell."

"Very well, *monsieur*, I'll give you twenty-five," said Mme Borel.

Whereupon M. Mounier folded the piece of cloth up again, and put it frostily back into its compartment.

"But *monsieur, monsieur!*" said Mme Borel in astonishment, "I'll gladly go up to twenty-five *livres* ten *sous*."

"*Madame*, an honest man has only his word." The good bourgeoise was greatly shocked.

This same love of hard work among the young, which today would make my grandfather so guilty, led him to take young Barnave under his wing.

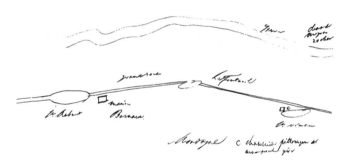

Isère.—Dent de Moirans. Rocks. Main road.—Le Fontanil.—St-Robert.—Barnave house.—St-Vincent.—Mountain.—C. My grandfather's picturesque cottage.

Barnave,[*] our neighbour in the country, he at Saint-Robert, ourselves at S[ain]t-Vincent (road from Grenoble to Voreppe and Lyon). Séraphie detested him and soon afterwards welcomed his death and the scant inheritance that remained to his sisters, one of whom was called, I fancy, Mme St-Germain. Every time we went past Saint-Robert: "Ah, there's the Barnave house," Séraphie would say.

[*]23 Dec 35. Tired of working *after* three o'clock.

Her attitude towards him was one of affronted piety. My grandfather was very well received by the nobility and was the oracle of the bourgeoisie, and I believe the immortal Barnave's mother, who grieved to see him neglecting his lawsuits for Mably[16] and Montesquieu, had her mind set at rest by my grandfather. In those days, our fellow-countryman Mably counted for something and two years later they gave his name to the Rue des Clercs.*

16. Gabriel Bonnot de Mably (1709–1785), historian and *philosophe* and another native of Grenoble.

*To be fitted in. Secret of Messrs Rothschild's fortune seen by Dominique 23 December 1835.

They sell what everyone wants, stocks and shares, and moreover have turned themselves into manufacturers (*id est* by taking on loans).

I would need a map of Grenoble and to paste it in here; get hold of the death certificates of my parents, which would give me the dates, and the birth certificate O F M Y D E A R E S T M O T H E R and my worthy grandfather.

December 1835.

Who thinks of them today apart from me, and how fondly of my mother dead these forty-six years! So I can speak freely of their faults. The same justification for Mme la Baronne de Barcoff, Mme Alex[andrine] Petit, Mme la Baronne Dembowski (how long it is since I wrote that name!), Virginie, 2 Victorines, Angela, Mélanie, Alex[andrine], Métilde, Clémentine, Julia, Albert[e] de Rub[empré] adored for one month only:

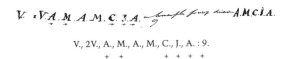

V., 2V., A., M., A., M., C., J., A. : 9.
+   +   + + + +

A positive man would say A., M., C., J., A.

The right I have to write these *Memoirs*: what human being doesn't like to be remembered!

20 December 1835.

Facts to be fitted in in their place, put behind here so as not to forget them: appointment as inspector of furnishings, behind page 254 of the present numbering: At age seven, started Latin, so in 1790.

Facts set down here so as not to forget them, to be put in in their place:

Why [Rome] weighs heavily on me.

The fact is I have no company in the evenings to distract me from my thoughts of the morning. When I was writing a book in Paris, I used to work until my head spun and I was unable to walk. When it struck six, I had to go and dine however, on pain of upsetting the restaurant-owner's waiters and for a 3fr 50 dinner, which was often the case, and I blushed at that. I would go to a salon; there, unless it was very third-rate, I was totally distracted from my work of that morning, to the point where I had even forgotten its subject when I got home at one a.m.

Tiredness in the mornings. That's what I miss in [Rome]: the company is so lacklustre (Mme Sandre, THE MOTHER OF Marietta), the Comtesse Koven, the Princesse de Da[a blank] aren't worth the effort of getting into a carriage.

None of this can distract me from my thoughts of the morning so that when I resume working in the afternoon, instead of being fresh and reinvigorated, I am exhausted, done in.

And after four or five days of this life, my work disgusts me, I have actually worn out my ideas by thinking about them too continuously. I take a fortnight's trip from C[ivit]a-V[ecchi]a to Ravenna (October 1835). This is too long a gap, I have *forgotten* my work. That is why *Le Chasseur vert* [*trans*. the novel which Stendhal was then writing, never finished, but which was published posthumously in 1855 as *Lucien Leuwen*] languishes, this is what, along with the complete absence of good music, displeases me about Rome.

CHAPTER 6

After my mother's death, my grandfather was in despair. I can see, but only today, that he was a man whose character must have been of the Fontenelle kind, modest, prudent, discreet, extremely amiable and amusing before the death of his beloved daughter. Afterwards he would often withdraw into a discreet silence. That daughter was all that he loved in the world.

His other daughter, Séraphie, bored and irritated him, he loved peace and quiet before all else, and she thrived only on scenes. My worthy grandfather, thinking of his paternal authority, reproached himself keenly for not baring his teeth; *that is a local expression*; I preserve them, subject to translating them later into the French of Paris; I preserve them at this moment the better to recall the facts which come crowding in on me. M. Gagnon esteemed and feared his sister, who in youth had preferred to him a brother who had died in Paris, something that the surviving brother had never forgiven her for; but with his amiable and pacific, Fontenelle-like character, this in no way showed; I guessed it later on.

M. Gagnon had a sort of aversion towards his son, Romain Gagnon, my uncle, a brilliant and thoroughly amiable young man.

It was the possession of this last quality, I fancy, which came between father and son; the two of them, though in different styles, were the most attractive men in the town. My grandfather never overstepped the mark with his pleasantries, and his subtle, dry wit could pass unnoticed. He was moreover a prodigy of science for those days (when the most comical ignorance flourished). To get their revenge, the stupid and the envious (Messrs Champel, Tournus [the cuckold], Tourte) were constantly complimenting him on his memory. He knew, believed and quoted the approved authors on all sorts of subjects.

"My son has read nothing," he would sometimes say gruffly.

This was only too true, but it was impossible to be bored in a company that included M. Gagnon junior. His father had given him a charming apartment in his house, had made him a lawyer. In a town with a parlement everyone loved chicanery and lived off chicanery and made witty remarks about chicanery. I still know a number of jokes about the *petitoire* and the *possessoire*.[1]

My grandfather gave his son room and board, plus an allowance of one hundred francs a month, a huge sum in Grenoble pre-1789, as pocket-money, and my uncle bought embroidered thousand-*écu* coats and kept actresses.

I caught only glimpses of these things which I worked out from my uncle's hints. I presume my uncle used to receive presents from his rich mistresses, with which money he dressed luxuriously and supported his poor mistresses. You must know that, in our part of the country and at that time, there was nothing wrong with receiving money from Mme Delauron or Mme de Marcieu or Mme de Sassenage, provided you spent it *hic et nunc* and didn't hoard it. *Hic et nunc* was a form of words that Grenoble owed to its parlement.

It happened several times that my grandfather would arrive at M. de Quinsonas's or in some other circle, and would catch sight of an expensively dressed young man to whom everyone was listening: it was his son.

"My father didn't know I had that coat," my uncle would say to me; "I vanished as soon as I could and went home to

1. Legal terms: the *petitoire* was a legal claim made on a property, the *possessoire* the opposing claim to *de facto* possession.

put my modest frock-coat back on. When my father said to me: 'But do me the small pleasure of telling me where you get the money to dress like that.' 'I gamble and I'm lucky,' I answered. 'Then why don't you pay off your debts?' 'And Mme Such-and-Such who wanted to see me in the fine coat she had bought me!' my uncle went on. 'I got out of it by some piece of nonsense or other.'"

I don't know whether my reader of 1880 knows a novel still very celebrated even today: *Les Liaisons dangereuses* had been composed in Grenoble by an artillery officer, M. Choderlos de Laclos, and depicted the mores of Grenoble.

I even knew Mme de Merteuil[2]; she was Mme de Montmaur, who used to give me crystallized nuts, a lame woman who had the Drevon house in Le Chevallon, near the church of S[ain]t-Vincent, between Le Fontanil and Voreppe, but nearer to Le Fontanil. The width of the road divided Mme de Montmaur's property (or the one Mme de Montmaur rented) from that of M. Henri Gagnon. The wealthy young person who is forced to go into a convent must have been a Mademoiselle de Blacons, from Voreppe. This family was of an exemplary sadness, piety, orthodoxy and ultraism, or at least it was exemplary around 1814, when the Emperor sent me as a commissioner to the army's 7th Division along with the old senator, the Comte de St-Vallier, one of the roués from my uncle's day and who talked a lot about him to me as having caused Mme This and Mme That to commit some notable follies; I've forgotten their names. At that time I was aflame with the sacred fire and could think only of ways of driving the Austrians back or at least of preventing them from coming in so quickly.

Thus I saw Mme de Merteuil's way of life at its close, as a child of nine or ten consumed by a temperament of fire may see those things which everyone avoids spelling out to him.

2. The selfish and sadistic female schemer of Laclos's novel.

CHAPTER 7

At the time of my mother's death then, around 1790, my family consisted of Messrs Gagnon senior, aged sixty; Romain Gagnon, his son, twenty-five; Séraphie, his daughter, twenty-four; Elisabeth, his sister, sixty-four; Chérubin Beyle, his son-in-law, forty-three; Henri, his son, aged seven; Pauline, his daughter, four; Zénaïde, his daughter, two.

These were the characters in the unhappy drama of my youth, which I remember as nearly all suffering and profound moral frustrations. But let's see briefly what they were like, these characters.

My grandfather, Henri Gagnon, aged sixty; his daughter Séraphie, that she-devil whose age I never knew, she may have been twenty-two or twenty-four; his sister Elisabeth Gagnon, aged sixty-four; a tall, lean, spare woman, with a fine Italian face, an altogether noble character, but noble with the refinements and scruples of conscience of a Spaniard. In this respect she formed my own heart and it's to my aunt Elisabeth that I owe the ghastly illusions of nobility *à l'espagnole* into which I fell during the first thirty years of my life. I presume that my aunt Elisabeth, who was rich (for Grenoble), had remained a spinster after an unhappy love affair. I learnt something to that effect from the lips of my aunt Séraphie in early childhood.

The family consisted finally of my father.

Joseph-Chérubin Beyle, a lawyer in the Parlement, later an ultra and a chevalier of the Légion d'Honneur, deputy-mayor of Grenoble, died in 1819 aged seventy-two, so they say; which assumes he was born in 1747. So in 1790 he was aged forty-three.

He was an extremely unattractive man, his thoughts forever on the acquisition and selling of land, excessively artful, used to selling to peasants and to buying from them, the complete Dauphinois. Never was there a soul less Spanish, less extravagantly noble than his, hence my aunt Elisabeth's antipathy for him. He was moreover excessively wrinkled and ugly, and ill at ease and silent with women, whom he needed all the same.

This latter quality had given him an insight into *La Nouvelle Héloïse* and other works by Rousseau, of whom he only ever spoke adoringly even as he cursed him for his impiety, for my mother's death had plunged him into the most exalted and ridiculous religiosity. He took it on himself to say all the priestly offices; for three or four years there was even talk of his taking holy orders, but he was probably held back by the wish to leave me his lawyer's position: he was on the point of being made a *consistorial*[1]; this was a noble distinction among lawyers which he spoke of in the way a young grenadier lieutenant speaks of the cross. He didn't love me as an individual, but as a son who would carry on his family.

It would have been very hard for him to love me: 1, he could easily see that I had no love for him; I never spoke to him unless I needed to, for he was a stranger to all the fine literary and philosophical ideas which formed the basis of my questions to my grandfather and the excellent replies of that amiable old man. I saw very little of him. My passion for escaping from Grenoble, i.e. from him, and my passion for mathematics, the one means I had of escaping from that town which I abhorred and which I hate still, for it was there I learnt to know humankind, my mathematical passion plunged me into a profound solitude from 1797 to 1799. I can say that

1. One of forty lawyers in the Parlement responsible for professional discipline.

in those two years and even during part of 1796 I laboured as Michelangelo laboured in the Sistine.

Once I had left at the end of October 1799, I remember the date because on the 18 Brumaire, the 9 November,[2] I was in Nemours, I was nothing to my father except a demander of money; the coldness increased all the time, he couldn't open his mouth without upsetting me. My horror was of selling a field to a peasant after a week of haggling to make a profit of 300fr: that was his passion.

Nothing more natural. His own father who bore, I believe, the great name of *Pierre* Beyle[3] died unexpectedly of gout, in Claix, at the age of sixty-three. At eighteen (so it was around 1765) my father found himself with an estate in Claix which brought in 800 or 1800fr, one or the other, an attorney's practice and ten sisters to provide for, a mother who was a wealthy heiress, that is with 60,000 [francs] perhaps, and an absolute devil in her capacity as heiress. For a long time in my childhood she used to smack me when I pulled the tail of her dog Azor (a Bologna spaniel with a long white coat). So money was, and with cause, my father's one big idea, while I've only ever thought about it with distaste. The thought evokes cruel torments for me, because having it gives me no sort of pleasure, but being without it is a vile misfortune.

Never perhaps has chance brought two more fundamentally antipathetic beings together than my father and myself.

Whence the absence of all pleasure in my childhood, from 1790 to 1799. Thanks to my father the season everyone says is that of life's true pleasures was for me no more than a bitter succession of grief and discouragement. Two devils had been unleashed against my poor childhood, my aunt Séraphie and my father who, from 1791 on, became her slave.

2. This was the date of the *coup d'état* by which Napoleon took power in France, with the rank of First Consul.

3. Pierre Bayle (1647–1706) was the author of a celebrated *Dictionnaire historique et critique* which established him as a tolerant and sceptical forerunner of the *philosophes*, and hence an anathema to such as Chérubin Beyle.

The reader may take comfort concerning the account of my misfortunes, in the first place he can skip a few pages, a course I implore him to follow: because I'm thoughtlessly writing down things that are very tedious even for 1835 perhaps, what will they be like in 1880?

Secondly, I have almost no memories of the miserable period 1790–5, during which I was a poor little persecuted bambino, forever being told off for the least thing and defended only by a Fontenelle-like sage who refused to do battle on my behalf, and all the more so because in the event of a battle his supreme authority would command him to raise his voice more; which is the thing he most dreaded; as my aunt Séraphie, who for some reason or other had taken against me, knew very well.

Fifteen or twenty days after my mother's death, my father and I returned to sleep in the cheerless house, I in a small varnished cot with bars, standing in my father's alcove. He sent his servants away and ate at my grandfather's, who would never hear of being paid. I believe it was out of friendship for me that my grandfather thus inflicted on himself the habitual company of a man he found antipathetic.

They were united only in their feeling of profound grief. On the occasion of my mother's death my family broke off all its ties with society and, as a crowning annoyance for myself, lived thereafter in constant isolation.

M. Joubert, a mournful pedant from the mountains (in Grenoble they call them *bet*, meaning an uncouth man born in the mountains of Gap), M. Joubert who taught me Latin, very stupidly God knows, by making me recite the rules out of the primer, something which revolted my intelligence, and it was allowed I had plenty of that, died. I used to go and have lessons from him on the little Place Notre-Dame; I can say that I never went there without recalling my mother and the perfect gaiety of the life I had led in her day. At present, I felt a dislike even for my kindly grandfather when he kissed me.

The pedantic Joubert with the terrible face left me as a

legacy the second volume of a French translation of Quintus Curtius, that worthless Roman who wrote the life of Alexander.

Though this frightful pedant, five foot six inches tall, horribly thin, clad in a dirty, black, torn frock-coat, wasn't so wicked deep down.

But his successor, M. *l'abbé* Raillane, was a wicked scoundrel in the full sense of the term. I am not claiming he had committed crimes, but it would be hard to meet with a soul more dried-up, more opposed to all that is honourable, more completely detached from all human feeling. He was a priest, a native of a village in Provence, he was short, thin, very tight-lipped, with a green complexion, a false stare and an abominable smile.

He had just completed the education of Casimir and Augustin Périer and their four or six brothers.

Casimir has been a minister, and celebrated, and in my opinion the dupe of Louis-Philippe. Augustin, the most pompous of m[en], died a peer of France. Scipion died a little mad around 1806. Camille has been a worthless prefect and has just married for the second time a very wealthy woman; he's a little mad like all his brothers. Joseph, the husband of a pretty, extremely affected woman, who has had some celebrated affairs, was perhaps the most sensible of the lot. Another one, Amédée I believe, having been robbed at the gaming table around 1815, chose to spend five years in Sainte-Pélagie rather than pay up.

All these brothers were mad during the month of May. Well, I believe they owed that advantage in part to our common tutor, M. *l'abbé* Raillane.

Either out of artfulness, or education, or priestly instinct, this man was the sworn enemy of logic and all right reasoning.

My father took him on seemingly out of vanity. M. Périer *Milord*, the minister Casimir's father, passed for being the richest man in the locality. In point of fact, he had ten or eleven children and left each of them three hundred and fifty thousand fr. What an honour for a lawyer in the Parlement to take on for his own son the tutor who had come from M. Périer's house!

Perhaps M. Raillane had been dismissed for some misdemeanour. What puts that suspicion into my mind today is that there were still three very young children in the Périer household, Camille of my own age, Joseph and Amédée, I believe, much younger.*

I have absolutely no idea what financial arrangements my father came to with the *abbé* Raillane. To give any attention to money matters was deemed supremely low and contemptible in my family. To talk about money was somehow infra dig, money was a sad necessity, as it were, and its role alas indispensable, like that of the privy, but it was never to be spoken of. They spoke none the less, and exceptionally, about the tidy sums a building had cost, the word building being uttered with respect: M. Bellier paid 20,000 *écus* for his property in Voreppe. Pariset cost our cousin Colomb more than 12,000 *écus* (of 3fr).

I don't know where this revulsion against talking about money, so contrary to the usages of Paris, came from, but it took complete hold in my character. The sight of a large sum of gold awakens no other thought in me than the bother of keeping it safe from thieves; this feeling has often been taken for an affectation, and I shall say no more about it.

All honour, all the exalted, extravagant sentiments in the family we got from my aunt Elisabeth; these sentiments reigned despotically over the household, yet she spoke of them only very rarely, perhaps once in two years; generally they were led up to by a eulogy of her father. This woman of a rare loftiness of character was adored by me, and may then have been sixty-five years old; always very neatly dressed and using expensive materials for her very modest wardrobe. You

*Idea. If I don't correct this first draft, perhaps I shall manage not to tell lies out of vanity.

can well imagine that it is only today, and when I think about it, that I discover these things. For example, I don't know the physiognomies[4] of any of my relations, yet their features are present to me down to the smallest detail. If I can partly picture to myself my excellent grandfather's physiognomy, it is because of the visit I made to him when I was already a commissioner or assistant in the Com[missariat of War]; the date of that visit has completely gone. I became a man very late on where character is concerned; that is how I now explain my lack of memory for physiognomies. Up until the age of twenty-five, what am I saying, even now I often have to hold on to myself with both hands so as not to be totally absorbed by the sensations produced in me by objects and to be able to judge them rationally, from my experience. But what the devil does this matter to the reader? What does any of this book matter? Yet if I don't probe more deeply into the character of Henri, which is so hard for me to know, I am not conducting myself as an honest author trying to tell all he can know about his subject. I beg my publisher, if I ever have one, to cut these longueurs severely short.

One day my aunt Elisabeth Gagnon grew sad at the memory of her brother, who died young in Paris; we were alone one after-dinner in her room overlooking the Grenette. Obviously that lofty soul was responding to its own thoughts, but because she was fond of me, she addressed me for form's sake.

"What character!" (which meant: what will-power). "What energy! Ah, how different!" (This meant: how different from *this* one, my grandfather, Henri Gagnon.)

And she at once caught herself up and, remembering before whom she was talking, she added: "*I've never gone so far before.*"

---

4. Stendhal makes much use of this term, now rather rare, but which was in vogue early in the nineteenth century as the result of the works of Lavater and others, who taught that people's characters might be determined from close study of their features.

I: "How old was he when he died?"

Mlle Eli[sabeth]: "Twenty-three."

The dialogue lasted a long time, she got on to talking about her father. Among a hundred details forgotten by me she said: "At such and such a time, *he wept with rage hearing that the enemy was approaching Toulon.*"

(But when did the enemy approach Toulon? Around 1736 perhaps, during the war signalled by the battle of L'Assiette, of which I have just seen in [18]34 an engraving interesting for being *truthful*.)

He would have wanted the militia to march. Now nothing in the world was more contrary to the sentiments of my grandfather Gagnon, a veritable Fontenelle, the wittiest and least patriotic man I have ever known. Patriotism would have been an ignoble distraction for my grandfather from his elegant, literary ideas. My father would instantly have worked out what it might bring in. My uncle Romain would have said with a look of alarm: "Dammit, that might put me in some danger." My old aunt's heart and my own throbbed with concern.

Perhaps I am advancing things somewhat in respect of myself and ascribing to the age of seven or eight the feelings I had at nine or ten. It's impossible for me to distinguish between my feelings on the same subjects from two adjoining periods.

What I'm certain of is that the solemn and rebarbative portrait of my grandfather in its frame gilded with large roses half a foot across, which I had found almost frightening, became dear and sacred to me once I learnt of the valiant and generous sentiment inspired in him by the enemy's advance on Toulon.

CHAPTER 8

This was the occasion when my aunt Elisabeth told me how my grandfather had been born in Avignon, a town in Provence, a country *where oranges grew*, she said in a tone of regret, and much nearer to Toulon than Grenoble. You must know that the town's great splendour was sixty or eighty orange-trees in boxes, provided perhaps by the Connétable de Lesdiguières, the last great personage produced by the Dauphiné, which on the approach of summer were set down with great ceremony in the vicinity of the magnificent avenue of chestnut trees, also planted, I believe, by Lesdiguières.

"So there's a country where orange-trees grow out in the open?" I said to my aunt.

I realize today that, without knowing it, I had reminded her of the everlasting object of her nostalgia.

She told me of how we had originated from a country even more beautiful than Provence (we, the Gagnons that is), that as the result of a most disastrous event, her grandfather's grandfather had come to seek refuge in Avignon in the retinue of a pope; that there he had been obliged to change his name slightly and go into hiding, that he had then made his living from the trade of surgeon.

With what I know today about Italy I shall translate as follows: that a M. Guadagni or Guadaniamo, having committed some unimportant murder in Italy, had come to Avignon around 1650, in the retinue of some legate. What then struck me forcibly, was that we had come (for I saw myself as a

Gagnon and never thought of the Beyles except with a repugnance which still endures in 1835), that we had come from a country where orange-trees grow out in the open. What a land of delight, I thought!

What may have confirmed me in this notion of an Italian origin, was that the language of that country was greatly honoured in the family, a very odd thing in a bourgeois family of 1780. My grandfather knew and honoured Italian; my poor mother read Dante, something very hard even in our own day; M. Artaud, who has spent twenty years in Italy and has just published a translation of Dante, has committed not fewer than two mistranslations and one absurdity per page. Of all the Frenchmen known to me, two only: M. Fauriel, who gave me the Arab love stories, and M. Delécluze, of the *Débats*,[1] understand Dante, yet all the hacks in Paris endlessly take away from that great name by quoting him and claiming to explain him. Nothing makes me more indignant.

My respect for Dante is of long standing; it dates from the copies which I found on the shelf in my father's library occupied by my poor mother's books and which provided my one consolation during the *Raillane tyranny*.

My revulsion for that man's profession and for what he taught professionally reached a point verging on mania.

Will you believe that only yesterday, 4 December 1835, coming from R[ome] to C[ivita-V[ecchia], I had the opportunity of rendering a very great service, without putting myself out, to a young woman whom I don't suppose to be so very unwilling? Along the way she found out my name without my wanting it; she was the bearer of a letter of recommendation for my secretary. She has very beautiful eyes and those eyes gazed at me none too unfavourably for the last eight leagues of the journey. She begged me to find her some inexpensive lodgings; in short it was probably entirely up to me

1. The "Arab love stories" were supplied for inclusion in Stendhal's treatise *On Love*, published in 1822; the *Débats* is the newspaper *Le Journal des Débats*, a liberal daily which lasted from 1789 until 1940.

whether she looked kindly on me, but in the past week as I've been writing this, the fateful memory of the M. *l'abbé* Raillane has been revived. The aquiline but rather too small nose of that pretty Lyonnaise, Mme [*a blank*], reminded me of that of the *abbé*, and from then on it was impossible for me even to look at her, and I made pretence of sleeping in the carriage. Even after having taken her aboard as a favour and for eight *écus* instead of twenty-five, I hesitated from going to visit the new quarantine house so as not to be obliged to see her and receive her thanks.

Since there is no consolation, nothing but dirt and ugliness in my memories of the *abbé* Raillane, for twenty years at least I have been averting my eyes in horror from the memory of that terrible time. That man should have made a scoundrel of me; he was, I can now see, the complete jesuit; he would take me aside on our walks along the Isère, from the Porte de la Graille to the mouth of the Drac, or simply to a small wood past the far end of the island A, in order to explain to me that I had spoken out of turn:

"But *monsieur*," I would say to him in other words, "it's true, that is what I feel."

"No matter, my young friend, you mustn't say so, it's not done."

If these maxims had taken hold today I should be rich, for good fortune has knocked on my door three or four times. (In May 1814, I refused the overall command of supplies [wheat] in Paris, under the orders of M. le C[om]te Beugnot whose wife had the keenest friendship for me; next to her lover, M. Pépin de Belle-Isle, my close friend, I was perhaps who she liked best.) I should be rich then, but I should be a scoundrel, I shouldn't have the delightful visions of the *beautiful* which still often fill my head at my age of FIFTY-TWO.

The reader is perhaps thinking that I'm trying to remove from me the fateful cup of having to speak of the *abbé* Raillane.

He had a brother who was a tailor at the end of the

Grande-Rue near the Place Claveyson and who was ignominy personified. This jesuit lacked only one disagreeable quality, he wasn't dirty but, on the contrary, very clean and well cared-for. He had a liking for canaries; he bred them and kept them very tidy, but next to my bed. I can't conceive how my father tolerated something so unhygienic.

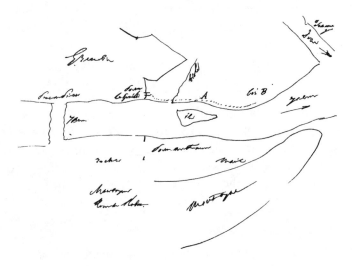

Grenoble.—Drac.—Sassenage.—Stone bridge.—Porte de la Graille.—Biole.—Wood B.—Isère.—Island.—Isère.—Porte de France.—Rocks.—Mall.—Mountain.—Rabot tower.—Mountain.

My grandfather had never come back up into the house after the death of his daughter, he wouldn't have put up with it; my father Chérubin Beyle, as I have said, loved me as the upholder of his name but not at all as his son.

The canaries' cage was of wire fastened to wooden uprights, themselves fastened to the wall by plaster clamps, and may have been nine feet long, by six high and four deep. Within this space there fluttered sadly far from the sunlight thirty or so wretched canaries of every hue. When they were nesting, the *abbé* fed them on the yolks of eggs, and of all the things he did this one alone interested me. But those accursed birds used to wake at first light; soon afterwards I would hear the *abbé*'s shovel as he arranged his fire with a care that I recognized later as peculiar to the jesuits. But the aviary gave off a strong smell, and only two feet from my bed and in a damp, dark room, into which the sun never came. We had no window overlooking the Lamouroux garden, only an *ancient light* (parlement towns are full of legal terms) which gave a brilliant light to the staircase L, shaded by a fine lime-tree, although the staircase was at least forty feet from the ground. That lime-tree must have been very tall.

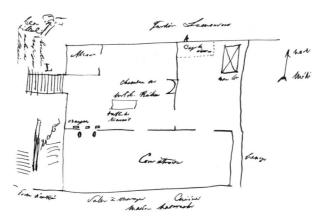

Fine lime-trees.—Lamouroux garden.—Staircase joining the one in the house.—Alcove.—M. *l'abbé* Raillane's room.—Work-table. —Orange-trees.—Bird-cage.—My bed.—Staircase.—Narrow courtyard.—North.—South.—Passageway.—Main entrance.—Dining-room.—Kitchen.—My father's house.

The *abbé* would get into a calm, gloomy, spiteful temper like some phlegmatic diplomat whenever I ate my dry crust at teatime near his orange-trees. These orange-trees were a veritable obsession, far more inconvenient than that with the birds. Some were three inches and the others a foot tall, and they stood over the window O, which got a little sun during two months in the summer. The *abbé* inevitably claimed that the crumbs falling from our bread attracted the flies, which ate the orange-trees. This *abbé* could have given lessons in pettiness to the most bourgeois, the most *patets* (*patet*, pronounced *patais*, paying excessive attention to the most trivial matters) of the town's bourgeois.

My companions, Messrs Chazel and Reytiers, were much less unfortunate than myself. Chazel was a good lad, already grown up, whose father, a southerner I believe, meaning a brusque, outspoken, coarse man and Messrs Périer's commissioning clerk, didn't much hold with Latin. He used to arrive *alone* (without a servant) around ten o'clock, do his Latin *exercise* badly and go off at half-past twelve; often he didn't come in the evenings.

Reytiers was an exceedingly pretty boy, fair-haired and as timid as a young girl, who didn't dare look the terrible *abbé* Raillane in the face. He was the only son of a father who was the most timid and most religious of men. He used to arrive as early as eight o'clock in the stern custody of a manservant who came to collect him as midday sounded from Saint-André (the fashionable church of the town, whose bells we could hear very clearly). No later than two the man would bring Reytiers back with his tea in a basket. In summer, around five, M. Raillane would take us out for a walk, in winter rarely, and then it was at around three. Chazel, who was *grown up*, became fed up with the walk and very soon left us.

Our great ambition was to go in the direction of the island in the Isère; in the first place there is a delightful view of the mountains from there, and one of the *literary* failings of my father and M. Raillane was endlessly to exaggerate the beauties of nature (which those beautiful souls can have had very little sense of, they thought only about making money). By dint of talking to us about the beauty of the rocks of La Buisserate, M. *l'abbé* Raillane had made us raise our heads. But it was a quite different object which caused us to like the riverbank near the island. There we poor captives could see young people *enjoying their freedom*, coming and going *on their own* and later bathing in the Isère and a tributary stream called the Biole. An excess of happiness of which we couldn't even glimpse the possibility in the most distant future.

Like a true ministerial newspaper of our own day, M. Raillane knew only how to talk to us about the dangers of freedom. He could never see a child bathing without predicting that he would end by drowning himself, thus doing us the service of turning us into cowards, and he succeeded perfectly where I am concerned. I have never managed to learn to swim. When I was free two years later, around 1795, I think, and still deceiving my parents and making up a new falsehood every day, I had thoughts already of escaping from Grenoble whatever the cost, I was in love with Mme Kubly and swimming was no longer an object of sufficient interest for me to learn it. Every time I got into the water Roland (Alphonse) or some other *expert* pushed my head under.

I have no dates during the frightful Raillane tyranny; I became gloomy and hated everyone. My great unhappiness was not to be able to play with other children; my father, probably very proud at having a tutor for his son, feared nothing so much as seeing me *mix with the common children*: that was the phrase the aristocrats used in those days. One thing alone might supply me with a date: Mlle Marine Périer (the sister of the minister Casimir Périer) came to see M. Raillane, who may have been her confessor, shortly before her marriage to that madman Camille Teisseire (a fanatical patriot who later burnt his copies of Voltaire and Rousseau), who, in 1811, he being a sub-prefect through the good graces of M. Crétet, his cousin, was so astounded by the favour whereby he saw me established in the salon of Mme la Comtesse Daru (on the ground floor overlooking the garden of the Hôtel de Biron, I fancy, a Civil List residence, the last house on the left in the Rue Saint-Dominique, on the corner of the Boulevard des Invalides). I can still see his envious expression and his awkward politeness towards me. Camille Teisseire had become rich, or rather his father had become rich manufacturing *cherry ratafia*,[2] which made him deeply ashamed.

Were I to have a search made in the records of the registry in Grenoble (which Louis XVIII called Grelibre) for the marriage certificate of M. Camille Teisseire (Rue [des] Vieux-Jésuites or Place Grenette because his enormous house had two entrances) with Mlle Marine Périer, I should get the date of the Raillane tyranny.

I was gloomy, sly, discontented; I translated Virgil; the *abbé* exaggerated the beauties of that poet to me and I greeted his eulogies as the poor Poles of today must greet the eulogies of Russian good nature in their venal news-sheets; I hated the *abbé*, I hated my father, the source of the *abbé*'s authority, I hated even more the religion in whose name they tyrannized over me. I proved to my fellow galley-slave, the timid Reytiers, that everything we were taught was an old wives' tale. Where had I got these ideas from? I don't know. We had a large illustrated bible bound in green with wood engravings inserted into the text; just the thing for children. I can remember that I was constantly looking for absurdities in that wretched bible. Reytiers, more timid and more of a believer, adored by his father and his mother who wore rouge a foot thick and had been a beauty, granted my doubts out of kindness to me.

We were toiling away translating Virgil then when I discovered in my father's library a translation of Virgil in four handsomely bound octavo volumes by that *scoundrel* the *abbé* Desfontaines, I think it was. I found the volume corresponding to the *Georgics* and to Book Two which we were massacring (in reality we knew no Latin at all). I hid this blessed volume in the privy, in a cupboard where we used to store the feathers from the capons eaten in the house, and there we would go two or three times during our painful *version*, to consult that of Desfontaines. I fancy that the *abbé*

2. A liqueur based on brandy.

got wind of it from Reytier's good humour: there was a terrible scene. I became more and more gloomy, spiteful and unhappy. I execrated everyone and my aunt Séraphie in the superlative.

One year after my mother's death, around 1791, or 92, I now fancy that my father fell in love with her; hence interminable walks to the Granges, on which I was taken as a chaperon but with the precaution of making me walk forty paces ahead of them once we had passed the Porte de Bonne. Aunt Séraphie had taken against me, I don't know why, and was forever getting me told off by my father. I execrated them and it must have shown, for even today, when I feel an aversion for someone, those present notice it at once. I detested my younger sister Zénaïde (today Mme Alexandre Mallein) because she was the favourite of my father who lulled her to sleep every evening on his lap and was vigorously defended by Mlle Séraphie. I covered the plaster in the house (daubed on the cramps) with caricatures of Zénaïde the teller of tales.* My sister Pauline (today the widow Mme Périer-Lagrange) [and I] used to accuse Zénaïde of playing the role of spy on us, and I firmly believe with good reason. I always dined at my grandfather's, but we had finished dinner as it struck a quarter past one from St-André, and at two o'clock we had to leave the lovely sunshine of the Place Grenette for the cold, damp rooms that the *abbé* Raillane occupied overlooking the courtyard of my father's house, in the Rue des Vieux-Jésuites. Nothing pained me more; being gloomy and sly, I made plans of escape: but where to get the money?

One day my grandfather said to the *abbé* Raillane: "But, m[onsieur], why teach this child the Ptolemaic system when you know it to be false?"

"M[onsieu]r, it explains everything and anyway it is approved by the Church."

---

*I recall one which was most amusing. Z. was depicted spooling thread placed on a spindle; she was shown full length, fairly grotesquely, with this caption at the bottom: "Zénaïde, jealousy telling tales, Caroline Beyle."

My grandfather couldn't stomach this reply and would often repeat it, though with a laugh; he never grew indignant against anything that was the responsibility of others. But my education was my father's responsibility, and the less respect M. Gagnon felt for his knowledge, the more he respected his rights as a father.

But this reply of the *abbé*'s, frequently repeated by the grandfather I adored, finally turned me into a fanatical unbeliever and the gloomiest of creatures to boot. My grandfather knew astronomy, although he understood nothing of the calculus; we would spend the summer evenings on the splendid terrace of his apartment, where he would show me the Great and Little Bear and talk poetically to me about the shepherds of Chaldea and about Abraham. Thus I developed a certain respect for Abraham, and said to Reytiers: "He's not a scoundrel like those other characters in the bible."

My grandfather either owned, or had else borrowed from the Public Library, of which he had been the instigator, a quarto edition of Bruce's *Travels in Nubia and Abyssinia.* These travels had engravings, hence their huge influence on my education.

I execrated everything my father and the *abbé* Raillane taught me. My father had made me recite by heart Lacroix's geography; the *abbé* had kept on with it; I knew it well, necessarily, but I execrated it.

Bruce, a descendant of the kings of Scotland, so my excellent grandfather told me, gave me a keen taste for all the sciences that he spoke of. Hence my love of mathematics and finally the idea, I dare say of *genius*: *Mathematics can get me away from Grenoble.*

CHAPTER 9

For all his Dauphinois shrewdness, my father Chérubin Beyle was a passionate man. To his passion for Bourdalue and Massillon[1] there had succeeded a passion for agriculture, which was subsequently overturned by his love for the mason's trowel (or for building) that he had always had, and finally by ultraism and the passion for administering the town of Grenoble in the Bourbon interest. My father dreamt night and day of whatever was the object of his passion. He had much shrewdness, had much experience of the shrewdness of the other Dauphinois and I'm quite ready to conclude from all this that he had ability. But I have no clearer idea of this than of his physiognomy.

My father took to going twice a week to Claix. This is a *domaine* (a local term meaning a small landholding) of one hundred and fifty *arpents*, I believe, situated to the south of the town on the slopes of the mountain beyond the Drac.

The ground in Claix and Furonières is all of it dry, chalky, full of stones. Around 1750, a free-thinking *curé* had the idea of cultivating the *marsh* to the west of the Pont de Claix; this marsh made the district's fortune.

My father's house was two leagues from Grenoble, I have made this journey on foot a thousand times perhaps. It's to this exercise no doubt that my father owed his perfect health which carried him through to the age of seventy-two, I

---

1. Two prominent seventeenth-century preachers whose sermons had been published.

believe. A bourgeois in Grenoble is well regarded only in so far as he has a *domaine*. Lefèvre, my father's wigmaker, had a *domaine* in Corenc and was often absent from his business "because he'd gone to Corenc," an excuse which always went down well. Sometimes we took a short cut by crossing the Drac by the Seyssins ferry at point A.

My father was so full of his new passion that he never stopped talking to me about it. *He sent for*, as the locals put it, apparently he sent to Paris or to Lyon for the *Bibliothèque agronomique ou économique*, which had illustrations; I often leafed through this book, and that earned me frequent visits to Claix (i.e. to our house in Furonières) on Thursdays, when I had a holiday. I would walk with my father in his fields and listen with an ill grace to him explaining his schemes; all the same the pleasure of having someone to listen to these romances, which he called calculations, meant that on several occasions I only came back to town on the Friday; sometimes we had set out as early as Wednesday evening.

I didn't like Claix because I was under constant siege there from agricultural schemes, but soon I discovered a major compensation. Soon afterwards I stole some volumes of Voltaire from the edition in forty vo[lumes] with engravings perfect bound in imitation marble calf which my father kept at Claix (his *domaine*). There were forty vo[lumes], I believe, packed tightly together; I took down two and spread all the rest out a little, it didn't show. In any case this dangerous book had been placed on the topmost shelf of the fine cherrywood, glass-fronted bookcase, which was often kept locked.

By God's grace, even at that age I found the engravings absurd, and what engravings, the ones in *La Pucelle*![2]

This miracle might almost make me believe that God had ordained I should have good taste and should one day write *L'Histoire de la peinture en Italie*.

We always spent the *holiday months* in Claix, i.e. the

2. This was Voltaire's iconoclastic version of the story of Joan of Arc.

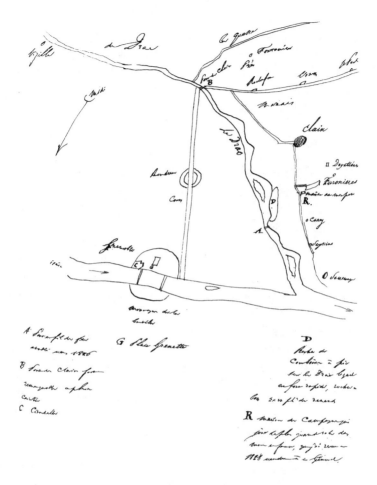

Vizille.—La Gresse.—Pont de Claix.—Fontanieu.—Meadows.—
Rochefort.—Varces.—St-Paul.—South.—Roundel.—Walk.—The
Drac.—Marsh.—Claix.—Doyatières.— Furonières.—My father's
house.—Cossey.—Seyssins.—Sassenage.—Grenoble.—Isère.—
Mountain of La Bastille.

A. Wire bridge erected around 1826.—B. Pont de Claix very
remarkable with round arches.—C. Citadelle.—G. Place Grenette.
—D. Rocks of Comboire sheer above the Drac, which is very fast-
flowing, rocks and woods full of foxes.--R. Country house which
played a very big part in my childhood, which I revisited in 1828,
sold to a general.

months of September and August. My teachers complained that I forgot all my Latin during this time of pleasure. I hated nothing more than when my father called our outings to Claix our *pleasure*. I was like a galley-slave who was forced to call *pleasure* a system of chains only slightly less onerous than the others.

I was outraged and, I think, very spiteful and unfair towards my father and the *abbé* Raillane. I admit, but by a great effort of reason, even in 1835, that I am unable to judge of these two men. They poisoned my childhood in the full sense of the word poison. They had stern faces and constantly prevented me from exchanging a single word with a child of my own age. It was only at the time of the Ecoles Centrales (the admirable handiwork of M. de Tracy) that I made my début in the society of children of my own age. But not with the gaiety and insouciance of childhood; I arrived there sly, spiteful, filled with thoughts of vengeance for the slightest blow from a fist which to me was what a slap on the cheek is between grown men; in short everything, except treacherous.

The great evil of the Raillane tyranny was that I was conscious of my afflictions. I was constantly seeing children of my own age crossing the Place Grenette going for a walk or running *together*; but that was what I had not once been allowed to do. When I let the vexation that was gnawing at me be glimpsed, I was told:

"You'll go in the carriage."

And Mme Périer-Lagrange (the mother of my late brother-in-law), the saddest of figures, would take me in her carriage when she went out in it for a constitutional; she berated me at least as much as the *abbé* Raillane; she was dried-up and devout and like the *abbé* had one of those unbending faces that never smile. Some substitute for a walk with young urchins of my own age! Who would believe it? I have never played *gobilles* (marbles) and I only got a spinning-top when my grandfather spoke up for me, on which account his daughter Séraphie made a *scene*.

I was very sly then, very spiteful, when in the beautiful bookcase in Claix I came upon a *Don Quijote* in French. The book had illustrations; it was old-looking and I loathed anything old, because my relations had stopped me from meeting young people and they struck me as exceedingly old. But anyway, so as to understand the illustrations which I found amusing: Sancho Panza mounted on his pack-saddle which is supported on four posts, Gines de Passamont has taken away the donkey.

Don Quijote made me die laughing. Kindly deign to consider that since the death of my poor mother I hadn't laughed; I was the victim of the most unwaveringly aristocratic and religious education. My tyrants hadn't let up for a moment. All invitations were refused. I often came in on arguments in which my grandfather was of the view that I should be allowed to accept. My aunt Séraphie opposed him in terms hurtful to myself; my father was under her thumb and made jesuitical replies to his father-in-law that I knew quite well committed him to nothing. My aunt Elisabeth shrugged her shoulders. Should a projected excursion have survived such a debate, my father would get the *abbé* Raillane to intervene on behalf of an exercise I had left unfinished the day before and that had to be done at the precise moment of the excursion.

Judge of the effect of *Don Quijote* in the midst of such awful joylessness! The discovery of that book, read beneath the second lime-tree in the walk beside the sunken parterre where the ground was a foot lower, and where I used to sit, is perhaps the greatest period of my life.

And would you believe it? My father seeing me in fits of laughter, came and reprimanded me, threatened to take the book away, which he did several times, and led me off into his fields in order to explain to me his schemes for repairs (improvements, betterments).

Disturbed even when reading D[on] Quijote, I hid in the arbour, a small walled den of greenery at the eastern end of the clos (small park).

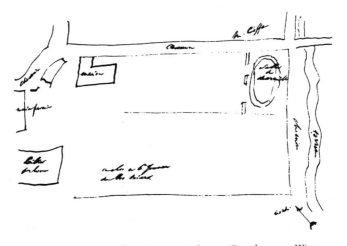

Lane.—Lane.—M. Coffe.—House.—Arbour.—Farmhouse.—Wine cellar.—This enclosure is of six acres of 600 fathoms.—Lane.—Torrent.—North.

I discovered a Molière with illustrations, the illustrations I thought absurd and I understood only L'Avare. I discovered the comedies of Destouches and one of the more absurd of them moved me to tears. There was a love story mixed in with noble feelings; I had a weakness for that. I have searched my memory in vain for the title of this comedy, unknown even among the unknown comedies of that worthless diplomat.[3] I

3. Destouches was the pseudonym of Philippe Néricault (1680–1754), who was both a playwright and at one time a diplomat in London.

was much amused by *Le Tambour nocturne*, which includes an idea copied from the English.

I find it as an established fact in my head that from the age of seven I had determined to write comedies like Molière. Only ten years ago I could still remember the *how* of that determination.

My grandfather was charmed by my enthusiasm for *Don Quijote*, which I told him about, for I told him more or less everything; in fact that excellent man of sixty-five was my one comrade.

He lent me, unbenownst to his daughter Séraphie, the *Orlando Furioso*, translated, or rather, I think, imitated from Ariosto by M. de Tressan (whose son, today an army brigadier, and in 1820 a fairly worthless ultra, but in 1788 a charming young man, had played so large a part in my learning to read by promising me a little book full of pictures which he never gave me, greatly shocking me by breaking his word).

Ariosto formed my character; I fell madly in love with Bradamante, whom I pictured to myself as an ample girl of twenty-four with charms of the most dazzling whiteness.

I felt a revulsion for all those ignominious bourgeois details which served Molière in making his ideas known. Such details reminded me too much of my unhappy life. Not more than three days ago (December 1835) when two bourgeois of my acquaintance were about to perform a comic scene between them of petty dissimulation and semi-quarrelling, I moved ten paces away so as not to hear them. I have a horror of these things, which has stopped me from gaining experience. This is *no small misfortune*.

Whatever is mean and commonplace in the bourgeois kind reminds me of Grenoble, whatever reminds me of Grenoble fills me with horror; no, *horror* is too distinguished, makes me feel *sick*.

For me Grenoble is like the memory of a terrible indigestion; there is no danger, but a frightful nausea. Whatever is irredeemably mean and commonplace, whatever is opposed to the faintest impulse of generosity, whatever takes delight in the misfortune of anyone who loves his country or is generous: that for me is Grenoble.

Nothing has astonished me more on my travels than hearing it said by officers of my acquaintance that Grenoble was a charming town, effervescent with wit and where the pretty women "knew how to look after themselves." The first time I heard this remark was dining with General Moncey (today a marshal, Duc de Conigliano), in 1802 in Milan or Cremona; I was so astonished I asked for details right across the table; a *rich* (150fr a month) subaltern at the time, I was full of myself. My detestation of the state of nausea and perpetual indigestion from which I had only just escaped was at its height. The staff officer defended his statement very stoutly: he had spent fifteen or eighteen months in Grenoble; he maintained that it was the pleasantest town in the province; he named for me Mmes Allemand-Dulauron, Piat-Desvials, Tournus, Duchamps, de Montmaur, the Mlles Rivière (daughters of the innkeeper, Rue Montorge), the Mlles Bailly, m[illin]ers, friends of my uncle, Messrs Drevon, Drevon senior and Drevon the Similar, M. Dolle of the Porte de France, and, where aristocratic society was concerned (the term of 1800 replaced by *ultra*, then by legitimist), M. le Ch[evalie]r de Marcieu, M. de Bailly.

Alas, I had hardly ever heard these delightful names uttered; my relations evoked them only in order to deplore their folly, for they censured everything, they were *jaundiced*. This needs repeating if a reasonable explanation is to be given of my unhappiness; at my mother's death, my despairing relations had broken off all connection with society; my mother had been the life and joy of the family. My father, gloomy, timid, rancorous, unfriendly, had the character of Geneva: there they calculate and never laugh; and I fancy had only ever socialized because of my mother. My grandfather, an amiable man, a man of the world, the man whose conversation was the most sought after of anyone in the town, by everyone from the artisan up to the grand seigneur, from Mme Barthélemy, the shoemaker's wife, a woman of wit, up to M. le Baron des Adrets, at whose house he continued to dine once a month, cut to the very heart by the death of the one person he loved and finding he had reached the age of sixty, had broken with the world out of a weariness with life. My aunt Elisabeth alone, independent, rich even (for Grenoble in 1789), had kept houses where she went to play cards in the evenings (before supper, from seven till nine). She thus left the house two or three times a week, and sometimes, though full of respect for a father's rights, out of compassion for me, when my father was at Claix, she would claim to have need of me and take me with her as her squire, to Mlle Simon's, in the brand-new Maison des Jacobins, who put on rouge a foot thick. My worthy aunt even made me attend a big supper-party given by Mlle Simon. I can still remember the brilliance of the lights and the magnificence of the place settings, in the middle of the table there was a centrepiece with silver statues. The next day my aunt Séraphie denounced me to my father and there was a scene. These arguments, formally very polite, but in the course of which cutting things were said of the kind one doesn't forget, constituted the one amusement of that morose family into which my ill fate had cast me. How I envied the nephew of Mme Barthélemy, our shoemaker's wife!

I suffered, but I couldn't see the causes of it all; I put everything down to the spitefulness of my father and of Séraphie. To be fair, one could see them as bourgeois, puffed up with pride, who wanted to give their *only son*, as they called me, an aristocratic education. These ideas were far too advanced for my age, and in any case who might have given me them? For friends I had only Marion, the cook, and Lambert, my grandfather's manservant, and Séraphie was constantly calling me back hearing me laughing with them in the kitchen. In their gloomy state of mind, I was their sole preoccupation;

they dressed this vexation up under the name of education, and were probably sincere. By this continual contact my grandfather passed on to me his reverence for literature. Horace and Hippocrates were very different men, as I saw it, from Romulus, Alexander and Numa. M. de Voltaire was a very different man from that imbecile of a Louis XVI, of whom he had made fun, or that roué Louis XV, whose unsavoury habits he had condemned, and had talked disgustedly of *la* du Barry, and I was much struck by the absence of the word *madame*, in the midst of our own very polite ways, I felt a revulsion for these people. We always said M. de Voltaire and my grandfather only ever uttered that name with a smile which combined respect with affection.

Soon there came politics. My family was among the more aristocratic in the town, which meant that I instantly felt I was a raging republic[an]. I saw the handsome regiments of dragoons go by on their way to Italy; there was always someone billeted in the house; I devoured them with my eyes; my relations execrated them. Soon the priests went into hiding; there were always one or two priests hiding in the house. The gluttony of one of the first to come, a gross man whose eyes bulged from his head when he ate pickled pork, struck me as disgusting. (We had excellent *pickled pork* which I used to go and fetch from the cellar with Lambert the manservant, it was kept in a stone hollowed out into a basin.) In our house we were unusually clean and refined at table. I was told for example never to make noises with my mouth. The majority of these priests were vulgar men, they made noises with their tongues against their palates, they broke their bread messily; this was more than enough for me to feel a revulsion for these men, who sat on my left. One of our Lyon cousins (M. Santerre) was guillotined, and the gloom in the family and its state of hatred and discontent with everything redoubled.

In the old days, when I heard speak of the simple joys of childhood, of the thoughtlessness of that age, of the happi-

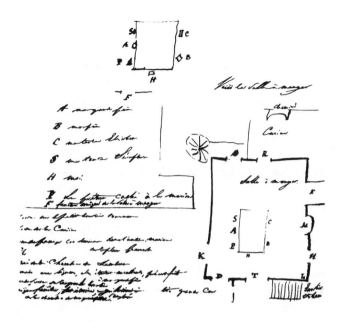

Here is the lay-out of the table at my grandfather's house where I ate from the age of seven to sixteen [and a] half:

A. My grandfather.—B. My father.—C. My aunt Elisabeth.—S. My aunt Séraphie.—H. Me.—P. The priest hiding in the house.—F. Only window in the dining-room.

Here is the dining-room.—Fireplace.—Kitchen.—Dining-room. —Very large courtyard.—Very fine staircase.

O. Door on to the little winding staircase.—R. Door to the kitchen.—E. Large passageway leading into the other house on the Place Grenette.—M. Stove.—N. Entrance to Lambert's room. —T. Large door on to the main staircase.—D. Only window, very narrow, sashes, English-style.—K. Door of my grandfather's room.

ness of early youth, the one true happiness in life, my heart would contract. I experienced none of all that; what's more, for me that age was a time of continual unhappiness, and of hatred, and of always impotent hopes of revenge. The whole of my unhappiness can be summed up in two words: I was never allowed to talk to a child of my own age. And my relations, greatly bored as a consequence of their isolation from all company, honoured me with their continual attention. For these two reasons, at what is such a cheerful time of life for other children, I was spiteful, gloomy, unreasonable, in a word a *slave*, in the worst sense of the term, and I gradually acquired the feelings to go with that condition. The little bit of happiness I was able to secure was preserved by lying. In other respects I was absolutely like the present-day populations of Europe: my tyrants always addressed me in the honeyed tones of the fondest solicitude, and their staunchest ally was religion. I had to endure continual homilies about a father's love and the duties of children. One day, fed up with my father's pathos, I said to him:

"If you love me so much, give me five *sous* a day and let me live as I want. You can be sure of one thing anyway: as soon as I'm old enough I shall enlist."

My father advanced on me as if to annihilate me, he was beside himself:

"You're nothing but an impious wretch," he said to me.

The tsar Nicholas, wouldn't you say, and the municipality of Warsaw, who are so much in the news on the day I write this (7 December 1835, C[ivit]a-Vecchia), so true is it that all tyrannies are alike.

By great good chance I fancy I haven't remained spiteful, but merely nauseated for the rest of my life by bourgeois, jesuits and hypocrites of every sort. I was cured of my spite perhaps by my successes in 1797, 98 and 99 and by becoming aware of my own strength. As well as my other fine qualities, I was unbearably arrogant.

Truth to tell, when I think hard about it, I haven't been cured of my unreasonable revulsion for Grenoble: in the true sense of the word I have *forgotten* it. My magnificent memories of Italy, of Milan, have erased everything.

All that remains is a notable gap in my knowledge of men and of things. All the details which make up the life of Chrysale in *L'Ecole des femmes*:

> Et hors un gros Plutarque à mettre mes rabats,[4]

fill me with horror. If I may be permitted an image *as distasteful as the sensation*, it is like the smell of oysters to a man who has had a terrible indigestion from oysters.

In me all the facts that make up the life of Chrysale are replaced by romance. This flaw in my telescope has been useful, I believe, for the characters in my novels, there's a sort of bourgeois baseness they can't have: and for their author it would be to talk the *Chinese* which he doesn't know. The term *bourgeois baseness* expresses a nuance only; it will perhaps be very obscure in 1880. Thanks to the newspapers, the provincial bourgeois is becoming a rarity, people no longer behave *according to their rank*: an elegant young man in Paris, with whom I used to meet in the gayest of company, was very well turned out, without affectation, and spent 8 or 10,000fr. I asked one day:

"What does he do?"

"He's a very busy attorney (procurator)," I was told.

As an example of bourgeois baseness then, I shall cite the style of my excellent friend M. Fauriel (of the Institute), in his excellent *Vie de Dante*, published in 1834 in the *Revue de Paris*. But alas, where will all these things be in 1880? Some clever fellow who knows how to write will have got hold of the excellent Fauriel's thorough researches, and the works of this good, highly conscientious bourgeois will be completely forgotten. He was the best-looking man in Paris. Mme Condorcet (Sophie Grouchy), who was a great *connaisseuse*, appropriated him for herself; the bourgeois Fauriel was fatuous enough to love her and when she died, around 1820, I believe, she left him 1,200fr a year as if to a lackey. He was profoundly humiliated. When he gave me ten pages for *L'Amour*, Arab adventures, I said to him: "When you're involved with

---

4. The line comes in fact from another Molière play, *Les Femmes savantes*, and might be translated as "But for a fat Plutarch to turn down my bands."

a princess or a woman with too much money, you must beat her or love is extinguished."

This remark horrified him, and he no doubt told it to little Miss Clarke who is shaped like a question-mark, ?, like Pope. Which is why shortly afterwards she had me reprimanded by a dunce among her friends (M. Augustin Thierry, a member of the Institute[5]), and I dropped her there and then. There was a pretty woman in that circle, Mme Belloc, but she used to make love with another question-mark, black and crooked, Mlle de Montgolfier, and the truth is I approve of these poor women.

5. Augustin Thierry (1795–1856), far from being a "dunce," was one of the most learned and interesting French historians of the Romantic age, second only to Michelet.

CHAPTER 10

MY TEACHER DURAND

I find I have no memory of the manner of my delivery from the Raillane tyranny. That scoundrel ought to have turned me into an excellent jesuit, worthy of succeeding my father, or a crapulous soldier running after women and taverns. Like in Fielding, temperament would have completely masked the *ignominy*. So I would have been one or other of these delightful things but for my excellent grandfather who, without realizing it, passed on to me his cult of Horace, Sophocles, Euripides and elegant literature. Happily, he despised all the worthless writers who were his contemporaries, and I wasn't poisoned by the Marmontels, Dorats[1] and other riff-raff. For some reason he was forever protesting the respect he felt for p[riests], who in actual fact filled him with revulsion as for something dirty. Seeing them installed as masters in his own drawing-room by his daughter Séraphie and my father, his son-in-law, he was perfectly polite towards them as with everyone else. To make conversation he talked literature and, for example, about sacred authors, though he had little liking for them. But politest of men though he was, he had all the difficulty in the world disguising the deep distaste he felt for their ignorance.

"What, they don't even know the *abbé* Fleury, their own historian!" I overheard this remark one day which renewed my confidence in him.

1. The pseudonym of Jean Dinemandi (1508–1588), humanist and poet—and hardly a contemporary of Stendhal's grandfather.

I found out soon after that he very rarely went to confession. He was extremely polite towards religion, rather than a believer. He would have been devout had he been able to believe that in heaven he would meet his daughter Henriette again (M. le Duc de Br[oglie] said: "To me it's as if my daughter were in America"), but he was merely sad and silent. As soon as someone came, he would talk out of politeness and recount anecdotes.

Perhaps M. Raillane was forced to go into hiding for refusing to take the oath for the civil constitution of the clergy.[2] However that may be, his removal was for me the greatest event imaginable, and I have no memory of it.

This constitutes a defect in my brain, of which I have discovered several instances in the three years since there came to me, on the esplanade of San Pietro in Montorio (Janiculum), the luminous thought that I was about to be fifty and that it was time to be thinking of my departure and, before that, of giving oneself the pleasure of looking back for a moment. I have no memory at all of the periods or moments when I felt too intensely. One of my reasons for thinking myself brave is that I remember, with perfect clarity, the least circumstances of the duels in which I have found myself involved. In the army, when it was raining, and I was on the march in the mud, this bravery just about sufficed, but when I hadn't got soaked during the previous night, and my horse wasn't sliding around underneath me, taking the most foolhardy risks was for me literally a genuine pleasure. My sensible comrades would grow serious and white-faced, or else quite red, Mathys became more cheerful and Farine more sensible. It's like nowadays: I never contemplate the possibility of WANTING OF A THOUSAND francs, yet that seems to be the dominant idea, the great thought of friends of my own age far more comfortably off than myself (for example, Messrs Besan[çon], Colomb, etc.). But I'm digressing. The

2. The oath whereby priests swore allegiance to the Revolutionary constitution.

great problem in writing these *Memoirs* is to have and to write down just those memories relating to the period I have firm hold of; for example, we come now to the time, less unhappy obviously, which I spent under my teacher Durand.

He was a good fellow of maybe forty-five, fat and round in every way, who had a very amiable grown-up son of eighteen whom I admired from afar and who later on, I believe, was in love with my sister. No one could have been less jesuitical or underhand than poor M. Durand; he was polite moreover, dressed strictly on the cheap but never untidily. Truth to tell, he knew not a word of Latin, but then neither did I, and that wasn't calculated to set us against one another.

I knew by heart the *Selectae e profanis*,[3] and especially the story of Androcles and his lion; I likewise knew the Old Testament and perhaps a bit of Virgil and of Cornelius Nepos. But if I had been given permission for a week's holiday, written in Latin, I wouldn't have understood a word of it. To me the wretched Latin written by moderns, the *De Viris illustribus*,[4] in which there was talk of Romulus, of whom I was very fond, was unintelligible. Well, M. Durand was the same! He knew by heart the authors he had been expounding for the last twenty years, but my grandfather having tried once or twice consulting him over some crux in his Horace that wasn't explained by Jean Bond (I rejoiced at that word, how pleasant in the midst of so many irritations to be able to laugh at *Jambon*!), M. Durand didn't even understand what the point under discussion was.

His method then was pitiful and, if I wanted to, I could teach Latin in eighteen months to a child of normal intelligence. But was it nothing, to have grown accustomed to having a hard time of it for two hours in the morning and three in the evening? That is a big question. (Around 1819, I taught

3. A selection of extracts from "profane" Latin authors published in 1727.

4. This volume of potted lives of famous Romans was the work of an eighteenth-century humanist, C.-F. Lhomond.

English in twenty-six days to M. Antonio Clerichetti of Milan, who was suffering under a miserly father. On day thirty he *sold* to a bookseller his translation of the interrogation of the Princess of Wales (Caroline of Brunswick), a notable strumpet, whom her husband, a king and lashing out millions, was unable to convict of having made him what ninety-five out of every hundred husbands are.)[5]

I have no recollection then of the event which separated me from M. Raillane.

After the ceaseless hardship resulting from the tyranny of that spiteful jesuit, I see myself suddenly installed in my excellent grandfather's house, sleeping in a small trapezium-shaped closet next to his room and receiving Latin lessons from the kindly Durand who came, I fancy, twice a day, from 10 till 11 and from 2 till 3. My relations still held firmly to the principle of allowing me no intercourse "with the common children." But M. Durand's lessons took place in the presence of my excellent grandfather, in winter in his room at point M, in summer in the large drawing-room next to the terrace at M', sometimes at M" in an anteroom into which we hardly ever went.

My memories of the Raillane tyranny filled me with horror up until 1814; around that time I forgot them, the events of the Restoration had absorbed my horror and my disgust. It is with this last feeling alone that I am filled by the memories of my teacher Durand at *home*, because I also took his course at the Ecole Centrale, but then I was happy, or relatively so; I was beginning to be aware of the beautiful landscape formed by the view of the hills of Eybens and of Echirolles and by the beautiful meadow on the *glacis* of the Porte de Bonne, which you looked down on from the window of the Ecole situated fortunately on the third floor of the college; the rest was under repair.

5. A reference to the divorce case brought in 1820 by the Prince Regent, about to become King George IV, against his wife, on grounds of her adultery.

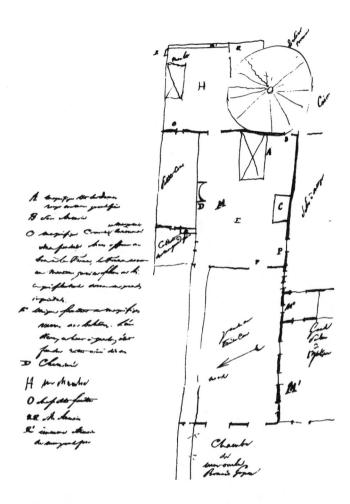

My bed.—Winding staircase.—Courtyard.—Small courtyard.—
My grandfather's study.—Dining-room.—Large, cheerless court-
yard.—North.—Large Italian drawing-room.—My uncle Romain
Gagnon's room.

A. My grandfather's magnificent red damask bed.—B. His cupboard.—C. Magnificent inlaid chest-of-drawers surmounted by
a clock: Mars offering France his arm; France wore a cloak decorated with fleurs-de-lis, which later on caused great anxiety.—
Solitary window with panes of magnificent Bohemian glass. One
of them, top left, was cracked and stayed that way for ten years.—
D. Fireplace.—H. My room.—O. My little window.—RR. My cupboards.—R. My grandfather's huge cupboard.

It would appear that in winter M. Durand came to give me lessons from 7 until 8 in the evening. At least I can see myself over a small table lit by a tallow candle, M. Durand almost forming a row of onions* with the family in front of my grandfather's fire and by a half turn to the right coming to face the little table at which I, H, was sitting.

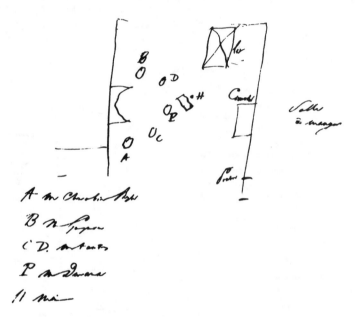

Bed.—Chest-of-drawers.—Door.—Dining-room.—A. M. Chérubin Beyle.—B. M. Gagnon.—C. D. My aunts.—H. Me.

It was here that M. Durand began to construe Ovid's *Metamorphoses* with me. I can still see him as well as the yellow or boxroot colour of the book's cover. I fancy that because the subject was too light-hearted there was an argument between Séraphie, who was more of a harridan than

*Lord Onion [*trans.* a reference to a certain Baron d'Oignon who, in the sixteenth century, had been responsible for arranging the seating-plan for the deputies attending the States of Blois].

ever, and her father. Thanks to his love of good literature he stood firm, and instead of the gloomy horrors of the Old Testament, I got the loves of Pyramus and Thisbe and especially Daphne, who was turned into a laurel-bush. Nothing amused me as much as this tale did. For the first time in my life, I realized that it might be agreeable to know Latin, which had for so many years past been my torment.

But here the chronology of this important history demands: For how many years?

The truth is, I haven't the least idea; I had started Latin at the age of seven, in 1790. I assume that Year VII of the Republic corresponds to 1799 because of the rebus:

Lancette
Laitue
Rat[6]

which was posted up on the Luxembourg *à propos* the Directory.

I fancy that in the Year V I was at the Ecole Centrale.

I had been there for a year, because we were occupying the large mathematics room on the first floor when the assassination of Roberjot [*a blank*] occurred in Rastadt.[7] It was in 1794 perhaps that I was construing Ovid's *Metamorphoses*. My grandfather sometimes allowed me to read the translation by M. Dubois-Fontanelle, I believe, who later on was my teacher.

I fancy that the death of Louis XVI, 21 January 1793, took place during the Raillane tyranny. Amusingly enough, and posterity will find this hard to believe, my family, which was

---

6. As pronounced in French these three words, meaning literally "lancet," "lettuce" and "rat," give *L'an sept les tuera* or "The Year VII will kill them," a piece of agitprop against the regime of the Directory.

7. Claude Roberjot was one of two French envoys to the Congress of Rastadt in 1799 who were both assassinated there; the blank in the Ms was clearly intended for the name of the second envoy: Bonnier.

bourgeois but believed itself to be on the fringes of the nobility, my father especially who believed himself to be a ruined nobleman, read all the newspapers and followed the trial of the king as they might have followed that of a close friend or relation.

The news of the sentence came; my family was in absolute despair.

"But they'll never dare carry out that infamous sentence," they said.

"Why not," I thought, "if he's a traitor?"

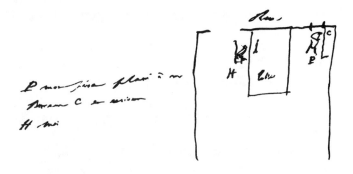

P. My father sitting at his desk C writing.—H. Me.—Street.—Table.

I was in my father's study in the Rue des Vieux-Jésuites, around seven o'clock in the evening, the night had closed in, reading by the light of my lamp and separated from my father by a very large table.

I was pretending to be working, but was reading the *Mémoires d'un homme de qualité* by the *abbé* Prévost, a copy of which I had discovered badly marked by age. The house was shaken by the postal carriage arriving from Lyon and Paris.

"I must go and find out what those monsters have done," said my father getting to his feet.

"I hope the traitor has been executed," I thought. Then I reflected on the extreme difference between my sentiments and those of my father. I had felt fond affection for our regiments that I had watched go past on the Place Grenette from my grandfather's window; I had imagined that the king was seeking to have them defeated by the Austrians. (You can see that, although I was barely ten years old, I wasn't so very far from the truth.) But I will confess that the interest shown in the fate of Louis XVI by the vicar-general M. Rey and the other priests, my family's friends, would have sufficed to make me desire his death. I considered at the time, on the strength of the couplet from the song I used to sing when I wasn't afraid of being overheard by my father or my aunt Séraphie, that it was one's *strict duty* to die for one's country if necessary. What was the life of a traitor who, by a secret letter, might bring about the slaughter of one of those handsome regiments I had watched go past on the Place Grenette? I was settling the case between my family and myself when my father returned. I can see him still in the white flannel frock-coat which he hadn't taken off to go the two steps to the post-office.

"It's all over," he said with a deep sigh, "they've murdered him."

I was gripped by one of the most intense feelings of joy I have ever felt in my life. The reader will perhaps think me cruel, but such I was at the age of ten and such I am at fifty-two.

When, in December 1830, that insolent rogue Peyronnet and the other signatories to the ordinances were not sentenced to death, I said of the bourgeois of Paris: they mistake the etiolation of their souls for civilization and generosity.[8] How after such feebleness dare they condemn to death a mere murderer?

It seems to me that what is happening in 1835 has justified my prediction of 1830.

8. The Comte de Peyronnet (1778–1854) was Charles X's chief minister, whose ordinances set off the 1830 "revolution" which removed the king. He was tried in 1834 and sentenced to perpetual imprisonment.

I was so carried away by that great act of national justice that I couldn't go on reading my novel, certainly one of the most affecting in existence. I hid it, I placed in front of me the serious book, probably Rollin,[9] that my father was making me read, and I closed my eyes so as to be able to savour this great event in peace. Which is exactly what I should do still today, adding that, short of some imperious duty, nothing could persuade me to set eyes on the traitor whom the interests of the country were sending to the scaffold. I could fill ten pages with the details of that evening, but if the readers of 1880 are as etiolated as is good society in 1835, then the scene, like its hero, will fill them with a feeling of profound aversion to the extent almost of what the papier-mâché souls call horror. As for myself, I would feel much more compassion for a murderer condemned to death on insufficient evidence than for a K[ING] who found himself in the same position. The DEATH OF A K[ING] when guilty is always useful *in terrorem* in order to prevent the strange abuses to which the *ultimate madness* brought on by absolute power drives such people. (Witness Louis XV's love for the newly filled-in graves in country cemeteries which he could see from his carriage on his excursions around Versailles. Witness the current mania of little Queen Doña Maria of Portugal.)

The page I have just written would greatly shock even my friends of 1835. I was reviled for my hard-heartedness at Mme Aubernon's in 1829, for having WICHED [*sic*] THE DEATH OF THE DUKE OF B[lac]as. M. Mignet even (today a councillor of state) was horrified by me and the mistress of the house, whom I liked (DID LIKE), because she looked like Cervantes, has never forgiven me: she said I was supremely immoral and was shocked, in 1833, at the baths in Aix, because Mme la Comtesse C[uri]al defended me. I can say that I am utterly indifferent to the approval of people

9. Author of a *History of Rome*.

whom I look upon as *weak*. To me they seem mad; I can clearly see that they don't understand the problem.

Well, suppose I am cruel, well yes, I am, you will see plenty more of it from me if I go on writing.

From this memory, so present to my gaze, I conclude that in 1793, forty-two years ago, I was engaged in the pursuit of happiness exactly as I am today; in other, more common terms: my character was absolutely the same as today. When one's *country* is involved, I still find all half-measures *puerile*.

I would say *criminal*, were it not for my boundless scorn for men who are weak. (Example M. Félix Faure, peer of France, first president, talking to his son, at St-Ismier, summer 1828, about the death of Louis XVI: "He was put to death by wicked men." This is the same man who is today sentencing, in the Chamber of Peers, the young and respectable madmen known as the April conspirators.[10] I would sentence them to spend one year in Cincinnati, during which year I should give them 200fr a month.)

The only other memory this distinct is of my first communion, which my father made me take in Claix in the presence of the devout carpenter Charbonot, of Cossey, around 1795.

Since in 1793 the post took five full days, and perhaps six, from Paris to Grenoble, the scene in my father's study was perhaps on the 28 or 29 of January, at seven in the evening. At supper my aunt Séraphie made a scene about my *atrocious* soul, etc. I was looking at my father: he didn't open his mouth, seemingly out of fear of being driven, and of my being driven to the ultimate extremes. However cruel and atrocious I am, at least my family didn't take me for a coward. My father was too much the Dauphinois and too shrewd not to have had some insight, even in his study (at seven o'clock), into the feelings of a child of ten.

10. See the note on p. 67.

At the age of twelve, a prodigy of knowledge for my age, I was constantly asking questions of my excellent grandfather whose happiness lay in answering them. I was the one person to whom he was willing to talk about my mother. No one in the family dared talk to him about that beloved being. At the age of twelve, then, I was a prodigy of knowledge and at twenty a prodigy of ignorance.

From 1796 to 1799, I gave my attention only to that which might provide me with the means of escaping from Grenoble, that is, to mathematics. In my anxiety I worked out ways of being able to devote half an hour more to my work each day. What is more I loved, and still do love, mathematics for itself as not allowing room for *hypocrisy* or *vagueness*, my two pet aversions.

In which state of mind, what did I care for my excellent grandfather's thorough and judicious answer including a report on Sanchoniathon, or an evaluation of the works of Court de Gébelin,[11] of whom my father had somehow or other got a fine quarto edition (perhaps there is no duodecimo edition) with a beautiful engraving showing the human speech organs?

At the age of ten I wrote in great secrecy a comedy in prose, or rather a first act. I did little work because I was waiting for the moment of genius, i.e. for that exalted state which used to take hold of me perhaps twice a month. This work was a great secret, my compositions have always inspired the same reticence in me as my love affairs. Nothing would have pained me more than to hear them spoken of. I still had this feeling very keenly in 1830, when Mme Victor de Tracy spoke to me about *Le Rouge et le noir* (a novel in two volumes).

11. Antoine Court de Gébelin (1725–1784), author of a work entitled *Le Monde primitif analysé et comparé avec le monde moderne.*

CHAPTER 11

AMAR AND MERLINO

They were two people's representatives* who arrived in Grenoble one fine day† and some time later published a list of 152 notorious suspects (of not loving the Republic, i.e. the government and the fatherland) and 350 mere suspects. The *notorious* were to be placed under arrest; as for the *mere*, they were merely to be kept under surveillance.

I saw all this from below as a child, perhaps if one were to search through the *Journal du département*, if it existed at that time, or in the Archives, one would find just the opposite so far as dates are concerned, but what isn't in doubt is its effect on me and on the family. But however that may be, my father was a notorious suspect and M. Henri Gagnon a mere suspect.

The publication of these two lists was a thunderbolt for the family. I hasten to say that my father was only freed on the 6 Thermidor (Ah, here we have a date: freed on the 6 Thermidor, three days before the death of Robespierre) and was placed on the list for twenty-two months.

This great event may date back therefore to [*a blank*] in the year [*a blank*]. In any case, I find in my memory that my father was twenty-two months on the list and spent only thirty-two or forty-two days in prison.

---

*Look up the date in Marrast's *Fastes* [*trans.* a well-known chronology of the Revolution].

†Chronology. Perhaps M. Durand only came to the Gagnon house after Amar and Merlino.

On this occasion my aunt Séraphie displayed much courage and urgency. She went to see the *members of the department*, i.e. of the departmental ad[ministrati]on; she went to see the people's representatives, and always obtained stays of a fortnight or three weeks, sometimes of fifty days.

My father put down the appearance of his name on the fateful list to an old rivalry between himself and Amar, who was also a lawyer I fancy.

Two or three months after this nuisance, which was the constant topic of conversation in the evenings among the family, I let fall a naive remark which confirmed the *atrociousness* of my character. In polite terms they were expressing the full horror with which the name of Amar filled them.

"But," I said to my father, "Amar put you on the list of those notoriously *suspected* of not loving the Republic; it seems to me *certain* you don't love it."

At which remark, the whole family went red with anger; I was on the point of being sent to prison in my room; and during supper, which they soon came to tell us was ready, no one addressed a word to me. I pondered deeply: "What I said was no more than the truth; my father takes pride in execrating the *new order of things* (an expression then fashionable among the aristocrats); what right have they to get angry?"

This form of argument: *What right has he?* had become habitual with me since the first arbitrary acts which followed the death of my mother soured my character and made me what I am.

The reader will no doubt remark that this formula rapidly led to an extreme indignation.

My father, Chérubin B[eyle], had come and installed himself in the room O, known as my uncle's room. (My amiable uncle Romain Gagnon had got married in Les Echelles, in Savoy, and when he came to Grenoble, every two or three months, for the purpose of revisiting his former lady friends, he lived in this room, magnificently furnished in red damask, magnificent for Grenoble in 1793.)

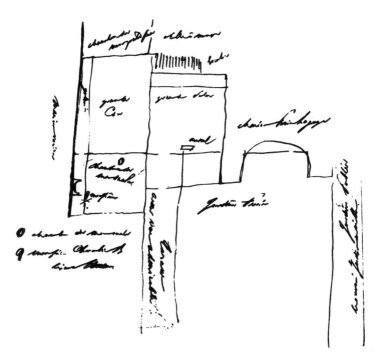

Nextdoor house.—My grandfather's room.—Dining-room.—
Staircase.—Gallery.—Large courtyard.—Large drawing-room.—
Altar.—Périer-Lagrange house.—My uncle's room.—My father.—
Terrace with admirable view.—Périer garden.—Public gardens
known as Jardin de Ville.

O. My uncle's room.—My father Chérubin B[eyle] reading Hume.

You will remark once again the wisdom of the Dauphinois
mind. For my father going into hiding meant crossing the
road and coming to sleep in his father-in-law's house, where
it was known he had been having dinner and supper for the
past two or three years. The Terror was very mild therefore,
and I shall boldly add very reasonable, in Grenoble. Despite
twenty-two years of progress, the Terror of 1815, or reaction
of my father's party, seems to me to have been crueller.[1] But
the extreme distaste which 1815 inspired in me has made me

1. I.e. at the time of the restoration of the monarchy, under King Louis XVIII.

forget the facts, and an impartial historian would perhaps be of another opinion. I entreat the reader, should I ever find one, to remember that I have no pretensions to truthfulness except in what concerns *my feelings*; as for the facts, I have never had much memory. Which meant, in parenthesis, that the celebrated Georges Cuvier always defeated me in the debates he sometimes condescended to have with me in his salon on Saturdays between 1827 and 1830.[2]

My room.—Staircase.—Small courtyard. Smell from M. Reyboz's kitchen.—My grandfather's room.—Large courtyard.

In order to escape from this terrible persecution, my father came and installed himself therefore in my uncle's room, O. It was wintertime, because he said to me: "It's like an icehouse in here."

2. Georges Cuvier (1769–1832) was a zoologist and palaeontologist, and often seen as the creator of modern comparative anatomy. His salons were held at the Jardin des Plantes in Paris.

I slept beside his bed in a pretty bed made like a bird-cage from which it was impossible to fall out. But that didn't last. Soon I found myself in the trapezium next to my grandfather's room.

It seems to me now that it was only at the time of Amar and Merlino that I went to live in the trapezium. I was much inconvenienced there by the smell from the kitchen of M. Reyboz or Reybaud, a grocer from Provence, whose accent made me laugh. I often heard him grumbling at his daughter, hideously ugly, otherwise I wouldn't have failed to make her the lady of my thoughts. I was crazy that way and it lasted a long time, but I always had the habit of a perfect discretion which I met with again in the melancholic temperament in Cabanis.

Seeing my father from closer to in my uncle's room, I was greatly astonished to find that he was no longer reading Bourdaloue, Massillon and his Sacy Bible in twenty-two volumes.[3] Like many others, the death of Louis XVI had driven him to Hume's History of Charles I; since he didn't know English, he read what was then the only translation by a Mme Belot or President Belot. My father, changeable but absolute in his tastes, was soon all politics. In my childhood I saw only the absurdity of this change; today I can see the reason. Perhaps my father's abandonment of all other ideas in pursuit of his passions (or his tastes) made him a man a bit above the common run.

Here he was then all Hume and Smollett and wanting to get me to enjoy their books just as two years earlier he had wanted to get me to revere Bourdaloue. You can imagine how this proposal from my enemy Séraphie's bosom friend was received.

3. The Lemaistre de Saci translation of the Bible first appeared in the later years of the seventeenth century.

The hatred of that devout sourpuss was redoubled when she saw me installed at her father's in the position of favourite. We had awful scenes together because I stood up to her very firmly; I would argue and that's what drove her into a fury.

Mmes Romagnier and Colomb, loved tenderly by me, our cousins, women at that time of thirty-six or forty, and the second the mother of M. Romain Colomb, my best friend (who in his letter of the—December 1835, received yesterday, took me to task over the de Brosses preface,[4] but no matter), used to come to play cards with my aunt Elisabeth. These ladies were surprised by the scenes I had with Séraphie, which often went so far as to interrupt their whist, and it was obvious to me that they took my side against that madwoman.

Having thought seriously about these scenes since that time, 1793, I fancy I would explain them thus: Séraphie, who was quite pretty, was flirting (an Italianism to be removed) with my father and felt a passionate hatred for me as the person who had come and put a moral or legal obstacle in the way of their marrying. It remains to find out whether in 1793 the ecclesiastical authorities would have allowed a marriage between brother-in-law and sister-in-law. I think they would. Séraphie belonged to the town's leading sanhedrin of the devout along with a Mme Vignon, her close friend.

During these violent scenes, which were repeated once or twice a week, my grandfather said nothing; I have already given warning that his character was Fontenelle-like, but deep down I worked out that he was for me. What, reasonably, could there be in common between an unmarried woman of twenty-six or thirty and a child of ten or twelve?

The servants, to wit Marion, Lambert first of all and then the man who succeeded him, were in my camp. My sister

4. A reference to a preface written by Stendhal for Colomb's edition of De Brosses' *Letters from Italy in 1739–40*, but which was rejected by Colomb.

Pauline, a pretty girl who was three or four years younger than me, was in my camp. My second sister Zénaïde (today Mme Alexandre Mallein) was in Séraphie's camp and had been accused by Pauline and myself of spying on us on her behalf.

I made a caricature, drawn in graphite on the plaster of the large passageway from the dining-room to the rooms on the Grenette in my grandfather's old house. Zénaïde was shown in what was supposed to be a portrait two feet high, underneath I wrote: "Caroline-Zénaïde B . . . , teller of tales."

This triviality was the occasion of a ghastly scene, the details of which I can still see. Séraphie was furious, the card-game was broken off. I fancy that Séraphie went for Mmes Romagnier and Colomb. It was already eight o'clock. These ladies were rightly offended by that madwoman's outbursts and finding that neither her father (M. Henri Gagnon) nor her aunt (my great-aunt Elisabeth) could or dared force her to be silent, made up their minds to leave. Their departure was a signal for the storm to redouble in strength. Some stern word was spoken by my grandfather or my aunt; Séraphie was trying to throw herself on me, to drive her back I took up a straw chair which I held between us, and went off into the kitchen where I was quite sure that the good Marion, who adored me and loathed Séraphie, would protect me.

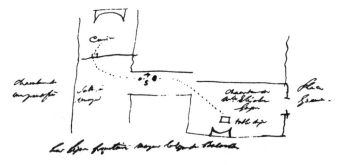

My grandfather's room.—Kitchen.—Dining-room.—Mlle Elisabeth Gagnon's room.—Card-table.—Place Grenette.—The dotted line marks the line of battle.

Next to the clearest mental pictures I find *gaps* in this memory, it's like a fresco, large parts of which have fallen away. I can see Séraphie retreating from the kitchen and myself escorting the enemy along the passageway. The scene had taken place in my aunt Elisabeth's room.

I can see myself and I can see Séraphie at point S. As I was very fond of the kitchen, occupied by my friends Lambert and Marion and my father's maid who had the great advantage of not being my superiors, there alone I experienced a sweet equality and freedom, I took advantage of this scene not to appear before suppertime. I fancy I wept with fury at the atrocious abuse (impious, criminal, etc.) which Séraphie had hurled at me, but I was bitterly ashamed by my tears.

I have been questioning myself for the past hour to find out whether this scene is actually true, real, just like twenty others which have reappeared in part, summoned back from the shadows after years of oblivion. Yes indeed, it is definitely real, though I've never observed the like of it in other families. It's true I haven't seen the inside of many bourgeois homes, distaste keeping me away from them and the fear induced by my rank or my wit (may I be forgiven this vanity) might perhaps have prevented such scenes from taking place in my presence. In the end, I can't doubt the reality of the one over the caricature of Zénaïde nor of several others. I triumphed especially when my father was at Claix; that was one enemy the less and the only really powerful one.

"Vile child, I should eat you," my father said to me one day, advancing on me in fury.

But he never struck me, or only two or three times at most. Those words: "Vile child, etc." were addressed to me on a day when I had beaten Pauline, who was raising the roof with her crying.

As my father saw it I had an atrocious character; this was a truth established by Séraphie and *based on fact*: the murder of Mme Chenevaz, my biting Mme Pison-Dugalland on the forehead, my remark about Amar. Soon there came the famous anonymous letter signed Gardon. But explanations are required if that great crime is to become comprehensible. It really was a spiteful trick, I felt ashamed of it during the several years when I was still reflecting on my childhood before my passion for Mélanie, a passion that ended in 1805 when I was twenty-two. Today, when the action of writing my life is causing large shreds of it to appear to me, I very much approve of the Gardon initiative.

CHAPTER 12

GARDON LETTER

They had formed the battalions of Hope or the army of Hope[1] (strange I can't even recall with certainty the name of something which so excited me as a child). I longed to be in these battalions which I watched marching past. I can see today that they were an excellent institution, the only one which might be able to extirpate priestism in France. Instead of playing at priests, children's imaginations think about war and accustom themselves to danger. What's more, when their country calls them at the age of twenty, they know about *drill* and, instead of shuddering at the *unknown*, recall the games of their childhood.

So unterrible was the Terror in Grenoble that the aristocrats didn't send their children.

The army of Hope was run by a certain *abbé* Gardon, who had thrown away his cassock. I committed a forgery: I took a piece of paper broader than it was long, shaped like a bill of exchange, I can see it still, and, disguising my handwriting, I invited Citizen Gagnon to send his grandson Henri B . . . to Saint-André, so that he could be enrolled into the battalion of Hope. It ended with: "Greetings and fraternity, Gardon."

---

1. Paramilitary formations for young boys, founded in 1794.

The mere idea of going to Saint-André was for me the ultimate happiness. My relations demonstrated a distinct lack of intelligence; they allowed themselves to be taken in by this childish letter which must have contained a hundred implausibilities. They needed the advice of a little hunchback called Tourte, a veritable TOAD-EATER, who had insinuated himself into the house by way of this infamous trade.[2] But will they understand this in 1880?

M. Tourte, who was hideously hump-backed and a copying clerk in the departmental ad[ministration], had insinuated himself into the house in a subordinate role, taking offence at nothing, fawning ignominiously on everyone. I had placed my sheet of paper in the space between the doors forming an anteroom on the winding staircase, at point A.

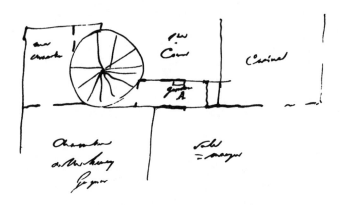

My room.—First courtyard.—A. Gardon.—Kitchen.—M. Henri Gagnon's room.—Dining-room.

My parents were greatly alarmed and summoned little Tourte to a council, who, in his capacity of official scribe, obviously knew M. Gardon's signature. He asked for some of my handwriting, compared them like the shrewd copying

2. I.e. the trade of sycophancy.

clerk he was, and my poor little ruse for escaping from the cage was uncovered. While they deliberated on my fate, I had been sent away into my grandfather's natural history room which formed a lobby on our magnificent terrace. There I amused myself making a ball of red clay that I had just kneaded *jump into the air* (a local expression). I was in the moral situation of a young deserter about to be shot. The act of committing a *forgery* rather *told against me*.

In that lobby on the terrace there was a magnificent map of the Dauphiné four feet across hanging on the wall. On its way down from the very high ceiling, my ball of red clay brushed against this precious map so greatly admired by my grandfather, and being very damp, left a long red *stripe* across it.

"Oh, that's done for me," I thought. "This is another matter altogether; I have offended my one protector." At the same time I was very upset at having done something displeasing to my grandfather.

At that moment, I was summoned to appear before my judges, Séraphie at their head and next to her the hideous hunchback Tourte. I had intended answering them like a Roman, i.e. that I desired to serve my country, that it was my duty as well as my pleasure, etc., etc. But my awareness of my fault towards my excellent grandfather (the mark on the map), who I could see was pale from the fright the note signed Gardon had given him, affected me, and I think I was pitiful. I have always had the weakness of letting myself be affected like a ninny by the least word of submission from the people I was most angry with, *et tentatum contemni*.[3] In vain, later on, did I write this observation of Livy's everywhere; I've never been certain of preserving my anger.

Thanks to the weakness of my heart (not my character), I unfortunately wasted a superb position. My plan had been to threaten to go myself to the *abbé* Gardon to declare my determination to serve my country. I made this declaration,

3. "And tempted to despise": this appears to be a bogus Latin quotation.

but in a weak and timid voice. My idea alarmed them and they could see I lacked conviction. Even my grandfather condemned me, the sentence was that for three days I shouldn't eat at table. Hardly had I been sentenced before my weakness passed and I became a hero once again.

"I much prefer eating alone," I told them, "rather than with tyrants who are constantly reprimanding me."

Little Tourte tried to perform his function:

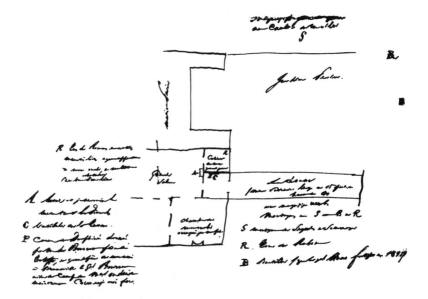

Magnificent garden set in the centre of the town.—Périer house.—
Périer garden.—Large drawing-room.—My grandfather's study.—
The terrace (saracen wall 15 foot long by 40 high).—Magnificent
view of the mountains at S, B, and R.—My uncle's room occupied
by my father. R. Pile of novels and other cheap books having belonged to my uncle and smelling of amber or musk from a league
away.—A. Altar where I served at mass every Sunday.—C. Lobby
on the terrace.—P. Map of the Dauphiné drawn up by M. de
Bourcet father of the Tartuffe and grandfather of my friend at
Brunswick G[ener]al Bourcet aide-de-camp to M[arsh]al Oudinot,
now a cuckold and, I believe, mad.—S. Mountains of Seyssins and
Sassenage.—R. Rabot tower.—B. Bastille (which G[ener]al Haxo is
fortifying in 1835).

"But, *monsieur* Henri, it seems to me . . ."

"You ought to be ashamed and keep quiet," I said interrupting him. "Are you a relation, to talk to me in that way?" etc., etc.

"But *monsieur*," he said, all red in the face behind the spectacles with which his nose was equipped "as a friend of the family . . ."

"I shall never allow myself to be reprimanded by a man such as you."

This allusion to his enormous hump dampened his eloquence.

As I left my grandfather's room, in which this scene had taken place, to go and do my Latin all on my own in the large drawing-room, I was in a grim mood. I felt confusedly that I was a feeble creature; the more I thought about it the angrier I felt with myself.

The son of a notorious suspect, still out of prison thanks to successive *stays of execution*, going to ask the *abbé* Gardon to serve his country, what could my relations answer to that, with eighty people coming to their mass every Sunday?

And so from the very next day they made up to me. But it was as if this business, which Séraphie didn't fail to bring up against me the first time she made a scene, had erected a wall as it were between my relations and myself. I say it with regret, I began to love my grandfather less, and I at once saw clearly what his failing was: "He's afraid of his daughter, he's afraid of Séraphie!" Only my aunt Elisabeth had stayed loyal to me. So my affection for her redoubled.

She opposed, I remember, my hatred for my father, and reprimanded me roundly because once when speaking of him I called him "that man."

On which I shall make two observations.*

---

*I'm well aware that all this is too long, but I get amusement from finding these early if unhappy times reappear, and I ask M. Levavasseur to shorten it should he publish. H. Beyle.

1. This hatred of my father for myself and of myself for him was something so firmly settled in my head that my memory has retained nothing of the part he must have played in the terrible business of the *Gardon* letter.

2. My aunt Elisabeth had the soul of a Spaniard. Her character was the quintessence of honour. She passed this way of feeling on to me in full measure, hence an absurd succession of follies committed out of delicacy and greatness of soul. This foolishness only ceased in me somewhat in 1810, in Paris, when I was in love with Mme Petit. But still today, the excellent Fiori (condemned to death in Naples in 1800) tells me:

"You stretch your nets too high" (Thucydides).

My aunt Elisabeth would still commonly say when she admired something to excess: "That's as fine as the Cid."

She felt, but never expressed, a considerable scorn for the *fontenellisme* of her brother (Henri Gagnon, my grandfather). She had adored my mother, but didn't grow sad when talking about her as my grandfather did. I don't think I ever saw my aunt Elisabeth cry. She would have forgiven me anything at all rather than having called my father "that man."

"But how can you expect me to like him?" I said. "Except for combing my hair when I had ringworm, what has he ever done for me?"

"He is kind enough to take you out for walks."

"I much prefer staying at home, I loathe the walk to *Les Granges.*"

(Near Saint-Joseph's church and to the south-east of that church which is now contained within the Place de Grenoble, which G[ener]al Haxo is fortifying, but, in 1794, the vicinity of St-Joseph was occupied by fields of flax and by infamous *routoirs* [holes half full of water for steeping the flax], in which I could make out the glutinous frog's-spawn which filled me with revulsion: *revulsion* is the right word, I shudder to think of it.)

Talking to me one day about my mother, my aunt let slip that she had had no affection for my father. This remark was for me of immense import. In the depths of my soul, I was still jealous of my father.

I went to tell Marion of this remark, who delighted me by saying that at the time of my mother's marriage, around 1780, she had said one day to my father who was courting her:

"Let me alone, you horrid ugly man."

At the time I didn't see how shameful and implausible such a remark was, I saw only the sense of it, which delighted me.

Tyrants are frequently clumsy, that perhaps is the thing that has made me laugh most in my life.

We had a cousin Santerre, too much of a womanizer, too light-hearted and as such rather disliked by my grandfather, who was much warier and perhaps not entirely immune from envy of poor Santerre, now getting on in years and quite badly off. My grandfather claimed only to look down on him because of his immoral ways in the past. Poor Santerre was very tall, pitted (marked) by small-pox, with red-rimmed, rather weak eyes; he wore spectacles and a broad-brimmed hat turned down.

Every other day, I fancy, in fact whenever the post arrived from Paris, he would come to my grandfather's bringing five or six newspapers addressed to other people but which we read before these other people.

M. Santerre used to come in the morning, around eleven o'clock; he was given lunch of half a glass of wine and some bread, and my grandfather's dislike several times went so far as to recall in my presence the fable of the grasshopper and the ant[4] (for *cigale* M . . . used to write *six gales*), meaning that poor Santerre had been attracted to the house by this finger of wine and *crochon* [*a blank*] of bread.

The meanness of this reproach revolted my aunt Elisabeth, and myself even more so perhaps. But the essential thing about the stupidity of tyrants was that my grandfather put on

4. The celebrated fable of "la Cigale et la fourmi" by La Fontaine; in which the grasshopper's improvidence is contrasted with the industry of the ant.

his spectacles and read all these newspapers out loud to the family. I didn't miss a syllable.

And in my heart I passed comments the exact opposite of those I heard being made.

Séraphie was a raging bigot; my father, often missing from these readings, an extreme aristocrat; my grandfather an aristocrat, but much more moderate, he hated the Jacobins above all as people who were badly dressed and unfashionable.

"*Fancy being called Pichegru!*"[5] he would say.

This was his great objection to that famous traitor, who was then conquering Holland. My aunt Elisabeth felt horror only at the death sentences.

The titles of these newspapers, which I drank in, were:

Le Journal des hommes libres.

Perlet, whose title I can still see, the final word of which was formed by a scrawl imitating Perlet's signature so:

Le Journal des débats;
Le Journal des défenseurs de la Patrie.

Later on, I fancy, a newspaper which had left Paris by special courier, caught up the stagecoach that had left twenty-four hours earlier.

I base my idea that M. Santerre didn't come to the house every day on the number of papers there were to be read. But perhaps, instead of several issues of the same paper, there was merely a large number of papers.

Sometimes, when my grandfather had a cold, I was responsible for the reading. How clumsy of my tyrants! This was like THE POPES founding a library instead of burning all

5. Charles Pichegru (1761–1804) was a general in the Revolutionary armies, and of humble origins.

the books like Omar[6] (whose splendid action has been called in question).

During all these readings which lasted, I fancy, for another year after the death of Robespierre and took up a good two hours each morning, I don't remember having once been of the same opinion as I heard expressed by my relations. As a precaution, I took good care not to speak, and if I sometimes tried to speak, instead of refuting me they imposed silence on me. I can see now that this reading was a remedy for the frightful tedium into which my family had plunged itself three years before, on the death of my mother, by breaking altogether with society.

Little Tourte took my excellent grandfather into his confidence over his love affair with one of our female relations whom we looked down on as being poor and a blot on our nobility. He was yellow, hideous, sickly looking. He began teaching my sister Pauline how to write, and I fancy the brute fell in love with her. He brought to the house the *abbé* Tourte, his brother, whose face was disfigured by *cold sores*. My grandfather having said that he felt *disgust* when he invited the *abbé* to dinner, that feeling became excessive in my own case.

M. Durand continued to come to the house once or twice a day, but I fancy it was twice; here's why: I had reached that incredibly stupid stage where the student of Latin is made to write verses; they're trying to find out whether he has the genius of poetry. My horror of verse dates from this time. Even in Racine, who strikes me as very eloquent, I find plenty of *padding*.

In order to develop the poetic genius in me, M. Durand brought a large duodecimo volume, whose black binding was horribly greasy and dirty.

Such dirtiness would have turned me against M. de Tressan's Ariosto which I adored; judge then of the black volume of M.

6. The caliph Omar I, supposed to have given orders for the burning of the library of Alexandria in the year 641.

Durand, who was none too well turned out himself. This volume contained a poem by a jesuit about a fly drowning in a jug of milk. The whole point turned on the antithesis produced by the whiteness of the milk and the blackness of the fly's body, the sweetness it was looking for in the milk and the bitterness of death.

These lines were dictated to me, leaving out the epithets, for example:

Mosca ep[ithet] *duxerit annos* ep[ithet]
synonyme

multos

I opened my *Gradus ad Parnassum*[7]; I read all the epithets for flies: *volucris, acris, nigra,* and, to get my hexameters and pentameters to scan, I chose *nigra,* for example, for *mosca, felices* for *annos.*

The dirtiness of the book and the banality of the ideas so filled me with disgust that regularly every day, around two o'clock, it was my grandfather who wrote my verses while appearing to be helping me.

M. Durand would come back at seven in the evening and make me remark and admire the difference there was between my verses and those of the jesuit f[ather].

Emulation is absolutely essential if we are to be got to swallow such ineptitudes. My grandfather used to tell me of his exploits at college and I yearned for the college; there at least I would have been able to exchange words with children of my own age.

Soon I was to have that joy: an Ecole Centrale was started, my grandfather was on the organizing committee, he got M. Durand appointed as master.

7. The primer from which many generations of French schoolboys learnt to write Latin verse. It is worth noting that Stendhal has mistaken the Italian form *mosca* for the correct Latin *musca*—and perhaps also that Mosca is the name of the supremely worldly politician and lover in his great novel of *La Chartreuse de Parme.*

CHAPTER 13*

I must speak of my uncle, that amiable man who brought joy into the family when he came to Grenoble from Les Echelles (Savoy), where he had got married.

In writing my life in 1835, I am making many discoveries, these discoveries are of two kinds: first 1, they are large fragments of frescos on a wall, long since forgotten and suddenly appearing, and next to these well preserved fragments there are, as I've several times said, large gaps where only the brickwork of the wall is to be seen. The rough coating of plaster on which the fresco had been painted has fallen away, and the fresco has been lost for ever. There is no date next to the preserved fragments of fresco; I have to go in pursuit of the dates now in 1835. Luckily, an anachronism hardly matters, a confusion of one or two years. As from my arrival in Paris in 1799, since my life merged with the events in the newssheets, all the dates are certain.

2. In 1835, I'm discovering the physiognomy of, and the reason for events. My uncle (Romain Gagnon) probably only

* 18 December 1835.

First visit to Les Echelles. To be fitted in before 1792. G[ener]al Mont[esquiou] takes possession of Savoy.

Les Echelles: to be fitted in in the first volume.

Dictate this and get it written on blank paper at the end of the first volume. Bind this chapter in at the end of second volume. 18 Dec 1835.

To be fitted in before 1792. G[ener]al Mont[esquiou] takes possession of Savoy, so aged eight.

To be fitted in in its place before the conquest of Savoy by General Montesquiou, before 1792. To get copied on blank paper put at the end of the second volume.

came to Grenoble, around 1795 or 96, in order to visit his former mistresses or to relax from Les Echelles, where he reigned, because Les Echelles is a small market-town, consisting at that time of country bumpkins grown rich from smuggling and from farming and whose one pleasure was hunting. My uncle could find the *elegances* of life, pretty, light-hearted women, frivolous and smartly dressed, only in Grenoble.

I made a visit to Les Echelles; it was like staying in heaven: everything about it I found ravishing. The noise of the *Guiers*, the torrent that flowed two hundred paces in front of my uncle's windows, became a sacred sound for me, which carried me instantly up into heaven.

Here already I don't have the phrases; I shall have to work on and transcribe these bits, as will happen later on for my stay in Milan. Where to find words to depict the perfect happiness savoured with delight and without surfeit by a soul sensitive to the point of annihilation and madness?

I don't know whether I may not abandon this work. It seems to me I could depict this rapturous, pure, fresh, heavenly happiness only by enumerating the troubles and the tedium of which it was the total absence. But that has to be a sad way of conveying happiness.

A drive of seven hours in a light cabriolet through Voreppe, La Placette and St-Laurent-du-Pont brought me to the Guiers, which then divided France from Savoy. So Savoy had not then been conquered by G[ener]al Montesquiou, whose plumes I can still see; it was occupied around 1792, I fancy. My heavenly stay in Les Echelles was in 1790 or 91 then. I was seven or eight years old.

This was a sudden, complete, perfect happiness, brought about in an instant by a change of scene. An amusing seven-hour journey had caused Séraphie, my father, my school primer, the Latin teacher, the dismal Gagnon house in Grenoble, the even more dismal house in the Rue des Vieux-Jésuites to vanish for ever.

Séraphie, priestism, all that was so terrible and so potent

in Grenoble, was hidden from view at Les Echelles. My aunt Camille Poncet, married to my uncle Gagnon, was a tall, good-looking woman, and kindness and gaiety personified. A year or two before this visit, near the Pont de Claix, on the Claix side, at point A, I had caught a momentary glimpse of her white skin two fingers above the knee as she got down from her covered wagon.

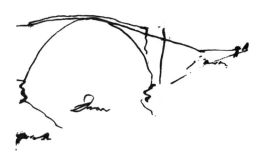

Bridge.—Drac.

For me, when I thought about her, she was an object of the most burning desire. (She is still alive, I haven't seen her these thirty or thirty-three years, she has always been of a perfect kindness.) Being young, she was genuinely susceptible. She resembled closely the charming women of Chambéry (where she often went; five leagues from her house) so well described by J.-J. Rousseau (*Confessions*), she had a sister of the most delicate beauty and the purest complexion, with whom my uncle, I fancy, used to flirt a little. I wouldn't like to swear that he didn't also honour with his attentions *la Fanchon*, the maid-of-all-work, the best and gayest of girls, though by no means pretty.

That visit was nothing but exquisite and poignant sensations of happiness, about which I could write twenty pages of superlatives.

The difficulty, my profound regret at describing things badly and so spoiling a heavenly memory in which the *subject surpasses the teller* makes writing genuinely painful for me rather than a pleasure. Later on, I may very well not describe at all my crossing of the Mont S[ain]t-Bernard with the army of reserve (16 to 18 May 1800) and my stay in Milan in the *casa* Castelbarco or the *casa* Bovara.

Anyway, so as not to leave this visit to Les Echelles as a blank, I shall record a few memories which must give as inaccurate an idea as possible of the objects which occasioned them. I was eight years old when I had this vision of heaven.

An idea occurs to me. Perhaps all the unhappiness of my frightful life in Grenoble, from 1790 to 1799, was a happiness since it brought about the happiness, which nothing for me can surpass, of my stay in Les Echelles and my stay in Milan at the time of Marengo.[1]

Once at Les Echelles, I became friends with everyone, everyone smiled at me as at a high-spirited child. My grandfather, a man of the world, had said to me: "You're ugly, but no one will ever hold your ugliness against you."

I learnt, ten or so years ago, that one of the women who loved me the most or at least the longest, Victorine B[igillion], used to speak of me in exactly the same terms, after an absence of twenty-five years.

At Les Echelles, I made a bosom friend of *la Fanchon*, as she was called. I was awed by the beauty of my *auntie* Camille and, hardly daring to speak to her, devoured her with my eyes. I was taken to the house of the Messrs Bonne or de Bonne, for they had great pretensions to nobility, they may even have said they were related to the Lesdiguières.

A few years afterwards I discovered the portrait of these good people feature by feature in Rousseau's *Confessions*, under the heading of "Chambéry."

The elder Bonne, who worked the *domaine* of Berlander,

1. The Piedmont village near the battlefield where Napoleon defeated the Austrians in 1800.

ten minutes from Les Echelles, where he gave a delightful party with cakes and milk, at which I was put on a donkey led by Grubillon the son, was the best of men; his brother, M. Blaise, the notary, was the most simple-minded. They made fun all day long of M. Blaise who would laugh with the others. Their brother, Bonne-Savardin, a merchant in Marseille, was very elegant, but the courtier of the family, the roué whom they all regarded with respect, was in the service of the king in Turin, and I only caught a glimpse of him.

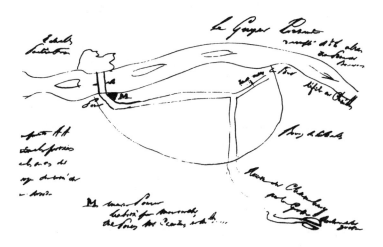

Echelles.—French part.—The Guiers, torrent full of islands, going to the Pont-de-Beauvoisin.—Bridge.—Street to the bridge.—Gorge of Chailles.—Village of Les Echelles.—Road to Chambéry via the cave.—Rocks round the cave.

At the points AA were the posts bearing the arms of Savoy on the right bank.—M. Poncet's house lived in by my uncle, Mme Poncet, Mme Camille and Mlles [a blank].

I remember him only by his portrait which Mme Camille Gagnon now has in her room in Grenoble (my late grandfather's room; the portrait, decorated with a red cross of which the whole family is proud, hangs between the fireplace and the small cabinet).

145

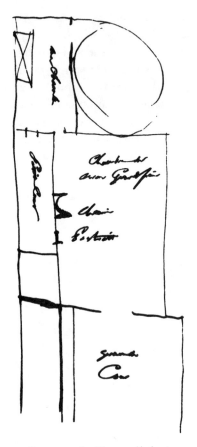

My room.—Small courtyard.—My grandfather's room.—
Fireplace.—Portrait.—Large courtyard.

At Les Echelles there was a tall, good-looking girl, a refugee from Lyon. (So the Terror had begun in Lyon, that might give me a reliable date. This delightful visit took place before the conquest of Savoy by G[ener]al Montesquiou, as they then put it, and after the royalists had fled from Lyon.)

Mlle Cochet was under the protection of her mother, but accompanied by her suitor, a handsome young man, M. [*a blank*], dark-haired and rather sad-looking. I fancy they had only just arrived from Lyon. Afterwards, Mlle Cochet married a good-looking imbecile from among my cousins (M. Doyat, from La Terrasse, and had a son at the Ecole Polytechnique. I fancy she was for a short time my father's mistress). She was tall, good-natured, quite pretty and, when I met her in Les Echelles, very jolly. She was charming at the Berlandets' party. But Mlle Poncet, Camille's sister (today the widowed Mme Blanchet), had a more delicate beauty, she spoke very little.

The mother of my aunt Camille and of Mlle [*a blank*], Mme Poncet, the sister of the Bonnes and of Mme Giroud, and my uncle's mother-in-law, was the best of women. Her house in which I was staying was the headquarters of jollity.

This delightful house had a wooden gallery and a garden alongside the torrent, the Guiers. The garden was traversed at an angle by the embankment of the Guiers.

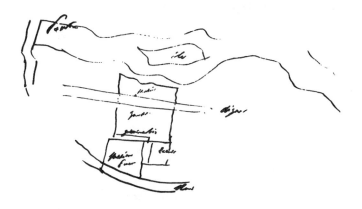

Bridge.—Island.—Garden.—Embankment.—Garden.—Wooden gallery.—Poncet house.—Stable.—Street.

At a second party at Berlandet I rebelled out of jealousy: a young lady whom I loved had looked kindly on a rival of twenty or twenty-five. But who was the object of my affections? Perhaps that will come back to me like many things that are coming back to me as I write. Here is the setting for the scene which I can see as clearly as if I had left it a week ago, though not its physiognomy.

House.—Hedge.—Steep lawn.—From B to C slope of eight or ten feet on which all the ladies were sitting. They were laughing, drinking ratafia from Teisseire (Grenoble), there were no glasses, out of the lids of tortoiseshell snuff-boxes.—Pont Jean-Lioud.— The cave.

After my jealousy-inspired rebellion, I threw stones at these ladies from point A. The big Corbeau (an officer on six months' leave) took me and set me in an apple or mulberry tree at M, at point O, between two branches from which I didn't dare climb down. I jumped, I hurt myself, I ran off towards Z.

I had slightly sprained my foot and ran off limping; the excellent Corbeau came after me, caught me and carried me on his shoulders as far as Les Echelles.

He played the role of *patito* a little bit by saying that he had been in love with Mlle Camille Poncet, my aunt, who had instead preferred the dazzling Romain Gagnon, a young Grenoble lawyer just returned from emigration to Turin.[2]

On this visit I caught a glimpse of Mlle Teresina Maistre, sister of M. le Comte de Maistre, nicknamed Bance.[3] (And it is Bance [*a blank*], author of the *Voyage autour de ma chambre*, whose mummy I saw in Rome around 1832; he is nothing more than a very polite ultra, dominated by a Russian wife, and still occupying himself with painting. The genius and gaiety have gone, only the kindness remains.)

What shall I say about an excursion to the cave? I can still hear the silent drips falling from the tops of the tall rocks along the road. We took a few steps into the cave with the ladies: Mlle Poncet was afraid, Mlle Cochet showed more courage. On the way back we crossed the Pont Jean-Lioud (God knows what its real name is!).

What shall I say about a hunting party in the woods of Berland, left bank of the Guiers, near the Pont Jean-Lioud?

I often used to slip off under the immense beech trees. M. [*a blank*], Mlle Cochet's suitor, hunted with [*a blank*]: the names and the mental pictures have gone from me. My uncle gave my father an enormous dog, called Berland, blackish in colour. After one or two years this reminder of a country I had found delightful died of some illness, I can see him still.

---

2. Where he had gone as a monarchist and ultra, to escape persecution.

3. Xavier, Comte de Maistre (1763–1852) was a soldier and author, of Romantic inclinations. His nickname of Bance derived from an imitation he used to give of someone of that name.

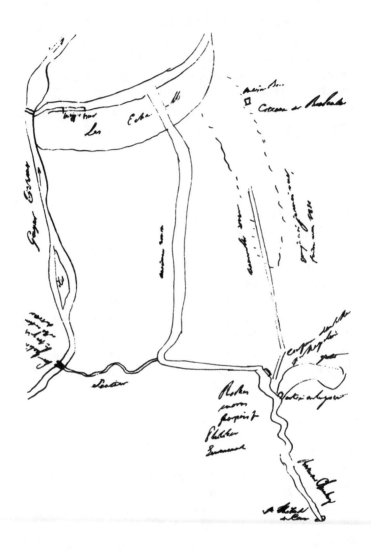

Guiers torrent.—Island.—Poncet house.—Les Echelles.—Bonne
house.—Slopes of Berlandet.—Old road.—New road which I've
never seen, made around 1810.—Pont Jean-Lioud 100 or 80 feet
above the torrent.—Path.—Enormous rocks cut through by
Philibert-Emmanuel.—Cutting in the rock by Napoleon.—Cave.—
Entrance to the cave.—St-Thibaud-de-Couz.—Road to Chambéry.

I set the scenes from Ariosto beneath the woods of Berland.

The forests of Berland and the cliff-like precipices bordering them on the side of the road to St-Laurent-du-Pont became for me a dear and sacred ideal. It was there that I set all the enchantments of Ismen in the *Jerusalem Delivered*. When I got back to Grenoble, my grandfather let me read the translation of the *Jerusalem* by Mirabaud, despite all the comments and objections of Séraphie.

My father, the least elegant, the most artful, the most politic, or, put in one word, the most Dauphinois of men, couldn't not be jealous of the amiability, the gaiety, the physical and moral elegance of my uncle.

He accused him of *embroidering* (telling lies). Wishing to be as amiable as my uncle on this visit to Les Echelles, I sought to embroider in imitation of him.

I made up some story or other about my Latin primer (a volume concealed by me under my bed so that my Latin teacher [was it M. Joubert or M. Durand?] shouldn't mark [with his fingernail] the lessons I had to learn at Les Echelles).

My uncle had no difficulty uncovering the falsehood of a child of eight or nine; I didn't have the prudence[4] of mind to say: "I was trying to be amiable, like you!"

Because I liked him, I was affected, and this lesson made a deep impression on me.

Had I been *reprimanded* (corrected) as reasonably and justly as this, they might have made anything of me. I shudder to think of it: had Séraphie had the politeness and wit of her brother, she might have made a jesuit of me.

(Today I am quite *eaten up with contempt*. Such baseness and cowardice among the generals of the Empire! This is the true defect of Napoleon's kind of genius: to raise a man to the highest positions because he is brave and has the gift of leading an attack. What an abyss of moral baseness and cowardice the peers are who've just sentenced the war[rant] of[ficer]

4. A lapsus: "prudence" should obviously be "presence."

Thomas to perpetual imprisonment, under the sun of Pondichéry, for a fault barely meriting six months in prison![5] And these poor young fellows have already done twenty months [18 Dec 1835]!

As soon as I have received my copy of M. Thiers's *Histoire de la Révolution*, I must write on the blank pages of the 1793 volume the names of all the generals who are now peers and have just sentenced M. Thomas, so as to be able to feel sufficient contempt for them as I read about the fine actions which got them known around 1793. Most of these infamous wretches are now sixty-five to seventy years old. My worthless friend Félix Faure has the infamous baseness without the fine actions. And M. d'Houdetot! And Dijon! I shall say with Julien: Scum! Scum! Scum![6])

Forgive this lengthy parenthesis, oh reader of 1880! By that time everything I'm speaking of will have been forgotten. The generous indignation which causes my heart to throb and stops me from writing more will be absurd. If in 1880 they have a passable gov[ernment], the waterfalls, the rapids, the anxieties through which Fr[ance] will have passed in order to get there will have been forgotten, history will write only one word beside the name of [*a blank*]: *the most scoundrelly of* K[INGS].[7]

M. de Corbeau, who had become my friend since carrying me on his back from Berlandet to Les Echelles, took me angling for trout in the Guiers. He used to fish between the Portes de Chailles, at the foot of the precipices in the gorge of Chailles, and the Pont des Echelles, sometimes over towards

---

5. Thomas was one of the "April conspirators" and was sentenced to be deported.

6. A reference to the cry of Stendhal's young hero, Julien Sorel, in *Le Rouge et le noir*. The Comte Frédéric Christophe d'Houdetot (1778–1870) was a former colleague of Stendhal on Napoleon's Conseil d'Etat, who became a peer of France and thus a judge of the 1834 conspirators. "Dijon" is a pseudonym for the Comte Molé (1781–1855), another trimmer who served first Napoleon, then the Bourbons and finally Louis-Philippe, as both foreign and prime minister.

7. The contemptuous allusion is to Louis-Philippe.

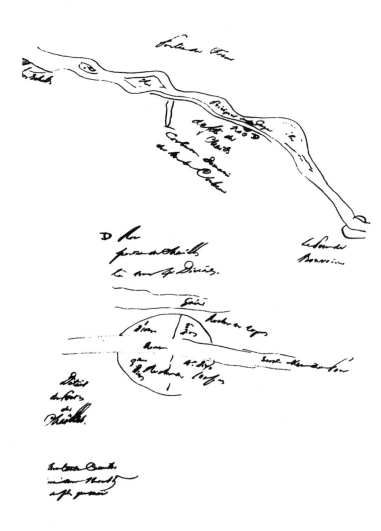

French part.—Island.—Precipices of the Guiers.—Island.—
Les Echelles.—Gorge of Chailles.—Corbaron, M. de Corbeau's
domaine.—The Pont-de-Beauvoisin.—D. Rock. Porte de Chailles;
four dioceses here.—Guiers.—20-foot rock.—First diocese.—
Second diocese.—Road.—Road going to Pont.—Third diocese.—
Fourth diocese.—100-foot rock.—Detail of the Portes de Chaille.
—My aunt Camille must have been twelve or fifteen years older
than me.

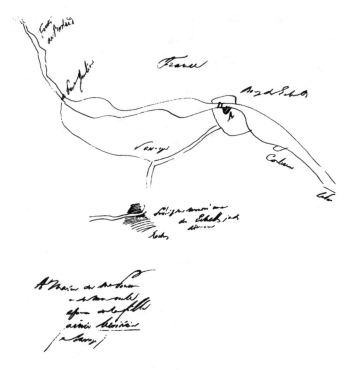

Forests of Berland.—Pont Jean-Lioud.—France.—Village of
Les Echelles.—Savoy.—Corbaron.—The Pont.—Precipices climbed
with ladders in the old days, it was said.—Rocks.

A. House of Mme Poncet or of my uncle husband of the elder
daughter *the heir* (in Savoy).

the Pont Jean-Lioud.* His l[ine] was fifteen or twenty feet
long. Near Chailles, as he lifted the hook quickly out, his line
of white horsehair went over a tree, and his trout of three-
quarters of a pound (those are the good ones) appeared before
us dangling twenty feet above the ground on top of a leafless
tree. How I enjoyed that!

* 18 December 1835. At 4.50, not enough daylight. I stop.

18 Dec[ember] 1835, from 2 to half-past 4, twenty-four pages. I am so absorbed by
the memories unveiling themselves to my gaze I can scarcely form my letters. Fifty-
two years eleven months.

CHAPTER 14*

DEATH OF POOR LAMBERT

I insert here, so as not to waste it, a drawing with which I this morning decorated a letter I'm writing to my friend R. Colomb who, at his age, careful man that he is, has been bitten by the bug of metromania, which has led him to reproach me because I have written a preface for the new edition of De Brosses but he too had written a preface.

This map has been made in answer to Colomb, who says I'm going to despise him.

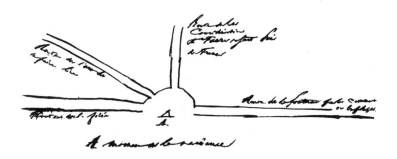

Road to madness.—Road to the art of getting oneself read.—Road to consideration: F[élix] Faure makes himself a peer of France.—Road to a fortune made through trade or job-seeking.—A. Moment of birth.

---

*Death of poor Lambert.
  The two guillotined priests; death of poor Lambert falling from the mulberry tree; Chorier terrace; trousers smelling of the makers.

155

I add: if there is another world, I shall go and kneel before Montesquieu; he will perhaps say to me: "My poor friend, you were quite without talent in the other world."

I shall be annoyed, but hardly surprised; the eye can't see itself.

But my letter to Col[omb] will only make all the men of money turn pale; once they have become prosperous, they start to hate the people who've been read by the public. The clerks in the Foreign Ministry would be very glad to cause me some small setback in my career.[1] This sickness is more malignant when the man of money reaches fifty and acquires the obsession of turning himself into a writer. It's like those generals of the Empire who, finding around 1820 that the Restoration had no need of them, developed a *passionate* love of music, i.e. as a second best.

Let us return to 1794 or 95. I protest once again that I don't claim to be describing things in themselves, but only their effect on me. How could I not be persuaded of this truth by this simple observation: I can't remember the physiognomies of my relations, my excellent grandfather for example, whom I looked at so often and with all the affection of which an ambitious child is capable.

Since, in accordance with the barbaric system adopted by my father and Séraphie, I had no friend or comrade of my own age, my *sociability* (inclination to speak freely about everything) had been divided into two branches.

My grandfather was my serious and respectable comrade.

My friend, to whom I told everything, was a very intelligent boy called Lambert, my grandfather's manservant. My confidences often annoyed Lambert and, when I pressed him too hard, he would give me a brisk clip round the ear befitting my age. I only liked him all the more. His main task,

1. I.e. as French consul in Civitavecchia.

156

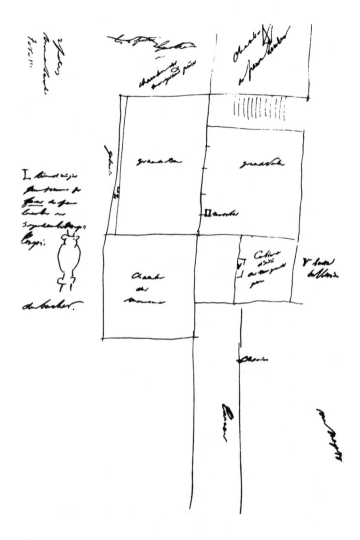

Two priests.—Death of Lambert. Chorier terrace.—My grandfather's room.—Poor Lambert's room.—L. Place from where I *forced* myself to remember poor Lambert by looking at the spinning-tops of the woodstore.—Gallery.—Large courtyard.—Large drawing.—My table.—My uncle's room.—My grandfather's summer study.—V. Bust of Voltaire.—Chorier.—Terrace.—Magnificent view.

which he greatly disliked, was to go and fetch peaches from St-Vincent near Le Fontanil (my grandfather's *domaine*). Next to this cottage, which I adored, were some very well situated espaliers which produced magnificent peaches. There were trellised vines that produced an excellent *lardan* (a sort of chasselas grape, of which the Fontainebleau one is simply a copy). All this arrived in Grenoble in two baskets placed at either end of a flat stick, and this stick was balanced on the shoulders of Lambert who had to cover in this way the four miles separating St-Vincent from Grenoble.

Lambert had ambition: he was discontented with his lot; in order to better it he set to breeding silkworms, after the example of my aunt Séraphie who had ruined her chest *doing* silkworms in St-Vincent. (During which time I breathed freely, the house in Grenoble, run by my grandfather and the sensible Elisabeth, became agreeable to me. I sometimes risked going out without the indispensable company of Lambert.)

This best friend of mine had bought a mulberry tree (near St-Joseph); he bred silkworms in the room of some mistress or other.

While *gathering* (picking) the leaves of this mulberry tree, he fell; he was brought back to us on a ladder. My grandfather tended him like a son; but there was a disturbance of the brain, the light no longer made any impression on his pupils; he died after three days; in his delirium, which never left him, he let out piteous cries which pierced me to the heart.

I experienced grief for the first time in my life. I thought about death.

The wrench caused by the loss of my mother had been a madness into which there entered, as it seems to me, a great deal of love. My grief at the death of Lambert was grief such as I have known it during all the rest of my life, a thoughtful grief, dry-eyed, without tears, without consolation. I was heartbroken and on the verge of falling (for which I was roundly reprimanded by Séraphie) when I went ten times a day into my friend's room and gazed at his handsome face: he was dying

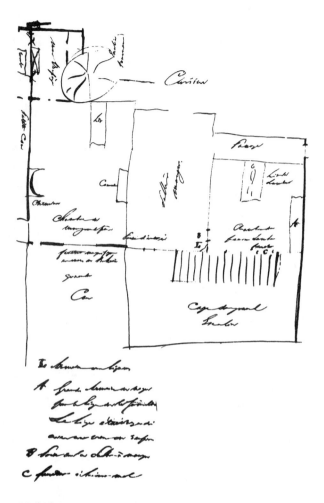

My bed.—My trapezium.—Winding staircase.—Kitchen.
—Small courtyard.—Bed.—Fireplace.—Chest-of-drawers.—
My grandfather's room.—Dining-room.—Main entrance.—
Passageway.—Lambert's bed.—Poor Lambert's room.—Window.
—Magnificent window of Bohemian glass.—Well of main
staircase.

L. Liqueur cupboard.—A. Large walnut cupboard for the
family linen. The linen was regarded with a kind of awe.—
B. Door into the dining room.—C. Window giving poor light,
opening on to the staircase, but very big and very handsome.
—North.

and expiring. I shall never forget his fine black eyebrows and that air of vigour and good health which his delirium had only heightened. I watched him being bled, after each bleeding I watched them try the experiment of the light in front of his eyes (a sensation I was reminded of on the evening of the battle of Landshut, I believe, 1809).[2]

In Italy once I saw the face of a St John gazing at his crucified friend and God, which all of a sudden seized me thanks to the memory of what I had experienced twenty-five years before at the death of *poor Lambert*, that was the name he acquired in the family after his death.

I could fill another five or six pages with *clear* memories I still have of that great grief. He was nailed into his coffin, he was taken away . . .

Sunt lacrimae rerum.[3]

The same side of my heart is moved by certain of Mozart's accompaniments in *Don Giovanni*.

Poor Lambert's room was situated on the main staircase, next to the liqueur cupboard A.

A week after his death, Séraphie flew quite rightly into a rage because she was served some soup or other (*soupe* in Grenoble) in a little chipped earthenware bowl, which I can still see (forty years after the event), which had been used to collect Lambert's blood during one of his bleedings. I suddenly dissolved in tears to the point where my sobs were suffocating me. I had never been able to cry at my mother's death. I only began to be able to cry more than a year later, alone, during the night, in my bed. Seeing me crying over Lambert, Séraphie made a scene. I went off to the kitchen repeating under my breath and as if to get my revenge: "Vile woman! Vile woman!"

2. A town in Bavaria; Stendhal arrived there on the day following the battle.

3. A line from Virgil's *Aeneid*, Book I, meaning literally "There are tears for things."

My sweetest effusions with my friend had come while he worked sawing wood by the woodstore, divided from the courtyard, at C, by an open partition, formed of uprights of walnut-wood turned on a lathe, like a garden balustrade.

Woodshed.—Large courtyard.—North.—On the second floor, here, my uncle's room.

After his death I used to take up a position on the gallery, from the second storey of which I had an ideal view of the uprights of the balustrade which seemed to me wonderful for making spinning-tops.

What age might I then have been? The idea of a spinning-top indicates at least the age of reason. I have a thought: I can have a search made for poor Lambert's death certificate; but was *Lambert* a baptismal or a household name? I fancy that his brother, who kept a dubious small café, Rue de Bonne, near the barracks, was also called Lambert. But how different, good Lord! At the time I thought nothing could have been more *common* than this brother to whose house Lambert sometimes took me. For it has to be admitted, although my opinions were then thoroughly and fundamentally republican, my relations had passed on to me in their entirety their aloof and aristocratic tastes. This defect has remained with me, and prevented me only ten days ago, for example, from taking advantage of a fortunate chance.[4] I loathe the hoi-polloi (to have dealings with), while at the same time, under the

4. I.e. the girl in the carriage whose advances he ignored.

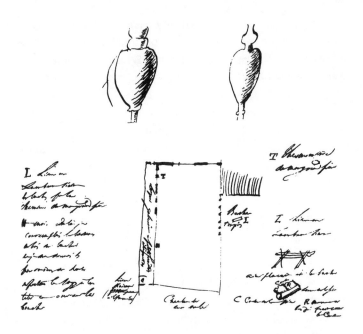

Long gallery with elegant small windows.—Privy (reserved for the family).—My uncle's room.—Woodstore.—Spinning-tops.

L. Place where Lambert used to saw logs for my grandfather's fireplace.—H. Me. From here I used to contemplate the wooden bars of the woodstore and give myself paroxysms of pain by letting the blood go to my head and opening my mouth.—T. My grandfather's thermometer.—L. Place where Lambert did the sawing. He placed the log thus.—Rope.—Teeth of the saw.—C. Saw rope. —R. Piece of wood which tightened the rope.

name of *the people*, I long passionately for their happiness, which I think isn't to be got except by putting questions to them on an important subject. That is, by summoning them to appoint deputies for themselves.

My friends, or rather purported friends, go on from this to cast doubt on my sincere liberalism. I have a horror of anything dirty, but the people are always dirty, as I see it. The one exception is in Rome, but there the dirt is concealed by ferocity. (For example, the unique dirtiness of the little

162

Sardinian *abbé* Crobras, but my boundless respect for his energy. His five-year lawsuit against his leaders. *Ubi missa, ibi mensa.*[5] Few men have that much strength. The Princes Caetani know the full story of M. Crobras of Sartene, I believe, in Sardinia.)

The paroxysms of love I gave myself at point H. were unbelievable. To the point where I might have burst a bloodvessel. I have just hurt myself *mimicking* them at least forty years later. Who remembers Lambert today, other than the heart of his friend!

I will go further, who remembers Alexandrine, dead in January 1815, twenty years ago?

Who remembers Métilde, dead in 1825?

Do they not belong to me, I who love them better than all the rest of the world, I who think passionately of them, ten times a week, and often for two hours at a time?

---

5. "Where the mass is, there is the table": a phrase meaning that a priest should be fed by the community in which he says mass. Nothing is known of the *abbé* Crobras.

CHAPTER 15

My mother had had a rare gift for drawing, it was often said in the family.

"Alas, what wasn't she good at?" they went on with a deep sigh.

After which, a long, sad silence. The fact is that before the Revolution, which changed everything in those remote provinces, drawing was taught in Grenoble as ridiculously as Latin. Drawing meant making perfectly parallel hatchings in red chalk in imitation of engravings; they paid little attention to outline.

I often came upon large heads in red chalk drawn by my mother.

My grandfather brought up this example, this all-powerful *precedent*, and Séraphie notwithstanding, I went to learn drawing from M. Le Roy. This was a big step forward: as M. Le Roy lived in the Teisseire house, before the big Jacobins doorway, I was gradually allowed to go to him and especially to come back on my own.

For me this was tremendous. My tyrants, I called them that as I watched other children running about, had tolerated my going alone from P to R. I realized that if I went very fast, for they counted the minutes, and Séraphie's window looked out precisely on to the Place Grenette, I could take a turn round the Place de la Halle, which was reached through the gateway L. I was exposed to view only when getting from R to L. The clock of St-André, from which the town took its time, sounded the quarter-hours, I had to leave from M. Le Roy's at

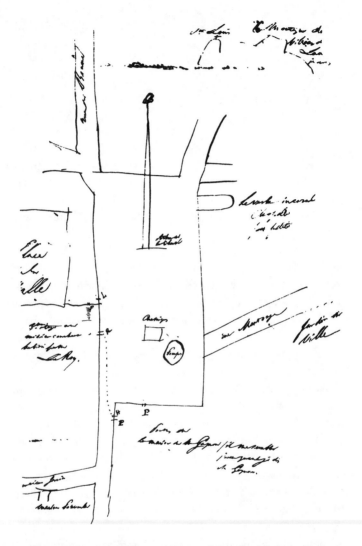

Rue de Bonne.—St-Louis.—Mountain of Le Villard-de-Lans, I
believe.—Place de la Halle.—Tree of liberty.—The Verbe Incarné.
Very small chapel.—Third-floor apartment on the south and west
lived in by M. Le Roy.—Chestnut-trees.—Pump.—Rue Montorge.
—Jardin de Ville.—Rue [des] Vieux-Jésuites.—Father's house.
—Doors of the Gagnon house (I fancy I am swearing when I
say M. Gagnon).

half-past three or four o'clock (I don't well remember which) and be back indoors five minutes later. M. Le Roy, or rather Mme Le Roy, a shrewish thirty-five-year-old, very appetizing and with beautiful eyes, had had special instructions, I fancy, on pain of losing a very profitable pupil, not to let me out before a quarter past three. Sometimes, as I came back up, I would pause for whole quarters of an hour at the window on the stairs, at F, pleased simply at feeling myself free; in these rare moments, instead of being employed working out the moves my tyrants would make, my imagination began to enjoy everything.

Soon my great concern was to guess whether Séraphie would be at home at half-past three, the time of my return. My good friend Marion (Marie Thomasset, from Vinay), a servant straight out of Molière and who loathed Séraphie, was of great assistance to me. One day when Marion had told me that Séraphie had left after coffee, around three o'clock, to go and see her good friend Mme Vignon, the *boime*,[1] I risked going to the Jardin de Ville, full of young street urchins (*gamins*). To that end I crossed the Place Grenette passing behind the chestnut shed and the pump and slipping under the archway into the gardens.

I was spotted; some friend or protégé of Séraphie's gave me away; a scene in the evening in front of the grandparents. I lied, very properly, when Séraphie asked:

"Have you been to the Jardin de Ville?"

Thereupon, my grandfather reprimanded me quietly and politely, but firmly, for the falsehood. I felt keenly what I couldn't express. Is lying not the one expedient of the slave? An old manservant, poor Lambert's successor, a sort of La Rancune,[2] a faithful executor of my relations' orders and who

1. A dialect term meaning hypocrite.

2. A disagreeable character in the *Roman comique* of Paul Scarron (1610–1660), a picaresque novel about a troop of strolling players. *Rancune* is the French for "rancour" or "bile."

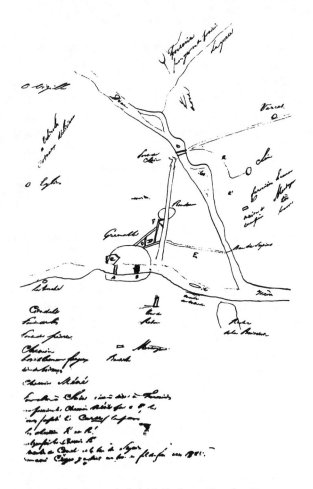

Vizille.—Echirolles. Delightful hillsides.—Church.—Drac.—
Fontanieu (we had meadows there).—La Gresse.—North.—Pont
de Claix.—Varces.—Roundel.—Grenoble.—Islands.— Seyssins
ferry.—Claix.—Furonières, hamlet.—My father's house.—Very
high mountain.—La Tronche.—Rabot tower.—Island.—Isère.—
Montée de St-Martin.—Rocks at La Buisserate.—Mountain.

C. Citadel.—A. Wooden bridge.—B. Stone bridge.—D. Horribly
muddy lane known as Les Boiteuses.—F. Méné lane. In order to go
to Claix, i.e. to Furonières, we used to take the Méné lane through
O F, the Cours (known as the Course), the bridge and the lane R
and R', sometimes the lane E from the Moulin de Canel and the
bottom of Seyssins. My friend Crozet created a wire bridge there
around 1826.

used to say morosely when speaking of himself: "I'm a mur-derizer of chamber-pots," was made responsible for taking me to M. Le Roy's. I was free on the days when he went to St-Vincent to fetch fruit.

This glimmer of freedom drove me wild. "What will they turn me into after all," I said to myself. "What child of my age doesn't go around on his own?"

I went several times to the Jardin de Ville; if I was spotted, I was told off, but I didn't answer back. They threatened to put an end to the drawing teacher, but I went on with my ex-cursions. Tempted by this little bit of freedom, I had become fierce. My father was beginning to acquire his great passion for agriculture and went frequently to Claix.

I thought I could tell that, when he was away, I was begin-ning to frighten Séraphie. My aunt Elisabeth, with her Span-ish pride, had no legitimate authority and remained neutral; my grandfather, true to his Fontenelle-like character, loathed shouting; Marion and my sister Pauline supported me openly. Séraphie passed for crazy in the eyes of many people, for ex-ample, in the eyes of our cousins, Mmes Colomb and Roma-gnier, excellent women. (I was able to appreciate them after I reached the age of reason and had some experience of life.) In those days, a word from Mme Colomb would make me with-draw into myself, which gives me to suppose that by showing gentleness they might have made me into anything, probably a *worthless*, very *devious* Dauphinois. I began to stand up to Séraphie; in my turn I had terrible fits of rage.

"You won't go to M. Le Roy any more," she said.

If I think hard about it, I fancy Séraphie scored a victory and that as a consequence my drawing lessons were inter-rupted.

The Terror had been so mild in Grenoble that now and again my father would go to live in his own house, Rue des Vieux-Jésuites. There I can see M. Le Roy giving me my les-son on the big black table in my father's study, and saying to me at the end of the lesson:

"*Monsieur*, tell your *dear* father I can no longer come for 35 francs, or 45 francs, a month."

It was a question of the *assignats*,[3] which were *collapsing* steadily a (local expression). But what date to put on this very distinct mental picture which has suddenly come back to me? Perhaps it was much later on, at the time when I was painting in gouache.

Rue des Vieux-Jésuites.—Study.—L. M. Le Roy.—H. Me.

Drawing and M. Le Roy were what mattered least to me. This teacher made me do eyes in profile and from the front, and ears in red chalk copying other drawings engraved, I fancy, in the style of pencil drawings.

M. Le Roy was a very polite *Parisian*, dried-up and enfeebled, aged by the most excessive debauchery (such is my impression, but how could I justify the words "the most excessive"?), polite besides, civilized as people are in Paris, which had the effect on me of an excessive politeness, accustomed as I was to the cold, discontented, far from civilized manner which constitutes the normal expression of those

3. The promissory notes issued under the Revolution between 1790 and 1796.

very shrewd Dauphinois. (See the character of Sorel *père* in the *Rouge*, but where the devil will the *Rouge* be in 1880? It will have crossed the stygian banks.)[4]

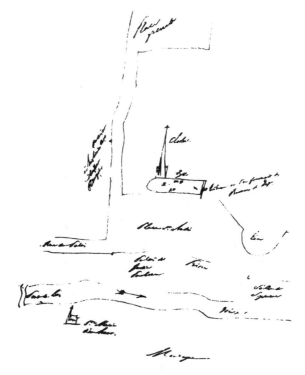

Place Grenette.—House where Mmes Colomb and Romagnier lived.—Belfry.—Church.—Gallery reached from the dep[artmen]tal offices.—Rue du Palais.—Place St-André.—Tower.—Palais de Justice. Parlement.—Prison.—Theatre.—Wooden bridge.—Isère.— Ste-Marie-d'en-Haut.—Mountain.

One evening, as night was falling, it was cold, I was bold enough to make my escape, apparently to go and join my aunt Elisabeth at Mme Colomb's, I ventured into the

4. Julien Sorel's father in the novel is the essential Dauphinois countryman. The "stygian banks" are no doubt intended for those of the River Styx itself.

Jacobin Club, which held its meetings in the church of St-André.[5]

I was full of the heroes of Roman history, I saw myself one day as a Camillus and a Cincinnatus all in one. God knows what punishment I'm laying myself open to, I said to myself, if some *spy of Séraphie's* (that was my thought at the time) catches sight of me here? The president was at P, some badly dressed women at F, myself at H.

People demanded the floor and spoke somewhat confusedly. My grandfather habitually, and *light-heartedly*, made fun of their manner of speaking. It seemed to me straight away that my grandfather was right, my impression wasn't favourable: I found these people that I should like to have loved horribly vulgar. The church was tall and narrow and very dimly lit, I could make out many women of the lowest kind. In a word, I was then as I am today: I love the people, I detest its oppressors; but it would be a constant torment for me to live with the people.

I shall borrow for a moment the language of Cabanis.[*] My skin is too delicate, a woman's skin (later on I always got blisters after having held[†] my sabre for an hour); the least thing takes the skin off my fingers, which are very good; in a word, the surface of my body is that of a woman. Hence maybe an insurmountable revulsion for whatever looks *dirty*, or *damp*, or *blackish* in colour. Many of which things were to be seen at the Jacobins in St-André.

On my return, an hour later, to Mme Colomb's, my aunt of the Spanish character gave me a very serious look. We came out; when we were alone in the street, she said to me:

---

5. The Jacobins were a party which began as moderates in 1789, but became the most extreme of revolutionary factions and the supporters of Robespierre and the Terror. The church of St-André had been deconsecrated in 1790.

*Style. The words *for a moment* offer respite to the mind. I would have erased them in 1830, but in 35 I regret not finding [any] like them in the *Rouge*.

† FIRST word written on my Tronchin bureau.

"If you run off like that, your father will notice . . ."

"Never on your life, unless Séraphie gives me away."

"Let me speak . . . And I don't care to have to talk about you to your father. I shan't take you to Mme Colomb's any more."

Wooden pyram[id] illuminating Chépy.[6]

These words spoken with great simplicity affected me; the ugliness of the Jacobins had made an impression on me. I was thoughtful the next day and the days following: my idol was tottering. Had my grandfather guessed my feelings, and I would have told him everything if he'd spoken to me at the moment when we were watering the flowers on the terrace, he could have made the Jacobins seem ridiculous once and for all and brought me back into the fold of the *Aristocracy* (as it was then known, today the legitimist or conservative party). Instead of treating the Jacobins as gods, my imagination might have been employed picturing to itself and exaggerating the filth of their hall in St-André.

This filth left to itself was soon erased by the account of some victorious battle which brought lamentations from my family.

Around this time, the arts took possession of my imagination, by way of the senses, a preacher would say. In M. Le Roy's studio there was a large and beautiful landscape: a steep mountainside seen from very close to, decorated with tall trees; at the foot of the mountain a stream, shallow but broad

6. The Revolutionary government in Paris's envoy to Grenoble in 1793.

173

and limpid, flowed from left to right at the foot of the last trees. In it, three almost, or not almost, naked women were gaily bathing. This was almost the one point of light in that canvas of three and a half feet by two and a half.

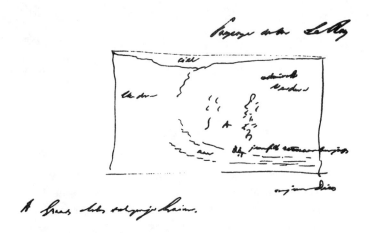

M. Le Roy's landscape.—Sky.—Verdure.—Admirable verdure.—
Young girls holding up their skirts or young goddesses.—Water.
A. Tall trees such as I like them.

This landscape, of a delightful verdure, encountering an imagination prepared by *Félicia*,[7] became for me the ideal of happiness. It was a mixture of tender sentiments and soft voluptuousness. To bathe like that with attractive women!

The water was of a clearness which made a beautiful contrast with the evil-smelling streams of Les Granges, full of frogs and covered with a green putrescence. I mistook the green plant which grows on these filthy streams for something rotten. Had my grandfather said to me: "It's a plant; even the *mould* which spoils bread is a plant," my revulsion would have quickly passed. I overcame it fully only after M. Adrien de Jussieu, during our journey to Naples (1832) (a man

7. A popular novel by Andrea de Nerciat (1739–1801).

so very natural, so wise, so reasonable, so deserving of being loved), had talked to me at length about these little plants, which I still saw a little as a sign of putrescence, although I vaguely knew that they were plants.*

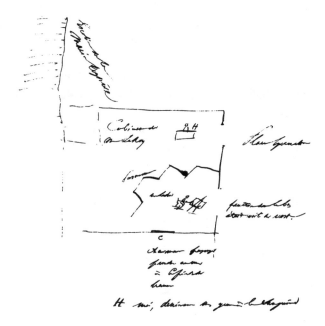

Staircase of Teisseire house.—M. Le Roy's study.—Screen.— M. Le Roy.—Place Grenette.—Window the bottom of which was draped in green.—Charming landscape hanging on the wall six feet up.

    H. Me drawing my eyes in red chalk.

I have only one means of preventing my imagination from playing tricks on me, that is to march straight to the objective. I can see this clearly as I march on the two cannons (of which mention is made in General Michaud's certificate[†]).

---

[*] I ought today to study the natural history of worms and beetles which still nauseate me. Around 1810, I bought two volumes by M. Duméril with that intention, but the Russian campaign, the 1813 one, my mission in the Seventh Division took my mind off it. In Grenoble, however, I read a bit of it in order to talk to Mme Gauthier about it.

[†] M. Colomb must have this certificate.

Later on, I mean around 1805, in Marseille, I had the delightful pleasure of watching my mistress, who had a superlative figure, bathing in the Huveaune crowned by tall trees (on the *bastide* of Mme Roy or . . .).

I vividly recalled M. Le Roy's landscape which, for four or five years, had been my *ideal* of sensual delight. I might have exclaimed, like some ninny out of an 1832 novel: *That is my ideal!*

All this, it may be sensed, is quite independent of the merits of the landscape which was probably a dish of spinach with no aerial perspective.

Later on, *Le Traité nul*, an opera by Gaveaux,[8] was for me the start of the passion which came to a halt with *Il Matrimonio segreto*, met with in Ivrea (end of May 1800), and *Don Giovanni*.[9]

8. This was a comedy in prose but with ariettas, first produced in 1797.

9. *Il Matrimonio segreto* is an opera by Cimarosa, the eighteenth-century Italian composer whom Stendhal rated remarkably highly.

CHAPTER 16

I was working on a small table at point P, near the second window in the large Italian drawing-room; I was translating with pleasure Virgil or Ovid's *Metamorphoses* when the dull murmur of a vast crowd, gathered on the Place Grenette, told me that two army brigadiers had been guillotined.[1]

This was the only blood shed by the 93 Terror in Grenoble.

Here is one of my great faults: my reader of 1880, far removed from the partisan fury and seriousness, will hold it against me when I confess to him that this death, which sent a chill of horror through my grandfather, which drove Séraphie into a fury, which reinforced the haughty Spanish silence of my aunt Elisabeth, gave me *pleasure*. There, the great word is written.

There's more, there's far worse. I AM still IN 1835 THE MAN OF 1794.

(Here is one more way of securing a genuine date. The registers of the criminal tribunal, now the Cour Royale, Place St-André, must give the date of the deaths of Messrs Revenas and Guillabert.)

My confessor, M. Dumolard, from Bourg d'Oisans (a priest with only one eye and quite a good fellow outwardly, since 1815 a raging jesuit), showed me, with gestures I found ridiculous, some prayers or Latin verses written by Messrs Revenas and Guillabert, whom he wanted at all costs to make me see as martyrs.

1. In fact, not brigadiers but priests, as we shall see.

"My grandpa (grandfather) has told me that twenty years ago they hanged two protestant ministers in that same spot."

I answered him haughtily:

"Ah, that was quite different!"

"The Parlement sentenced the first two for their religion, the criminal tribunal has just sentenced these ones for having betrayed their country."

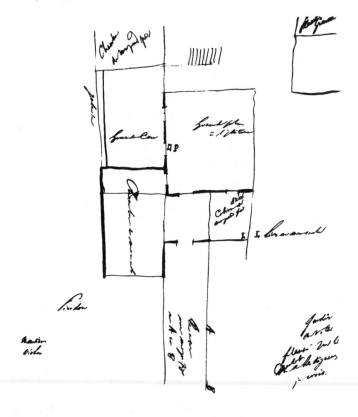

Gallery.—My grandfather's room.—Place Grenette.—Large courtyard.—Large Italian drawing-room.—My uncle's room.—My grandfather's summer study.—L. My uncle's books.—Pirodon.—Mention, violin.—Terrace with magnificent view at A and B.—Jardin de Ville planted by the Connétable de Lesdiguières, I believe.

If those aren't the words, that at least was the sense.

But I didn't yet know that arguing with tyrants is dangerous; they must have read in my eyes my lack of sympathy for two traitors to the fatherland. (There wasn't in 1795 and isn't, in 1835, in my eyes an even *comparable* crime.)

They picked a terrible quarrel with me, my father turned on me in one of the greatest rages of which I have any recollection. Séraphie was triumphant. My aunt Elisabeth lectured me in private. But I believe, may God forgive me, I convinced her that it was the punishment of an eye for an eye.

Luckily for me my grandfather didn't join with my enemies; in private he was wholly of the opinion that the deaths of the two protestant ministers were just as much to be condemned.

"Much less, under the tyrant Louis XV the country wasn't in danger."

I didn't say tyrant, but my face must have said it.

If my grandfather, who had already been against me in the *abbé* Gardon battle, had shown himself the same in this affair, that would have been the end, I would no longer have loved him. Our conversations about good literature, Horace, M. de Voltaire, Chapter XV of *Bélisaire*, the beautiful passages from *Télémaque, Séthos*,[2] which formed my mind, would have ceased and I would have been far unhappier throughout the whole time which elapsed from the death of the two unfortunate pr[iests] up until my exclusive passion for mathe[matics]: spring or summer 1797.

All the winter afternoons* were spent with our legs in the sun in the room of my aunt Elisabeth which looked out on to the Grenette at point A.

---

2. *Bélisaire* is a novel by Marmontel, whose fifteenth chapter contains a vigorous attack on intolerance; *Télémaque* is a prose epic by the author and archbishop, Fénélon (1651–1715), which was interpreted by Louis XIV as a satire on his reign; *Séthos* was a three-volume novel set in ancient Egypt, published in 1731.

*Chorier terrace to be done. Summer trousers smelling of the makers. My uncle's books near the corner of the big desk Rue des Vieux-Jésuites. Marriage and life of my uncle.

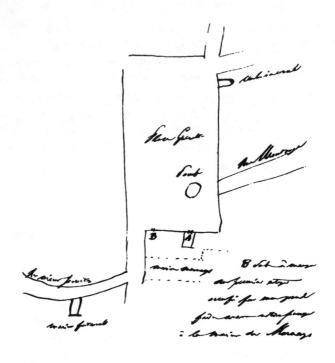

Place Grenette.—Pump.—Verbe Incarné.—Rue Montorge.—
Rue [des] Vieux-Jésuites.—Father's house.—Marnais house.
  B. First-floor dining-room occupied by my grandfather before
our move to the Marnais house.

Above the church of Saint-Louis, or rather beside it, one
could see the trapezium T of the mountain of Villard-de-Lans.
That was where my imagination was, formed by M. de
Tressan's Ariosto; [it] dreamt only of a meadow in the midst of

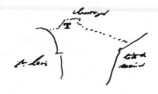

Mountain.—St-Louis.—Roofs of the houses.

high mountains. My scrawls of those days closely resembled the handwriting herewith of my illustrious fellow-countryman[3]:

It was my grandfather's custom to say, as he took his most excellent coffee around two in the afternoon, with his legs in the sun:

"From 15 February on, *in this climate*, it's *good* in the sun."

He loved geological ideas and would have been a supporter or opponent of the upheavals of M. Elie de Beaumont, which I find enchanting.[4] My grandfather used to talk to me *with passion*, that was the essential thing, about the geological ideas of a M. Guettard, whom he had known, *I fancy*.

Together with my sister Pauline, who was in my camp, I remarked that the conversation at this best moment of the day, while we had coffee, always consisted of moaning. They moaned about everything.

---

3. The writing is that of Antoine-Pierre-Joseph-Marie Barnave (1761–1793), mentioned earlier in the text, a lawyer from Grenoble and delegate to the States-General who was guillotined under the Terror.

4. Léonce Elie de Beaumont (1798–1874) drew up a geological map of France and speculated about its geological history.

I can't give the reality of the facts, I can only present their *shadow*.

We spent summer evenings, from seven until half past nine (at nine the *sein* or *saint*[5] sounded from St-André, the

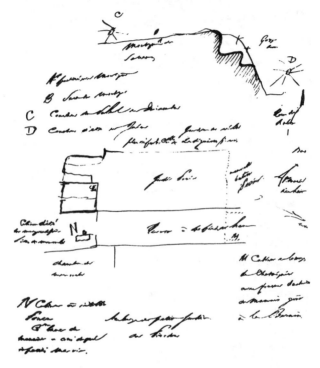

Mountain of Sassenage.—Vertical gorges.—Rabot tower.—
Bas[tille].—Ste-Marie-d'en-Haut.—North.—Jardin de Ville planted
by the C[onnéta]ble de Lesdiguières, I believe.—Périer garden.—
New Périer building.—Terrace: 40 feet high.—My uncle's room.—
Inn and Pirodon's small garden.—Poor Mention.

   A. First mountain.—B. Second mountain.—Sunset in
December.—D. Summer sunset in June.—L. My grandfather's
summer study.—My uncle's books.—M. Cabinet with lozenges
of chestnut-wood architectural in form and in bad taste *à la*
Bernini.—N. Study where Poncet was installed.—G. Carpenter's
bench beside which I spent my life.

---

5. The bell which was rung to signal that the gates of the town were being shut.

lovely sound of that bell caused a keen emotion in me). My father, insensitive to the beauty of the stars (I was forever talking constellations with my grandfather), said he was catching cold and went off to make conversation in the adjoining room with Séraphie.

This terrace, formed out of the thickness of a so-called *saracen* wall, a wall which was fifteen or eighteen feet high, had a magnificent view over the mountains of Sassenage; that was where the sun set in winter; above the [rocks] of Voreppe, the summer sunset, and to the north-west above the Bastille whose mountain (now transformed by General Haxo) rose above all the houses and above the Rabot tower which was, I fancy, the old entrance to the town before they cut through the rock at the Porte de France.

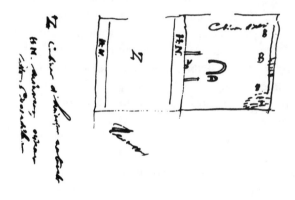

Summer study.—Terrace.—Z. Natural history room.—H, N. Minerals, Birds.—Small crocodile.

My grandfather spent large sums on this terrace. Poncet the carpenter came and installed himself for a year in the natural history room, whose whitewood cupboards he made; next he made some boxes out of chestnut, eighteen inches across and two feet high, filled with good soil, vines and flowers. Two vinestocks climbed up from the garden of M. Périer-Lagrange, a good-natured imbecile, our neighbour.

My grandfather had had porches erected out of chestnut-wood slats. This was a major undertaking entrusted to a carpenter called Poncet, a good-natured drunkard of thirty, quite cheerful. He became my friend because with him at last I discovered the charms of equality.

My grandfather watered his flowers every day, twice rather than once, Séraphie never came out on to the terrace, it was a moment of respite. I always helped my grandfather water his flowers, and he would talk to me about Linnaeus and Pliny, not out of duty but with pleasure.

This is the great and extreme obligation I'm under to that excellent man. As if that weren't happiness enough, he had no time at all for the pedants (the Lerminiers, the Salvandys, the [a blank] of our own day), his intelligence was of the same kind as that of M. Letronne who has just toppled Memnon from his throne, "nothing more nor less than the statue of Memnon."[6] My grandfather talked to me with the same interest about Egypt, he showed me the mummy he had persuaded them to buy for the Public Library; there the excellent Father Ducros (the first superior man I ever spoke to in my life) showed me a thousand kindnesses. My grandfather, much criticized by Séraphie, supported by the silence of my father, made me read *Séthos* (a ponderous novel by the *abbé* Terrasson), which at the time I thought divine. A novel is like a violin-bow, the box which *gives off the sounds* is the soul of the reader. My soul at that time was mad, and I shall tell you why.

While my grandfather was reading, sitting in his armchair at D opposite the small bust of Voltaire at V, I was looking at his bookcase situated at B, I was opening the quarto volumes of Pliny, a translation with facing text. In it I was looking especially for the natural history of *woman*.

The excellent smell was either amber or musk (which have made me feel ill these past sixteen years; perhaps it's the

6. The reference is to a French archaeologist who had just published a study showing that the sounds produced by the statue of Memnon in Thebes were physical and not supernatural in origin.

same amber and musk smell). Anyway, I was drawn to a pile of sewn volumes, thrown down higgledy-piggledy at L. These were cheap unbound novels which my uncle had left behind in Grenoble at the time when he went to install himself in Les Echelles (Savoy, near Le Pont-de-Beauvoisin). This discovery was decisive for my character. I opened some of these books; they were worthless novels of 1780; but for me they were the very essence of voluptuousness.

My grandfather forbade me to touch them, but I waited until such time as he was most engrossed in his armchair reading the new books, which he somehow or other always had in great abundance, and I stole a volume from my uncle's novels. My grandfather no doubt noticed my thefts, for I see myself installed in the natural history room, watching until a patient should come asking for him. In which circumstances my grandfather would groan at finding himself taken away from his beloved studies and would go to receive the patient in his room or in the anteroom to the main apartment. Presto, I went into the study at L, and stole a book.

I wouldn't be able to express the excitement with which I read those books. After one or two months I came across *Félicia ou mes fredaines*. I went absolutely berserk; the possession of a real-life mistress, then the object of all my desires, wouldn't have plunged me into such a torrent of voluptuousness.

From that moment on, my vocation was settled: to live in Paris writing comedies like Molière.

This was my *idée fixe* which I kept heavily disguised; the tyranny of Séraphie had given me the habits of a slave.

I have never been able to speak of what I adored; such discourse would have seemed to me a blasphemy.

I feel this as keenly in 1835 as I felt it in 1794.

These books of my uncle's bore the address of M. Falcon, who at that time kept the one public reading-room; he was a fiery patriot profoundly despised by my grandfather and altogether hated by Séraphie and my father.

I began as a result to like him, he was perhaps the Grenoblois for whom I had the greatest regard. There was in this former lackey of Mme de Brison's (or of some other lady in the Rue Neuve at whose house my grandfather had been waited on at table by him), there was in this lackey a soul twenty times nobler than that of my grandfather, of my uncle, let alone of my father and the jesuitical Séraphie. Perhaps my aunt Elisabeth alone was to be compared with him. Poor, earning little and disdaining to make money, Falcon set up a tricolour outside his shop at each triumph of arms and on the public holidays of the Republic.

He worshipped the Republic in the time of Napoleon as under the Bourbons and died at eighty-two, around 1820, still poor but of the most scrupulous honesty.

On my way past, I used to look out of the corner of my eye at this shop of Falcon's, who wore a large, perfectly powdered toupet, and flaunted a beautiful red coat with large steel buttons, then the fashion, on days auspicious to his beloved Republic. He was the finest specimen of the Dauphinois character. His shop was near the Place St-André; I can remember him moving to the Palais. Falcon came to occupy the shop A in the former Palais des Dauphins where the Parlement sat and then the Cour Royale. I used to go underneath the passageway B on purpose so as to see him. He had a very ugly daughter, the usual butt of my aunt Séraphie's pleasantries, who accused her of making love with the patriots who came to read the newspapers in her father's reading-room.

Later on, Falcon installed himself at A'. I was bold enough then to go and read there. I don't know whether, at that time when I was stealing my uncle's books, I was bold enough to become one of his subscribers; I fancy that one way or another I got books from him.

My rêveries were given powerful direction by *La Vie et les aventures de Mme de . . .* , *an extremely affecting novel, very silly*, because the heroine was captured by savages. I fancy I lent this novel to my friend Romain Colomb, who retains a memory of it even today.

Soon I got hold of *La Nouvelle Héloïse*: I think I took it off the top shelf of my father's bookcase at Claix.

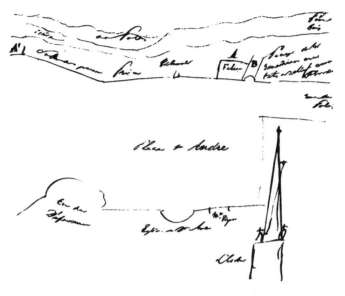

Isère.—Wooden bridge.—Theatre.—Prison.—Tribunal.—A. Falcon.—B. Renaissance passageway with heads in relief like in Florence.—Rue du Palais.—Place St-André.—Department tower.— Church of St-André.—Mme Vignon.—Belfry.

I read it lying on my bed in my *trapezium* in Grenoble, after having been careful to lock myself in, and in raptures of delight and voluptuousness impossible to describe. Today that book strikes me as pedantic and even in 1819, in the raptures of the maddest love affair, I couldn't read twenty consecutive pages of it. From then on stealing books became my main business.

I had a corner beside my father's desk in the Rue des Vieux-Jésuites where I stored, half-hidden by their humble position, the books I enjoyed: there were copies of Dante with strange wood engravings, translations of Lucian by Perrot d'Ablan-court (the *belles infidèles*), the Marquis d'Argens's *Corres-pondance de Milord All-eye avec Milord All-ear* and lastly the *Mémoires d'un homme de qualité retiré du monde.*[7]

I found a means of getting them to open up my father's study for me, which had been abandoned since the fateful Amar and Merlino list, and I made a careful inspection of all the books. He had a superb collection of elzevir editions, but unfortunately I understood nothing of Latin although I knew the *Selectae e profanis* by heart.

I found some duodecimo volumes above the little door leading into the drawing-room and I tried to read a few arti-cles in the *Encyclopédie*. But what was any of this compared with *Félicia* and *La Nouvelle Héloïse*!

My literary confidence in my grandfather was extreme; I relied completely on his not giving me away to Séraphie and my father. Without admitting that I had read *La Nouvelle Héloïse*, I risked singing its praises to him. His conversion to jesuitry can't have been of long standing; instead of question-ing me sternly he told me how M. le Baron des Adrets (the only one of his friends with whom he had continued to dine two or three times a month since my mother's death), in the days when *La Nouvelle Héloïse* first appeared (wasn't it in 1770?), kept them waiting one day at dinner in his house; Mme des Adrets sent to tell him a second time, finally this most unemotional of men arrived all in tears.

"What is it, my friend?" said Mme des Adrets quite alarmed.

"Ah, *madame*, Julie is dead!" and he ate hardly anything.

I used to devour the advertisements of books for sale which came with the newspapers. My relations then received, I fancy, a newspaper in partnership with someone else.

---

7. This last is a work by the Abbé Prevost (1697–1763), author of *Manon Lescaut*; its full title is *Les Mémoires et aventures d'un homme de qualité qui s'est retiré du monde.*

I got the idea that Florian[8] must be a sublime book, seemingly from the titles: *Gonzalve de Cordoue, Estelle*, etc.

I put one small *écu* (3fr) into a letter and wrote to a bookseller in Paris to send me a certain work of Florian's. This was foolhardy, what would Séraphie have said when the package arrived?

But in the end it never came, and with a *louis* which my grandfather had given me on New Year's Day I bought a Florian. It was from the works of that great man that I derived my first comedy.

8. Jean-Pierre Claris de Florian (1755–1794) wrote plays, pastoral fictions and fables; he was the great-nephew of Voltaire.

CHAPTER 17

Séraphie had made a bosom friend of a certain Mme Vignon, the town's leading *boime*. (*Boime* in Grenoble means a smooth-talking hypocrite, a female je[sui]t.) Mme Vignon lived on the third floor, in the Place St-André, and was the wife of the attorney, I believe, but respected as a mother of the C[hurch], finding places for priests and always with some staying in her house on their way through. What concerned me was that she had a daughter of fifteen who looked rather like a white rabbit with her big red eyes. I tried, but in vain, to fall in love with her during a visit of a week or two which we made to Claix. There my father didn't stay in hiding but always lived in his own house, the finest in the canton.

On this visit there were Séraphie, Mme and Mlle Vignon, my sister Pauline, myself and perhaps a M. Blanc from Seyssins, an absurd personage who much admired Séraphie's bare legs. She went out bare-legged, without stockings on, in the mornings into the *clos*.

I was so carried away by my age that the legs of my cruellest enemy had an effect on me. I would gladly have fallen in love with Séraphie. I imagined to myself the delightful pleasure of taking that inveterate enemy in my arms.

In spite of her status of marriageable young lady, she had a large disused door opened up which led from her room on to the staircase in the Place Grenette, and, following a terrible scene in which I can still see her face, had a key made. Her father had apparently refused her the key to this door.

Through this door she let her woman friends in and among

others Mme Vignon, a female Tartuffe, who had her own private prayers for the saints and for whom my worthy grandfather would have felt revulsion, if his Fontenelle-like character had allowed him

1. To feel revulsion.

2. To express it.

My grandfather employed his great oath against this Mme Vignon: "May the devil spit up your bum!"

My father was still in hiding in Grenoble, i.e. was living in my grandfather's house, and didn't come out during the day. The political passion lasted only eighteen months. I can see myself going on his behalf to Allier's, the bookseller, Place St-André, with 50fr in *assignats* to buy Fourcroy's chemistry[1] which led him on to his passion for agriculture. I can well imagine how this taste originated: Claix was the one place where he could walk about.

But was all this not brought about by his love affair with Séraphie, if love affair there was? I can't see the physiognomy of events, I have only my child's memory. I can see mental images, I remember the effects on my emotions, but, as for causes and the physiognomy, nothing. It's like the frescos of [*a blank*] in Pisa again, where you can make out an arm easily enough, but the piece next to it, which showed the head, has fallen away. I can see a *very clear* succession of images, but not the physiognomy except as they appeared to me. Moreover, I can only see this physiognomy thanks to the memory of the effect it produced in me.*

Soon my father experienced a sensation befitting the heart of a tyrant. I had a tame thrush which usually remained underneath the chairs in the dining-room. It had lost a foot in battle and walked with a hop. It defended itself against cats and dogs and everyone protected it, which showed much con-

---

1. Antoine-François de Fourcroy (1755–1809), professor of chemistry and author of textbooks.

*Put in something about the enforced walks to Les Granges.

sideration for me, because it used to leave unwholesome white stains all over the floor. My manner of feeding this thrush wasn't the most wholesome, on *chaplepans* drowned in the *benne* in the kitchen (cockroaches that had drowned in the bucket of dirty water in the kitchen).

Kept strictly isolated from all human beings of my own age, living only with old people, such childishness appealed to me.

Suddenly, the thrush vanished; no one would tell me how: someone had inadvertently trodden on it when opening the door. I believed my father had killed it out of spite; he found out, the idea pained him, one day he spoke to me about it in very roundabout, very delicate terms.

I was sublime, I blushed to the whites of my eyes, but I didn't open my mouth. He urged me to reply: same silence; but my eyes which at that age were very expressive must have spoken.

Thus was I avenged, tyrant, for the mild, fatherly look with which you forced me so many times to go on that hateful walk to *Les Granges* through fields irrigated by the *midnight carts* (nightsoil from the town)!

For more than 1 month I felt proud of this act of vengeance, I like that in a child.*

---

*20 Dec 1835. Facts to be fitted in in their time, set down here so as not to be forgotten.

Following the Emp[eror]'s objection, I became inspector of furnishings by means of my birth certificate; 2. of the Michaud certificate; 3. by the addition to my name. The mistake was not having put Brulard de la Jomate (Jomate being *ours*).

M. de Baure was an altogether wise and courteous magistrate at the end of the eighteenth century; he liked what was honourable and upright, and would have done anything wrong only out of extreme necessity and under duress. For the rest, witty, voluble, eloquent, having a wide knowledge of authors, a particular friend of M. the C[ardin]al de Bausset and M. de Villaret, bishop (of the University), tall, thin, dignified, with cunning little eyes and an endless nose. He would have made an excellent and very dignified archb[ishop]. He put up with for money what I wouldn't have put up with for anything: being slandered by M. the Co[mt]e Da[ru] whose secretary-general he was. He it was who, to oblige Mme Petit (because I, with my thoughtlessness and notions of a lofty and outspoken virtue, must have shocked him twenty times a day), secured my appointment after the Emperor had objected. Appointed to Amsterdam Sept [*a blank*] or Nov 1811.

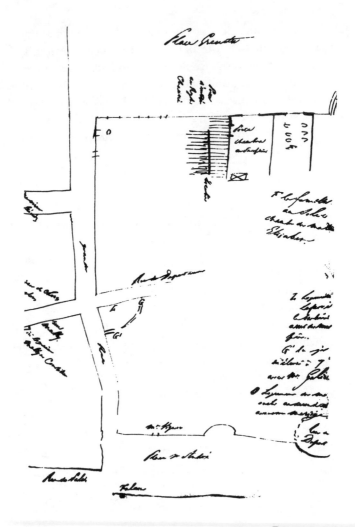

Place Grenette.—Ground-floor entrance.—Staircase.—Door.—
Séraphie's room.—Rue [des] Vieux-Jésuites.—Rue des Clercs then
Rue Mably.—Here Mably and Condillac lodged.—Rue du Palais.—
Grande-Rue.—Rue du Département.—Mme Vignon.—Place St-
André.—Falcon.—Department tower.

F. The family in the sunshine. My aunt Elisabeth's room.—
L. Lodgings of Lefèvre, my father's hairdresser friend. G'. Here I got
up to 7 with Mme Galice.—O. My uncle's lodgings on the second
floor before his marriage.

My father's passion for his *domaine* at Claix and for agriculture became extreme. He had major *repairs* done, improvements, *mining* the ground for example, breaking it up to a depth of two and a half feet and removing all the stones larger than an egg to one corner of the field. Jean Vial, our former gardener, Chorier, Mayousse, old [*a blank*], an ex-soldier, did this work for a *fixed sum*, for example 20 *écus* (60fr) for mining a *tière*, the amount of land contained between two rows of espaliers or else maples, which carried the vines.

My father planted the Grandes Barres, then La Jomate where he pulled out the creeping vine. By an exchange with the hospital (which had got it, I fancy, in the will of a M. Gutin, a cloth-m[erchan]t) he obtained the Molard vine (between the orchard and our own Molard), he pulled it out, mined it, burying the *murger* (a pile of stones from seven to ten feet high) and finally planted it.

He discussed all these projects with me at length, he had become a true *southern landowner*.

This is a form of madness frequently met with to the south of Lyon and Tours; the mania consists of buying fields which yield one or two per cent, withdrawing for the purpose money that has been lent out at five or six, and sometimes borrowing at five per cent in order to *round it up*, that is the expression, while buying fields which bring in two. A Minister of the Interior doubtful of his occupation might launch a campaign against this mania, which is destroying the prosperity and that whole portion of happiness that depends on money in the twenty departments to the south of Tours and Lyon.

My father was a memorable example of this mania which stems at once from avarice, vainglory and the mania for nobility.

CHAPTER 18

FIRST COMMUNION

This mania, which ended by ruining my father radically and reducing me, all told, to my third share of my mother's dowry, made life very comfortable for me around 1794.

But before going any further, I must despatch the story of my first communion prior, I fancy, to 21 July 1794.

What consoles me a little for the impertinence of writing so many *I*s and *me*s, is that I assume that many very ordinary people in this nineteenth century are doing as I am. So they will be inundated with *Memoirs* around 1880, with *Journals* and, with my *I*s and *me*s, I shall only be like everyone else. M. de Talleyrand, M. Molé are writing their *Memoirs*, M. Delécluze too.

It was a pr[iest], infinitely less of a scoundrel than the *abbé* Raillane, it must be admitted, who was entrusted with the major operation of my first communion, to which my father, at that time very devout, attached the greatest importance. The je[suitry] of the *abbé* Raillane had even frightened my father; just as M. Courier[1] frightened even the jesuit.

This worthy priest, outwardly so good-natured, was called Dumolard and was a peasant, full of simplicity and born in the neighbourhood of La Matheysine, or La Mure, near Le Bourg d'Oisans. He has since become a great jesuit and has obtained the delightful parish of La Tronche, ten minutes from Grenoble (this is like the sub-prefecture of Sceaux for a

---

1. Paul-Louis Courier (1772–1825), soldier and writer who became a fierce critic of the reactionary Establishment after 1814. He was eventually murdered.

sub-prefect, a ministerial stooge or who is marrying one of their bastard daughters). In those days, M. Dumolard was so good-natured I was able to lend him a small Italian edition of Ariosto in four volumes in 18mo. Perhaps though I only lent it to him in 1803.

M. Dumolard was not bad-looking, except for an eye that was always closed; he was one-eyed, it can but be said, but his features were good and expressed not only good nature but, what was far more ridiculous, a cheerful and complete candour. In actual fact he was not in those days a scoun[drel], or rather, now that I think about it, my twelve-year-old's insight, exercised in complete solitude, was wholly deceived, because he has since become one of the most thoroughgoing jesuits in the town, and moreover his most excellent parish within reach of the pious ladies of the town *testifies for him* and against my twelve-year-old's naivety.

M. le Premier Président de Barral, the most indulgent and well brought up of men said to me around 1816, I believe, as he walked me in his magnificent garden in La Tronche which adjoined the parish:

"That Dumolard is one of the most unmitigated scoun[drels] of the band."

"And what about M. Raillane?" I said.

"Oh, Raillane outdoes them all. How could *monsieur* your father have picked a man like that?"

"I don't know, I really don't, I was a victim and not an accomplice."

In the last two or three years M. Dumolard had often said mass in our house, in my grandfather's Italian drawing-room. The Terror, which in the Dauphiné never was the Terror, never noticed that eighty or a hundred devout women came out from my grandfather's house every Sunday at noon. I have forgotten to say that when I was very small I was made to serve at these masses and acquitted myself only too well. I wore a very respectable and very serious look. All through my life religious ceremonial has greatly moved me. For a long

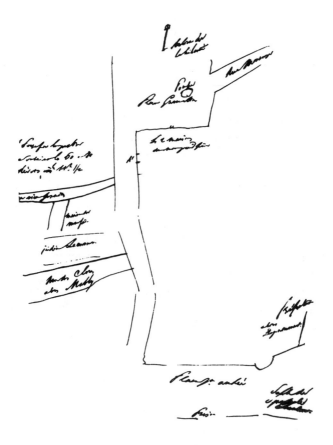

A'. Door out of which the 60–80 devout women came around half-past eleven.—Rue [des] Vieux-Jésuites.—My father's house.—Lamouroux garden.—Rue des Clercs then Mably.—Tree of Liberty.—Pump.—Place Grenette.—Rue Montorge.—My grandfather's 2 houses.—Prefecture then Department.—Place St-André.—Prison.—Theatre.

time I served at mass for that scoun[drel] of an *abbé* Raillane who went to say it at the Propagation, at the end of the Rue Saint-Jacques, on the left; it was a convent and we said our mass in the gallery.

Such children were we, Reytiers and I, that it was a big event one day when Reytiers, apparently out of timidity, peed himself on a pine prie-dieu during the mass I was serving at. The poor devil tried to absorb, wipe away, soak up the moisture he had produced to his deep shame, by rubbing his knee against the horizontal bar of the prie-dieu. There was a great scene. We often went in to the nuns; one of them, tall and with a good figure, I admired very much; this was noticed no doubt, for I have always been extremely clumsy in matters of that kind, and I didn't see her again. One thing I observed was that *madame* the abbess had a large number of black spots at the end of her nose, I thought that was horrible.

The government had sunk to the dreadful folly of persecuting the priests. The good sense of Grenoble and its distrust of Paris saved us from the harsher aspects of that folly.

The priests may have said they were being persecuted, yet sixty devout women used to come at eleven o'clock in the morning to hear their mass in my grandfather's drawing-room. The police can't even have pretended not to know. A crowd used to form in the Grande-Rue as they emerged from mass.

CHAPTER 19

My father was struck off the list of suspects (which for twenty-one months had been the sole object of our ambitions) on 21 July 1794, with the help of the lovely eyes of my pretty cousin Joséphine Martin.

At that time he paid long visits to Claix (i.e. to Furonières). My independence was born, like liberty in the towns of Italy around the eighth century, out of the weakness of my tyrants.

During my father's absences I took it into my head to go and work in the drawing-room of our apartment in the Rue des Vieux-Jésuites where no one had set foot for the past four years.

This notion, born of the needs of the moment like all mechanical inventions, had huge advantages. First of all, I used to go to the Rue des Vieux-Jésuites on my own, two hundred paces from the Gagnon house; secundo, I was safe there from the incursions of Séraphie, who at my grandfather's, when she was even more worked up than usual, would come to examine my books and rummage in my papers.

Undisturbed in the silent drawing-room where the beautiful piece of furniture was that my poor mother had embroidered, I began working with pleasure. I wrote my comedy, whose title, I believe, was *Monsieur Piklar*.

Before writing I always waited for the moment of genius.

I was only cured of this mania very belatedly. Had I expelled it sooner I would have finished my comedy of *Letellier et St-Bernard*, which I took to Moscow and, what's more,

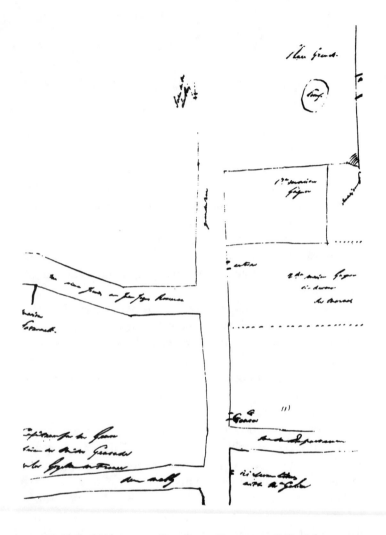

Rue [des] Vieux-Jésuites or Jean-Jaques Rousseau.—Father's house.
—Café kept by M. Genou the father of M. de Genoude of the
Gazette de France.—Rue Mably.—M. Le Roy's door.—Place
Grenette.—Pump.—Grande-Rue.—First Gagnon house.—Périer
house.—Entrance.—Second Gagnon formerly de Marnais house.
—Genou.—Rue du Département.—Here SEVEN TIMES WITH
Mme Galice.

brought back (it is among my papers, in Paris).[1] This foolishness proved very damaging to the quantity of my writings. Even in 1806, I was waiting for the moment of genius before writing.* All through my life, I have never talked of the thing I was passionate about, the least objection would have pierced me to the heart. So I have never talked literature. My close friend of that time M. Adolphe de Mareste (born in Grenoble around 1782) wrote to me in Milan to give me his views on the *Vie de Haydn, Mozart et Metastase*. He had no idea that I was THE AUTHOR.[2]

Had I spoken around 1795 of my intention of writing, some man of good sense would have told me:

"Write for two hours every day, genius or no."

A remark that would have led to my making use of ten years of my life fatuously spent waiting for *genius*.

My imagination had been employed forestalling the harm my tyrants did me and cursing them; as soon as I was free, at H, in my mother's drawing-room, I had the leisure to develop a taste for something. My passion was: medallions moulded in plaster from hollow moulds of sulphur. Before I had had a minor passion: a love of thorn-sticks, gnarled sticks cut from hawthorn hedges, I believe; game-shooting.

My father and Séraphie had curbed both of them. That for thorn-sticks vanished under the jibes of my uncle; that for shooting, based on the voluptuous rêveries nurtured by M. Le Roy's landscape and the lively images my imagination had manufactured when reading Ariosto, became a frenzy, meant that I adored *La Maison rustique*, Buffon,[3] that I wrote about

1. That he should have brought the Ms back with him is remarkable given the terrible conditions under which Napoleon's Grande Armée retreated from Russia in the winter of 1812.

*The medallions of F[ather] Ducros—2. The Ecole Centrale.

2. This multiple biography was Stendhal's first published work; it appeared in 1815 under the sardonic pseudonym of Louis-Alexandre-César Bombet.

3. Georges Louis Leclerc, Comte de Buffon (1707–1788) was the greatest French naturalist of the century.

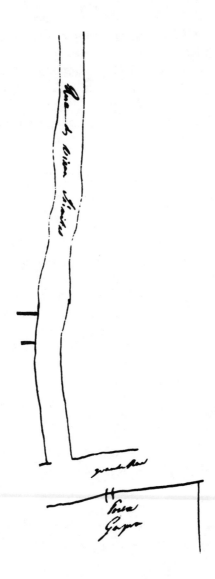

Rue des Vieux-Jésuites.—Grande-Rue.—Gagnon door.

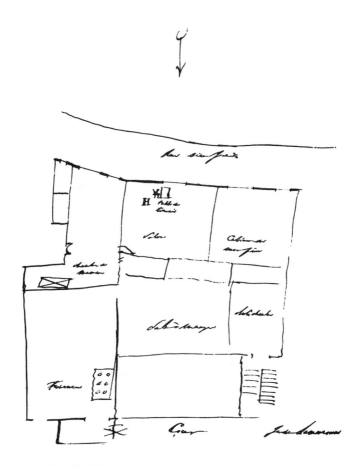

Rue [des] Vieux-Jésuites.—H. Work-table.—Drawing-room.—
Mamma's bedroom.—My father's study.—Dining-room.—
Anteroom.—Range.—Courtyard.—Lamouroux garden.

animals, and expired finally only from a surfeit. At Brunswick, in 1808, I was one of the leaders on shoots on which we killed fifty or sixty hares with peasants as beaters. Killing a doe horrified me, that horror has grown. Today I can think of nothing more contemptible than turning a charming bird into four ounces of dead flesh.

If my father in his bourgeois fearfulness had allowed me to go out shooting, I would have been more agile, which would have helped me in the war. There I was agile only by dint of being *strong*.

I shall speak again about shooting, let us return to the medallions.*

*26 Dec 1835. To be fitted in: Character O F M Y F A T H E R Chérubin B. He was not avaricious but a great enthusiast. Money was no object in satisfying his dominant passion; thus, in order to *mine a tière*, he didn't send me the 150fr a month in Paris without which I couldn't live. He had a passion for agriculture and for Claix, then a year or two of a passion for building (the house in the Rue de Bonne, for which I was foolish enough to draw up the plan with Mante). He borrowed at 8 or 10 per cent with the intention of finishing a house that would one day yield him 6. Bored with the house, he gave himself up to the passion for administration on behalf of the Bourbons, to the unbelievable extent of spending seventeen months without going to Claix, two leagues outside the town. He was ruined between 1814 and 1819, I believe, the time of his death. He loved women to excess, but as timid as a boy of twelve. Mme Abraham Mallein, *née* Pascal, used to find this a great source of amusement.

CHAPTER 20

After four or five years of the dreariest, most profound unhappiness, I drew breath only when I found myself alone and locked into the apartment in the Rue des Vieux-Jésuites, hitherto abhorrent to me. During these four or five years, my heart was full of a feeling of impotent hatred. But for my taste for the voluptuous, I would perhaps have become, thanks to an education about which those who provided it never had any doubts, a *blackguard* or a graceful and insinuating scoundrel, a true jesuit, and I would no doubt be very rich. My reading *La Nouvelle Héloïse* and the moral scrupulousness of St-Preux[1] made a profoundly honest man of me; for all that I wept as I read it and was transported by a love of virtue, I might still afterwards have done scoundrelly things, but would have been aware I was a scoundrel. So it was a book read in the greatest secrecy and in spite of my relations which made an honest man of me.

The Roman history of the woolly Rollin, for all its worthless observations, had furnished my head with deeds of a solid virtue (based on *utility* and not on the self-regarding honour of monarchies; Saint-Simon is a fine proof of Montesquieu's maxim: *honour* the foundation-stone of monarchies; not bad to have grasped this in 1734, the date of the *Lettres persanes*, at a time when reason among the French was still in its infancy).[2]

1. The exceedingly upright hero of Rousseau's moralistic and highly influential epistolary novel.

2. Montesquieu's *Lettres persanes* (1721) consists of letters imagined as having been written by Persian travellers in Europe critical of contemporary French customs and institutions.

What with the feats I learnt about in Rollin, confirmed, explained and illustrated in constant conversation with my excellent grandfather and the theories of St-Preux, nothing could equal the repugnance and profound contempt I felt for the com[mandments] OF GOD AND THE CHURCH expounded by pr[iests] whom I saw every day bewailing the *victories of the fatherland* and hoping for the French armies to be defeated.*

The conversation of my excellent grandfather, to whom I owe everything, his veneration for the benefactors of mankind so contrary to the ideas of Ch[ristian]ity, no doubt prevented me from being caught like a fly in a spider's web by my respect for ceremonial. (I can see today that this was the earliest form of my love of music 1, painting 2, and the art of Viganò 3.)[3] I would gladly believe that my grandfather was newly converted around 1793. Perhaps he had taken to religion on the death of my mother (1790); perhaps the need to have the support of the clergy in his profession of doctor had imposed a thin veneer of hypocrisy on him at the same time as the wig with three rows of curls. I would rather believe the latter, for I discovered he was a friend, and of long standing, of M. *l'abbé* Sadin, the *curé* of St-Louis (his parish), of M. *le chanoine* Rey and of Mlle Rey, his sister, to whose house we often went (my aunt Elisabeth played cards there), a little street behind Saint-André, later Rue du Département, even of the amiable or over-amiable *abbé* Hélie, *curé* of St-Hugues, who had baptized me as he reminded me later at the Café de la Régence, in Paris, where I lunched around 1803 during my real education in the Rue d'Angivilliers.

It should be pointed out that in 1790 the pr[iests] hadn't adopted the consequences of their theory and were far from

*27 Dec 1835. WRITTEN BAD CHARACTERS on purpose FOR THE POLICEMEN. I HAVE ALWAYS THIS PRECAUTION. I FEAR ALSO THE BOOKBINDER.

3. Salvatore Viganò (1769–1821), Neapolitan dancer and choreographer, one of the pioneers of modern ballet.

being as intolerant and absurd as we find them in 1835. My grandfather was left perfectly free to work in front of his little bust of Voltaire and for his conversation to be, except on one topic alone, what it would have been in Voltaire's drawing-room, and the three days he had spent in that drawing-room he recalled as the best of his life when occasion arose. He certainly didn't forbid himself a critical or scandalous anecdote about the pr[iests], and during his long and observant career that wise and dispassionate spirit had collected hundreds. He never exaggerated, he never lied, which permits me, I fancy, to claim today that, where his mind was concerned, he was no bourgeois, but he was quick to conceive an undying hatred for the most trivial offence and I can't absolve his soul from the reproach of being bourgeois.

I have met the bourgeois type again, even in [Rome], at M. 120[4] and his family's, especially M. Bois the Simonetti brother-in-law who has become rich.

My grandfather felt a veneration and love for great men which quite shocked M. the current *curé* of St-Louis and M. the current vicar-general to the bis[hop] of Gre[noble], who makes it a point of honour not to return the visit of the prefect in his capacity as *prince* of Gre[noble], I believe (told me by M. Rubichon and approvingly, C[ivit]a-V[ecchi]a, Jan 1835).

Father Ducros the Franciscan whom I assume to be a man of genius, had ruined his health by stuffing birds with poisons. He suffered badly with his innards, and from my uncle's jokes I gathered he had a priapism. I didn't really understand this malady, which to me seemed perfectly natural. Father Ducros was very fond of my grandfather, his doctor, to whom he was partly indebted for his librarian's position, but he couldn't help feeling a *tiny bit contemptuous* of his weakness of character; he couldn't tolerate the outbursts of Séraphie which often went so far as to interrupt the

---

4. A pseudonym concealing the name of a Roman lawyer who lived at No 120 Via Vignaccia.

conversation, disturbing the company and forcing their friends to withdraw.*

Fontenelle-like characters are very sensitive to any such hint of unspoken contempt; thus my grandfather often contested my enthusiasm for Father Ducros. Sometimes, when Father Ducros came to the house with something interesting to tell us, I was sent to the kitchen; I wasn't in the least offended, but cross at not learning what this intriguing thing might be. This *philosophe* was conscious of my eagerness and of the keen liking I showed for him, and which meant I never left the room while he was there.

He used to give his friends, male and female, presents of gilt frames two and a half feet by three, set with a large sheet of glass, behind which he had arranged six or eight dozen plaster medallions eighteen *lignes*[5] in diameter. They were all the Roman emperors and empresses; another frame displayed all the great men of France, from Clément Marot to Voltaire, Diderot and d'Alembert.[6] What would the M. Rey of today say to such a sight?

These medallions were set very gracefully in small cardboard mounts with gilded edges, and scrolls made from the same material filled the gaps between the medallions. Ornaments of this sort were very uncommon at that time and I

---

*Answer to a criticism: how can I be expected to write well, forced to write so quickly in order not to waste my ideas?

5. An archaic measurement: twelve *lignes* made one inch.

6. Clément Marot (1496–1544) was a court poet, though not always in favour at the court, and a bridge between medieval and renaissance verse in France; Voltaire, Diderot and d'Alembert were the three most militant of the eighteenth-century *philosophes*. Father Ducros's conception of the nation's "great men" was clearly a provocative one.

can own that the contrast between the matt white of the medallions and the light, delicate, carefully drawn shadows that marked the features of these personages, together with the gilded edges of the mounts and their golden yellow colour created a very elegant effect.

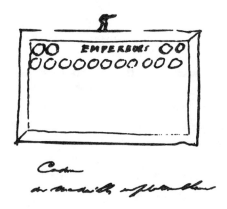

Frame of white plaster medals by Father Ducros, librarian in the town of Grenoble (around 1790), died around 1806 or 1818.

The bourgeois from Vienne, Romans, La Tour-du-Pin, Voiron, etc., who came to my grandfather's to dine, never tired of admiring these frames. For my own part, standing on a chair, I didn't tire of studying the features of these *illustrious men* whose lives and whose writings I would have liked to imitate or read.

Father Ducros used to write along with his gilt-edged pieces of cardboard right at the top of his frames:

ILLUSTRIOUS MEN OF FRANCE or
EMPERORS AND EMPRESSES

In Voiron, for example, at my cousin Allard-Duplantier's (a descendant of the historian and antiquary Allard), these frames were admired as antique medallions; I don't know even whether this cousin, who was none too bright, didn't mistake them for antique medallions. (He was a son outshone by a father who was a wit, like Monseigneur by Louis XIV.)

One day Father Ducros said to me:

"Would you like me to teach you to make medallions?"

For me this was for the heavens to open.

I went to his apartment, truly delightful for a man fond of thinking, I would dearly love to have something of the sort myself to end my days in.

Four small rooms ten foot high, facing south and west, with a very pretty view over St-Joseph, the slopes of Eybens, the Pont de Claix and the endless mountains towards Gap.

These rooms were filled with bas-reliefs and medallions moulded from the antique or from decent modern work.

The medallions were most of them in red sulphur (reddened by a cinnabar mixture), which looks handsome and serious; in fact not one square foot of that apartment but prompted a thought. There were pictures also.

"But I'm not rich enough," said Father Ducros, "to buy the ones I would like."

The principal picture showed a snowstorm, it wasn't altogether bad.

My grandfather had taken me a number of times into this delightful apartment. The moment I was alone with my grandfather outside the house, out of range of my father and of Séraphie, I was perfectly cheerful. I walked very slowly because my worthy grandfather had rheumatic pains which I assume were gout (because I, his true grandson and who have the same body, I had gout in May 1835 in C[ivit]a-V[ecchi]a).

Father Ducros who was comfortably off, because he made M. Navizet of St-Laurent, a former dealer in chamois-leather, his heir, was very well looked after by a tall, fat valet, a good-natured fellow who helped in the library, and an excellent maidservant. I used to tip them all on the advice of my aunt Elisabeth.

I was as green as could be thanks to the miracle of my awful solitary education and of a whole family hounding one wretched child in order to indoctrinate him, whose system had been followed very strictly because the family's grief meant this system was to their liking.

This inexperience in the simplest things caused me to commit many gaucheries at M. Daru senior's between November 1799 and May 1800.

To return to the medallions. Father Ducros had somehow or other got hold of a large number of plaster medallions. He soaked them in oil and on to the oil poured sulphur mixed with a very dry, powdered slate.

Once this mould was quite cold, he put in a little oil, surrounded it with a piece of oiled paper, three *lignes* high from A to B, with the mould at the bottom.

The mould

On to the mould he poured liquid plaster newly made, then straight away some less fine, stronger plaster, in such a way as to give the plaster medallion a thickness of four *lignes*. This was what I never succeeded in doing properly. I didn't mix my plaster quickly enough or rather I let the air get into it. Saint-[*a blank*,] the old manservant, brought me powdered plaster but it was no good. I found my plaster had jellified, five or six hours after placing it on the sulphur mould.

But these moulds, the hardest part, I made on the spot, and very well, only too thick. I didn't stint on materials.

I set up my plasterer's studio in my poor mother's dressing-room. I entered this room, into which no one had been for five years, only with a religious feeling, I avoided looking at the bed. I would never have laughed in that room hung with a paper from Lyon closely imitating red damask.

Although I never succeeded in making a frame of medallions like Father Ducros, I was everlastingly preparing myself for such great renown by making a large number of sulphur moulds (at B in the kitchen).

I bought a large cupboard containing twelve or fifteen drawers three inches deep, in which I hoarded my riches.

I left all this behind in Grenoble in 1799. After 1796 it no longer meant anything to me; they could have turned my precious slate-coloured sulphur moulds or hollows into matches.

I read the dictionary of medallions in the *Encyclopédie méthodique.**

An astute teacher able to exploit this inclination might have set me enthusiastically to studying the whole of ancient history; I needed to be made to read Suetonius then Dionysius of Halicarnassus, as and when my young brain was capable of absorbing serious ideas.

But the then prevailing taste in Grenoble was for reading and quoting the epistles of one M. de Bonnard; he was, I think, a lesser Dorat (as one might talk about a lesser Macon). My grandfather would allude with respect to Montesquieu's *Grandeur des Romains*, but that proved beyond me, which isn't hard to believe: I knew nothing of the events on which Montesquieu has provided his splendid commentary.

I should at least have been made to read Livy. Instead of which they made me read and admire the hymns of Santeuil: *Ecce sed tonantes . . .*[7] You can imagine how I greeted this religion of my tyrants.

The priests who dined at the house sought to acknowledge the hospitality of my relations by sentimentalizing over

---

*I FEEL tired after three and a half h[ours] working and reading. I feel sleepy.

7. Another misquotation: the line should read *Ecce sedes hic Tonantis*, or "Here is the throne of the Thunderer"; Jean de Santeuil was a seventeenth-century hymn-writer.

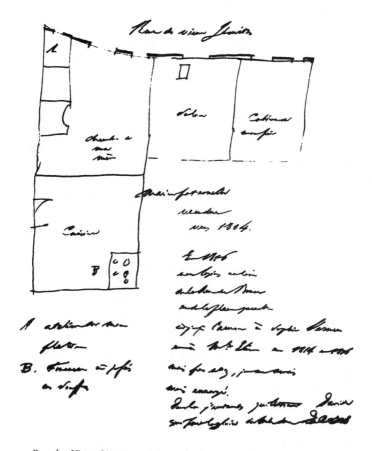

Rue des Vieux-Jésuites.—My mother's room.—Drawing-room.—
My father's study.—Kitchen.

A. My plaster studio.—B. Range where I made my sulphur.
Father's house sold around 1804. In 1816 we were lodging on the
corner of the Rue de Bonne and the Place Grenette where I made
love to Sophie Vernier and to Mlle Elise in 1814 and 1816 but not
enough, I'd have been less bored. From here I heard the guillotin-
ing of David, the glorious act of M. Decazes.[8]

8. David was involved (as it is just possible Stendhal himself may have been) in a
Bonapartist plot—the "Didier affair"—centred on Grenoble in 1816. Decazes was the
Minister of Police at the time.

the Royaumont Bible whose honeyed, smarmy tones filled me with the most profound disgust. I infinitely preferred the New Testament in Latin the whole of which I had learnt by heart in an 18mo edition. My relations, like the kings of to-day, asked that religion should keep me in abjection, while I breathed only rebellion.

I watched the Allobroge legion going past (the one commanded by M. Caffe, I believe, who died in Les Invalides, at 85, in November or December 1835), my great thought was this: "Would I not do well to enlist?"

I often went out on my own, I went to the gardens but I found the other children too familiar; from a distance I longed to play with them, close to I found them uncouth.

I was even beginning, I believe, to go to the theatre, from which I came out at the most interesting moment, at nine o'clock in summer, when I heard the *sin* (or the *saint*) ringing.

Anything tyrannical repelled me and I had no love of authority. I *did my schoolwork* (compositions, translations, verses about the fly drowned in a jug of milk) on a pretty little walnut-wood table in the anteroom to the big Italian drawing-room; except on Sundays for our mass the door on to the main staircase was always shut. I took it into my head to write the names of all the royal assassins on the wood of this table, for example: Poltrot, Duc de Guise, at..., in 15... While he was helping me write my verses, or rather writing them himself, my grandfather saw this list; his gentle, peaceable soul, opposed to all violence, was greatly distressed; he almost decided that Séraphie was right to portray me as possessing an atrocious soul. Perhaps I'd been led to make my list of assassins by the action of Charlotte Corday—11 or 12 July 1793—which I was wild about.[9] In those days I was a great enthusiast for Cato of Utica,[10] the sickly Christian

9. Charlotte Corday had murdered Marat, the Revolutionary extremist, in his bath, in order to try and prevent further extremism; she was herself guillotined.

10. A Roman politician who sided with Pompey against Julius Caesar and is notable mainly for his stoical suicide.

Bibliothèque de Grenoble.—Rue Neuve.—Library.—Courtyard.—
Entrance.—Natural history room around 1804.

A. Librarian's main office.—BB. Books.—I fancy the natural
history room was turned into quite a pretty museum which I saw
in 1816 when I came for the Didier affair.—N. Portrait room.—
P. Portrait of M. Mounier.—O. Staircase to Father Ducros's pretty
little apartment.—E. Anteroom to the library.—M. Mummy.—
C.C.C. Stuffed birds.—R. Antiquities.

reflections of the *good Rollin*, as my grandfather used to call him, seemed to me the height of stupidity.

At the same time I was such a child that, having discovered in Rollin's *Histoire ancienne*, I believe it was, a personage called *Aristocrate*, I marvelled at this circumstance and shared my enthusiasm with my sister Pauline, who was a liberal and in my camp against Zénaïde-Caroline, who was attached to Séraphie's camp and called a spy by us.

Inclined mirror.

Before or after this, I had had a violent liking for optics, which led me to read Smith's *Optics* in the Public Library. I made some spectacles for seeing the person next to you while seeming to look straight ahead. By this means, and with a bit of adroitness, they could very easily still have launched me on the science of optics and made me *pick up* a good chunk of mathematics. From where it was only a short step to astronomy.

CHAPTER 21

When I had every right to ask my father for money, for example because he had promised it to me, he muttered, became angry, and instead of the 6fr promised gave me 3. This outraged me: what, not be true to his promise!

The Spanish sentiments passed on to me by my aunt Elisabeth carried me up into the clouds, I dreamt only of honour, of heroism. I hadn't the least skill, the smallest art of getting by, none of the plausibility of the hypocrite (or jesuit).

This defect has withstood experience, argument, remorse at having been taken in infinitely many times because of my *espagnolisme*.

I still have no skill in such things: every day, thanks to my *espagnolisme*, I am swindled out of a *paolo* or two, buying anything at all. The remorse which I feel an hour later has finally given me the habit of not buying very much. I allow myself to go without some small item of furniture that will cost me 12fr for a whole year on end in the certainty of being swindled, which will put me in a bad mood, and this bad mood outweighs the pleasure of possessing the small item of furniture.

I am writing this standing up at a Tronchin bureau made by a joiner who had never seen anything of the kind; I had been depriving myself of it for the past year out of anxiety not to be swindled. Finally I took the precaution of not going to talk to the joiner when I came back from the café at 11 a.m. —at that hour my character is at its fieriest (just as in 1803, when I used to drink *scalding hot* coffee in the Rue St-Honoré, on the corner of the Rue de Grenelle or d'Orléans)— but in moments of fatigue, and my Tronchin bureau only cost me four and a half *écus* (or 4.5 × 5.45 = 24.52).

This characteristic meant that my conferences about money, so very thorny a topic between a father aged . . . and a son of fifteen, normally ended on my side in a fit of profound contempt and compressed indignation.

Sometimes, not out of cleverness but purely by chance, I would talk eloquently to my father about whatever it was I wanted to buy; without suspecting it I *excited* him (passed on to him a little of my own passion), and then he gave me all I needed without any trouble, with pleasure even. One market-day in the Place Grenette, while he was in hiding, I talked to him of my desire of owning some of those movable characters cut from a sheet of brass the size of a playing-card. He gave me six or seven 15-*sou assignats*; on my return I had spent the lot.

"You always spend all the money I give you."

Since in giving me these 15-*sou assignats* he had exhibited what in so graceless a character might be called a good grace, I found his criticism very just. If my relations had known how to manage me, they would have turned me into the kind of simpleton I have seen so many of in the provinces. The indignation that I felt from my childhood on and in the highest degree, because of my Spanish sentiments, created the character that I have in spite of them. But what is that character?

I would be very hard put to say. Perhaps I shall see the truth at sixty-five if I get there.*

A poor man addressing me in the *tragic style* like in Rome, or the *comic style* like in France, makes me indignant: 1. I hate my rêverie being broken into; 2. I don't believe a word of what he says to me.

Yesterday, as I went down the street, a woman of the people, forty years old, but quite presentable, said to a man who was walking with her:

"Bisogna campar." ("One has to live all the same.")

There was nothing theatrical about the remark, which moved me to tears. I never give to the poor who ask me: I don't think this is out of meanness. When the fat quarantine official (11 Dec) in C[ivit]a-V[ecchi]a spoke to me about a poor Portuguese in the lazar-house who only asks for six *pagnotte*[1] a day, I at once gave him six or eight *paolos* in loose change. Since he refused them, for fear of compromising himself with his chief (a coarse peasant, a native of Fiuminata, called Romanelli), I thought it would be more dignified for a reigning consul to give an *écu*, which I did; six *paolos* therefore out of genuine humanity and four because of the gold braid on my coat.

A propos financial conversations between a father and his son: the Marquis Torrigiani, of Florence (a great gambler in his youth and strongly accused of winning by improper

*To be fitted in. Concerning my character. People will say to me: But are you a prince or an Emile, that some J.-J. Rousseau should take the trouble to study and to guide your character? I shall reply: My whole family took a hand in my education. After having very unwisely given everything up on my mother's death, I was their one remedy against tedium and they gave to me all the tedium I took away from them. Never to speak to a living being of my own age!

Handwriting: my thoughts go at a gallop, if I don't record them quickly I lose them. How should I write quickly [*sic*]? This, Monsieur Colomb, is how I have acquired the habit of writing badly.

Rome, THIRTIETH DECEMBER 1835, returning from San Gregorio and from the Foro Boario.

1. An Italian word meaning hunks of bread.

means), finding that his three sons were sometimes losing 10 or 15 *louis* at the tables, so as to spare them the bother of asking him for it, handed 3,000fr to a faithful old porter with orders to hand this money to his sons when they had lost, and to ask him for more when the 3,000fr had been spent.

This is very good in itself, and was a method moreover his sons found touching, and they became more moderate. This marquis, an of[fice]r in the Légion d'Honneur, is the father of Mme Pazzi, whose lovely eyes filled me with so intense an admiration in 1817. The anecdote about his father's gambling would have pained me terribly in 1817 because of the accursed *espagnolisme* of my character of which I complained formerly. This *espagnolisme* prevents me from having the *comic genius*: 1. I avert my gaze and my memory from anything low; 2. I sympathize, as at the age of ten when I was reading Ariosto, with anything in the way of tales of love, of forests (woods and their vast silence), of generosity.

If there is generosity in it, the most commonplace Spanish tale brings tears to my eyes, whereas I avert my eyes from the character of Chrysale in Molière and even more so from the underlying malice of *Zadig, Candide, Le Pauvre Diable* and other works by Voltaire of whom I only really adore:

> Vous êtes, lui dit-il, l'existence et l'essence
> Simple avec attribut et de pure substance.[2]

Barral (the Comte Paul de Barral, born in Grenoble around 1785) brought me early on to share his liking for these lines which his father, the first president, had taught him.

This *espagnolisme*, which was passed on to me by my aunt Elisabeth, means that I pass, even at my age, for a child de-

---

2. A couplet coming from one of Voltaire's satirical poems. A literal translation would be:

You are, he said to him, existence and essence
Simple with attribute and pure substance.

void of experience, for a madman "increasingly incapable of any serious business," in the view of my cousin Colomb (whose very words these are), who is a true bourgeois.

The conversation of the true bourgeois about *men* and *life*, which is no more than a collection of such ugly details, brings on a profound attack of *spleen* when I am obliged out of propriety to listen to it for any length of time.

This is the secret of the revulsion I felt for Grenoble around 1816, which at the time I couldn't explain to myself. I still can't explain to myself today, at the age of fifty-two, why Sundays tend to make me miserable. And this to the point where I am cheerful and contented; but after two hundred paces down the street, I notice that the shops are shut: "Ah, *it's Sunday*," I say to myself.

Instantly any inner tendency towards happiness vanishes.

Is it envy for the contented air of the workmen or the bourgeois in their Sunday best?

It's no good my telling myself: "But I waste fifty-two Sundays a year in this way and ten public holidays perhaps." It's stronger than I am. My one recourse is determined hard work.

This defect, the revulsion I feel for Chrysale, has perhaps kept me young. It would then be a fortunate misfortune, like that of not having possessed many women (women like Bianca Milesi, whom I failed with in Paris, one morning around 1829, solely from not having realized the moment was ripe— she had on a dress of black velvet that day—near the Rue du Helder or the Rue du Mont-Blanc).

Since I have possessed hardly any of these women (true bourgeoises), I'm not in the least blasé at the age of fifty. I mean morally blasé, because physically it's only right I should be considerably worn down, to the extent of easily going for a fortnight or three weeks without a woman, a lenten fast which troubles me only during the first week.

Most of my apparent follies, especially the stupidity of not having *gone bald-headed* (as D[on] Japhet of Armenia has it[3]) after the opportunities that offered; all the times I've been taken in when buying things etc., etc., stem from the *espagnolisme* passed on to me by my aunt Elisabeth, for whom I always had the most profound respect, a respect so profound it prevented my friendship from being affectionate, and, I fancy, from my having read Ariosto when I was so young and with so great a pleasure. (These days, Ariosto's heroes strike me as stableboys whose sole virtue is their physical strength, which sets me at odds with clever people who openly prefer Ariosto to Tasso [here M. Bontadossi, Don Filippo Caetani], whereas in my view, when happily Tasso forgets to imitate Virgil or Homer, he is the most affecting of poets.)

In less than an hour, I have just written these twelve pages, and pausing now and again in order to try not to write things which are not very clear and that I would be obliged to erase.

How *physically* could I have written well, Monsieur Colomb? My friend Colomb, who heaps this criticism on me in his letter of yesterday and its predecessors, would face torture for a promise, and for me. (He was born in Lyon around 1785, his father, a former merchant, very honest, retired to Grenoble, around 1788. M. Romain Colomb has 20 or 25,000 fr a year and three daughters, Rue Godot-de-Mauroy, Paris.)

The famous siege of Lyon (the commander of which, M. de Précy, I later got to know so well in Brunswick, 1806–9, my earliest model of a man of breeding after M. de Tressan in my early childhood), the siege of Lyon was exciting the whole of the Midi; I was for Kellermann and the republicans, my relations for the besieged and Précy (without the *monsieur*, as they used to say).

Our cousin Santerre, from the post office, whose cousin or nephew Santerre was fighting in Lyon, came to the house

---

3. In a comedy by the seventeenth-century playwright Scarron.

Sunday altar.—Mountains.—Périer garden.—Terrace 40 feet high decked with vines and flowers.—My uncle's room.

J. My private garden next to the water stone.—A. Natural history room.—F. Locked cupboards containing minerals, seashells. —T. Lunch table containing excellent *café au lait* and very good small rolls well baked, perfect *griches*.—S. M. Santerre with his hat with the broad brim because of his weak, red-rimmed eyes.— H. Me devouring the news reports.—B. My grandfather's (M. Henri Gagnon) study.—L. Pile of my uncle's books smelling of musk which provided my education.

twice a day; as it was summer, we would be having our morning *café au lait* in the natural history room on the terrace.

It was at point H that I perhaps experienced the most intense raptures of love for my country and hatred for the *aristocrats*, the *legitimists* of 1835, and the priests, its enemies.

M. Santerre worked in the post office and regularly brought us six or seven newspapers purloined from the subscribers, who only got them two hours later because of our curiosity. He would have his finger of wine and bit of bread and listen to the papers. Often he had had news from Lyon.

In the evenings I would go out on to the terrace on my own, to see if I could hear the cannon from Lyon. I see from the *Table Chronologique*, the one book I have in Rome, that Lyon was taken on 9 October 1793. So it was during the summer of 1793, at the age of TEN, that I went out to listen to the cannon from Lyon. I never heard them. I gazed enviously at the mountain of Méaudre (pronounced Mioudre), from where they could be heard. Our worthy cousin Romagnier, a cousin from having married a Mlle Blanchet, a relation of my grandfather's wife, I believe, came from Mioudre where he went every other month to visit his father. When he got back he would make my heart pound by telling me:

"We can hear the cannon from Lyon very clearly, especially in the evening at sunset and when the wind is in the north-west (norwest)."

I used to contemplate point B with the most intense desire to go there, but that was a desire I had to be very careful not to express.

I should perhaps have placed this detail much higher up, but I repeat that where my childhood is concerned I only have very clear mental pictures, without *dates* and without any *physiognomy*.

I write them down more or less as they come to me.

I have no books and I don't want to read any books; I have the help just of the stupid *Chronologie* which bears the name of that shrewd, dried-up man M. Loève-Veimars. I shall do the same for the Marengo campaign (1800), for that of 1809, for the Moscow campaign, for that of 1813 when I was an intendant in Sagan (Silesia, on the Bober); I don't at all claim to be writing a history, but quite simply to be recording my memories so as to work out what sort of man I have been:

Horizon visible at sunset from my grandfather's terrace.—Two
mountains.—Grenoble.—Isère.

Méaudre or Mioudre at M in the valley between the two
mountains A and B.—V. Valley of Voreppe adored by me as being
the road to Paris.—S. Sunset in August; in summer at V, in winter at D, which gives two hours of twilight.

stupid or intelligent, fearful or courageous, etc., etc. This in answer to the great saying: *Gnoti seauton*.[4]

During that summer of 1793, I was much excited by the siege of Toulon; it goes without saying that my relations approved of the traitors who surrendered it, whereas my aunt Elisabeth in her Castilian pride said to me [*a blank*]

I watched the departure of General Carteau or Cartaud, who paraded on the Place Grenette. I can still see his name on his wagons filing slowly and very noisily past over the paving-stones along the Rue Montorge to go to Toulon.

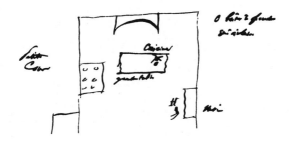

Small courtyard.—Kitchen.—Big table.—O. Powder-box which blew up.—Me.

For me a great event was at hand; I felt it very strongly at the time, but it was too late: all ties of friendship between my father and myself had been broken once and for all, and my revulsion for bourgeois pettiness and for Grenoble was from now on invincible.

My aunt Séraphie had had a long illness. Finally, there was talk of her being in danger; it was the good Marion (Marie Thomasset), my friend, who uttered the great word. The danger became urgent, the pr[iests] flocked in.

One winter evening, I fancy, I was in the kitchen around

4. The injunction "Know thyself" inscribed over the entrance to the temple at Delphi.

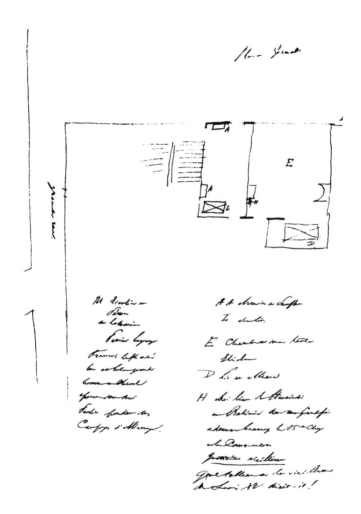

Grande-Rue.—Place Grenette.

M. Staircase and entrance steps of the Périer-Lagrange house. François, the eldest son, good-natured and stupid, a great horseman, married my sister Pauline, when I was campaigning in Germany.—A, A. Séraphie's cupboards.—L. Her bed.—E. My aunt Elisabeth's room.—D. Bed and alcove.—H. Me reading *La Henriade* or *Bélisaire*, the fifteenth chapter of which my grandfather admired greatly for its opening: "Justinian was growing old." "What a portrait of the old age of Louis XV!" he used to say.

seven o'clock in the evening, at point H facing Marion's cupboard. Someone came in and said: "She's gone."

I dropped to my knees at point H to thank God for this mighty deliverance.

If Parisians are as fatuous in 1880 as in 1835, this reaction to the death of my mother's sister will make me be thought barbaric, cruel, atrocious.

However that may be, such was the truth. After the first week of masses for the dead and prayers, everyone in the house felt a great relief. I believe even my father was glad enough to be delivered from that hellish mistress, always assuming she had been his mistress, or else from that hellish friend.

One of her last actions had been, one evening when I was sitting on my aunt Elisabeth's chest-of-drawers, at point H, reading *La Henriade* or *Bélisaire*,[5] which my grandfather had just lent me, to exclaim: "How can anyone give such books to that child! Who gave him that book?"

My excellent grandfather, at my untimely request, had just been kind enough in spite of the cold to go with me as far as his study adjoining the terrace, at the far end of the house,

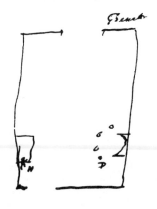

Grenette.

<hr/>

5. Both are works by Voltaire.

in order to give me the book for which I had felt a desire that evening.

The whole family formed a string of onions in front of the fire at point D. This was a phrase often repeated in Grenoble: a string of onions. My grandfather, with a shrug, made no reply to his daughter's insolent rebuke other than: "She isn't well."

I have absolutely no idea of the date of this death; I shall be able to get it taken from the records of the registry in Grenoble.

I fancy that soon afterwards I went to the Ecole Centrale, something that Séraphie would never have stood for. I think that was around 1797 and that I went to the Ecole Centrale for three years only.

CHAPTER 22

ECOLE CENTRALE

Many years later, around 1817, I learnt from M. de Tracy that it was he who was largely responsible for the excellent law creating the Ecoles Centrales.[1]

My grandfather was the very worthy head of the committee responsible for presenting the departmental administration with the names of the teachers and for organizing the School. My grandfather adored literature and education, and for the past forty years had taken the lead in everything literary and liberal that had been done in Grenoble.

Séraphie had criticized him roundly for having accepted these duties as a member of the organizing committee, but the founder of the Public Library owed it to his reputation in the world to be the head of the Ecole Centrale.

My teacher Durand, who came to the house to give me lessons, taught Latin; how could I not go to his classes at the Ecole Centrale? Had Séraphie lived, she would have found a reason; but as things stood, my father limited himself to making weighty and profound remarks concerning the risk to morals of making undesirable acquaintances. I felt no joy; there was an official opening of the School in the rooms of the Library at which my grandfather made a speech.

It is this very crowded gathering in the first room SS, perhaps, the picture of which I find in my head.

The teachers were Messrs Durand for the Latin language;

---

1. These schools were instituted by two laws of 1795, inspired though not drawn up by Destutt de Tracy.

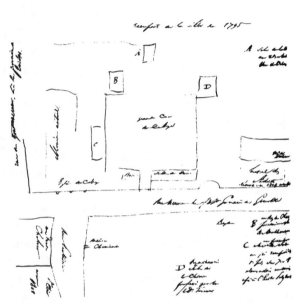

Collège de Grenoble.—Pont de Claix.—Eternal snows or snows at least for eight months of the year.—Mountains of Echirolles.—Comboire.—Magnificent view.—Town ramparts in 1795.—Rue du Gouvernement. Here the Day of Tiles. Present-day museum.—College church.—Main courtyard of the College.—Drawing-in-the-round.—Art classroom.—Latin classroom on second or third floor. Delightful view.—Mme de Valserre.—Des Adrets mansion demolished around 1804 and rebuilt.—Rue Neuve, the *faubourg St-Germain* of Grenoble.[2]—My aunt Chalvet.—Ste-Claire before 1802.—Rue Pertuisière.—Cheminade house.—Beyle.

D. ground-floor classroom where M. Trousset taught chemistry.—B. On the ground floor, first mathematics classroom.—C. On the first floor, second classroom where I won first prize ahead of seven or eight pupils admitted one month later to the Ecole Polytechnique.

2. I.e. the smartest residential quarter of the town.

Gattel, general grammar and even logic, I fancy; Dubois-Fontanelle, author of the tragedy of *Ericie ou la Vestale* and editor for twenty years of the *Gazette des Deux-Ponts*, literature; Trousset, a young doctor, a protégé and, it might be said, pupil of my grandfather's, chemistry; Jay, a great braggart of five-foot-ten, without any hint of ability but good at firing up the children (getting them excited), drawing; he soon had three hundred pupils; Chalvet (Pierre-Vincent), a penniless young libertine, a genuine author without any talent, history, and

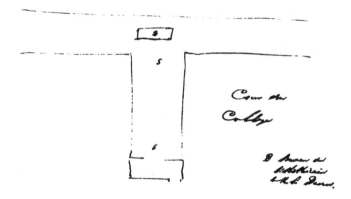

Rue Neuve.—College yard.—B. The librarian Father Ducros's office.

responsible for collecting the enrolment fees which he partly squandered with the help of three sisters, complete whores by profession, who gave him a fresh dose of p[ox] from which he died soon afterwards; lastly Dupuy, the most bombastic and fatherly bourgeois I have ever met, taught mathematics, without any hint of a hint of ability. He was barely even a surveyor and was appointed in a town which possessed a Gros![3] But my grandfather knew not the first thing about mathematics and hated them, and in any case Father Dupuy's (as we called

3. Louis-Gabriel Gros (1765–1812) was a Grenoblois admired by Stendhal as much for his ardent Jacobinism as his mathematical ability.

him; to us he would say, *my children*) pomposity was certainly calculated to earn him general esteem in Grenoble. This very vacuous man did however say one great thing:

"My child, study Condillac's *Logic*,[4] it is the basis of everything."

One couldn't say better than that today, provided Condillac's name be replaced by that of de Tracy.

The funny thing is that I don't believe M. Dupuy understood the first word of this Condillac's *Logic* that he recommended to us; it was a very thin small volume in duodecimo. But I am anticipating, which is my failing, I shall need perhaps to reread, erasing all these sentences which offend against a chronological order.

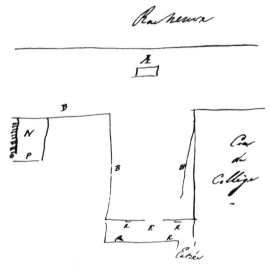

Rue Neuve.—College yard.—Entrance.

The one man who was perfectly at home was M. *l'abbé* Gattel, a dapper, flirtatious *abbé*, always in the company of

4. Etienne Bonnot de Condillac (1715–1780) was a leading *philosophe*, born in Grenoble; he was a convinced empiricist, a follower of John Locke.

women, a genuine seventeenth-century *abbé*. But in class he was very serious and knew, I believe, all that was then known about the habits, the principles of the instinctive impulses and the secondary impulses of facility and analogy which nations have followed in forming languages.

M. Gattel had compiled a very good dictionary, in which he had dared to record pronunciations and which I have always used. Indeed, he was a man who knew how to work for five or six hours a day, which is an enormous amount in the provinces, where they only know how to *fritter away the time* all day long.

The idiots in Paris criticize this healthy and natural description of pronunciation. This is out of cowardice and out of ignorance. They're afraid of looking ridiculous if they give the pronunciation of *Anvers* (town), of *cours*, of *vers*. They don't know that in Grenoble, for example, people say: I have been to the *Cour-ce*, or I have been reading some *ver-ces* about *Anver-se* and *Calai-se*. If they speak like this in Grenoble, a town of intelligence and still partly dependent on the north, which has crushed the south linguistically, what must it be like in Toulouse, Bazas, Pézenas, Digne? Regions where a French pronunciation ought to be posted up on the doors of the churches.

A Minister of the Interior who wanted to do his job properly, instead of plotting with the king and in the Chambers like M. Guizot,[5] should demand credits of two million a year to bring the populations who live in the fateful triangle between Bordeaux, Bayonne and Valence up to the same level of education as other Frenchmen. In these parts they believe in witchcraft, can't read and don't speak French. They may accidentally produce a superior man such as Lannes, Soult,[6] but the general [*a blank*] there is unbelievably ignorant. I believe

5. François Guizot (1787–1874), historian and politician; a monarchist and arch-bourgeois, he was not admired by Stendhal.

6. Lannes and Soult were both Napoleonic generals, born in the south.

that, because of the climate and the love and vitality it endows our mechanism with, this triangle ought to produce the leading men of France. Corsica leads me to think this.[7]

With its 180,000 inhabitants, this small island gave eight or ten men of merit to the Revolution, and the department of the Nord, with its 900,000 inhabitants, scarcely a single one. I don't even know the name of that *one*. It goes without saying that the priests are all-powerful in this fateful triangle. Civilization goes from Lille to Rennes and stops around Orléans and Tours. To the south-east Grenoble is its brilliant limit.

Appointing the teachers at the Ecole Centrale—Messrs Gattel, Dubois-Fontanelle, Trousset, Villars (a peasant from the Hautes-Alpes), Jay, Durand, Dupuy, Chalvet, there you have them in approximate order of their usefulness to the children, the first three had some ability—didn't cost much and was soon done, but there were major repairs to be done to the buildings. Despite the war, everything got done in those energetic days. My grandfather was forever demanding funds from the departmental administration.

Classes began in the spring, I believe, in temporary classrooms.

M. Durand's had a delightful view, and at the end of a month I finally became aware of it. It was a lovely summer's day and a gentle breeze was stirring the hay on the *glacis* of the Porte de Bonne, beneath our eyes, sixty or eighty feet below.

My relations were forever extolling to me, *ad nauseam*, the beauty of the fields, the greenery, the flowers, etc., ranunculi, etc.

These worthless phrases have given me a distaste for flowers and flower-beds that still survives.

Happily, the magnificent view which I discovered *for myself* at a window of the college, next to the Latin room, where I used to go to daydream on my own, overcame the deep dis-

---

7. Corsica was of course the birthplace of Napoleon, the Stendhalian hero.

taste resulting from the phrases of my father and of the pr[iests], his friends.

Thus it was, all those years later, that the rhythmical and pretentious phrases of Messrs Chateaubriand and Salvandy made me write *Le Rouge et le noir* in too jerky a style. A great foolishness, for who in twenty years' time will have a thought for those gentlemen's hypocritical twaddle? As for myself, I am taking a ticket in a lottery first prize in which boils down to this: to be read in 1935. This is the same attitude of mind which led me to close my eyes to the landscapes about which my aunt Séraphie went into ecstasies. I was in 1794 like the common people of Milan are in 1835: the German authorities that they abhor want to give them a taste for Schiller whose beautiful soul, so different from that of the worthless Goethe, would be greatly shocked to find itself being glorified by apostles like these.

For me it was a very strange thing to start in the spring of 94 or 95 at the age of eleven or twelve in a school where I had ten or twelve classmates.

I found the reality far inferior to the wild pictures I had imagined. These classmates weren't light-hearted enough, not wild enough, and they had the vilest manners.

I fancy that M. Durand, all puffed up by finding himself teaching in an Ecole Centrale, but still good-natured, set me to translating Sallust, *De bello Jugurtino*. Freedom produced its first fruits: good sense returned as I lost my anger and much enjoyed Sallust.

The whole college was full of workmen, many of the rooms on our third floor were open, I went there to daydream on my own.

Everything astonished me in this longed-for freedom, to which I had finally attained. The attractions I discovered in it were not the ones I had dreamt of: I hadn't met with the gay, friendly, noble companions I had pictured to myself, but in their stead some very selfish young brats.

I have suffered this same disappointment more or less all

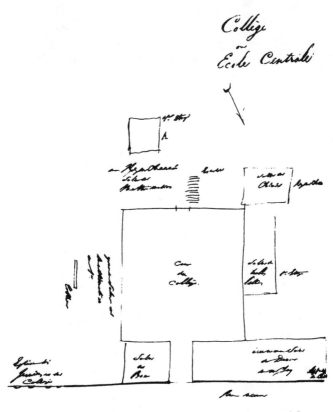

College or Ecole Centrale.—Third floor.—On the ground floor,
mathematics classroom.—Staircase.—Chemistry classroom.—
Ground floor.—Large mathematics classroom on the first floor.—
Blackboard.—College yard.—Literature classroom.—First
floor.—Jesuit and College church.—Drawing-in-the-round classroom.—M. Jay's vast art classroom.—M. Chalvet's ap[artmen]t.—
Rue Neuve.

through my life. The happiness that goes with ambition has
alone been exempt from it, when, in 1812, I became a commissioner and, a fortnight later, an inspector of furnishings, I
was drunk with contentment for three months at no longer
being a com[missioner] of war and exposed to the envy and
abuse of those coarsest of heroes who were the Emperor's
navvies at Jena and at Wagram. Posterity will never know just

how stupid and how coarse these men were away from their battlefield. And even on the battlefield, how cautious! They were men like Admiral Nelson, the hero of Naples (see Coletta and what M. di Fiori has recounted to me), like Nelson forever wondering what each wound might bring in by way of a grant of money or a medal. What contemptible animals, compared to the exalted virtue of General Michaud, of Colonel Mathis! No, posterity will never know what worthless *jeansucres* they were, these heroes of Napoleon's despatches, and how I laughed when I got the *Moniteur* at Vienna, Dresden, Berlin, Moscow, which almost no one in the army got so that they couldn't make fun of its lies! The despatches were an engine of war, *fieldworks* and not historical documents.

Luckily for poor truth, the extreme cowardice of these heroes, who have become peers of France and judges in 1835, will let posterity into the secret of their heroism in 1809. I make exception only for the amiable Lasalle and for Exelmans who since . . .[8] But he hadn't then gone to call on Marshal Bourmont, the Minister of War. Moncey too wouldn't have committed certain contemptible acts, but Suchet [*a blank*]. I was forgetting the great Gouvion-Saint-Cyr before age turned him into a semi-imbecile, and his imbecility goes back to 1814.[9] After which date his only talent was for writing. And in the civilian world, under Nap[oleon], such worthless characters as M. de Barante coming to pester M. Daru at Saint-Cloud in the month of November at seven o'clock in the morning, and the Comte d'Argout, that miserable flatterer of General Sebastiani![10]

But great heavens, where was I? In the Latin class in the buildings of the college.

8. Lasalle was a cavalry general, killed at the battle of Wagram; Exelmans a Napoleonic marshal exiled under the Restoration and a hero to Stendhal for having later defended Marshal Ney when he was accused of treason (and executed).

9. Moncey refused to preside over the court-martial of Marshal Ney; Suchet was a Napoleonic marshal who went over to King Louis XVIII in 1814; Gouvion-Saint-Cyr also went over to the Bourbon cause, hence the accusation of semi-imbecility.

10. The Comte d'Argout and General Sebastiani were both part of the government which followed the revolution of 1830.

CHAPTER 23

I wasn't a great success with my classmates; I can see today that I was then a very ridiculous mixture of haughtiness and the need to have fun. To their very ruthless egotism I responded with my notions of Spanish nobility. I was desolate when they left me out of their games; to crown my misery, I didn't know these games, I brought to them a nobility of soul, a delicacy which they must have thought completely mad. Artfulness and a ready egotism, I believe, an outsize egotism, are the only things that succeed among children.

To round off my lack of success I was timid in front of the teacher; a restrained word of reproach spoken in kindness and in the proper tone of voice by that small bourgeois pedant brought tears to my eyes. These tears were cowardice in the eyes of Messrs the brothers Gaultier, Saint-Ferréol, I believe, Robert (currently director of the Théâtre-Italien in Paris) and especially Odru. This latter was a peasant, very strong and even more uncouth, who was a foot taller than any of us and whom we called Goliath; he had Goliath's grace but thumped us unmercifully when he got it into his thick head that we were making fun of him.

His father, a rich peasant from Lumbin or some other village in the valley. (This is the name par excellence of the admirable valley of the Isère, between Grenoble and Montmélian. In point of fact, the valley extends as far as the *Dent de Moirans*, as below.)

My grandfather had taken advantage of Séraphie's departure to make me attend classes in mathematics, chemistry and drawing.

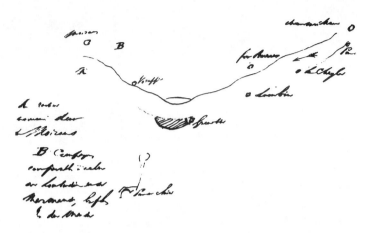

Moirans.—Voreppe.—Fort Barraux.—Montmélian.—Chambéry.—
Grenoble.—Lumbin.—Le Cheylas.—Pontcharra.—Pont de Claix.

A. Rock known as Dent-de-Moirans.—B. Countryside comparable with that of Lombardy and Normandy, the most beautiful in
the world.

Where civic importance was concerned, the very bombastic and very ridiculous bourgeois, M. Dupuy, was a sort of minor rival to M. *le Docteur* Gagnon. He went on all fours
before the nobility, but this advantage that he held over
M. Gagnon was made up for by the complete lack of amiability and of literary ideas which then formed as it were the
daily bread of our conversation. M. Dupuy, jealous at finding
M. Gagnon a member of the organizing committee and his
superior, didn't at all welcome the recommendation of this
fortunate rival in my favour and I only won my place in the
mathematics class on the strength of my ability, and finding
that ability called constantly into question for three years in
succession. M. Dupuy, who talked incessantly (but never too
much) about Condillac and his *Logic*, hadn't the faintest hint
of logic in his head. He talked exaltedly and with grace, and
he had an imposing figure and very polite manners.

In 1794, he had a very good idea: this was to divide the

hundred pupils who had filled the ground-floor classroom at the first mathematics lesson into brigades of five or seven each with its leader.

Mine was a *big boy*, i.e. a young man past puberty and a foot taller than we were. He used to spit on us, by placing a finger cleverly in front of his mouth. In the army such characters are referred to as *yobs*. We complained about this yob, Raimonet by name, I believe, to M. Dupuy, who with admirable highmindedness reduced him to the ranks. M. Dupuy was in the habit of giving lessons to the young artillery officers in Valence and was a stickler for honour (for the duel).

We were following the worthless textbook by Bezout, but M. Dupuy had the wit to talk to us about Clairaut and about the new edition of him that M. Biot (that industrious charlatan) had just brought out.[1]

Clairaut was calculated to open the minds which Bezout tended to leave forever stopped up. In Bezout each *proposition* is like a big secret learnt from some kind woman neighbour.

In the drawing room, I found that M. Jay and M. Couturier (with the broken nose), his deputy, did me a terrible injustice. But for want of any other virtue, M. Jay had that of bombast, which bombast, instead of making us laugh, enthused us. [*]

M. Jay was a great success, most important for the Ecole Centrale, which had been slandered by the pr[iests]. He had two or three hundred pupils.

These were all distributed on benches of seven or eight, and every day fresh benches needed to be built. And what models! Bad nudes drawn by Messrs Pajou, M. Jay himself: legs, arms, all more or less were very clumsy, very heavy, very ugly. The style was that of the younger M. Moreau or of M. Cochin,

1. Alexis-Claude Clairaut (1713–1765), author of textbooks on both geometry and algebra; Jean-Baptiste Biot (1774–1862) was an astronomer and mathematician and elsewhere commended by Stendhal.

[*]Lunch Monday to be paid to Robert.

who says such comical things about Michelangelo and Domenichino in his three small volumes on Italy.

The large heads were drawn in red chalk or engraved in the style of a pencil drawing. It must be admitted that our total ignorance of drawing showed up less in these than in the *académies* (nude figures). The great virtue of these heads, which were eighteen inches high, was that the hatchings were perfectly parallel; as for copying nature, that was out of the question.

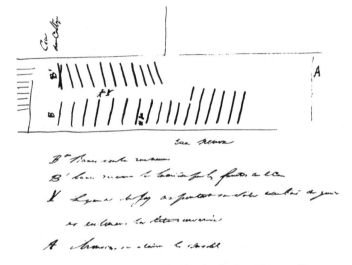

College yard.—Rue Neuve. B. Benches by the Rue Neuve.—B'. Benches getting their light from the window onto the yard.—Y. The tall M. Jay pacing his classroom with an air of genius and with his head thrown back.—A. Cupboard where the models were.

A certain Moulezin, a stupid, self-important donkey and today a rich and self-important bourgeois in Grenoble and no doubt one of the bitterest enemies of common sense, soon immortalized himself by the perfect parallelism of his red chalk hatchings. He had drawn nudes and had been the pupil of M. Bridone (of Lyon); I, a pupil of M. Le Roy, who had been prevented in his lifetime by illness and a Parisian good taste from being as great a charlatan as M. Bridone, a designer of fabrics in Lyon, I was only able to obtain the large heads, which greatly shocked me, but had the big advantage of being a lesson in modesty.

Of this I had great need, for I must speak frankly. The relations whose handiwork I was had congratulated themselves on my talents in front of me, and I thought myself the most distinguished young man in Grenoble.

My inferiority in games with my Latin classmates began to open my eyes. The bench of the large heads near H, where I was put right next to the two ridiculous-looking sons of a shoemaker who had ridiculous faces (how improper for the grandson of M. Gagnon!), filled me with the determination to get on or die in the attempt.*

Here is the story of my gift for drawing: my ever judicious family had decided, after a year or eighteen months of lessons from that most polite of men, M. Le Roy, that I drew very well.

The fact is I didn't even suspect that drawing is an imitation of nature. I drew a head in half-relief in hard black pencil. (In Rome, in the *Braccio Nuovo*,[2] I discovered that it was the head of Musa, Augustus's doctor.) My drawing was neat, lifeless, quite without merit, like the drawing of a young convent schoolgirl.

My relations, who for all their fine talk about the beauties of the countryside and beautiful landscapes, had absolutely no feeling for the arts, not one decent engraving in the house, declared me very good at drawing. M. Le Roy was still alive and painted landscapes in gouache (thick colour) which were less bad than the others.

I got permission to give up the pencil and paint in gouache.

*Rapidity. Bad handwriting (reason for). 1 Jan 1836. It's only two o'clock, I have already written sixteen pages; it's cold, the pens are malfunctioning. Instead of getting into a temper, I keep going ahead, writing as best I can.

2. The "New Wing" of the Vatican Museum.

M. Le Roy had done a view from the Pont de la Vence, between La Buisserate and Saint-Robert, as seen from point A.

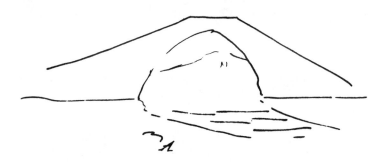

I crossed this bridge several times a year to go to Saint-Vincent, I found the drawing, especially the mountain at M., a strong likeness, the light dawned. So first and foremost, a drawing has to resemble nature!

It was no longer a matter of perfectly parallel hatchings. After this splendid discovery I made rapid progress.

Poor M. Le Roy chanced to die, I missed him. However I was still a slave at that time and all the young people went to M. Villionne, a fabric designer driven out of *Commune-Affranchie* by the war and the executions. Commune-Affranchie was the new name given to Lyon after its capture.[3]

I conveyed to my father (but inadvertently not having had the wit to think of it) my liking for gouache, and bought many of her husband's gouaches from Mme Le Roy for three times their value.

I greatly coveted two volumes of La Fontaine's *Fables* with engravings very delicately done but very clear.

"They're horrid," Mme Le Roy said to me with her lovely, so very hypocritical soubrette's eyes, "but they're masterpieces."

I saw I wasn't going to be able to wangle La Fontaine's

3. A name translatable literally as "Freed-Commune."

Fables for the price of the gouaches. The Ecole Centrale opened, I no longer thought about gouache, but my discovery [remained] with me: you had to imitate nature, and that perhaps prevented my large heads, copied from those worthless drawings, from being as execrable as they ought to have been. I recall the "Indignant Soldier" in Raphael's *Heliodorus chastized*; I never look at the original (in the Vatican) without recalling my copy; the wholly arbitrary technique of the pencil, a false virtue, excelled above all in the dragon that crowns the helmet.

When we had done fair work, M. Jay would sit in the pupil's place, emend the head slightly with some pompous argument, but an argument none the less, and finally sign the head on the back, *ne varietur* it would seem, so that it could be entered for the competition in the middle or at the end of the year. He fired our enthusiasm but hadn't the faintest notion of the *beautiful*. He had produced only one wretched picture in his life, a *Liberty* modelled on his wife, squat, bunched up, shapeless. To lighten it, he had filled the foreground with a tomb behind which there appeared Liberty concealed up as far as the knees.

The end of the year arrived, there were examinations in the presence of the committee and I believe of a member of the Department.

I obtained only a miserable *accessit* and then I think only so as to please M. Gagnon, the head of the committee, and M. Dausse, another member of the committee who was a good friend of M. Gagnon's.

My grandfather felt humiliated and told me as much with perfect politeness and restraint. His very simple words made the greatest possible impression on me. He added with a laugh:

"All you knew how to do was show us your fat bottom!"

This unattractive stance had been observed at the blackboard in the mathematics room.

This was a slate six feet by four, supported at a height of five feet on a very solid frame. You climbed up to it by three steps.

M. Dupuy would get us to demonstrate a proposition, the square on the hypotenuse for example, or the following sum: a piece of work is paid for at seven *livres*, four *sous*, three *deniers* the fathom; the workman has done two fathoms, five feet, three inches. How much does he get?

In the course of the year, M. Dupuy had always summoned to the blackboard the Messrs de Monval who were noblemen, M. de Pina, nobleman and ultra, M. Anglès, M. de Renneville, a nobleman, and never myself, or only once.

The younger Monval, a buzzard with a face like a buzzard but a good mathematician (a school expression), was slaughtered by bandits in Calabria around 1806, I believe. The elder one, who was on such good terms with Paul-Louis Courier, became a filthy old debauchee . . . He was a colonel, ruined a great lady in Naples in a vile fashion; tried to blow hot and cold in Grenoble around 1830, was found out and generally despised. He died of this general and richly merited contempt, much extolled by the church party (see the *Gazette* for 1832 or 1833). He was a right one, an all-round scoundrel.

M. de Pina, mayor in Grenoble from 1825 to 1830. An all-round ultra probity forgotten in favour of his nine or ten children, he amassed an income of 60 or 70,000 francs. A gloomy fanatic and, I think, an all-round scoundrel, a true jesuit.

Anglès, since a prefect of police, tireless worker, a lover of order, but in politics an all-round scoundrel, but in my opinion infinitely less of a scoundrel than the previous two, who hold first place in my mind in the scoundrel line.

The pretty Mme la Comtesse Anglès was a friend of Mme la Comtesse Daru, in whose drawing-room I met her. The pretty Comte de Meffrey (from Grenoble like M. Anglès) was her lover. The poor woman was very bored, I fancy, in spite of her husband's high positions.

This husband, son of a celebrated miser and a miser himself, was the saddest of creatures and had the falsest and most anti-mathematical of minds. Cowardly to the point of scandal moreover; I shall recount later on the story of his slap

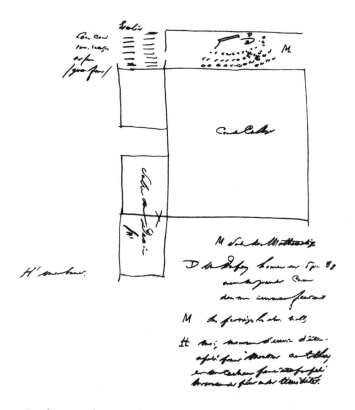

Death-trap without iron banisters (hand-rail).—Staircase.—College yard.—Art classroom.—H. My bench.—M. Mathematics classroom.—D. M. Dupuy, a man of 5 ft 8 inches, with his big cane, in his vast armchair.—His protégés, the aristocratic pupils.—H. Me, dying with envy to be called to go up to the blackboard and hiding so as not to be called, dying of fear and timidity.

across the face and its tailpiece. Around 1826 or 27 he lost his prefecture of police and went and built a fine château in the mountains, near Roanne, and died there very suddenly shortly afterwards, still young. He was a sad creature, he had all that's bad in the Dauphinois character, mean, artful, wily, attentive to the smallest detail.

M. de Renneville, a cousin of the Monvals, was good-looking and a complete dunce. His father was the dirtiest and most arrogant man in Grenoble. I haven't heard of him since school.

M. de Sinard, good character, my friend, reduced to beggary through emigration, protected and supported by Mme de Valserre, was my friend.

Having gone up to the blackboard, you wrote at O. The demonstrator's head was a good eight feet up. But, put on show once a month, without any support from M. Dupuy, who would be talking to Monval or M. de Pina as I demonstrated, I was overcome with timidity and mumbled. When in my turn I went up to the blackboard in front of the committee, my timidity was renewed, I became muddled as I gazed at these gentlemen and especially the terrifying M.

Way up to the blackboard.—Slate.

Dausse, sitting beside and to the right of the blackboard. I had the presence of mind not to go on staring at them, to pay attention only to what I was working out and I got through it correctly, though I bored them. How different from what happened in August 1799! I can say that it was on the strength of my ability that I broke through *in mathematics* and drawing as we used to say at the Ecole Centrale.

I was fat and not very tall, I had a light grey frock-coat. Hence the reproach:

"Why didn't you get a prize?" my grandfather said to me.

"I didn't have time."

The classes had only lasted four or five months that first year, I believe.

I went to Claix, still mad about shooting; but as I roamed the fields in spite of my father, I pondered deeply over this remark: "Why didn't you get a prize?"

I can't recall whether I attended the Ecole Centrale for four years or only three. I'm certain of the date of my leaving, the examination at the end of 1799, the Russians expected in Grenoble.

The aristocrats and my relations, I believe, used to say:

O Rus, quando ego te adspiciam![4]

For myself I feared for the examination which was to get me away from Grenoble! If ever I was to go there, a brief search in the archives of the departmental administration, in the Prefecture, will tell me whether the Ecole Centrale opened in 1796 or not until 1797.

At that time they reckoned by the Republican calendar, it was the Year V or the Year VI. It was only long afterwards, when the Emperor was stupid enough to want it, that I learnt to recognize 1796, 1797. I saw things from close to in those days.*

4. The line comes from Horace and means, literally, "Oh country, when shall I see you?" It was quoted punningly by the reactionaries, who took the word *rus* to refer to Russia, the Russians being seen as saviours by enemies of the Revolution such as Stendhal's family.

*Handwriting. 1 Jan 1836, 26 pages. All the pens malfunctioning; it is bitterly cold; instead of trying to form my letters properly and getting impatient, *io tiro avanti*. M. Colomb criticizes me every time he writes for writing badly.

The Emperor then began to raise up the throne of the Bourbons and was abetted by the boundless and inordinate cravenness of M. de Laplace.[5] A strange thing, poets show spirit, *savants* properly so called are servile and craven. What servility and baseness towards authority did M. Cuvier not show! Even the sensible Sutton Sharpe was repelled by it. In the Council of State M. le B[aro]n Cuvier was always of the most craven opinion.

When the order of the Réunion was created I was a true intimate at court, he came and *wept*, that is the word, so much did he want it. I shall report the Emperor's reply in its place. Given a pension for cravenness: Bacon, Laplace, Cuvier. M. Lagrange wasn't so contemptible, I fancy.

These gentlemen were certain of fame by their writings and hoped that the *savant* would be a cover for the statesman; in money matters, as in favours, they went after what was useful. The celebrated Legendre, a geometer of the highest class, on receiving the Légion d'Honneur, pinned it to his coat, looked at himself in the mirror and leapt for joy.

The apartment was a low one, his head bumped against the ceiling, he fell half-dazed. A worthy death that would have been for this successor to Archimedes!

To what baseness did they not stoop in the Académie des Sciences, between 1815 and 1830 and since, in order to wangle medals for themselves! It's unbelievable, I got the details from Messrs de Jussieu, Edwards, Milne-Edwards and via the salon of M. le Baron Girard. I have forgotten so many vilenesses.

A diplomat is less contemptible for saying openly: "I'll do whatever it takes to get ahead."[*]

5. The Marquis Pierre-Simon de Laplace (1749–1827), the greatest astronomer of his day but politically speaking an arrant time-server in Stendhal's judgment.

*1 Jan 1836, 29 pages. I stop for lack of light in the sky at 4.45. Mlle Kubly, after Victorine Big[illi]on. Pont de Bois. Duclos' *Mém[oires]*.

CHAPTER 24

Released from tyranny, my soul began to acquire some buoyancy. Gradually I was no longer obsessed* all the time by that very enervating emotion: impotent hatred.

My worthy aunt Elisabeth was the saving of me. She went almost every evening to have her game of cards with Mmes Colomb or Romagnier. The only bourgeois thing about these excellent sisters was a certain cautiousness of manner and certain habits. They had beautiful souls, something very rare in the provinces, and a fond attachment to my aunt Elisabeth.

I can't speak too highly of these good-hearted cousins; theirs were great, generous souls; they had given singular proof of that on the great occasions in their lives.

My father was more and more taken up with his passion for agriculture and for Claix, and spent three or four days a week there. He no longer found M. Gagnon's house, where he had had dinner and supper every day since my mother died, so agreeable, far from it. He could unburden himself only to Séraphie. He stood in awe of my aunt Elisabeth's Spanish sentiments; there had never been very much conversation between them. The unvarying Dauphinois pettiness and craftiness and unpleasant timidity of the one consorted badly with the noble sincerity and simplicity of the other. Mlle Gagnon had no liking for my father who, on the other hand, wasn't up to carrying on a conversation with M. *le Docteur* Gagnon: he

*Style. S[aint]-S[imon] says: filled. I can see no other word.

255

was respectful and polite, M. Gagnon was very polite, and that was all. My father was sacrificing nothing therefore by going to spend three or four days a week in Claix. He said to me two or three times, when forcing me to go with him to Claix, that it was sad at his age not to have somewhere of his own.

When I got home in the evenings to have supper with my aunt Elisabeth, my grandfather and my two sisters, I didn't have to fear any very severe questioning. Generally I said with a laugh that I had been to fetch my aunt from Mmes Romagnier and Colomb's house; indeed, I often accompanied her from these ladies' house as far as the door of the apartment then ran downstairs again to go and spend half an hour on the promenade in the Jardin de Ville which, on summer evenings, in the moonlight, beneath magnificent chestnut-trees eighty feet tall, served as a meeting-place for everything young and dazzling in the town.

Bit by bit I became bolder, I went more often to the theatre, always standing in the pit.

I felt a tender concern in watching a young actress called Mlle Kubly. Soon I was hopelessly in love with her; I never spoke to her.

She was a thin young woman, quite tall, with a Roman nose, pretty, slender, with a good figure. She still had the thinness of early youth, but a serious, often melancholy face.

Everything was new for me in the strange madness which suddenly found itself master of all my thoughts. All other interests evaporated. I scarcely recognized the sentiment whose description had enchanted me in *La Nouvelle Héloïse*, still less was this the voluptuousness of *Félicia*. I suddenly became indifferent and fair towards everyone around me; this [was] the moment when my hatred for my late aunt Séraphie died. Mlle Kubly played *jeune première* parts in comedy, she also sang in comic opera.

As you can well imagine, true comedy wasn't my thing. My grandfather was endlessly dinning the great saying into me: *knowledge of the human heart*. But what could I know of this *human heart*? A few *predictions* at most, seized on in books, in *Don Quijote* especially, almost the only book which didn't fill me with mistrust, all the others had been recommended to me by my tyrants, because my grandfather (newly converted, I believe) had refrained from teasing me about the books my father and Séraphie had made me read.

I needed romantic comedy therefore, i.e. dramas that weren't too grim, portraying the misfortunes of love and not money (grim, unhappy dramas based on the lack of money have always repelled me as being bourgeois and too lifelike; "my a . . . too is in nature," said Préville to an author).[1]

Mlle Kubly excelled in Florian's *Claudine*.

A young Savoyarde girl, who has had a child in Le Mont-envers by a fashionable young traveller, dresses up as a man and, with her small brat in tow, practises the trade of road-sweeper in a square in Turin. She meets her lover again, whom she still loves, she becomes his servant, but this lover is about to get married.

The actor playing the lover, whose name was Poussi, I fancy, that name suddenly comes back to me after all these years, said with total naturalness: "Claude! Claude!" at a particular moment when he was telling his servant off for speaking ill of his betrothed. The tone of his voice resounds still in my soul, I can see the actor.

For several months this work, frequently asked for again by audiences, afforded me the most intense pleasure, the most intense I might have said ever afforded me by a work of art, had my pleasure not for a long time past been the wildest and most devoted tender admiration.

I didn't dare pronounce Mlle Kubly's name; if someone named her in front of me, I felt a strange movement close to

1. Préville was an eighteenth-century actor reported as having replied in these terms to an author who had defended some very banal lines of dialogue on the grounds that they were "in nature." Préville answered "My a[rse] too is in nature; however, I don't display it."

my heart, I was on the verge of falling. There was like a storm in my blood.

If someone said *la* Kubly instead of Mlle Kubly, I felt an impulse of loathing and revulsion* that I was scarcely able to control.

With her poor thin little voice she sang in *Le Traité nul*, an opera by Gaveaux (feeble-minded, died mad a few years later).

That was when my love of music began, which has perhaps been my strongest and most costly passion; it survives still at the age of fifty-two and keener than ever. I don't know how many leagues I wouldn't do on foot, or how many days in prison I wouldn't submit to in order to hear *Don Giovanni* or *Il Matrimonio segreto*, and I know of nothing else I would go to such lengths for. But my misfortune is to loathe *second-rate* music (I see it as a satirical pamphlet against good music, for example Donizetti's *Furioso* yesterday evening, Rome, Valle²). The Italians are quite unlike me, they can't tolerate music once it is more than five or six years old. One of them said in front of me at Mme 120's:

"Can music that's more than a year old be beautiful?" What a parenthesis, great heaven!†

Rereading, half this manuscript needs to be erased or put in a different place.‡

I learnt by heart, and with what raptures, that continuous, jerky trickle of vinegar known as *Le Traité nul*!

A decent actor, cheerfully playing the role of the valet (I can see today that he had the genuine insouciance of a poor devil who only has sad thoughts at home and happily gives

*This passion is spelt thus: orror.

2. The reference is to a performance of Donizetti's opera *Il Furioso nell'isola di San Domingo* given at the Teatro della Valle.

†4 Jan 1836. Corrected 4 Jan 1836, beside my fire, my legs burning, dying from cold behind.

‡No, leave it as it stands. My Kubly story may be tedious for fifty-year-old Pasquiers. They however are the elite among readers. [*trans.* The Pasquier in question was president of the chamber of peers in Paris and Stendhal's example of a typical reader.]

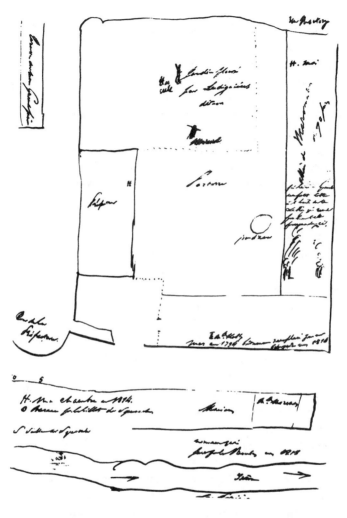

My grandfather's terrace.—Tower of the Prefecture.—Prefecture.—
Hercules.—Garden said to have been planted by Lesdiguières.—
Parterre.—Water fountain.—Rue Montorge.—H. Me.—Walk with
70-foot chestnut-trees.—I left behind in Grenoble a small oil
painting by M. Le Roy which is very good of this promenade.—
Mlle Kubly.—Wall in 1794 stupidly replaced by a handsome rail-
ing in 1814.—Houses.—Mlle Morénas.—New quay built by the
Bourbons in 1818.—Isère. La Perrière.—H. My room in 1814.—
O. Theatre ticket office.—S. Theatre.

himself up to his role), gave me my first notions of the *comic*, especially at the moment when he arranges the country dance which ends with: "Mathurine nous écoutait . . ."

A landscape the shape and size of a bill of exchange, in which there was a lot of gamboge strengthened with bistre, especially in the left foreground, that I had bought from M. Le Roy's and which I was then delightedly copying, seemed to me the same thing exactly as the playing of this comic actor who made me laugh wholeheartedly when Mlle Kubly wasn't on stage; if he addressed a word to her, I was moved, and charmed. Whence it happens perhaps that still today I often get the same sensation from a picture or a piece of music. How many times did I not experience this identity in the Brera museum in Milan (1814–21)!

So true and so forceful is it that I find it hard to express, and it will anyway be found hard to believe.

The marriage, the intimate union of these two arts was cemented once and for all when I was twelve or thirteen by four or five months of the most intense happiness and the most powerful upsurge of voluptuousness almost bordering on the painful that I have ever experienced.

At present* I can see (but I can see from Rome, at the age of fifty-two) that I had my taste for music before this *Traité nul*, so jerky, so thin and vinegary, so French, but which I still know by heart. These are my memories: 1. the sound of the bells of St-André, above all ringing for the elections one year when my cousin Abraham Mallein (my brother-in-law Alexandre's father) was president or simply an elector; 2. the noise of the pump in the Place Grenette in the evening, when the servant-girls were pumping with the big iron bar; 3. last but least of all, the sound of a flute which some shop assistant was playing on a fourth floor on the Place Grenette.

These things had already given me a pleasure which, though I didn't know it, was a musical pleasure.

*See sensations post-Kubly.

Mlle Kubly also performed in Grétry's *L'Epreuve villa-geoise*, infinitely less bad than *Le Traité nul*. A tragic situation made me shudder at *Raoul, sire de Créqui*; in short, all the bad minor operas of 1794 were raised to the sublime for me by the presence of Mlle Kubly; nothing could be vulgar or dull once she had come on.

One day I had the extreme courage to ask someone where Mlle Kubly was lodging. This was probably the bravest action of my life.

"Rue des Clercs," I was told.

Well before that, I had had the courage to ask whether she had a lover. To which the person questioned replied with some coarse commonplace: he knew nothing of her way of life.

On my days of high courage I went down the Rue des Clercs; my heart was pounding; I would have fallen down perhaps, had I met her; I was greatly relieved when I got to the end of the Rue des Clercs and was sure of not meeting her.

One morning, walking alone at the far end of the avenue of tall chestnut-trees in the Jardin de Ville, and with my mind on her as ever, I caught sight of her at the other end of the garden against the wall of the Intendance and coming towards the terrace.

I almost fell down and in the end, *I took flight*, as if the devil were bearing me off, along the line of railings F; she, I believe, was at K', and I was lucky enough not to be spotted by her. Bear in mind she had no idea at all who I was. This is one of the most notable traits of my character, such I have always been (even the day before yesterday). The happiness of seeing her from close to, five or six paces away, was too great, it was scorching me, and I fled from that burning sensation, which was a very real pain.

This singularity might lead me to think that, where love is concerned, I have Cabanis's melancholic temperament.

Indeed, for me love has always been the most important thing, or rather the only thing. I have feared nothing except to see the woman I love gazing intimately at a rival. I feel very little anger against that rival: he is going about his business, was my thought, but my grief is boundless, and poignant; to the extent where I feel the need to abandon myself on a stone seat at the door to her house. I admire everything about the preferred rival (the squadron commander Gibory and Mme Martin, Palazzo Anguissola, Milan). No other disappointment can produce a thousandth part of this effect on me.

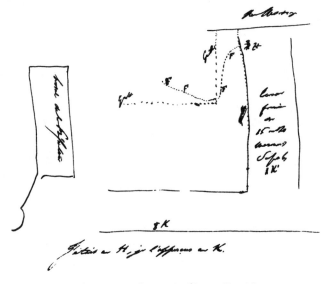

Hôtel de la Préfecture.—Railings.—Railings.—Rue Montorge.—
Terrace formed of fifteen or twenty superb chestnut-trees.—I was
at H, I caught sight of her at K.

With the Emperor I was attentive, zealous, with no thought of my *cravate*,[3] quite unlike all the others. (Example: at seven in the evening, at [*a blank*], in Lausitz, 1813 campaign, the day after the death of the Duc de Frioul.)

I am neither timid nor melancholy when I'm writing and laying myself open to the risk of a hostile reception; I feel full of courage and of pride when I write a sentence that would

3. The insignia of the Légion d'Honneur.

be rejected by one of those two giants (of 1835), Messrs de Chateaubriand or Villemain.[4]

In 1880, no doubt some astute, moderate charlatan will be in vogue, as these gentlemen are today. But if this is read I shall be thought envious, that distresses me; that contemptible bourgeois vice is, I fancy, wholly foreign to my nature.

In reality, I am mortally jealous only of the men who are paying court to a woman I love; what's more, I am even jealous of those who paid court to her ten years before me. For example, Babet's first lover (at Vienna, in 1809).

"You received him in your bedroom!"

"Everywhere was a bedroom for us, we were alone in the château, and he had the keys."

I can still feel the hurt these words caused me, yet that was in 1809, twenty-seven years ago; I can still see pretty Babet's perfect naivety; she was looking at me.

I have no doubt had great pleasure from writing this past hour, and from trying to describe my feelings of the time *exactly as they were*, but who on earth will be brave enough to go deeply into it, to read this excessive heap of *I*s and *me*s? I find it *stinks* myself. That is the defect of this kind of writing, whose insipidity, moreover, I can't relieve by any seasoning of charlatanism.

Dare I add: *like the* Confessions *of Rousseau*? No, despite the huge absurdity of the objection, I am again going to be thought envious or rather seeking to establish a comparison so absurd as to be frightening with the masterpiece of that great writer.

I protest again and once and for all my sovereign and sincere contempt for M. Pariset, M. de Salvandy, M. St-Marc Girardin and the other windbags, the salaried and pedantic jesuits of the *Journal des Débats*, but I don't for that reason believe I come any closer to the great writers. I don't believe

4. Abel François Villemain (1790–1870), liberal politician and professor of literature at the Sorbonne, sympathetic to Romanticism.

myself to have any other genius, any other guarantee of my worth, beyond 1. to depict a *likeness* of the nature which at certain moments appears to me with such clarity; 2. I am confident of my perfect good faith, of my reverence for what is true; 3. and of the pleasure I take in writing, a pleasure which became a mania in 1817 (in Milan, at M. Peronti's, Corsia del Giardino*).

*Perhaps the whole [of sheet] 370 is in the wrong place, the insipidity of my love for Kubly needs to be relieved by some more substantial idea.
  13 pages in an hour and a half. Damnably cold, 3 January 1836.

CHAPTER 25

But to return to Mlle Kubly. How far away I was from envy, or from the thought of fearing the *imputation of envy*, or from thinking about other people in any way at all in those days! Life was beginning for me.

There was only one human being in the world: Mlle Kubly; only one event: would she be performing that evening, or the day after?

What disappointment when she wasn't performing, and they put on some tragedy or other!

What a rapture of pure, tender, triumphant joy when I read her name on the playbill! I can see that playbill still, its shape, the paper, the characters.

I went to read that cherished name in turn at the three or four places where the bills were put up: on the door of the Jacobins, on the archway into the gardens, on the corner* against my grandfather's house. I didn't only read her name, I treated myself to the pleasure of rereading the whole bill. The slightly worn characters of the bad printer who had produced the bill became dear and sacred to me, and through long years, I preferred them to much handsomer characters.

I even recall this: when I arrived in Paris, in November 1799, the beauty of the characters shocked me, they were no longer those in which the name of Kubly had been printed.

---

*Engle: the orthography of passion, depicting the sound and nothing more. [*trans.* *Engle* rather than the correct *angle*, which would in fact be pronounced by most francophones indistinguishably.]

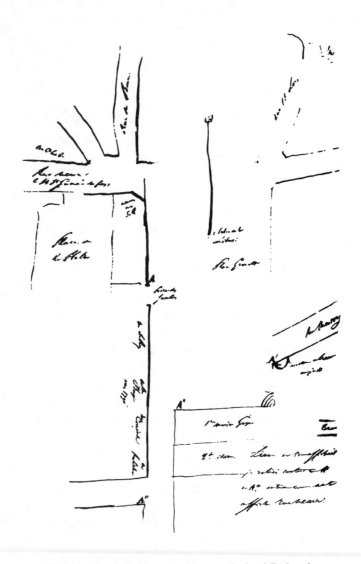

Rue de Bonne.—M. Chabert.—Rue Neuve, the local f[aubour]g
St-Germain.—Love-making with S[ophie] G[alice].—Place de la
Halle.—Mountain.—Tree of Liberty.—Place Grenette.—Jacobins
doorway.—M. Le Roy.—Mlle Bourg[eois] around 1796.—M.
Corréard.—M. Rubichon.—Rue Montorge.—Archway leading to
the gardens.—First Gagnon house.—Second Gagnon house.—
Terrace.—Place where playbills were posted. I read them again and
again above all at A' and A", as well as another in the Rue Neuve.

She left, I can't tell whenabouts that was. For a long time I couldn't go to the theatre any more. I got permission to learn music, not without difficulty: my father's religion was shocked by so profane an art, and my grandfather hadn't the least liking for this art.

I took a violin teacher named Mention, the most agreeable of men, the old French gaiety mixed in with bravery and love. He was very badly off, but he had the heart of an artist; one day, when I was playing worse than usual, he closed his book, saying:

"I am giving no more lessons."

I went to a clarinet teacher, called Hoffmann (Rue de Bonne), a worthy German; I played a little less badly. I don't know why but I left that teacher to move on to M. Holleville, Rue Saint-Louis opposite Mme Barthélemy, our shoemaker's wife. A very fair violinist, he was deaf, but could tell the slightest wrong note. There I met with M. Félix Faure (today a peer of France, first president, judge in August 1835). I don't know why, but I left Holleville.

Finally I went to have lessons in vocal music, unbenownst to my relations, at six o'clock in the morning, Place Saint-Louis, from a very good singer.

But there was nothing to be done: I was the first to be appalled by the sounds I produced. I bought Italian songs, one among others that I read as *Amore*, or something of the sort, *nell cimento*; I took this to mean: "in the cement," "in the mortar."[1] I adored these Italian songs, of which I understood not a word. I had started too late. If anything had been capable of turning me against music, it would have been the execrable sounds one has to produce in order to learn it. The *piano* alone might have been able to get round that difficulty for me, but I had been born into an essentially unmusical family.

When subsequently I wrote about music, the chief objection

1. This is an Italian phrase in fact meaning "the ordeal of love."

raised by my friends was this ignorance. But I have to say without any affectation that at the same time I was aware in the piece being performed of nuances they hadn't noticed. The same goes for facial nuances in copies of the same painting. I can see these things as clearly *as through a crystal*. But good Lord, I shall be thought a fool!

When I returned to life after several months of the absence of Mlle Kubly, I found I was a different man.

I no longer hated Séraphie, I had forgotten her; as for my father, I desired only one thing: not to find myself in his company. I remarked, with remorse, that I didn't have a *single drop* of tenderness or affection for him.

"I'm a monster then," I said to myself. And for long years I found no answer to this objection. In the family they talked incessantly and *ad nauseam* about being fond of one's relations. These good people gave the name of *fondness* to that perpetual vexation with which they had been honouring me for the past five or six years. I began to half-see that they were bored to death and that being too proud to take up again with the society they had unwisely left at the time of a cruel loss, I was their one recourse against tedium.

But nothing could move me any more after what I had just been feeling. I studied Latin and drawing intently and won a first prize in one or other of these subjects, and a second. I translated with pleasure Tacitus' *Life of Agricola*, it was almost the first time Latin had given me pleasure. This pleasure was marred, *amaregiato* [*sic*],[2] by the blows I received from big Odru, a large and ignorant peasant from Lumbin, who was in our class and understood nothing about anything. I fought stoutly with Giroud who had a red coat. I was still a child for a good half of my life.

All the same the moral tempest to which I had been exposed for several months had matured me, I began seriously to tell myself:

2. *Amareggiato* in Italian means "poisoned."

"I must make up my mind and get myself out of this mudhole."

I had only one possible means: mathematics. But they were explained to me so stupidly that I made no progress; it's true that my fellow pupils made even less, if that's possible. The great M. Dupuy explained propositions to us like a succession of recipes for making vinegar.

Bezout, however, was my one recourse for getting away from Grenoble. But Bezout was so stupid! He had a brain like that of M. Dupuy, our bombastic teacher.

My grandfather knew a small-minded bourgeois by the name of Chabert, who *gave home tuition in mathematics*. That was the local expression and it suited the man perfectly. With some difficulty I was allowed to go to this home of M. Chabert's; they were afraid of giving offence to M. Dupuy and what was more had to pay 12 francs a month, I fancy.

I answered that most of the pupils in the mathematics class at the Ecole Centrale went to M. Chabert's, and that if I didn't go too I would remain bottom at the Ecole Centrale. So I went to M. Chabert's. M. Chabert was a bourgeois, quite neatly turned out, but who always looked dressed up and in a panic about spoiling his coat or his waistcoat or his pretty *goose-shit* cashmere breeches; he also had quite a pretty bourgeois face. He lodged in the Rue Neuve, near the Rue St-Jacques and almost opposite Bourbon, the iron m[erchan]t, whose name impressed me, for it was only with signs of the most profound respect and genuine devotion that my bourgeois relations would utter that name. It was as if the survival of France had been attached to it.

But at M. Chabert's I again met with that lack of favour which had weighed on me at the Ecole Centrale and meant that I was never called to the blackboard. In a small room and in the midst of seven or eight pupils gathered around an oil-cloth blackboard, nothing could be more abject than to ask to go up to the blackboard, i.e. to go and explain for the fifth or sixth time a proposition that four or five pupils had already explained. Yet that is what I was sometimes forced to do at M. Chabert's, otherwise I would never have *demonstrated* anything. M. Chabert thought me a *minus habens*[3] and remained of that abominable opinion. Nothing could have been more comical subsequently than hearing him speak of my successes in mathematics.

But, in these early stages, it was a strange lack of concern, or rather intelligence, on the part of my relations not to have asked whether I was up to *demonstrating* and how many times a week I went up to the blackboard. They never descended to such details. M. Chabert, who professed a deep respect for M. Dupuy, hardly ever called anyone to the blackboard except those who went up to it at the Ecole Centrale. There was a certain M. de Renneville whom M. Dupuy called to the blackboard as being a nobleman and a cousin of the Monvals, he was a sort of imbecile, almost mute and with staring eyes; I was shocked to overflowing when I found M. Dupuy and M. Chabert preferring him to me.

I forgive M. Chabert: I must have been the most presumptuous and most contemptuous of little boys. My grandfather and my family had proclaimed me to be a wonder: hadn't they been bestowing all their care on me for the past five years?

M. Chabert was in point of fact less of an ignoramus than M. Dupuy. With him I discovered Euler and his problems concerning the number of eggs a peasant woman was carrying to market when a miscreant steals one fifth of them, then she drops half the remainder, etc., etc.

This opened my mind; I could half-see what it was to make use of the instrument known as algebra. I'm hanged if anyone had ever told me; M. Dupuy was always pontificating on the subject, but never said the simple thing: it is a *division of labour* which produces miracles like all divisions

3. Literally, someone who has less, i.e. a dunce.

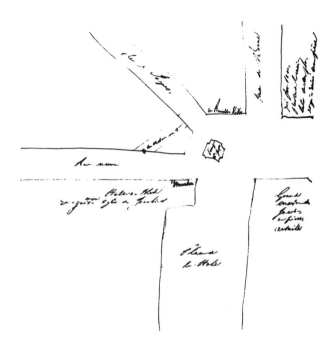

Rue Saint-Jacques.—M. Renauldon the cuckold.—Rue de Bonne.—
Here ten years later stood the house built to my plans and which
ruined my father.—M. Chabert on the third floor.—Saint-Jacques
pump.—Rue Neuve.—Bourbon.—Corn-market which I saw when
still the Jacobin church.—Place de la Halle.—Big Jacobin building
in natural stone.

of labour and enables the mind to concentrate all its powers
on a single aspect of its objects, on a single one of their
properties.

How different for us if M. Dupuy had told us: "This cheese
is soft or it's hard; it's white, it's blue; it's old, it's young;
it's mine, it's yours; it's light or it's heavy! Out of all these
properties let us consider absolutely none but the weight.
Whatever the weight may be, let's call it A. Now, with absolutely no further thought for the cheese, let's apply to A
everything we know about quantities."

No one told us this very simple thing in that provincial

backwater; since that time, the Ecole Polytechnique and the ideas of Lagrange will have flowed out into the provinces.

The masterpiece of the education of those days was a small scoundrel dressed in green, mild-mannered, hypocritical, gentle, who was scarcely three feet tall and learnt the propositions that were *demonstrated* by heart, without worrying in the least whether he understood them. The name of this favourite of M. Chabert no less than of M. Dupuy was, if I'm not mistaken, Paul-Emile Teisseire. The examiner for the Ecole Polytechnique, that imbecile of a Louis Monge, brother of the great geometer, who committed the famous howler (at the beginning of his *Statique*), didn't notice that Paul-Emile's sole virtue consisted of an astonishing memory.

He arrived at the Ecole; his total hypocrisy, his memory and his pretty girl's face didn't have the same success there as in Grenoble; he emerged as an officer all right but was soon touched by grace and became a priest. Unfortunately, he died of consumption; I should have followed his fortunes with pleasure. I had left Grenoble with an inordinate desire to be able one day to clout him to my heart's content.

I fancy I had already given him something on account at M. Chabert's, where he rightly came ahead of me thanks to his imperturbable memory.

As for him, nothing ever made him angry and he passed with perfect *sang-froid* beneath the volleys of "little hypocrite" which reached him from every quarter and were renewed one day when we saw him crowned with roses and playing the role of an angel in a procession.

He was almost the only character I took any notice of at the Ecole Centrale. He made a fine contrast with the gloomy Benoît, whom I met in M. Dubois-Fontanelle's literature class and who had it that the sublime science consisted in the Socratic love that Doctor Clapier, that madman, had taught him.

It's ten years perhaps since I thought about M. Chabert; it comes back to me bit by bit that he was in fact much less limited than M. Dupuy, though he spoke with even more of a drawl and was even more shabby and bourgeois in appearance.

He thought highly of Clairaut and it was something immense to put us in contact with that man of genius and take us away a little from the worthless Bezout. He had Bossut, the *abbé* Marie, and now and again made us study a theorem in these authors. He even had in manuscript some small things by Lagrange, of a kind suitable for our limited reach.

I fancy we worked with a pen on a paper exercise-book and at an oilcloth blackboard.

My unpopularity extended to everything; perhaps it stemmed from some gaffe by my relations who had forgotten to send a Christmas turkey to M. Chabert or to his sisters,

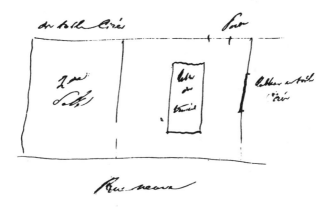

Door.—Second classroom.—Work-table.—Oilcloth blackboard.—
Rue Neuve.

for he had some and very pretty ones too and, but for my timidity, I would certainly have paid court to them. They had much consideration for the grandson of M. Gagnon, and what was more came to mass on Sundays in our house.

We used to go out surveying with a graphometer and surveyor's table; one day we surveyed a field beside the road to Les Boiteuses. This was the field BCDE. M. Chabert got all the others to draw the lines on the board; finally, my turn came, but last or one from last, before a mere child. I was humiliated and angry; I pressed too hard on the pen.

"But it was a line I told you to draw," said M. Chabert in his drawling tones, "what you've made is a bar."

He was right. I believe that this state of marked disfavour from Messrs Dupuy and Chabert and total indifference from

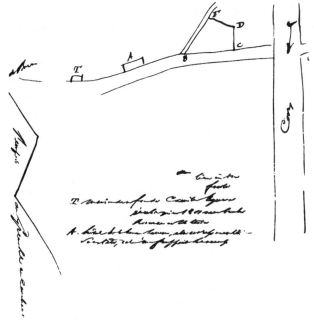

Porte de Bonne.—Ramparts of Grenoble at sunset.—Cours.—Moulin de Canel.—Place where people are shot.

    T. House of that madman, Camille Teisseire, the jacobin, who in 1811, wanted to burn Rousseau and Voltaire.—A. Hôtel de la Bonne Femme; she is shown without a head; that impressed me greatly.

M. Jay in his drawing lessons stopped me from becoming a fool. I had wonderful tendencies in that direction; my relations, who in their morose bigotry had declaimed ceaselessly against public education, had convinced themselves without much difficulty that in five years of all too assiduous attentions, they had produced a masterpiece and that masterpiece was me.

I said to myself one day, though truth to tell this was before the Ecole Centrale: "Might I not be the son of some great prince, and everything I hear about the Revolution, and the little I see of it, a fable intended to complete my education, like in *Emile*?"

For my grandfather, a man whose conversation was agreeable in spite of his pious resolutions, had cited *Emile* in front of me, had spoken about the *Confession de foi du vicaire savoyard*, etc., etc., etc. I had stolen this book in Claix, but couldn't understand it, not even the absurdities of the opening page, and had given it up after a quarter of an hour. To do justice to my father's tastes: he was keen on Rousseau and sometimes talked about him, for which, and for his rashness in front of a child, he was roundly reprimanded by my aunt Séraphie.

CHAPTER 26

I had and still have the most aristocratic tastes. I would do anything to make the people happy, but I would rather, I believe, spend fifteen days of each month in prison than live with the inhabitants of shops.

Around this time, I became friendly, I don't know how, with François Bigillion (who later killed himself, I believe, out of boredom with his wife).

He was a simple, natural, sincere man, who never tried to make you think, by some ambitious reply, that he knew the world, women, etc. That was our great ambition and our principal form of conceit at the college.* Every one of those young brats wanted to convince the others that he had possessed women and knew the world. Nothing of that sort with the good Bigillion. We went on long walks together, especially to the Rabot tower and the Bastille. The magnificent view to be enjoyed from there, especially towards Eybens, behind which rise the tallest of the Alps, lifted our souls. Rabot and the Bastille are the first an old tower, the second a small house, situated at two quite different altitudes, on the mountain enclosed within the walls of the town, quite absurd in 1795, now in 1836 being made good.

On these walks we shared with one another very frankly our thoughts on what seemed to us that terrible, gloomy and delightful forest we were on the point of entering. Of course, I mean: on society and the world.

*Father Morlon, Bigillion, Shakespeare, M. Dolle from the Porte de Fr[ance].

Bigillion had great advantages over me:

1. He had lived in freedom since childhood, the son of a father who was not overfond of him and knew how to find amusement other than by turning his son into a toy doll.

2. This father, a country bourgeois, very comfortably off, lived in St-Ismier, a village one post-stage outside Grenoble to the east, in a very pleasant position in the valley of the Isère. This worthy countryman, a lover of wine, good food and fresh peasant girls, had rented a small apartment in Grenoble for his two sons, who were getting their education there. The elder was called Bigillion, following the custom in our province, the younger Rémy, a humorist, an odd man, a true Dauphinois, but generous, a little jealous even then of the friendship Bigillion and I had for one another.

Based on the most complete sincerity, this friendship was very close by the end of a fortnight. He had had an uncle who was a learned monk, very unmonkish I fancy, the good Father Morlon, a Benedictine perhaps who, during my childhood, had been kind enough, out of friendship for my grandfather, to confess me on one or two occasions. I had been most surprised by his gentle and polite tone, very different from the harsh pedantry of the ill-bred sourpusses my father most often handed me over to, such as M. *l'abbé* Rambault.

The good Father Morlon had a great influence on my mind; he owned Letourneur's translation of Shakespeare and his nephew Bigillion borrowed all the volumes of this work for me one after the other, big for a child, eighteen or twenty volumes.

Reading it was like being born again. First of all it had the immense advantage of not having been extolled and preached at me by my relations like Racine. They needed only to praise something as being *pleasurable* for me to feel a revulsion for it.

So that nothing should be lacking in Shakespeare's hold over my heart, I even believe my father spoke ill of him.

I mistrusted my family over everything, but when it came

to the arts, their praises sufficed to give me a mortal distaste for the most beautiful things. My heart had far outrun my brain and I sensed that they were praising them as KINGS today praise religion, i.e. *in bad faith*. I sensed very confusedly but very intensely, and with an ardour *I no longer possess*, that any moral objective, i.e. of self-interest in the artist, spells death to a work of art. I read Shakespeare continuously from 1796 to 1799. Racine, endlessly extolled by my relations, struck me as a worthless hypocrite. My grandfather had recounted to me the anecdote of how he had died when Louis XIV lost his regard for him. In any case verse annoyed me because it dragged the sentences out and made them lose their clarity. I loathed *steed* instead of horse. I called that hypocrisy.

How, living in solitude within the bosom of a family that spoke very correctly, could I have sensed whether language was more or less exalted? Where could I have picked up a language other than elegant?

Corneille displeased me less. The authors I then revelled in were Cervantes, *Don Quijote*, and Ariosto in translation. Immediately afterwards came Rousseau, who had the double defect, DRAWBACK, of extolling the pr[iests] and religion and of being extolled by my father. I read with delight La Fontaine's *Fables* and *Félicia*. But they were not *literary pleasures*. They're the kind of books you read with only one hand, as Mme . . . used to say.[1]

When in 1824, at the moment of falling in love with Clémentine, I strove not to let my soul be absorbed in the contemplation of her attractions (I recall a great battle one evening, at Mme Dubignon's concert I was next to the celebrated General Foy; Clémentine, as an ultra, would not enter that house), when, as I say, I wrote *Racine et Shakespeare*, I was accused of play-acting and of denying my earliest feelings

---

1. A reference to a remark cited by Rousseau in his *Confessions*, such books being those which cause their readers to masturbate as they read (an odd thought where La Fontaine is concerned).

as a child, you can see how true it was, what I was careful not to say (as being unbelievable), was that my first love had been for Shakespeare, and among others for *Hamlet* and *Romeo and Juliet*.

The Bigillions lived in the Rue Chenoise (I'm not certain of the name), the street which came out between the archway of Notre-Dame and a small stream, over which the Augustinian convent had been built. There there was a famous second-hand bookseller I often visited. Beyond was the Oratory where my father had been imprisoned for a few days along with

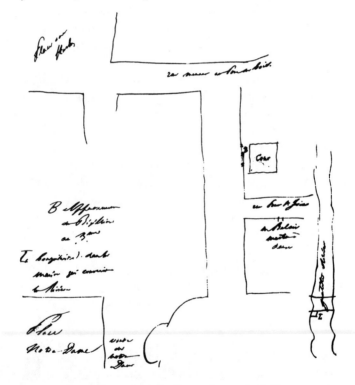

Place aux Herbes.—Street leading to the wooden bridge.—
Courtyard.—Rue Pont-St-Jaime.—M. Belair, dancing teacher.—
Place Notre-Dame.—Archway of Notre-Dame.—Small stream.
    B. Bigillion's third-floor apartment.—L. Bookseller in the
house spanning the stream.

M. Colomb, the father of Romain Colomb my oldest friend (in 1836). Here is that street whose name has more or less been erased, though not its appearance.

In that apartment, situated on the third floor, at B, there lived with the Bigillions their sister, Mlle Victorine Bigillion, very unaffected, very pretty, but no Greek-style beauty; on the contrary, her face was decidedly Allobrogian.[2] I fancy that these days they call this the Gaelic race (see Dr Edwards and M. Adrien de Jussieu; it's the latter at least who made me believe in this classification).

Mlle Victorine was clever and very thoughtful; she was freshness personified. Her face harmonized perfectly with the casement windows of the apartment she occupied along with her two brothers, gloomy, although south-facing and on the third floor, but the house opposite was enormous. This perfect harmony struck me, or rather I was conscious of its effect but couldn't at all explain it.

There I was often present at the two brothers' and their sister's supper. A servant-girl from their own region, as unaffected as themselves, prepared it for them; they ate brown bread, which to me seemed incomprehensible who had never eaten anything except white bread.

Therein lay my entire advantage in respect of them; they saw me as coming from a superior class: the son of M. Gagnon, member of the committee of the Ecole Centrale, was a *nobleman*, and they bourgeois, verging on peasant. It wasn't that they felt regret or a foolish admiration; for example they preferred brown bread to white bread and were perfectly free to get their flour sifted so as to have white bread.

We lived in complete innocence, around the walnut table draped in a cloth of grey holland: Bigillion, the elder brother, fourteen or fifteen years old; Rémy, twelve; Mlle Victorine, thirteen; me, thirteen; the servant-girl seventeen.

It was a very youthful society, as you can see, and no

2. The Allobrogi were the native inhabitants of the Dauphiné and Savoie at the time of the Roman conquest of Gaul.

grandparent to get in our way. When M. Bigillion senior came to town for a day or two, we didn't dare wish him absent, but he got in our way.

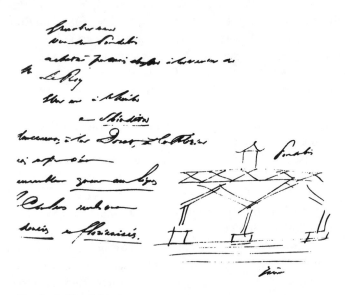

Wooden bridge. Isère.

I left behind in Grenoble a view of the wooden bridge bought by me at M. Le Roy's sale. It's in oils and *sbiadita*, oversweet, *à la* Dorat, *à la* Florian, but all said and done it's a good likeness where the lines are concerned; only the colours have been *sweetened* and Florianized.

We may all have been one year older, but that is all, my two last years, 1799 and 1798, were entirely taken up with mathematics and Paris at the end of them; so it was 1797 or rather 1796; and in 1796 I was thirteen.

We lived at that time like young rabbits playing in a wood and nibbling on the wild thyme. Mlle Victorine was the housekeeper; she kept bunches of dried grapes in a vine-leaf done up with thread, which she used to give me, and which I liked almost as much as her charming person. Sometimes I would ask her for a second bunch, and often she would refuse me, saying: "We've only got eight left and we have to get through the week."

The provisions came once or twice a week, from St-Ismier. This is the custom in Grenoble. Every bourgeois's passion is for his *domaine*, and he prefers a lettuce that has come from his *domaine* in Montbonnot, St-Ismier, Corenc, Voreppe, St-Vincent or Claix, Echirolles, Eybens, Domène, etc., etc., and

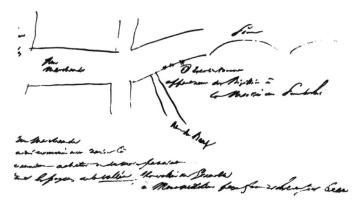

Place aux Herbes.—Rue Marchande.—Bridge.—Winding staircase. —Bigillions' apartment on the way up to the wooden bridge. Rue du Boeuf.

Rue Marchande, so called with good reason; here the peasants from the *valley* (the valley between Grenoble and Montmélian, a very rich and very beautiful region) came to buy, or at least passed by.

which has cost him four *sous*, to the same lettuce bought for two *sous* in the Place aux Herbes. This bourgeois had 10,000fr invested at 5 per cent with the Périers (father and cousin of Casimir, a minister in 1832); he invests them in a *domaine* which brings him in two or two and a half and he is overjoyed. His return on it, I imagine, is in vanity and the pleasure of saying with a self-important air: "I have to go to Montbonnot," or "I've come from Montbonnot."

I didn't feel love for Victorine; my heart was still badly bruised from the departure of Mlle Kubly, and my friendship with Bigillion was so close that I fancy that, in some abbreviated version, for fear of being laughed at, I had risked confiding my foolishness to him.

He wasn't in the least put off by this; he was the best and simplest of creatures, precious qualities which went with the shrewdest good sense, a good sense characteristic of that family and strengthened in his case by the conversation of Rémy, his brother and close friend, who was hardly sensitive but whose good sense was altogether more inexorable. Rémy often went whole afternoons without opening his lips.

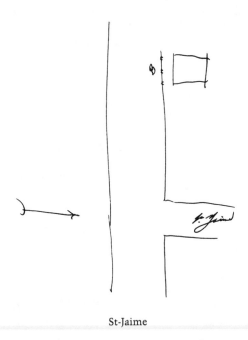

St-Jaime

The happiest moments of my life were spent on that third floor. Shortly afterwards, the Bigillions left that house to go and live on the rise leading up to the Pont de Bois; or rather quite the reverse, from the Pont de Bois they came into the Rue Chenoise, I fancy, certainly the one into which the Rue Pont-St-Jaime leads.

I'm certain of the three casement windows, at B, and of their position *vis-à-vis* the Rue Pont-St-Jaime.

I'm making more discoveries than ever as I write this (at Rome, in January 1836).

I have three-quarters forgotten all these things which I haven't thought about six times a year in the past twenty years.

I was very timid with Victorine whose developing bosoms I admired, but I confided everything to her; for example, my persecution by Séraphie from which I had only just escaped, and I remember that she refused to believe me, which grieved me mortally. She gave me to understand that I had a bad character.

CHAPTER 27

The stern Rémy wouldn't have taken at all kindly to my paying court to his sister. Bigillion gave me to understand as much and this was the one point on which we weren't completely open with one another. Often, towards nightfall, after our walk, as I was making as if to go upstairs to Victorine, I received a hurried goodbye which much frustrated me. I had need of friendship and to talk openly, my heart embittered by all the unkindness of which rightly or wrongly I firmly believed I had been the object.

I shall admit, however, that I much preferred having these very simple conversations with Victorine than with her brothers. Today I can see what my feeling was then; I found it incredible to be seeing that terrifying creature, a woman, from so close to; a woman moreover with magnificent hair, an arm exquisitely shaped, if on the thin side, and lastly a charming bosom often partly exposed because of the excessive heat. It's true that sitting against the walnut-wood table, two feet away from Mlle Bigillion, with the corner of the table between us, I spoke to the brothers only so as to be good. But for all that I didn't at all wish to be in love; I had been *scotato* (burnt, scalded), as they say in Italian: I had just had the experience of love as something serious and terrible. I didn't say so to myself, but I was well aware that all in all my love for Mlle Kubly had probably caused me more pains than pleasures.

While I felt like this towards Victorine, so innocent in

word and even in thought, I forgot my hatreds and especially the belief that people hated me.

I fancy that after some time Rémy's brotherly jealousy was stilled; or else he went to spend a few months in St-Ismier. He could see perhaps that in reality I wasn't in love, or had some love affair of his own: we were all of us thirteen- or fourteen-year-old politicians. But even at that age, the Dauphinois is very artful; we have neither the insouciance nor the [*a blank*] of the Paris *gamin*, and our passions take hold of us early on. Passions for mere trifles, yet the truth is we desire passionately. In fact, I used to go a good five times a week after dark or the *saint* (the 9 o'clock bell from St-André's), to spend the evening at Mlle Bigillion's.

Though I never mentioned the friendship that reigned among us, I was rash enough to name this family one day when having supper with my relations; I was severely punished for my thoughtlessness. I saw scorn poured on Victorine's family and brothers, with the most expressive pantomime.

"Isn't there a daughter? She'll be some young country miss."

I recall only dimly the terms of terrible contempt and the expression of cold disdain that accompanied them. I have a memory only of the burning impression which that contempt had on me.

It must have been absolutely the same air of cold and mocking contempt that M. le Baron des Adrets no doubt used when speaking of my mother or my aunt.

In spite of being only doctors and lawyers, my family believed itself to be on the fringes of the nobility, my father even claiming to be nothing less than a gentleman come down in the world. All the contempt that was expressed that evening, right the way through supper, was based on my friends' father M. Bigillion's rank of rural bourgeois, and on the fact that his younger brother, a very shrewd man, was governor of the departmental prison in the Place St-André, a sort of bourgeois jailer.

The family had received St Bruno at the Grande-Chartreuse

in [*a blank*].¹ That was proven beyond all doubt; it was far more respectable than the family of B[eyl]e, a judge in the village of Sassenage under the feudal lords of the Middle Ages. But the worthy Bigillion senior, a man of pleasure, very comfortably off in his village, never dined with M. de Marcieu, or Mme de Sassenage, and was the first to acknowledge my grandfather the moment he saw him in the distance and what was more spoke of M. Gagnon with the greatest consideration.

This outburst of haughtiness amused a family which was usually dying of boredom and lasted all through supper; I had lost my appetite hearing my friends treated in this way. I was asked what the matter was. I replied that I had *had tea* very late. A lie is the sole and simple expedient of the weak. I was dying of anger with myself: what, I'd been silly enough to talk to my relations about what concerned me?

Their contempt I found deeply disturbing, I have this minute seen the reason why: it was Victorine. Was it not then with that terrible creature, so greatly feared but so exclusively adored, a well-brought-up and pretty woman, that I had had the happiness of holding an almost intimate conversation every evening?

After four or five days of cruel torment, Victorine won the day; I declared her to be more agreeable and more worldly than my sad, *wizened* (that was my word), unsociable family, which never gave supper parties, never entered a drawing-room where ten people were gathered, whereas Mlle Bigillion often attended dinner-parties for twenty-five guests at M. Faure's in St-Ismier or at her late mother's parents' house in Chapareillan. She was even more aristocratic for having received St Bruno around 1080.*

Many years later, I understood the mechanism of what

1. St Bruno was the eleventh-century saint who founded the Carthusian order, and the great monastery of the Grande-Chartreuse, which is near Grenoble.

*Date: St Bruno, died in 1101 in Calabria.

289

then occurred in my heart, and, for want of a better word, I called it *crystallization* (a word that much shocked that great man of letters, Minister of the Interior in 1833, M. le Comte d'Argout: an entertaining scene recounted by Clara Gazul).[2]

This absolution from their contempt took five or six days, during which time I thought of nothing else. This insult very gloriously overcome introduced a *new fact* between Mlle Kubly and my present state. Although in my innocence I never suspected it, it was a large point gained: between our grief and ourselves we need to introduce new facts, even if it be only the breaking of an arm.*

I had just bought Bezout in a good edition, and had it carefully bound (perhaps it still exists in Grenoble at M. Alexandre Mallein's, the chief tax-collector); in it I drew a wreath of foliage, with in the centre a capital V. I gazed at this monument every day.

After Séraphie's death, out of my need to love, I might have been reconciled with my family, but this display of

2. "Crystallization" is the concept used by Stendhal in his treatise *On Love* to explain how one person comes to love another. "Clara Gazul" is a pseudonym used here for Stendhal's friend, the novelist Prosper Mérimée, who served in the Comte d'Argout's *cabinet*.

*Put this here, cut off too quickly, put it in its right place, in 1806 or 10. On one of my return visits to Grenoble, around 1806, a well-informed person told me that Mlle Victorine was in love. I felt very envious of this person. I assumed it was Félix Faure. Later on, someone else told me: "When she spoke to me about the person she has loved for such a long time, Mlle Victorine said to me: 'He's not handsome, but he will never be reproached with being ugly ... He was the wittiest and most amiable of the young men of my generation.' In a word," this someone added, "it's you." J[anuar]y 1836. (Have read De Brosses.)

haughtiness set an infinite distance between them and me; I might have forgiven the imputation of some crime to the Bigillion family, but to despise them! And my grandfather had been the one to express it most gracefully, and consequently most effectively!

I took good care not to mention to my relations other friends I made at this time: Messrs Gall, La Bayette [*a blank*].

Gall was the son of a widow who loved only him and respected him out of probity as the master of their fortune, the father must have been some old officer. This for me very strange spectacle both attracted and moved me. "If only my poor mother had lived!" I said to myself. "If only at least my relations had been of Mme Gall's sort: how I would have loved them!" Mme Gall had great respect for me as the grandson of M. Gagnon, the benefactor of the poor, whom he tended for nothing and even gave two pounds of beef to for making into stock. My father wasn't known.

Gall was pale, thin, puny, pock-marked, and in character moreover very cold, very restrained, very cautious. He sensed he was the absolute master of his small fortune and that he mustn't squander it. He was simple, honest and in no way boastful nor a liar. I fancy he left Grenoble and the Ecole Centrale ahead of me to go to Toulon and join the navy.

It was for the navy also that the amiable La Bayette was destined, the nephew or relation of Admiral (i.e. Vice-Admiral or Rear-Admiral) Morard de Galle.

He was as amiable and high-minded as Gall was estimable. I can still remember the delightful afternoons we spent, chatting together at the window of his small room. It was on the third floor of a house overlooking the new Place du Département. There I shared his *tea*: apples and brown bread. I was starved of any sincere, unhypocritical conversation. To these two virtues, common to all my friends, La Bayette added a great nobility of sentiment and manners and a tenderness of soul that was insusceptible of any profound passion like Bigillion's, but expressed itself with a greater elegance.

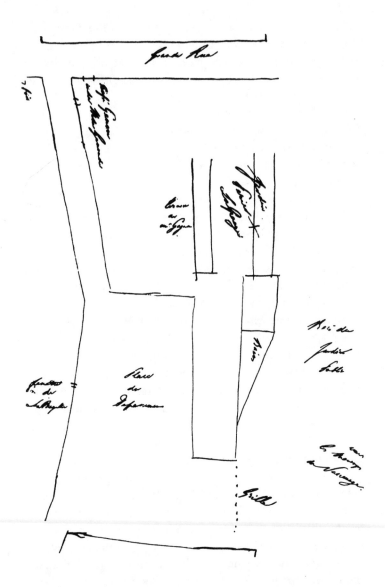

Grande-Rue.—Seven times.—Café Genou, *inde* M. de Genoude.—
M. Gagnon's terrace.—Périer-Lagrange garden.—La Bayette's win-
dow.—Place du Département.—Baths.—Wood in the Jardin de
Ville.—View of the mountains at Sassenage.—Railings.

I fancy he gave me sound advice at the time of my love for Mlle Kubly, which I risked talking to him about, so genuine and good-hearted was he. We pooled all our scant experience of women, or rather the scant knowledge we had derived from the novels we had read. We must have been comic to listen to.

Soon after my aunt Séraphie's departure, I had read and adored the *Mémoires secrets* of Duclos that my grandfather had been reading.[3]

It was, I fancy, in the mathematics class that I made the acquaintance of Gall and La Bayette; it was there certainly that I became friends with Louis de Barral (now my oldest and best friend, the person in the world who loves me the most, there is also, I fancy, no sacrifice I wouldn't make for him).

At that time he was very small, very thin, very puny, he was said to carry to excess a certain bad habit that we all had, and the fact is he looked like it. But his appearance was singularly enhanced by the superb uniform of a lieutenant of engineers; this was known as being an assistant engineer; it would have been a good way of attaching wealthy families to the Revolution or at least tempering their hatred.

Anglès too, later Comte Anglès and prefect of police, enriched by the Bourbons, was an assistant engineer, as well as an essentially inferior individual adorned with red hair whose name was Giroud, not the same as the Giroud with the red coat whom I quite often fought with. I used to tease the Giroud decorated with the gold epaulette unmercifully who was much more *grown-up* than me, i.e. he was a man of eighteen, whereas I was still a baby of thirteen or fourteen. At college this difference of two or three years is immense; it is roughly that between a nobleman and a commoner in Piedmont.

What quite won me over about Barral the first time we

3. The full title of this work, published in 1790, was *Mémoires secrets sur le règne de Louis XIV, la régence et le règne de Louis XV*.

spoke together (at that time, I fancy, he had as supervisor Pierre-Vincent Chalvet, the history teacher and very ill with the small pox's older sister), what then won me over about Barral was 1. the beauty of his coat the blue of which I found enchanting; 2. his way of reading these lines of Voltaire that I still remember:

> Vous êtes, lui dit-il, l'existence et l'essence,
> Simple . . .

His mother, a very great lady, *she was a Grolée*, as my grandfather used to say in awe, was the last of her order to wear the uniform; I can see her still next to the statue of Hercules in the gardens in a flowered dress, i.e. of white satin picked out with flowers, said dress being gathered up into the pockets like my grandmother (Jeanne Duperon, the widow B . . .), with a huge powdered chignon and perhaps a small dog under her arm. The street urchins would follow her admiringly at a distance, while I was taken, or carried, by the faithful Lambert; I might have been three or four at the time of this vision. This great lady had the manners of her class. M. le Marquis de Barral, her ex-president husband, or even first president in the Parlement, refused to emigrate. For which he was reviled in my family as if he had received twenty slaps across the face.

The wise M. Destutt de Tracy had the same idea in Paris, and was forced to take up posts, like M. de Barral who, before the Revolution, had been called M. de Montferrat, i.e. M. le Marquis de Montferrat (to be pronounced: Monfera, the *a* very long); M. de Tracy was reduced to living off the sa[lary] of his post as coun[cillor] for Public Education, I believe; M. de Barral had kept an income of 20 or 25,000 francs, of which in 1793 he donated half or two-thirds not to the fatherland but to his fear of the guillotine. Perhaps he had been kept in France by his love for Mme Brémond, whom he later married. I met M. Brémond *fils* in the army, where he was a battalion commander, I believe, then a *sous-inspecteur aux revues*[4] and still a man of pleasure.

I'm not saying that his father-in-law, M. le Premier Président de Barral (for Napoleon made him f[irst] pre[sident] when he created the royal courts) was a genius, but, as I saw it, he was so much the opposite of my father and had such a horror of pedantry and of ruffling his son's *amour-propre* that when they left the house to take a walk on the *cut-offs of the Drac*, if the father said . . . *bonjour,*

the son would answer . . . *toujours,*

the father . . . *oie,*

the son . . . *lamproie,*

and the walk would be spent in this way making up rhymes and trying to catch one another out.

The father taught his son the *Satires* of Voltaire (the one perfect thing according to me which that great reformer ever did).

That was when I first glimpsed true *good breeding* and it instantly won me over.

I was forever comparing this father who made up rhymes and was full of delicate consideration for his children's *amour-propre* with my own's grim pedantry. I had the most profound respect for M. Gagnon's knowledge; I loved him sincerely; I didn't go so far as to say to myself:

"Couldn't one have my grandfather's boundless knowledge and be as jolly and kind and friendly as M. de Barral?"

But my heart, so to speak, *had a presentiment* of this thought which later on was to become fundamental for me.

I had already met with good breeding, but half disfigured, masked by religiosity during the pious soirées at which Mme de Valserre would bring together, on the ground floor of the Adrets mansion, M. du Bouchage (a ruined peer of France), M.

---

4. This was a post without equivalent in the British Army. The *inspecteurs aux revues* were non-combatant administrative officers empowered to carry out inspections of troops in the field. They were highly unpopular (see Stendhal's further remarks concerning them in Chapter 40).

de Saint-Vallier (the great Saint-Vallier), his brother Scipion, M. de Pina (former mayor of Grenoble, a deep-dyed jesuit, 80,000 francs a year and seventeen children), Messrs de Sinard, de Saint-Ferréol, myself, Mlle Bonne de Saint-Vallier, whose beautiful arms white and plump in the Venetian style I found so very affecting.

Chelan the *curé*, M. Barthélemy d'Orban were models also. Father Ducros had the accents of genius. (The word *genius* was at that time for me like the word *God* for the bigots.)

CHAPTER 28

I didn't take such a rosy view of M. de Barral in those days, he was the *bête noire* of my relations for not having emigrated.

Necessity making of me a hypocrite (a fault for which I over-corrected and whose absence has done me so much harm, in Rome, for example), I mentioned to my family the names of Messrs de la Bayette and de Barral, my new friends.

"La Bayette! Good family," said my grandfather. "His grandfather was a ship's captain, his uncle, M. de [*a blank*], president in the Parlement. As for Montferrat, he's worthless . . ."

It has to be admitted that one night, at two in the morning, the municipal authorities, and M. de Barral with them, had come to arrest M. d'Antour, a former c[ouncillo]r in the Parlement, a thirty-year-old imbecile who lived on the first floor and who spent all his time pacing in his large drawing-room biting his nails. The poor devil was losing his sight and was moreover a notorious suspect like my father. He was religious to the point of fanaticism, but otherwise harmless. It was considered shameful of M. de Barral to have come to arrest one of the councillors who had formerly served under him when he was a president in the Parlement.

It must be agreed that a bourgeois of France was an amusing creature around 1794, when I began to be able to understand him, complaining bitterly about the arrogance of the nobility yet valuing a man among themselves entirely according to his birth. Virtue, goodness of heart, generosity were of no account, in fact the more distinguished a man was, the more vigorously they reproached him for his lack of birth, and what birth!

Around 1803, when my uncle Romain Gagnon came to Paris and lodged with me, in the Rue de Menars, I didn't introduce him at Mme de Neuilly's; there was a reason for this: that lady didn't exist.[1] Shocked by this absence of an introduction, my good aunt Elisabeth said:

"There must be something extraordinary here. Otherwise Henri would have taken his uncle to that lady's; one is only too glad to show *one wasn't born under a cabbage-leaf.*"

It was I, if you please, who wasn't born under a cabbage-leaf.

And when our cousin Clet, dreadfully ugly, the face of an apothecary, and an apothecary by trade in fact (an army pharmacist), was on the point of getting married, in Italy, my aunt Elisabeth replied to criticism of his frightful appearance:

"One has to agree he's a real tramp," said someone.

"True enough, but there's also birth! Cousin to the leading doctor in Grenoble, is that nothing?"

The character of this excellent old maid was a very striking example of the maxim, *Noblesse oblige.* No sacrifice would have been beyond her, so generous and disinterested was she. I owe it to her in part that I speak correctly, if a vulgarism escaped me she would say: "Oh, Henri!"

And her face would express a cold disdain the memory of which used to *haunt* me (pursued me for a long time).

I have known families in which they spoke just as correctly, but not one in which they spoke more correctly than in mine. This isn't to say that we didn't commonly commit the eight or ten faults of the Dauphiné.

But if I used an imprecise word or one *aiming* at *effect*, I would at once be the butt of some pleasantry and all the more happily, on my grandfather's part, in that these were almost the only pleasantries the poor man was allowed by the

---

1. A family invented by Stendhal in order to impress his own family by his aristocratic connections in Paris.

humourless piety of my aunt Séraphie. If you were to avoid the sardonic stare of that witty man, you had to use the simplest turn of phrase and the exact word, without however taking it into your head to use a vulgarism.

I have seen children, in the wealthy families of Paris, forever employing the most ambitious expressions so as to achieve an elevated style, and their parents applauding this attempt at bombast. Young Parisians would happily say *steed* instead of *horse*, hence their admiration for Messrs de Salvandy, de Chateaubriand, etc.

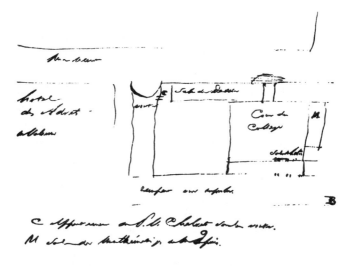

Rue Neuve.—The des Adrets mansion.—Mme de Valserre.—
Archway.—Art classroom.—College yard.—Latin classroom.—
Rampart: superb view.
  C. P.-V. Chalvet's apartment under the archway.—M.
Dupuy's mathematics classroom.

There was moreover at that time a depth and truthfulness of feeling in the young Dauphinois of fourteen that I have never observed in young Parisians. On the other hand, we used to say: "J'étais au *cour-se* ou M. *Passe-kin* (Pasquin) m'a lu une pièce de ver-*se* sur le voyage d'Anver-*se* à Calai-*ce*." It was only when I got to Paris in 1799 that I suspected there was another pronunciation. Subsequently I took lessons from the celebrated Larive and from Dugazon so as to expel the last remnants of my native *drawl*. Only two or three words remain (*côte*, *kote* instead of *kaute*, for a small rise in the ground; the worthy *abbé* Gattel was quite right therefore to give pronunciations in his worthy dictionary, something he was recently criticized for by a dim-witted *man of letters* in Paris), and the firm, passionate accent of the Midi which reveals the *strength of one's feelings*, the vigour of one's likes and dislikes, is instantly strange and hence *bordering on the ridiculous* in Paris.

So it was saying *chose* instead of *chause*, *cote* instead of *caute*, Calai-*ce* instead of Calai (Calais), that I made conversation with my friends Bigillion, La Bayette, Gall, Barral.

The latter came each morning, I fancy, from La Tronche to spend the day with Pierre-Vincent Chalvet, the history teacher, who lodged at the college underneath the archway. Over by B, there was quite a pretty avenue of lime-trees, very narrow, but the limes were old and bushy although they had been cut back, the view was delightful. There I used to walk with Barral who had come from point C very close by. M. Chalvet, preoccupied with his whores, his p[ox] and the books that he produced, and in any case the most casual of men, gladly allowed him to run off.

I believe it was when walking at P that we met Michoud, a face like an ox but an excellent man (whose only offence was to die as a corrupt supporter of the ministry and a councillor in the Cour Royale around 1827). I can almost believe that this excellent man believed that probity was an obligation only between individuals, and that it is always permissible to betray one's duties as a citizen in order to procure money for the government. I draw a vast distinction between him and his schoolfellow Félix Faure; the latter was born with a contemptible soul, and so he is a peer of France and first president in the Cour Royale in Grenoble.

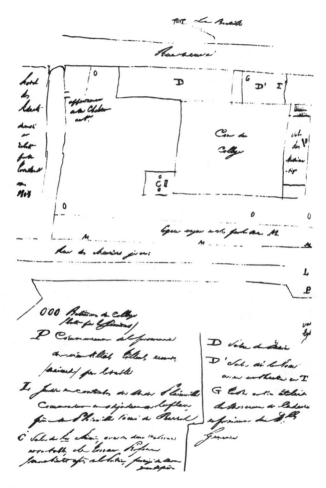

The Bastille.—Rue Neuve.—Des Adrets mansion demolished and rebuilt by M. Trouilloud around 1808.—M. Chabert's first-floor apartment.—College yard.—Mathematics classroom.—Waste ground enclosed by wall M.—Rue des Mûriers, I believe.

OOO. College building (built by the Jesuits).—P. Beginning of the Promenade of old lime-trees shortened (M A I M E D) by pruning.—L. Sunken garden of M. Plainville, commandant or adjutant of the place, the father of Plainville, Barral's friend.—C. Chemistry classroom with its two columns and its table. M. Trousset, teacher (died soon afterwards from consumption, my grandfather's protégé). —D. Art classroom.—D'. Drawing-in-the-round classroom with a stage at T.—G. Table where bits of corpses were laid out in the presence of the Mlles Genèvre.

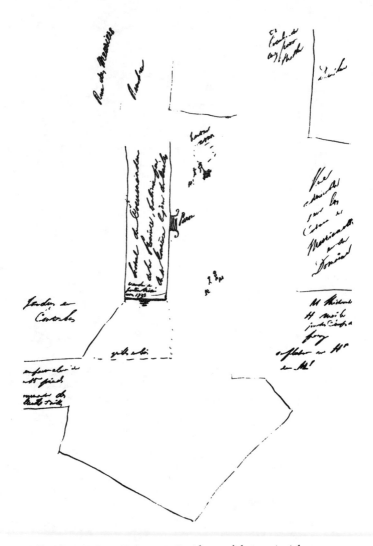

Rue des Mûriers.—Rampart.—Residence of the provincial com-
mandant lived in by M. de Tonnerre on the Day of Tiles, sold
partly destroyed around 1793.—Earth mound. Entrance steps.—
Sunken garden.—Rampart 12 or 15 feet high.—Promenade with
pruned lime-trees.—Tomb of MY POOR MOTHER.—
Demi-lune.—Admirable view over the slopes of Murianette and
Domène. M. Michoud. H. Me, on the day of the fight, or rather at
H' and M'.

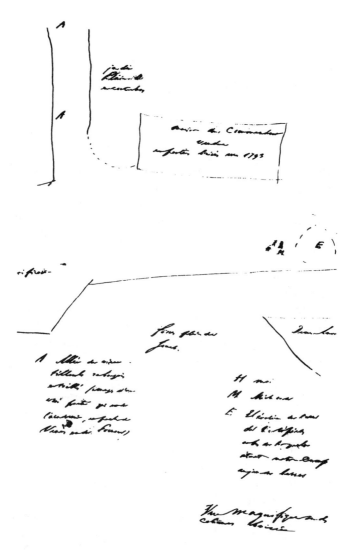

Plainville's sunken garden.—Commandant's house sold partly destroyed around 1793.—Fortifications.—Ditches full of reeds.—Demi-lune.—Magnificent view over the wooded hills.

A. Walk of old stunted and pruned lime-trees (images from a genuine poet who belongs to the Academy and talks of Venus and Pomona).—H. Me.—M. Michoud.—E. Earth mound 8 or 10 feet high at the foot of which was our camp for prisoner's base.

But whatever poor Michaud's motives may have been for selling his country to the wishes of the Attorney-G[enera]l, around 1795 he was the best, the most natural and the most unaffected of companions.

I believe he had learnt to read with Barral at Mlle Chavand's; they often spoke of their adventures in that small class. (Even then the rivalries, the friendships, the hatreds of society!) How I envied them! I even believe I lied once or twice by giving others of my companions to understand that I too had learnt to read at Mlle Chavand's.

Michaud loved me up until his death, and he didn't love an ingrate; I had the highest regard for his good sense and his kindness. Only once did we come to blows, and since he was twice my size, he thrashed me.

I reproached myself for my outburst, not because of the blows I received, but for having failed to recognize his extreme kindness. I was sly and made witty remarks that earned me many a blow, but, in Italy and in Germany, this same characteristic earned me something better and, in Paris, unforgiving critics among the minor *littérateurs*.

When a witticism occurs to me, I can see its attractions, never its malice. I'm always surprised by its malicious implications, for example, it was Ampère and A. de Jussieu who made me see the implications of my remark to that cad the Vicomte de La Passe (Civita-Vecchia, September 1831 or 1832): "Dare I ask you for your name?" for which La Passe will never forgive me. Nowadays I'm cautious, I no longer say these things, and one day recently D[on] Filippo Caetani did me the justice of saying that I was one of the least malicious men he had ever met, although my reputation was that of a man infinitely witty, but very malicious, and even more immoral (immoral because I wrote about women in *L'Amour*, and because, in spite of myself, I make fun of the hypocrites, an even more respectable body, would you believe, in Paris than in Rome?).

Recently, Mme d'Anvers, Mme Toldi, of the *Valle*, said, as

I was coming out of her house, to Prince C[aetani]: "But it's M. de S[tendhal], such a witty man but so *immoral*."

An actress who has a bastard by Prince Leopold of Syracuse in Naples! The worthy Don Filippo defended me very earnestly against the charge of immorality.

Even when recounting that a yellow cabriolet has just gone down the street I am unlucky enough to give mortal offence to the hypocrites, and even to the *simpletons*.

But at bottom, dear reader, I don't know what I am: kind, unkind, clever, stupid. What I know beyond question are the things that give me pain or pleasure, that I wish for or that I hate.

A drawing-room full of newly enriched provincials flaunting their luxury is my pet aversion for example. Next comes a drawing-room full of Marquis and holders of the Légion d'Honneur flaunting their morality.

A salon of eight or ten people where all the women have had lovers, where the conversation is light-hearted, anecdotal, and where a light punch is drunk at half past midnight, that's where I feel most at home in the world; there, deep down, I infinitely prefer hearing someone else talk to talking myself. I lapse gladly into the silence of *happiness* and, if I talk, it's only in order to *pay my entrance fee*, a term I introduced into Parisian society in this usage, it's like *fioriture* (imported by me) and which I come across incessantly. I more rarely come across, I have to agree, *crystallization** (see *L'Amour*). But I don't at all insist on it: if a better term be found, more in tune with the language, for the same idea, I shall be the first to acclaim it and make use of it.

---

*A sort of madness leading one to find every perfection and everything *turning to perfection* in the object affecting the womb. "He's poor"; ah, I love him all the more! "He's rich"; ah, I love him all the more!

CHAPTER 29

Today I can see that a quality common to all my friends was *naturalness* or the absence of hypocrisy. Mme Vignon and my aunt Séraphie had given me a revulsion for this first of qualifications for success in present-day society which has done me much harm and borders on a physical disgust. Prolonged exposure to a hypocrite and I start to feel sea-sick (just as a month ago the Ch[evali]er Scarabée's Italian obliged the C[omte]sse Sandre to loosen her corsets).

It wasn't at being *natural* that poor Grand-Dufay excelled, a boy of infinite wit; and so he was never anything more than my *literary* friend, i.e. full of jealousy on his side, and of mistrust on mine, and each of us with a high regard for the other.

He won first prize for general grammar in the same year, I fancy, as I won first prize for literature. But which year was that? Was it 1796 or 1795? I badly need the archives in the prefecture; our names were printed on a folio placard, and posted up. The sensible law of M. de Tracy (to be transcribed hereafter) had invested the examinations with much ceremony. Was the future of the country not at stake? It was as much an education for the member of the departmental administration, the moral product of Mme du Barry's despotism, as for the pupil.

What was to be done, in 1796, with all men over twenty? To save the country from the harm they were disposed to do it and as best one could wait for their DEATH.

This is as true as it is sad to say so. How much lighter the ship of state would be, in 1836, if everyone over fifty were suddenly gathered *ad patres*! Except, of course, for *the king, my wife and me*.

During one of the numerous illuminations that took place every month, from 1789 to 1791, a bourgeois set up this transparency:

LONG LIVE
THE KING
MY WIFE AND I

Grand-Dufay, the eldest of four or five brothers, was a small thin creature without much flesh on his bones, with a large head, a face heavily pock-marked yet very red, brilliant but shifty eyes and with something of the alarming vivacity of a wild boar. He was wary and kept close watch on his tongue; always busy bestowing praise, but in the most measured terms possible. Just like a Member of the Institute.[1] For the rest, very lively-minded and quick on the uptake, but even at that very tender age consumed with ambition. He was the eldest son and the *spoilt child* (a local expression) of a mother similar in character, and not without reason: the family was poor.

What an admirable Plougoulm Dufay would have made (i.e. an advocate-g[ener]al in the pocket of the authorities and knowing how to gloss over the worst iniquities)![2]

But he didn't live and, at his death in Paris around 1803, I

1. The Institut de France consists of the five learned academies of Paris, including the Académie Française. These were not bodies likely to be admired by Stendhal.

2. Pierre-Ambroise Plougoulm (1796–1863) was a lawyer detested by the liberals for having gone over to King Louis-Philippe.

shall have to accuse myself of one of the worst feelings of my life, of the kind which have most caused me to hesitate in going on with these memoirs. I had forgotten it since 1803 or 4, the date of that death. It's odd how many things I have remembered since I have been writing these confessions! They come upon me suddenly, and I fancy I judge them impartially. I am constantly seeing the *best thing* I didn't do.

But who on earth will have the patience to read these things?

When I go out into the street in a brand-new, well-made coat, my friends would give an *écu* for someone to throw a glass of dirty water over me. The sentence is ill-formed, but the thing itself is true (I make exception, naturally, of the excellent Comte de Barral; he is a La Fontaine by nature).

Where to find the reader who, after four or five volumes of *I* and *me*, won't be wanting them to throw, no longer a glass of dirty water, but a bottle of ink over me? But the whole trouble, oh my reader, lies only in the five letters: B,R,U,L,A,R,D, that form my name, and which concern my self-respect. Suppose I had written *Bernard*, this book would then only have been, like *The Vicar of Wakefield* (its rival in innocence), a novel written in the first person.[3]

The person to whom I have bequeathed this posthumous work will have at the very least to get all these details abridged by some hack editor, the M. Amédée Pichot or the M. Courchamps of the day. It's been said that we never go so far in an *opera d'inchiostro*[4] as when we don't know where we are going; if that were always the case, these memoirs, which depict *a man's heart*, as Messrs V[icto]r Hugo, d'Arlincourt, Soulié, Raymond, etc., etc., would say,* ought to be something very fine. The *I*s and *me*s were tormenting me

3. It was a favourite joke of Stendhal's, that his acidic and unforgiving "Memoirs" were somehow on a par with the benign, sentimental fiction of Oliver Goldsmith.

4. Literally, an "ink work."

* 14 Jan 1836. To be investigated by reading, or by going through twenty-four novels.

yesterday evening (14 January 1836) while I was listening to Rossini's *Moses*. Good music makes me reflect more lucidly and intensely on what is preoccupying me. But for that the moment of *judgment* has to have passed; it is so long since I passed judgment on *Moses* (in 1823) that I have forgotten what the verdict was and no longer think about it. I am simply now *the slave of the ring*, as the *Arabian Nights*[5] have it.

The memories are multiplying beneath my pen. I now realize I have been forgetting one of my closest friends, Louis Crozet, now Chief Engineer, and a very worthy Chief Engineer, in Grenoble, but entombed like the "Baron buried face to face with his wife"* and drowned by her in the narrow egotism of the jealous and small-minded bourgeoisie of a small town in our local mountains (La Mure, Corps or Le Bourg d'Oisans).

L[oui]s Crozet was cut out to be one of the most brilliant men in Paris; in a salon he would have outshone Koreff, Pariset, Lagarde and myself after them, if it be permitted to name oneself. Pen in hand, he would have been a wit in the style of Ducros, the author of the *Essai sur les mœurs* (but that book will be dead perhaps in 1880, the man who, in d'Alembert's words, "displayed the most wit within a given space of time").

It was I think *in Latin* (as we used to say), with M. Durand, that I became friends with Crozet, at that time the ugliest and most unprepossessing boy in the whole Ecole Centrale; he must have been born around 1784.

---

5. A confusing reference to the *Arabian Nights*, which contains a Slave of the Lamp, not of the Ring; Stendhal seems to have merged the Aladdin story with that of Angelica in Ariosto, whose ring made her invisible.

*Lines from *L'Homme du jour*:
  Ci-gît, sans avoir rendu l'âme,
  Le baron enterré vis-à-vis de sa femme.
[These might be translated as:
  Here lies the baron, though still in life,
  Buried face to face with his wife.]

He had a round, pasty face, heavily pock-marked, and small, very keen blue eyes, but whose rims had been affected and made bloodshot by that cruel malady. All this was rounded off by a small air of pedantry and ill-humour; walking badly and as if his legs were crooked, his whole life the very antithesis of elegance yet unfortunately seeking elegance, but for all that "Un esprit tout divin" (La Fontaine).[6]

Rarely sensitive, but when he was, a passionate lover of his country and, I think, capable of heroism. Had it been necessary, he might have been a hero in a deliberative assembly, a *Hampden*,[7] which for me is to say everything. (See the *Life of Hampden*, by Lord King or Dacre, his great-grandson.)

In short, he had incomparably more wit and sagacity than any other of my Dauphinois acquaintances, and he possessed that mixture of boldness and timidity needed in order to shine in a Paris salon, like G[enera]l Foy he grew animated from talking.

He was very useful to me by this latter quality, *sagacity*, which I lacked altogether by nature and with which, I fancy, he succeeded partially in inoculating me. I say *partially*, for I still have to force myself to it. And if I discover something, I am liable to exaggerate my discovery to myself and see only that.

I excuse this defect of my mind by calling it: the *necessary effect* and *sine qua non* of an extreme sensitivity.*

When a thought takes too strong a hold of me in the middle of the street, *I fall down*. Example: Rue de Richelieu, near the Rue des Filles-Saint-Thomas, my one fall in five or six years, caused around 1826 by this problem: should M. de

6. Literally, "A spirit quite divine."

7. John Hampden (1594–1643), one of the heroes of the Parliamentary struggle against King Charles I. There is no known life of him by a Lord King or Dacre.

*Handwriting. This is how I write when my thoughts are treading on my heels. If I write well, I waste them.

Belleyme, to further his ambitions, get himself appointed as a deputy or not?* This was the time when M. de Belleyme, the prefect of police (the one popular magistrate in the days of the senior branch of the Bourbons), was making clumsy attempts to become a deputy.

When thoughts come upon me in the middle of the street, I am always on the verge of colliding with a passer-by, falling or being run over by the carriages. One day in Paris, near the Rue d'Amboise (one occasion out of a hundred), I stared at Doctor Edwards without recognizing him. That is, there were two actions; the first said right enough: "There's Doctor Edwards," but the second was busy thinking, and failed to add: "You must say hello to him and speak to him." The doctor was greatly surprised, but not put out; he didn't think I was playing at being a genius (as Messrs Prunelle would have done, the ex-mayor of Lyon, the ugliest man in France, Jules-César Boissat, the most conceited man, Félix Faure and a great many other of my acquaintances, and friends).

I had the good fortune to re-encounter Louis Crozet frequently, in Paris, in 1800; in Paris, between 1803 and 1806; in Plancy, between 1810 and 1814, where I went to visit him, and where I put my horses into stables while I was on some mission or other for the Emperor. Finally, we slept in the same room together (Hôtel de Hambourg, Rue de l'Université) on the evening Paris was taken in 1814. Out of grief he got indigestion during the night; I, who had lost everything, looked on the affair more as a spectacle. And in any case I was in a bad mood from the stupid correspondence I had had with the Duc de Bassano, when I was in the 7th Division with that old *rimbambito*,[8] M. le Comte de Saint-Vallier.

I still felt badly, I admit it to the shame of my intelligence, about the Emperor's conduct towards the deputation from

*I am writing without being able to see 14 Ja[nuary] at 5.12.

8. An Italian term meaning "dotard."

the Corps Législatif, which included that susceptible and eloquent imbecile by the name of Lainé (from Bordeaux), later a viscount and peer of France, died in 1835, as well as that man *without a heart*, utterly devoid of all sensibility, by the name of Roederer.

With Crozet, so as not to waste our time in admiring chit-chat about La Fontaine, Corneille or Shakespeare, we used to write what we called *Characters*. (I would dearly like to see one of them today.)

They consisted of six or eight folio sheets analysing (under an assumed name) the character of someone whom we both knew to a jury made up of Helvétius, Tracy and Machiavelli, or Helvétius, Montesquieu and Shakespeare. That was who we then admired.

We read Adam Smith and J.-B. Say together, then abandoned that science on discovering obscure or even contradictory points in it. We were first-rate mathematicians, and after his three years at the Ecole Polytechnique, Crozet was so good at chemistry that he was offered a post similar to that of M. Thénard (today a peer of France but as we saw it then a man without genius; we revered only Lagrange and Monge. Even Laplace was simply *a source of enlightenment* intended to make things understood, to clarify, but not to invent). Crozet and I read Montaigne, Letourneur's Shakespeare I don't know how many times (though we had a very good knowledge of English).

We had working sessions lasting five or six hours after taking coffee in the Hôtel de Hambourg, Rue de l'Université, with a view over the Musée des Monuments Français, a charming creation very close to perfection, annihilated by those worthless Bourbons.

The description of excellent mathematician attributed to me above is arrogant perhaps. I have never known differential or integral calculus, but at one time I spent my life delightedly dreaming of the art of forming equations, of what, if I dared, I would call the metaphysics of mathematics. I won first prize (and without favouritism, on the contrary my haughtiness had antagonized them) ahead of eight young men who, one month later, at the end of 1799, all passed into the Ecole Polytechnique.

With Louis Crozet I worked through a good six to eight hundred working sessions *improbus*, each of five to six hours. This work, earnest and with furrowed brows, we called *mugging up*, after an expression in use at the Ecole Polytechnique. These sessions were my true literary education; it was with an extreme delight that we thus set off on the discovery of the truth, to the great scandal of Jean-Louis Basset (nowadays M. le Baron de Richebourg, commissioner, former subprefect, former lover of a rich Montmorency, conceited, no brains, but harmless). This creature, four foot three inches tall and in despair at being called Basset, lodged with Crozet at the Hôtel de Hambourg. His only virtue that I knew of was of having been stabbed in the chest with a bayonet, mainly in the lapels of his coat, one day when from the pit we took the stage by storm at the Théâtre-Français in honour of Mlle Duchesnois (but Lord alive, I am encroaching!), an excellent actress in two or three roles, died in 1835.

We overlooked nothing, Crozet and I, when we worked together; we were constantly afraid of letting ourselves be led astray by vanity, finding none of our friends capable of discussing these questions with us.

These friends were the two Bassets, Louis de Barral (my close friend, close friend also of Louis Crozet), Plana (professor in Turin, member of all the Academies and orders in that country). Crozet and Plana, both my friends, were a year behind me in mathematics, they were learning arithmetic, whereas I had got on to trigonometry and the rudiments of algebra.

CHAPTER 30

My grandfather didn't like M. Dubois-Fontanelle; he was altogether a man of a cultivated and implacable vanity, a man of the best society in respect of infinitely many people whom he said kind things about but whom he didn't like.

I think he was afraid of being despised, looked down on, as a literary man, by poor M. Dubois, who had written a tragedy, which had had the honour of sending its publisher into penal servitude. The work in question was *Ericie ou la Vestale.* This was obviously *Ericie ou la Religieuse*, or the *Mélanie* of that scheming Laharpe,[1] whose bloodless genius had, I believe, stolen the subject from poor M. Dubois-Fontanelle, always so impoverished that he had developed horribly small handwriting so as to save on paper.

Poor M. Dubois went quite young to Paris *with a love of the beautiful.* Constant poverty obliged him to seek out the useful; he was never able to raise himself into the ranks of leading *jean-sucres*, such as Laharpe, Marmontel, etc. Want obliged him to agree to become political editor of the *Journal des Deux-Ponts*, and, far worse, there he married a tall, fat German woman, a former mistress of the King of Bavaria, Maximilian-Joseph, at that time Prince Max and a French colonel.

Her eldest daughter, the King's daughter, was married to a

---

1. Jean François Delharpe (1739–1803) was a writer and critic, whose play was entitled *Mélanie ou la Religieuse*; Dubois-Fontanelle's play had been banned after its first and only performance in 1787.

M. Renauldon, a conceited personage expressly designed to be the worthy mayor of a large provincial town. Indeed, he was the worthy mayor of Grenoble from 1800 to 1814, I believe, and, what's more, was outrageously cuckolded by my cousin Pellat, the king of fools, who was thereby disgraced and was forced to leave the district with a post in the Customs and Excise given to him by the beneficent Français (of Nantes), a financier, influential under the Emperor, and who found a post for Parny. I knew him well as a literary man under the name of M. Jérôme around 1826. All these clever men, unfortunate in their ambitions, take up literature as their last resort. Thanks to their skill in intrigue and their political friends, they obtain a semblance of success, but, in point of fact, attract *ridicule*. Of this kind I have known M. Roederer, M. Français (of Nantes) and even M. le C[omt]e Daru when, thanks to his poem *L'Astronomie* (published after his death), he became an associate member of the Académie des Sciences. These three men, very clever, very shrewd and certainly in the front rank of Councillors of State and prefects, had never seen this little geometrical figure invented by myself, a simple commissioner, a month before.

If, when he got to Paris, poor M. Dubois, who took the name of Fontanelle, had found himself a pension of a hundred *louis* on condition he wrote (like Beethoven in Vienna around 1805), he would have cultivated the *beautiful*, i.e. imitated not nature but Voltaire.

Instead of which, he was obliged to translate Ovid's *Metamorphoses* and, far worse, English books. This excellent man gave me the idea of learning English and lent me the first volume of Gibbon, on which occasion I discovered he pronounced it "Te istory of te fall." He had learnt English without a teacher, out of poverty, and by recourse to the dictionary.

I learnt English only many years later, when *I invented the idea* of learning by heart the first four pages of the *Vicar of Wakefield* (Ouaikefield). This, I fancy, was around 1805. Someone had had the same idea in Scotland, I believe, but

I didn't find that out until 1812 when I got hold of some *Edinburg[h] Reviews* in Germany.

M. Dubois-Fontanelle was almost crippled by gout, his fingers no longer had any shape; he was polite, obliging, helpful, his character had moreover been shattered by constant ill-fortune.

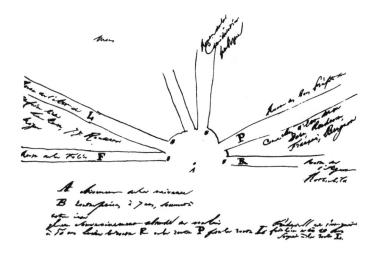

Road to madness.—L. Road to getting oneself read: Tasso, J.-J. Rousseau, Mozart.—R. Road to public regard.—P. Road of good prefects and councillors of State: Messrs Daru, Roederer, Français, Beugnot.—Road to money: Rothschild.

A. Moment of birth.—B. Roads taken at age seven, often without our knowing it. It is supremely ridiculous at the age of fifty to try and leave road R or road P for road C. Frederick II hardly got himself read yet from the age of twenty had been dreaming of road L.

Although the *J[ourn]al des Deux-Ponts* had been taken over by the armies of the Revolution, M. Dubois didn't for all that become an *aristocrat* but, strangely enough, still remained a *citoyen français*. This will seem straightforward around 1880, but was nothing short of miraculous in 1796.

Witness my father who, when the Revolution came, advanced himself thanks to his abilities, becoming first deputy

and acting mayor of Grenoble, a *chevalier* of the Légion
d'Honneur, yet who loathed the Revolution which had lifted
him out of the mire.

The poor and estimable M. Fontanelle, abandoned by his
journal, arrived in Grenoble with his large German wife who,
in spite of her earlier profession, had vulgar manners and little money. He was only too glad to be a live-in schoolteacher
and even went to occupy his apartment in the *south-west*
corner of the college yard before it was finished.

At B was his beautiful octavo edition of Voltaire, by Kehl,
the only one of his books which this excellent man wouldn't
lend. His books had notes in his own hand, luckily almost
impossible to read without a magnifying-glass. He had lent

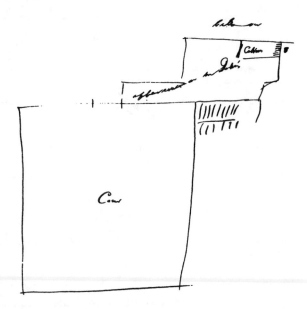

Beautiful view.—M. Dubois's apartment.—Cabinet.—Yard.

me *Emile* and was very worried because, at J.-J. Rousseau's
wild declamation, "The death of Socrates is that of a man,
that of J[esus]-C[hrist] that of a God," he had inserted a *papil-*

lon (a piece of glued paper), very reasonable and not at all eloquent and which ended with the contrary maxim.

This *papillon* would have done him great harm, even in the eyes of my grandfather. What would it have been like if

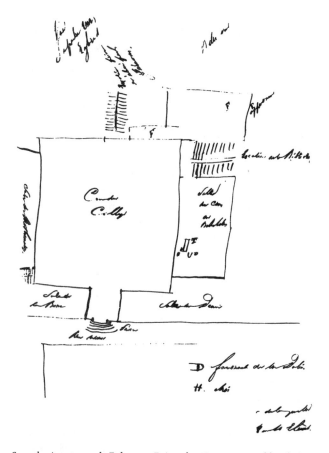

Superb view towards Eybens.—Painted staircase erected by the Jesuits.—Beautiful view.—Apartment.—Mathematics classroom. —College yard.—Staircase to the Library.—Literature classroom. —Drawing-in-the-round classroom.—Art classroom.—Entrance steps.—Rue Neuve.

D. M. Dubois's armchair.—H. Me.—T. Table round which the eight or ten pupils used to sit.

my father had seen it? Around that time, my father didn't buy Bayle's *Dictionary*, at the sale of our cousin Drier's (the man of pleasure), so as not to put my religion at risk, and told me as much.

M. Fontanelle was too broken by misfortune and by the character of his she-devil of a wife to be an enthusiast; he hadn't the faintest spark of M. *l'abbé* Ducros's fire, and so had hardly any influence over my character.

I fancy I attended these lessons with that little jesuit Paul-Emile Teisseire, the fat Marquis (a good lad, a rich young man from Rives or from Moirans); Benoît, a good lad who genuinely thought he was a Plato because the doctor, Clapier, had taught him that love (*à la* Bishop of Clogher).

This didn't revolt us because our parents would have been revolted by it, but it did surprise us. Today I can see that what we were ambitious for was victory over that terrible creature: an attractive woman, who judged men by their abilities, not pleasure. We found pleasure everywhere. The gloomy Benoît made no proselytes.

Soon the fat Marquis, who was some sort of relation of mine, I fancy, could no longer follow the lessons and left us. I fancy we also had a Penet, one or two Gautiers, *minus habens* of no consequence.*

In this class as in all the others there was an examination in the middle of the year. I had a distinct advantage over that little jesuit Paul-Emile who learnt everything by heart and who, for that reason, terrified me, for I have *no memory*.

This is one of the great defects of my brain: I ruminate endlessly on what concerns me, by dint of looking at it from different *positions of soul* I finally find something new in it and cause it to *change its appearance*.

*In an hour and a half, from 450 to 461: eleven pages.

I extend the tubes of my telescope in every direction, or retract them, to adopt the image used by M. de Tracy (see his *Logique*).*

This young villain of a Paul-Emile, with his false and honeyed tones, put me in great fear of this examination. Fortunately, a M. Teste-Lebeau from Vienne, a member of the departmental ad[ministration] plied me with questions. I was obliged to think up answers and I finished above Paul-Emile, who only knew by heart the summary of the course-work.

In my written composition, there was even a sort of idea concerning J.-J. Rousseau and the praises he had merited.

Everything I had learnt from M. Dubois-Fontanelle's l[essons] I looked on as knowledge both external and *false*.

I thought I had *genius*; where the devil had I got that idea from? Genius for the profession of Molière and Rousseau.

I had a supreme and sincere contempt for the talents of Voltaire: I thought him *childish*. I had a sincere regard for Pierre Corneille, Ariosto, Shakespeare, Cervantes and verbally for *Molière*. My difficulty was to reconcile them.

My idea about literary beauty is basically the same as in 1796, but every six months it improves or, if you like, changes somewhat.

This has been *the one task of my whole life*.

Everything else has been simply *a way of earning money* combined with a certain vanity at earning it as well as the next man; I make exception for my *intendancy* at Brunswick after Martial had left. That had *the attraction of novelty* and,

---

* 16 J[anuary] 1836. 25 $^2\sqrt{4}$ + $^3\sqrt{9}$.

[*trans.* The calculation is intended to show Stendhal's present age of fifty-three, as the sum of 25 times 2 plus 1 times 3. He should however have taken the square, not the cube root of 9 in the second half of the sum.]

I fancy, the criticisms M. Daru made of the intendant of Magdeburg, M. Chaalons.

My literary ideal has more to do with enjoying the works of others and evaluating them, with ruminating on their worth, than in writing myself.

Around 1794, I was waiting fatuously for the moment of *genius*. More or less like the voice of God speaking to Moses out of the *burning bush*. This simple-mindedness made me lose a lot of time, but may have prevented me from being content with the *semi-worthless* as so many writers of merit are (M. Loève-Veimars for example).

When I start to write I no longer think about my literary ideal, I am beset by ideas that I need to record. I presume that M. Villemain is beset by forms of sentences; and that what is called a poet, a Delille, a Racine, by forms of verse.

Corneille was excited by forms of rejoinder: Emilie to Cinna:

Eh bien! prends-en ta part et laisse-m'en la mienne[2]

As my idea of perfection has changed every six months therefore, it is impossible for me to record what it was around 95 or 96 when I wrote a drama whose name I have forgotten. The principal character was called Picklar perhaps and had perhaps been taken from Florian.

The one thing I can see clearly is that, for the past forty-six years, my ideal has been to live in Paris, on the fourth floor, writing a drama or a book.

The countless servilities and sense of decorum it takes to get a drama put on have stopped me from writing one, much though I would have liked to, and only a week ago I was full of a terrible remorse about this. I have roughed out more than twenty, always too much detail and too profound, insuffi-

---

2. A line from Corneille's play *Cinna*, translatable as "Well, take your share and leave me mine." It is, as usual, slightly misquoted by Stendhal.

ciently intelligible for audiences as stupid as M. Ternaux, with which the Revolution of 1789 has populated the pit and the boxes.[3]

When, by his immortal pamphlet, *What is the Third Estate? We are on our knees, let us stand up*, M. *l'abbé* Sieyès struck the first blow against the political aristocracy, he founded, without knowing it, the literary aristocracy.

(This idea came to me in November 1835, writing a preface to De Brosses which shocked Colomb.)

3. Louis-Mortimer Ternaux (1808–1871) served on the Council of State in the 1830s and later wrote a vast history of the Terror.

CHAPTER 31

I had a certain idea of literary *beauty* then in my head in 1796 or 97 when I was taking M. Dubois-Fontanelle's course; this beauty was very different from his. The most marked characteristic of the difference was my reverence for the simple, tragic truthfulness of Shakespeare, in contrast to the *puerile bombast* of Voltaire. I remember among other things M. Dubois enthusiastically reciting to us certain lines by Voltaire, or by himself, in which there occurred:

> retourner le couteau
> dans la plaie.[1]

The word *couteau* I found thoroughly, profoundly shocking, because it failed to apply my rule: my love of simplicity. Today I can see the *reason why*. I have felt intensely all my life, but I only see the reason why long afterwards.

Only yesterday, 18 January 1836, the festival of the *cattedra* at St Peter's, coming out from St Peter's at four o'clock and turning round to look at the dome, *for the first time in my life* I looked at it as I look at other buildings. I saw the iron balcony on the tambour. I said to myself: "I am seeing what is there for the first time; up until now I have looked at it the way you look at the woman you love." I liked everything about it (I mean about the tambour and the dome), how could I have found fault with it?*

---

1. Literally: "to turn the knife/in the wound."

*Poetry. [*trans.* The second part of Stendhal's sentence in French forms an alexandrine: "comment aurais-je pu y trouver des défauts?"]

So here by another route, another aspect, I come back within sight of that defect I noted higher up in this veracious account of mine: *the lack of sagacity*.

Heavens, how I digress! I had a private doctrine then when I was taking M. Dubois's course; I learnt everything he told me only as a *useful falsehood*. Above all when he criticized Shakespeare, I blushed inwardly.

But I learnt this literary doctrine *all the better* for not being an enthusiast for it.

One of my misfortunes has been not being liked by the people I was enthusiastic about (e.g. Mme Pasta and M. de Tracy), seemingly I liked them in my fashion and not in theirs.

Similarly, I often fail when expounding a doctrine I *revere*; someone contradicts me; the tears come into my eyes and I can no longer speak. I would say if I dared: "Oh, you cut me to the heart!" I recall two very striking instances.

Praise of Correggio in connection with Prud'hon,[2] talking to Mareste in the Palais-Royal, and going to a picnic with Messrs Duvergier de Hauranne, the amiable Dittmer and the wretched Cavé.[3]

The second, talking about Mozart to Messrs Ampère and Jussieu (Adrien de) coming back from Naples around 1832 (one month after the earthquake that knocked bits off Foligno).

Literarily speaking, M. Dubois's course (later printed in four vol[ume]s by his grandson, Ch. Renauldon) was useful for giving me an overall view of the literary field and preventing my imagination from exaggerating the parts of it I didn't know like Sophocles, Ossian, etc.

This course was very useful to my vanity for confirming

2. Pierre Prud'hon (1758–1823), a painter.

3. Prosper Duvergier de Hauranne (1798–1881), politician and publicist; Adolphe Dittmer (1795–1846), inspector of stud-farms; François Cavé (1794–1852), civil servant. All three were part of Stendhal's set in Paris in the 1820s.

the others definitively in the opinion that numbered me among the seven or eight clever boys in the Ecole. I fancy all the same that Grand-Dufay came ahead of me. I have forgotten the names of the others.

M. Fontanelle's golden age, the time he talked feelingly about, was his arrival in Paris around 1750. All the talk then was of Voltaire and the works by him endlessly issuing from Ferney. (Was he already at Ferney?)

All this failed in its effect on me, who loathed Voltaire's *childishness* in his history and his *contemptible envy* of Corneille; I fancy that even then I had remarked the priestly tone of Voltaire's *Commentary* in the beautiful engraved edition of Corneille, which occupied one of the top shelves in my father's glass-fronted bookcase at Claix, a bookcase to which I had stolen the key and in which I had discovered, I fancy, *La Nouvelle Héloïse* a few years before and, certainly later on, *Grandison*[4] which I read moved to floods of tears in a second-floor garret in the house at Claix where I thought I was safe.

M. Jay, that great windbag, who had so little talent for painting, had a very great talent for inspiring us to emulation and, as I now see it, that is the first gift of a teacher. How different my ideas were in 1796! I worshipped genius and talent.

A temperamental man doing everything *by fits and starts*, as men of genius ordinarily behave, wouldn't have had four hundred or three hundred and fifty pupils like M. Jay.

Indeed we choked the Rue Neuve when we came out from his class, which caused that teacher to wear an even more pompous and self-important air.

I was overjoyed, as at the most hard-won and finest promo-

4. *Charles Grandison*, the novel by Samuel Richardson (1689–1761), a writer greatly admired in France at the end of the eighteenth century.

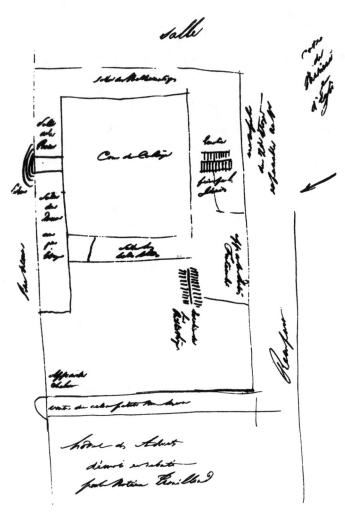

Classroom.—Mathematics classroom.—Entrance steps.—Rue
Neuve.—Drawing-in-the-round classroom.—First-floor art classroom.—College yard.—Literature classroom.—Staircase painted
by the Jesuits.—M. Dubois-Fontanelle's apartment.—Staircase to
the Library.—M. Chabert's ap[artment].—Archway over this small
deserted street.—Des Adrets mansion demolished and rebuilt by
the lawyer Trouilloud.—Superb view from the second floor and
fair one from the first.—Rampart.—Slopes of Muriannette and
Eybens.

tion possible, when around the middle of the year, I fancy, M. Jay said to me with his majestic, fatherly air:

"Come on, *monsieur* B., take your portfolio and go to the drawing-in-the-round room."

The word *monsieur*, in such common use in Paris, was altogether unwonted in Grenoble, when talking to a child, and always startled me when addressed to myself.

I don't know whether I owed this promotion to some remark addressed to M. Jay by my grandfather or to my ability at making perfectly parallel hatchings in the life class to which I had recently been admitted. The fact is it surprised both me and the others.

Once admitted among the twelve or fifteen *drawers-in-the-round*, my work in black or white crayon, copying the heads of Niobe and Demosthenes (so christened by us), surprised M. Jay who looked shocked at finding I had as much talent as the others. The best in the class was a M. Ennemond Hélie (later a court notary); he was the coldest of men; he was said to have been in the army. His work tended to the manner of Philippe de Champagne, but he was a man not a child like the rest of us, it was unfair to make him compete with us.

I soon won a prize for drawing in the round. Two or three of us got it; we drew lots and I got the *abbé* Ducros's *Essai sur la poésie et la peinture* which I read with the keenest pleasure. This book spoke to the feelings in my soul, feelings I didn't know I had.

Moulezin, the typical timid provincial, quite void of ideas but very painstaking, excelled at drawing perfectly parallel hatchings with a well sharpened red chalk crayon. A man of talent in M. Jay's place would have said to us pointing to Moulezin:

"*Messieurs*, that is what you should not be like."

Instead of which Moulezin was the rival of Ennemond Hélie.

The witty Dufay did very original drawings, said M. Jay. He especially distinguished himself when M. Jay had the excellent notion of getting us all to pose one by one for a study of heads. We also had the gross Hélie, nicknamed *le Bedot* (the stupid, the clod), and the two Monvals whose favourable treatment in mathematics had followed them to the drawing class. We worked with an incredible ardour and rivalry for two or three hours every afternoon.

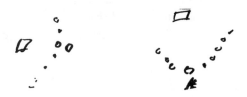

One day when there were two models, big Odru, from the Latin class, was in my line of sight, and I clouted him with all my might at O. A moment later, I having sat down again in my place at H, he pulled my chair back and made me fall on my behind. He was a man; he was a foot taller than me, but he disliked me intensely. On the stairs up to the Latin room I had drawn, in concert with Gautier and Crozet, I fancy, a caricature that was enormous like him, underneath which I had written: *Odruas Kambin*. He went red when he was called *Odruas*, and said *kambin* instead of *quand bien*.

It was at once decided that we should fight with pistols. We went down into the yard; M. Jay attempting to intervene, we took to our heels. M. Jay went back to the other classroom. We went outside, but the whole college followed us. We had perhaps two hundred followers.

I had asked Diday, who happened to be there, to act as my second; I was greatly agitated, but full of ardour. For some reason or other we happened to make for the Porte de la Graille, much impeded by our cortège. We needed to get some pistols; that wasn't easy. I finally obtained a pistol eight inches long. I could see Odru walking twenty paces away; he was showering me with insults. They didn't let us get near one another; one punch from him would have killed me.

I didn't reply to his insults, but I was shaking with anger. I don't say that I would have been exempt from fear if this duel had been arranged in the normal way, four or six people going cold-bloodedly together, at six o'clock in the morning, in a fiacre, a good league outside the town.

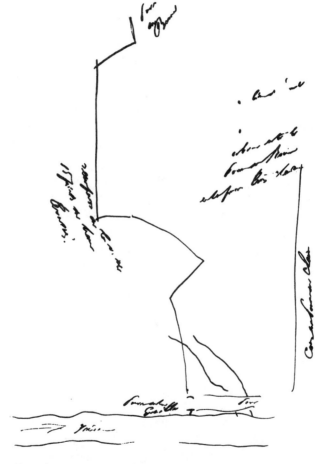

Porte de Bonne.—Town ramparts, fifteen feet high, terraced.—Porte de la Graille.—Isère.—Bridge.—Site of the duel or else between the Porte de Bonne and the Porte Très-Cloîtres. Cours du Pont-de-Claix.

The guard at the Porte de la Graille was on the point of taking up its weapons.

The procession of street urchins, absurd and highly inconvenient for us, renewed its shouting: "Will they fight? Won't they fight?" whenever we stopped for any reason. I was greatly afraid of being thrashed by Odru, taller by a foot than his own seconds and mine. I recall only Maurice Diday as my second (later a worthless ultra, mayor of Domène, and writing *badly spelt* ultraist letters to the newspapers). Odru was enraged.

At last, after pursuing us for an hour and a half, as darkness was approaching, the urchins granted us a little peace and quiet between the Porte de Bonne and the Porte Très-Cloîtres. We went down into the town moat, laid out by Louis Royer at a depth of ten feet, or halted on the edge of the moat.

There the pistols were loaded; a frightening number of paces, perhaps twenty, were measured out, and I said to myself: "Now is the moment to feel courage." For some reason or other, Odru was to fire first. I stared fixedly at a small trapezium-shaped bit of rock that happened to be above him, A, the same one you could see from my aunt Elisabeth's window next to the roof of the church of St-Louis.

For some reason or other we didn't fire. Probably the seconds hadn't loaded the pistols. I fancy I didn't have to aim. Peace was declared, but without any shaking of hands let alone an embrace. Odru was in a rage and would have thrashed me.

In the Rue Très-Cloîtres, walking with my second Baudry, I said to him:

"So as not to feel afraid while Odru was aiming at me I stared at the small rock above Seyssins T."

"You should never say that; no such words should ever pass your lips," he said to me taking me severely to task.

I was very surprised and, on reflection, very shocked by this telling-off.

But the very next day, I felt a terrible remorse at having let this affair be settled. It offended against all my dreams of Spanishness, how could I dare admire *Le Cid* after not having

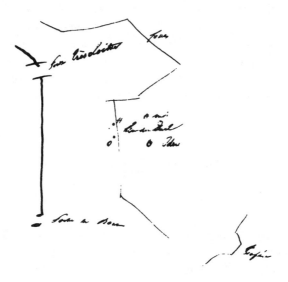

Porte Très-Cloîtres.—Porte de Bonne.—Moat.—Site of the duel.—H. Me.—O. Odru.

fought? How think of the heroes of Ariosto? How admire and criticize the great figures of Roman history of whose mighty deeds I had often reread in the insipid Rollin?

As I write this I have the sensation of passing a hand over the scar of a healed-up wound.

I haven't thought twice about this duel since my other duel arranged with M. Raindre (a squadron commander or colonel of light artillery), in Vienna in 1809, over Babet.

I can see that this was the great regret of the whole early part of my youth, and the real reason for my effrontery (insolence almost) in the duel in Milan when Cardon was a second.

In the Odru affair I was surprised, agitated, letting things take their course, distracted by the fear of being thrashed by the colossal Odru; from time to time I prepared myself to feel fear. During the two hours that the procession of two hundred street urchins lasted I was saying to myself: "When the paces are measured out, that's when there will be danger." What I had a horror of was of being carried back to the house *on a ladder*, as I had seen poor Lambert carried back. But I never for a moment had the remotest idea that the affair would be settled.

When the great moment arrived, as Odru was taking aim at me and I fancy his pistol misfired several times, I was studying the outline of the small rock T.

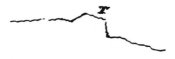

The time didn't seem at all long to me (as it seemed long at the Moskova to that very brave and excellent officer Andrea Corner, my friend).

In short, I wasn't play-acting; I was perfectly natural; not boastful, but very brave.

I was wrong; I should have *shown bravado*. By my genuine

determination to fight, I would have earned myself a reputation in our town where they fought a great deal, not like the Neapolitans of 1836 among whom duels produce very few or no corpses, but as brave men. In contrast to my extreme youth (it must have been in 1796, so thirteen years old, or perhaps 1795), and my aloof ways as *a child of the nobility*, had I had the wit to say something, I would have made an admirable reputation for myself.

M. Chatel, an acquaintance and neighbour of ours, Grande-Rue, had killed six men. In my day, i.e. between 1798 and 1805, two of my acquaintances, Bernard *fils* and Royer Gros-Bec, were killed in duels, M. Royer at forty-five paces, as it was getting dark on the *cut-offs* of the Drac, near to the spot where the wire bridge was later erected.

That coxcomb of a Bernard (son of another coxcomb, later a judge in the Appeal Court, I fancy, and an ultra), that coxcomb of a Bernard received a brief thrust from a sword at the Moulin de Canel from the amiable Meffrey (M. de Meffrey, collector of taxes, husband of the lady-in-waiting to the obliging Mme la Duchesse de Berry and later the fortunate heir of the fat Vourey). Bernard fell dead, M. de Meffrey fled to Lyon; the quarrel was almost one *of caste*. Mareste, I fancy, was de Meffrey's second and told me of the affair.

However that may be, I acquired a profound regret:

1. Because of my *espagnolisme*, a defect that still existed in 1830, which Fiori recognized and which he, like Thucydides, calls: "You stretch your nets too high."

2. Want of bravado. In moments of great danger I am natural and simple. This was in good taste at Smolensk in the opinion of the Duc de Frioul. M. Daru, who didn't like me, wrote the same thing to his wife, from Vilna, I believe, after the retreat from Moscow.

But in the eyes of the common herd, I haven't played the brilliant role which I needed only to stretch out my hand to attain.

The more I think about it, the more it seems to me that

this quarrel was in 95, and well before my passion for mathematics, my friendship for Bigillion, my tender friendship for Mlle Victorine.

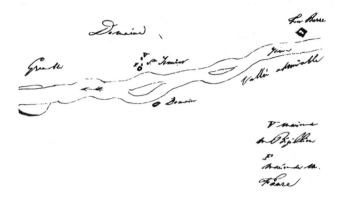

Grenoble.—St-Ismier.—Fort Barraux.—Isère.—Domène.—
Admirable valley.
  V. M. Bigillion's house.—F. M. Faure's house.

I felt infinite respect for Maurice Baudry:

1. because my excellent grandfather, a close friend of his mother's perhaps, was full of praise for him;

2. I had seen him several times in the uniform of an artilleryman and he had gone further than Montmélian to join his corps;

3. finally, and especially, he had the honour of being in love with Mlle Letourneau, perhaps the prettiest girl in Grenoble and the daughter of certainly the jolliest, most carefree, most philosophical man, and the one most criticized by my father and my relations. Indeed, M. Letourneau wasn't at all like them; he had ruined himself and had married a Mlle Borel, I believe, a sister of the mother of Victorine Mounier who was the reason for my abandoning the military state and for my flight to Paris in 1803.

Mlle Letourneau was a beauty of the heavy kind (like the figures of Tiarini, "Death of Cleopatra" or "of Anthony," in the Louvre). Baudry subsequently married her, but soon suffered the sorrow of losing her after six years of love; he was said to have been stunned by this and he retired into the countryside at Domène.

After my mid-year prize for drawing in the round, which scandalized all the courtiers better placed than myself at the court of M. Jay, but which no one dared say was undeserved, my standing *in drawing,* as we used to say, changed. I would have gone through fire to get a prize at the end of the year also. I fancy I did get one, otherwise I should remember the disappointment of having missed it.

I got first prize for literature with acclamation; I got an accessit, or second prize, for mathematics, and that was a hard one to carry off. M. Dupuy showed a marked distaste for my mania for arguing.

Every day he summoned to the blackboard, addressing them familiarly as *tu,* Messrs de Monval—or the Monvaux as we used to call them—because they were noblemen and he himself had pretensions to nobility; Sinard, Saint-Ferréol, noblemen; the worthy Aribert who was his protégé, the amiable Mante, etc., etc.; and myself as rarely as he could, and, when I was up there, he didn't listen to me, which humiliated me and very much disconcerted me, because he never took his eye off the others. In spite of which my love of mathematics was beginning to get serious and meant that, when I came across a difficulty, I pointed it out to him, I being at the blackboard, H, and M. Dupuy in his huge sky-blue armchair, at D.

A. Slate.

My indiscretion forced him to respond and that was the trouble. He was forever asking me to explain my doubts to him in private, claiming it wasted the class's time.

He made the worthy Sinard responsible for removing my doubts. Sinard, far more knowledgeable, but honest, would devote an hour or two to refuting these doubts, then to understanding them, admitting finally he didn't know how to answer them.

I fancy all these brave young fellows, with the exception of Mante, had turned mathematics into a simple matter of memory. M. Dupuy appeared very much caught out by my triumphant first prize in the literature class. My examination which took place, like all the others, in the presence of members of the Department, of the committee members, of all the teachers and of two or three hundred pupils, was entertaining for these gentlemen. I spoke well, and the members of the departmental ad[ministrati]on, astonished not to have been bored, complimented me and, my examination over, said to me:

"Monsieur B[eyle], you have got the prize, but be so good as to answer a few questions for our own pleasure."

This triumph preceded, I believe, the mathematics examination and gave me a standing and self-confidence which the following year forced M. Dupuy to call me frequently up to the blackboard.

(If ever I go back through Grenoble, I must have a search made in the archives of the Prefecture for the years 1794–9 inclusive. The printed record of the prize-giving will give me the dates of all these small events the memory of which, after so many years, comes back to me with pleasure. I was on the up-slope of life, and how my imagination was fired picturing the pleasures to come! I am now on the down-slope.)

After this triumphal month of August, my father no longer dared oppose so firmly my passion for the chase. With an ill grace he allowed me to take his own gun and even a more solid gun with a larger bore, which had been made to order for the late M. Rey, the notary, his brother-in-law.

My aunt Rey was a pretty woman whom I used to go and visit in a pretty ap[artment] in the courtyard of the Palais. My

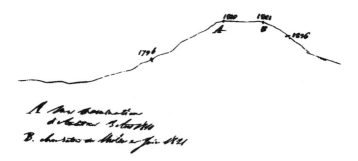

1796.—1810.—1821.—1826.
  A. My appointment as commissioner, 30 August 1830.—B. My return from Milan in June 1821.

father didn't want me to become friendly with Edouard Rey, her second son, a notorious young rogue who mixed with the vilest riff-raff. (Today he is Colonel Rey of the artillery, a notable in the Dauphiné, craftier and more deceitful in his own person than any four lawyers from Grenoble, an arch-cuckold for the rest, far from pleasant, but who must be a good colonel in that arm which goes in so much for detail. I fancy that in 1831 he was used in Algiers. He was the lover of M.P.)*

*In seven quarters of an hour, from 483 to 500: seventeen pages.

CHAPTER 32

I am making big discoveries about myself as I write these memoirs. The difficulty is no longer to discover and speak the truth, but to find someone who might read it. Perhaps the pleasure of these discoveries and of the judgments or appreciations that follow them will decide me to continue; the idea of being read grows more and more faint. Here I am at page 501 and I haven't yet left Grenoble! This picture of the revolutions of a heart would make a fat octavo volume before I get to Milan. Who would read such twaddle? What talent one would need as a painter to portray them properly, and I loathe almost equally the descriptions of Walter Scott and the bombast of Rousseau. For a reader I would need a Mme Roland, and even then perhaps the lack of descriptions of the delightful shady places in our valley of the Isère would cause her to throw the book away. So much to say for anyone with the patience to describe accurately! The beautiful groups of trees! The vigorous and luxuriant vegetation of the plain! The pretty chestnut woods on the lower slopes and above them, the impression of grandeur given to the whole by the eternal snows of Taillefer! A sublime bass to this beautiful melody!

It was that autumn, I believe, that I had the delightful pleasure of killing a thrush on the path to the vineyard above the Grande-Pièce, exactly opposite the white, rounded summit of the mountain of Le Taillefer. This was one of the most intense pleasures of my life.

I had just been roaming in the vineyards of Doyatières, I was starting on the narrow path, between two very tall, thick hedgerows, which comes down to the Grande-Pièce from H to P, when all of a sudden a plump thrush flew out with a brief cry from the vines at T' right at the top of the tree T, a cherry I believe, very elongated and without many leaves on.

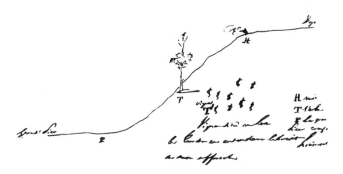

Grande-Pièce.—Vineyard.—Doyatières.
 T. Vineyard from which the thrush flew up hearing me approach.—H. Me.—T. The tree.—P. The Grande-Pièce rela[tively] horizontal.

I saw it, I fired from a more or less horizontal position, because I hadn't yet started down. The thrush fell, I can still hear the thud it made hitting the ground. I came down the path, intoxicated with joy.

I went home, I went to tell a grouchy old servant who was something of a sportsman:

"Barbier, your pupil is worthy of you!"

Grande-Pièce.—Doyatières.

The fellow would have been far more appreciative of the gift of a twelve-*sou* coin and anyway didn't understand a word of what I was telling him.

As soon as I become excited I lapse into the *espagnolisme* passed on to me by my aunt Elisabeth who still used to say: "As beautiful as the Cid."

I used to be deep in rêverie as I scoured, gun in hand, the vines and espaliers in the neighbourhood of Furonières. My father took pains to cross me and forbade me to shoot, or at most put up with it very reluctantly out of weakness, so I went out rarely and hardly ever with real sportsmen. Sometimes after foxes among the precipices of the Rocher de Comboire with Joseph Brun, who used to prune our espaliers.

There, having taken up my position to wait for a fox, I used to tell myself off for daydreaming to the point where I would have had to be woken up had the animal appeared. It did appear one day fifteen paces away, it came trotting towards me, I fired and saw nothing. I missed it completely. The dangers of the sheer precipices above the Drac I found so dreadful that I was thinking hard that day about the perils of the return journey.

You slid along ledges like A and B with the prospect of the Drac roaring at the foot of the rocks. The peasants I was with (Joseph Brun and his son, Sebastien Charrière, etc.) had been keeping their flocks of sheep on these precipitous slopes since the age of six and barefoot; if need be they would take off their shoes.

There was no question of my taking mine off, and I went among those rocks two or three times at most.

I was in a complete fright the day I missed the fox, much greater than the one I felt when, after stopping in a *field of flax* in Silesia, campaign of 1813, I was on my own and saw eighteen or twenty Cossacks coming towards me. That day at Comboire, I looked at my watch, which was gold, as I do on great occasions so as to have a clear memory at least of the time, and as M. de Lavalette did at the moment when he was

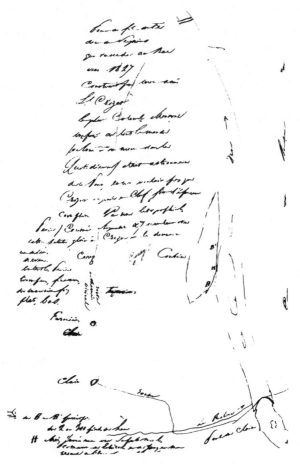

Wire bridge known as the Pont de Seyssins which succeeded the ferry around 1827 built by my friend L[ouis] Crozet; the worthless Colonel Monval universally despised (and eulogized at his death in *La Quotidienne*) was a shareholder in this bridge and didn't want Crozet, the engineer in chief, to test it thoroughly. By means of a lithograph the Périers (Casimir, Augustin, etc.) tried to take this small achievement away from Crozet and give it to one of their nephews. In everything the Périers deceitful, sly, insincere, worthless, mean.

Drac.—Cossey.—Comboire.—Road or country lane.—Furonières.—Claix.—Road.—La Robine.—Pont de Claix.—Valley.—Roundel.—Echirolles.—Cours.—Drac.

From B to B' precipices 2 or 300 feet high. H. Me, I had a superb view over the slopes of Echirolles and Jarrie and could look right down the valley.

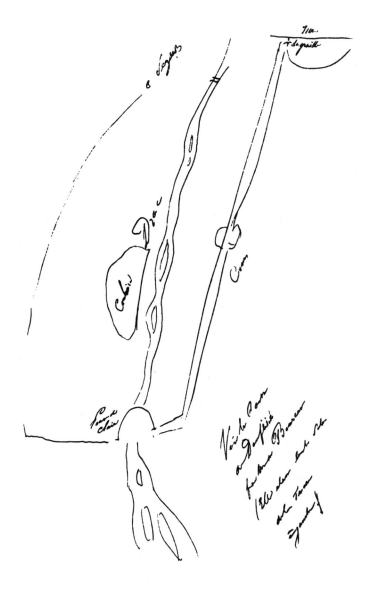

Seyssins.—Drac.—Comboire.—Pont de Claix.—Isère.—La
Graille.—Cours.

See M. de Bourcet's map of the Dauphiné (it was in the
drawing-room on the terrace to the left).

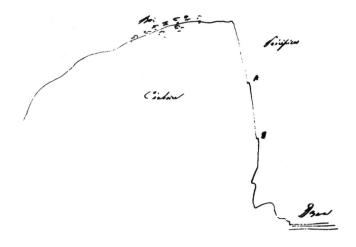

Comboire.—Cossey.—Woods.—Precipices.—Drac.

sentenced to death (by the Bourbons).[1] It was eight o'clock; I
had been made to get up before it was light, which always
blurs the whole morning for me. I was dreaming of the beautiful landscape, of love and probably also of the dangers of the
return journey, when the fox came trotting towards me. Its
bushy tail told me it was a fox, because to start with I took it
for a dog.

At S, the path may have been two feet wide, and at S' two
inches, the fox must have had to jump to get from S' to H,
when my gun went off, and jump on to the bushes at B five or
six feet below us.

The possible paths, practicable even for a fox, are very few
in number along this precipice; they are blocked by three or
four hunters, another one unleashes the dogs, the fox walks
along and very probably comes upon a hunter.

One form of the chase these hunters were constantly talking about was after chamois at Le Peuil-de-Claix, but my

1. The Comte de Lavalette was sentenced to death during the White Terror of 1815,
when there was a purge of Bonapartists. His wife however helped him to escape.

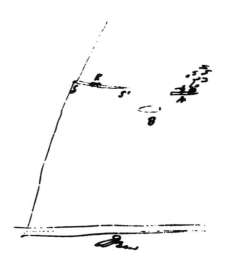

Drac.

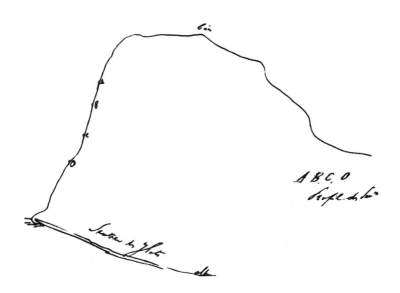

Comboire.—Woods.—Path from the small islands leading to the
ferry.—A,B,C,D, profile of the paths.

father had specifically forbidden that: none of them ever dared take me there. It was in 1795, I believe, that I felt that fine fear among the rocks of Comboire.

I soon killed my second thrush (*turdus*), but smaller than the first, as darkness fell, barely able to make it out, on a walnut-tree in the field belonging to M. de la Peyrouse, I believe, above *our Pelissone* (*id est*: our Pelissone vineyard).

I killed the third and last on a small walnut-tree bordering the road to the north of our *small orchard*. This very small thrush was almost vertically above me and practically fell on my head. It fell on to the dry-stone wall and with it large drops of blood that I can still see.

That blood was the sign of victory. It was only in Brunswick in 1808 that pity turned me against shooting. Today, I find it a distasteful and inhuman form of murder, and I wouldn't kill a gnat unless I had to. I felt no pity for the last quail I killed in C[ivit]a-V[ecchi]a though. Partridges, quail, hares, seem to me chickens born to go on a spit.

If they were consulted before being hatched in the Egyptian ovens at the end of the Champs-Elysées, they probably wouldn't refuse.[2]

I remember the delightful sensation one morning, setting off before daybreak with Barbier and finding a beautiful moon and a warm wind. It was the time of the vendange, I have never forgotten it. That day I had wrung permission from my father to follow Barbier, his factotum who managed the agricultural side of his *domaine*, to a fair in Sassenage or Les Balmes. Sassenage is the cradle of my family. They were judges there or b[eyles] and the *elder branch* (Louis-Philippe certainly says "the eldest of my race") was still established there in 1795 with fifteen or twenty thousand fr a year which, but for a certain law of 13 Germinal, I fancy,

2. These "Egyptian ovens" had been installed by a dramatist, Marie-Emmanuel Théaulon (1787–1841), in order to incubate bird's eggs by a method borrowed from the ancient Egyptians.

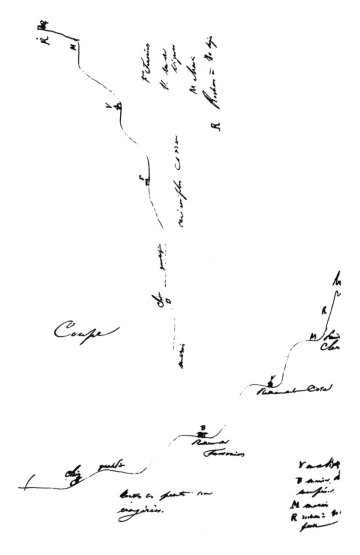

Section.—Claix.—Grande-Pièce.—Hamlet of Furonières.—Plateau of La Côte.—Peuil-de-Claix.—Rocks.—All these slopes are exaggerated.—M. M. de Vignon.—B. My father's house.—M. Marsh.—R. Rocks with an 80-degree slope.

    Marsh.—Claix.—Grande-Pièce.—Rocks.—This is more accurate.—F. Furonières.—V. M. de Vignon. R. 80-degree rocks.

would have come to me *in its entirety*. Not that my patriotism was at all shaken by this; it's true that at that age, not knowing what it was to *be without* and do disagreeable work in order to earn the needful, money for me was simply the satisfaction of my whims. But I had no whims, never going into society and never meeting a *woman*; so in my eyes money was nothing. At most I would have wanted to buy a double-barrelled gun.

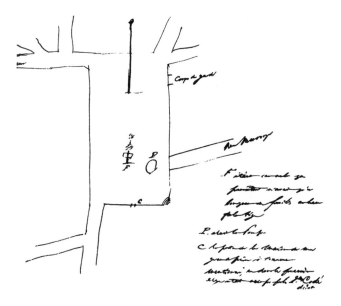

Rue Neuve.—Guardhouse.—Rue Montorge. F was the tree which perhaps had only one clump of leaves at the foot of the trunk.—P was the pump.—C, the door of my grandfather's house, mentioned so frequently, whose first floor was occupied by the devout Mlles Codé.

At that time I was like a great river which is about to hurl itself over a waterfall, like the Rhine, above Schaffhouse, still flowing peacefully but about to hurl itself down a huge waterfall. My waterfall was the love of mathematics which, first as a means of getting away from Grenoble, the embodiment of everything bourgeois and quite literally *of nausea*, and then for their own sake, absorbed me totally.

Hunting, which had led me to read *La Maison rustique* with feeling and to make extracts from Buffon's history of animals, whose bombast shocked me, even at that tender age, as being second cousin to the hypocrisy of my father's pr[iests], shooting was the last sign of vitality in my soul, prior to mathematics.

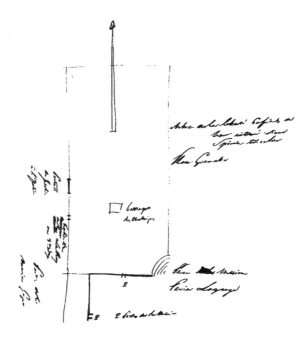

Italianate portal of the Jacobins.—M. Le Roy's third-floor home.—
Door of the Gagnon house.—Chestnut shack.—Tree of Liberty,
sixty feet tall, surrounded by a tricolour spiral.—Place Grenette.—
Entrance steps of the Périer-Lagrange house.—F. Door of the
house.

I certainly went as often as I could to Mlle Victorine Bigillion's, but I fancy that in those years she made long visits to the country. I also saw much of Bigillion, her elder brother,

La Bayette, Gall, Barral, Michoud, Colomb, Mante,* but my heart was in mathematics.

One more story and I shall be bristling all over with xs and ys.

It is a conspiracy against the Tree of Fraternity.

I don't know why I conspired. The tree was a luckless young oak, very elongated, thirty feet tall at least, which had been transplanted to its great regret into the middle of the

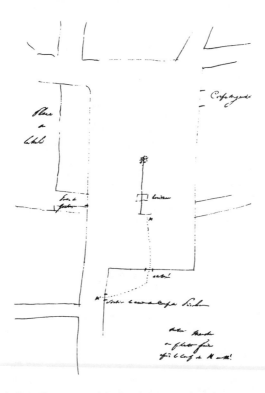

Place de la Halle.—Door of the Jacobins.—Signboard.—
Guardhouse.—Entrance.—Exit on the night of the pistol-shot.—
Direction we walked or rather fled in after firing from M to M'.

*I became friends with Mante, a tough, perfectly unemotional young man, and through him with Treillard his friend. Mante later, in Paris in 1804, almost dragged me into the Moreau conspiracy, but he made me read Tracy and Say (Rue de l'Echelle, house of the younger P [*illegible*]) and the second as much as the first.

Place Grenette, well this side of the Tree of Liberty, which had all my affection.

The Tree of Fraternity, as a rival to the other perhaps, had been planted immediately against the chestnut shed opposite the windows of the late M. Le Roy.

At some time or other a white signboard had been attached to the Tree of Fraternity on which M. Jay had painted in yellow, and with his usual skill, a crown, a sceptre, some chains, all of them underneath an inscription and in the attitude of things now vanquished.

The inscription was of several lines and I likewise have no memory of it, although it was against it that I conspired.

Which is certainly proof of the principle: that a little passion enlarges the mind, a lot extinguishes it. Against what did we conspire? I don't know. I remember, and then only vaguely, only this maxim: "It is our duty to do as much harm as we have in us to that which we hate." And even this is very vague. For the rest not the faintest recollection of what we hated or the motives for our hatred, simply the mental picture of the fact and that's all, but a very clear picture.

The idea was mine alone, it needed to be conveyed to the others who at first were unenthusiastic:

"The guardhouse is so close!" they said.

But in the end they were as resolved as I was. The conspirators were: Mante, Treillard, Colomb and I, perhaps one or two others.

Why didn't I fire the pistol? I don't know. I fancy it was Treillard or Mante.

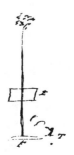

This pistol had had to be procured: it was eight inches long. We loaded it right to the muzzle. The Tree of Fraternity may have been thirty-six or forty feet tall, the board was attached ten or twelve feet up; I fancy there was a fence round the tree.

The danger might come from the guardhouse C, the soldiers from which often used to walk in the unpaved area between P and P'.

Passers-by coming from the Rue Montorge or the Grande-Rue might have stopped us. The four or five of us who didn't fire kept watch on the soldiers in the guardhouse; perhaps that was my post as being the most dangerous, but I have no recollection of it. Others kept watch on the Rue Montorge and the Grande-Rue.

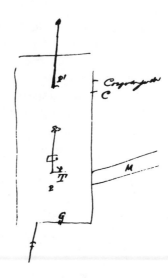

Guardhouse

Around eight o'clock in the evening, it was pitch black, and not very cold, we were in autumn or spring, the square was momentarily deserted, we walked nonchalantly across and gave the word to Mante or Treillard.

The shot went off and made a terrifying noise; the silence was profound and the pistol loaded to bursting-point. At the same instant the soldiers were upon us from the post at C. I imagine we weren't the only ones to detest that inscription and that they thought it might come under attack.

The soldiers were almost touching us; we ran off into the doorway G of my grandfather's house, but we were clearly visible; everyone was at their windows, many had brought up candles and were shining them.

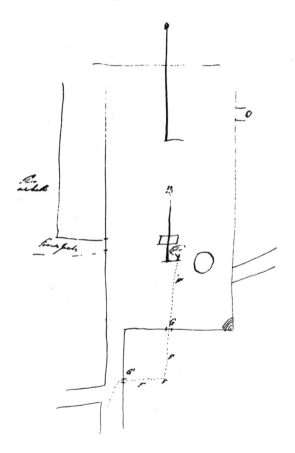

Place de la Halle.—Doorway of the Jacobins.

This doorway G on the Grenette led by a narrow passageway on the second floor to the door G' on the Grande-Rue. But this passageway was common knowledge.

To make our escape, therefore, we followed the line FFF. Some of us also escaped, I fancy, through the big doorway into the Jacobins, which would lead me to believe that there were more of us than I have been saying. Prié was perhaps one of us.

I and one other, Colomb perhaps, found ourselves being pursued the most vigorously. "They went into this house," we heard them shouting close by.

We didn't continue on up as far as the passageway above the second floor; we rang urgently at the first floor overlooking the Place Grenette, my grandfather's old ap[artment], currently let to the Mlles Codé, very devout old milliners. Luckily, they opened the door; we found them greatly frightened by the pistol-shot and busy reading the Bible.

Briefly, we told them:

"They're chasing us, say we spent the evening here."

We sit down; at almost the same moment there is a ringing fit to wrench out the bell; as for us, we are sitting listening to the Bible; I fancy one of us even picks up the book.

The officers enter. Who they were, I have no idea; obviously I hardly looked at them.

"Have these citizens spent the evening here?"

"Yes, *messieurs*; yes, citizens," said the poor terrified old ladies, correcting themselves.

I believe their brother M. Codé, an old clerk employed for the last forty-five years at the hospital, was with them.

These officers or zealous citizens must have been very imperceptive or else well disposed towards M. Gagnon, who was revered by the whole town from M. le Baron des Adrets down to Poulet, who kept the cheap eating-house, because our agitation must have made us look strangely out of place* in the

* TO CUTT [sic].

midst of those poor devout old women who were beside themselves with fear. That fear, which was as great as our own, may perhaps have saved us; the whole gathering must have worn the same scared expression.

The officers repeated their question two or three times:

"Have these citizens spent the whole evening here? Has no one come in since you heard the pistol-shot?"

The miraculous thing, at which we wondered later, was that those jansenist old maids were willing to tell a lie. I believe they yielded to this sin out of veneration for my grandfather.

The officers took our names and finally decamped.

The compliments from ourselves to those ladies were brief. We listened; when we could no longer hear the officers we left and continued on up to the passageway.

Mante and Treillard, more agile than we were and who had entered the doorway G ahead of us, told us the next day that when they came to the door G', on the Grande-Rue, they found it occupied by two guards. These gentlemen began talking about how friendly the young ladies they had spent the evening with had been, the guards didn't ask them any questions and they sped off.

Such was the impression of reality made on me by their story that I couldn't say whether it wasn't Colomb and I who came out talking about the friendliness of the young ladies.

It would seem more natural to me that Colomb and I entered the house, then [that] he left half an hour later.

What added spice was the arguments in which my father and my aunt Elisabeth indulged over the presumed perpetrators of the uprising. I fancy I told everything to my sister Pauline, who was my friend.

The next day, at the Ecole Centrale, Monval (later a colonel and despised), who didn't like me, said to me:

"So, you and yours fired a pistol at the Tree of Fraternity!"

What was delightful was to go and examine the state of the signboard: it had been riddled.

The sceptres, crowns and other *vanquished* attributes had been painted on the south side, overlooking the Tree of Liberty. The crowns etc. had been painted in bright yellow on paper stretched on canvas or on a canvas prepared for oil-paints.

It is fifteen or twenty years since I last thought about this affair. I must admit I find it very fine. In those days I often used to repeat to myself with enthusiasm, and I repeated it again not four days ago, the line from *Horace*:

Albe vous a nommé, je ne vous connais plus![3]

This action fitted well with that admiration.

The odd thing is that I didn't fire the pistol myself. But I don't think that was out of a blameworthy caution. I fancy, but I glimpse this only doubtfully and as if through a mist, that Treillard who had just arrived from his village (Tullins, I believe) absolutely insisted on firing the pistol as if this would give him the right of residence among us.

As I write this, the image of the Tree of Fraternity appears before my eyes; my memory is making discoveries. I think I can see that the Tree of Fraternity was surrounded by a two-foot wall clad in ashlar and supporting an iron railing five or six feet high.

Jomard was a beggarly pr[iest], like Ming[rat] later on, who got himself guillotined for having poisoned his father-in-law, a M. Martin of Vienne, I fancy, a former *Member of the Department*, as they used to say. I saw him sentenced, the scoundrel, and then guillotined. I was on the pavement in front of M. Plana's pharmacy.

Jomard had let his beard grow, his shoulders were draped in a red cloth as being a parricide.

3. A line from Corneille's play: "Alba has named you, I no longer know you!" Alba was reputedly the ancient city of Latium, or Rome.

I was so close that after the execution I could see the drops of blood forming along the blade before falling. That horrified

me and for I don't know how many days afterwards I couldn't eat *bouilli* (beef).

CHAPTER 33

I think I have despatched everything I wanted to talk about before embarking on the last story I shall have to tell concerning matters in Grenoble; I mean of my cascading down into mathematics.

Mlle Kubly had long since departed and all that remained to me of her was a fond memory; Mlle Victorine Bigillion was in the country a great deal. My one pleasure in reading was Shakespeare and the *Memoirs* of Saint-Simon,[1] at that time in seven volumes, which I later bought in twelve, an ed[ition] in Baskerville type, a passion that has endured like the physical passion for spinach and which is at least as strong at fifty-three as it was at thirteen.

I loved mathematics all the more as my contempt grew for my teachers, Messrs Dupuy and Chabert. For all his bombast and good manners, and the gentle aristocratic air he wore when addressing someone, I had sufficient insight to guess that M. Dupuy was infinitely more of an ignoramus than M. Chabert. M. Chabert who, in the social hierarchy of bourgeois Grenoble, found himself so far below M. Dupuy, would sometimes, on a Sunday or a Thursday morning, pick up a volume of Euler or [*a blank*] and get firmly to grips with the problem. Yet he always had the look of an apothecary who knows some good prescriptions, but there was nothing to

1. The Duc de Saint-Simon (1675–1755), soldier, courtier, diplomat and, in his later life, the greatest of French memorialists. His very extensive *Memoirs* record the court life of Versailles in the closing years of Louis XIV's reign and began to be published in 1830.

show how these *prescriptions* led on from one to the next, no *logic*, no philosophy in that brain; because of some mechanical effect or other of his education, or of vanity, or out of religion perhaps, the worthy M. Chabert detested the very names of these things.

With my mind of today, I was unjust enough, two minutes ago, to be surprised how I didn't realize straight away what the remedy was. I had nowhere to turn: out of vanity my grandfather found mathematics repellent, which was the one limitation on his almost universal knowledge. "That man," or rather "Monsieur Gagnon has never forgotten anything he has read," they used to say with awe in Grenoble. Mathematics were his enemies' one answer to that. My father detested mathematics on religious grounds, I believe; he forgave them a little only because they teach you how *to draw up the plan of an estate*. I was forever making copies for him of the plan of his properties in Claix, Echirolles, Fontagnieu, Le Cheylas (valley near [*a blank*]) (where he had just pulled off a successful deal).

I despised Bezout as much as Messrs Dupuy and Chabert.

There were a good five or six *experts* at the Ecole Centrale who passed into the Ecole Polytechnique in 1797 or 98, but they wouldn't stoop to answering my questions, not very clearly explained perhaps, or rather which stumped them.

I either bought or received as a prize the works of the *abbé* Marie, one volume in 18mo. I read this volume as avidly as a novel. In it I found the same truths differently expressed, which gave me great pleasure and rewarded me for my trouble, but otherwise nothing new.

I don't mean to say there really was nothing new in it; perhaps I didn't understand it, I wasn't sufficiently well informed to see it.

In order to meditate with less disturbance, I had installed myself in the drawing-room furnished with twelve handsome armchairs embroidered by my poor mother, and which was opened only once or twice a year for the dust to be removed.

This room inspired me to contemplation; in those days I could still picture to myself the pretty supper-parties given by my mother. As ten o'clock sounded we would leave the glittering lights of this drawing-room to go into the dining-room where an enormous fish was to be found. This was my father's luxury; this instinct remained with him even in the state of piety and agricultural speculation to which I saw him reduced.

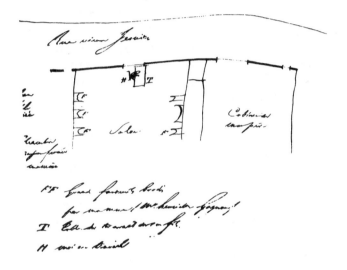

Rue [des] Vieux-Jésuites.—Oilcloth blackboard.—My mother's room kept permanently shut.—Drawing-room.—My father's study.
    FF. Big armchairs embroidered by my mother (Mme Henriette Gagnon).—T. Her son's work-table.—H. Me working.

It was on the table T that I had composed the first act or the five acts of my play, which I called a comedy, as I awaited the moment of genius more or less as if an angel had been due to appear to me.

My enthusiasm for mathematics was based principally perhaps on my horror of hypocrisy; hypocrisy as I saw it, was my aunt Séraphie, Mme Vignon, and their pr[iests].

In my opinion, hypocrisy wasn't possible in mathematics and, in my youthful simplicity, I thought the same went for all the sciences in which I had heard it said they were applied. What then when I realized that no one could explain to me how it is that a minus times a minus equals a plus $(- \times - = +)$? (This is one of the fundamental bases of the science known as *algebra*.)

They did far worse than not explain this difficulty to me (which is no doubt explicable because it leads to the truth), they explained it to me by reasons that were obviously far from clear to those who advanced them to me.

Under pressure from me, M. Chabert grew flustered, and repeated *his lesson*, the selfsame one to which I had raised objections, and finally seemed to be saying to me:

"But it's the custom; everyone accepts this explanation. Euler and Lagrange, who were just as good as you, obviously, accepted it all right. We know you're very clever (this meant: 'We know you won a first prize for *literature* and spoke well to M. Teste-Lebeau and the other members of the Department'), you clearly want to make yourself conspicuous."

As for M. Dupuy, he treated my timid objections (timid because of his own emphatic tone) with a haughty smile verging on antipathy. Although much less expert than M. Chabert, he was less of a bourgeois, less limited, and perhaps took a sound view of his own mathematical knowledge. If I were to meet with these gentlemen for a week today, I would know at once what line to take. But I am always having to come back to this point.

Raised under a bell-jar by relations whose despair had made their minds even narrower, denied all contact with humanity, I felt intensely at the age of fifteen, but was far less capable than other children of judging humanity and divining the various games it played. So I don't have great confidence fundamentally in all the judgments I have been writing in the foregoing 536 pages. All that is true for certain is the *feeling*; only to attain to the truth I need to raise the words I write by four sharps. I am expressing them with the coldness of a man of forty whose senses have been dulled by experience.

Four sharps

I distinctly recall that when I mentioned my difficulty over *minus times minus* to one of the *experts*, he laughed in my face; they were all more or less like Paul-Emile Teisseire and learnt by rote.

I often watched them up at the blackboard after a demonstration saying:

"It's evident therefore that, etc."

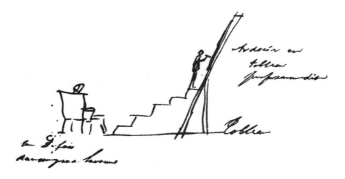

Slate or blackboard properly so called.—M. Dupuy in his big armchair.—Blackboard.

"Nothing could be less evident for you," I thought. But the things in question were evident for me and, with the best will in the world, it was impossible to doubt them.

Mathematics take into account only one small corner of objects (their quality), but are pleasing thereby for saying about it only things which are certain, only the truth, and almost the whole truth.

At the age of fourteen, in 1797, I imagined that higher mathematics, which I have never known, contained *every* or almost every aspect of objects, so that by going on I would come to know certain, indubitable things, which I could prove to myself whenever I wanted, *about everything.*

I was a long time convincing myself that my objection concerning $- \times - = +$ could never possibly enter M. Chabert's head, that M. Dupuy would only ever answer it with a lofty smile, and that the *experts* I questioned would always make fun of me.

I was thereby reduced to what I still tell myself today: that – times – equals + must be true, since self-evidently, by continually employing this rule in a calculation, you end up with results that *are true and indubitable.*

My great misery was this figure:

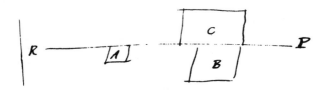

Let RP be the line separating the positive from the negative, everything above it is positive, just as everything below it is negative; how, by taking square B as many times as there are units in square A, can I manage to make it change sides to square C?

Or, to adopt a clumsy comparison that was made even clumsier by M. Chabert's supremely Grenoblois drawl, suppose the negative quantities are a man's debts, how by multiplying 10,000 francs of debt by 500 francs, will he or can he manage to acquire a fortune of 5,000,000, five million?

Were M. Dupuy and M. Chabert hypocrites like the pr[iests] who came to say [mass] in my grandfather's house and were my beloved mathematics only a confidence trick? I didn't know how to get at the truth. How avidly I would then have listened to a word about logic or the art of *discovering the truth*! What a moment to have had M. de Tracy's *Logic* explained to me! Perhaps I would have been a different man, perhaps I would have had a much better brain.

I concluded, by my own poor little efforts, that M. Dupuy might well be a deceiver, but that M. Chabert was a conceited bourgeois who couldn't understand that objections might exist unrecognized by him.

My father and grandfather possessed the folio *Encyclopédie* of Diderot and d'Alembert; this is, or rather was, a work costing seven or eight hundred francs. It takes a terrible amount of persuasion for a provincial to lay out that much capital on books, from which I conclude, today, that before I was born my father and grandfather must have belonged wholeheartedly to the party of the *philosophes*.

My father could but be upset seeing me leafing through the *Encyclopédie*. I had the most complete confidence in that book because of my father's antipathy and the resolute hatred it inspired in the pr[iests] who frequented the house. The vicar-general Canon Rey, a great papier-mâché figure five foot ten inches tall, pulled a strange face when he mispronounced the names of Diderot and d'Alembert. Deep inside me I felt joy at this grimace; I am still very susceptible to this kind of pleasure.* I enjoyed it at times in 1815 when I saw the noblemen refusing to recognize the courage of Nicolas Buonaparte, for such then was that great man's name, and yet, as early as 1807, I had hoped passionately he wouldn't conquer England; where to take refuge then?

I sought therefore to consult d'Alembert's mathematical articles in the *Encyclopédie*; their self-satisfied tone, the lack

---

*Who on earth could be interested in the simple movements of a heart described without rhetoric? Rome 36.

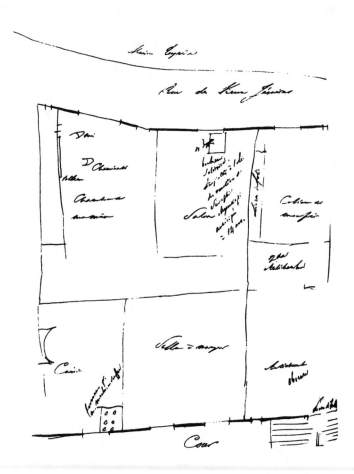

Teisseire house.—Rue des Vieux-Jésuites.—Me.—Cheminade.—
Blackboard.—My mother's room.—Drawing-room.—Solitary
happiness. Here I found shelter from the vexations of Séraphie.
Accentuated misanthropy at age fourteen.—Folio books.—My
father's study.—Second anteroom.—Kitchen.—Stove for the
sulphur moulds.—Dining-room.—Dark anteroom.—Front
door.—Courtyard.

   H. Me swotting up the *abbé* Marie.

of any reverence for the truth shocked me greatly and in any case I understood them little. How ardently I then worshipped the truth! How sincerely I believed it to be the queen of the world I was about to enter! Absolutely the only enemies I could find it had were the p[riests].

If $- \times - = +$ had caused me much sorrow, imagine the darkness that took possession of my soul when I began on the *Statics* of Louis Monge, the brother of the illustrious Monge who was to come and set the examinations for the Ecole Polytechnique.

At the beginning of geometry, it says: "We give the name of PARALLELS to two lines which, extended to infinity, would never meet." But right at the beginning of the *Statics*, that famous blockhead of a Louis Monge has put something like this: "Two parallel lines may be considered as meeting if extended to infinity."

I thought I was reading a catechism and one of the clumsier ones moreover. In vain did I ask for explanations from M. Chabert.

"My boy," he said, adopting that fatherly air so ill-suited to the foxy Dauphinois, the air of Edouard Mounier (peer of France in 1836), "my boy, you'll find that out later on."

And going up to his oilcloth blackboard and drawing two parallel lines very close together, that monster said to me:

"You can see very well that at infinity they may be said to meet."

I almost gave the whole thing up. An astute confessor, a good jesuit, might have converted me at this point by glossing this maxim:

"You can see that all is error, or rather that nothing is false, nothing true, all is convention. Adopt the convention which will earn you the best reception from the world. But the riff-raff are patriotic and will always besmirch that side of the question; make yourself an aristocrat like your relations and we shall find a means of sending you to Paris and recommending you to ladies of influence."

CHAPTER 34

This said winningly and I would have become a scoundrel and would today, in 1836, have a large fortune.

At thirteen I pictured the world to myself solely in terms of the *Mémoires secrets* of Duclos and S[ain]t-Simon's *Memoirs* in seven volumes. The supreme happiness was to live in Paris writing books on a hundred *louis* a year. Marion had told me my father would leave me more.

I fancy I said to myself: "*True or false, mathematics will get me out of Grenoble,* out of this mire that turns my stomach."

But I find this argument very advanced for my age. I continued to work hard; it would have upset me too much to break off, but I was profoundly anxious and dejected.

Finally chance willed that I should encounter a great man and that I should not become a scoundrel. Here for the second time *the subject surpasses the teller*. I shall try not to exaggerate.

In my reverence for mathematics, I had been hearing speak for some time of a young man, a well-known Jacobin, a great and fearless sportsman, and who knew far more mathematics than Messrs Dupuy and Chabert, but who hadn't made them his profession. Only, being far from rich, he had given lessons to that untrustworthy character Anglès (later on a count and prefect of police, enriched by Louis XVIII at the time of the loans).

But I was timid, how could I dare approach him? And then his lessons were horribly expensive: twelve *sous* a lesson; how to afford it? (This price strikes me as too ridiculous, perhaps it was twenty-four or forty *sous*.)

I recounted all this with a full heart to my good aunt Elisabeth who was by then perhaps eighty years old, but her excellent heart and her better brain, if that's possible, were no more than thirty. In her generosity she gave me a lot of six-franc *écus*. But what must have cost that soul filled with the most just and delicate pride wasn't the money but the fact that the lessons I took must be kept *secret from my father*, and to what well founded, legitimate reproaches was she not exposing herself? Was Séraphie still alive? I wouldn't answer to the contrary. Yet I was certainly a child when my aunt Séraphie died because, when I learnt of her death in the kitchen facing Marion's cupboard, I threw myself down on my knees to give thanks to God for so great a deliverance.

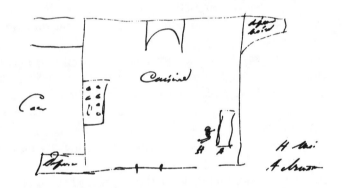

Courtyard.—Pantry.—Kitchen.—Dark pantry.—H. Me.—
A. Cupboard.

This event, the *écus* so nobly given me by my aunt Elisabeth so that I could have lessons in secret from that frightful Jacobin, stopped me once and for all from becoming a scoundrel. To meet a man who took after the Greeks and Romans and to wish to die rather than not be like him was the work of an instant: *punto (Non sia che un punto)* [Alfieri].[1]

How I, timid as I was, came to approach M. Gros I have no idea. (The fresco has fallen away at this point and I would be no more than a worthless novelist, like Don Ruggiero Caetani, were I to undertake to make it good. Allusion to the frescos in the *Campo Santo* in Pisa and to their present condition.)

Without knowing how I got there, I see myself in the small room that Gros occupied in St-Laurent, the oldest and poorest quarter of the town; this is a long narrow street squeezed between the mountains and the river. I didn't enter that small room on my own, but who was my fellow-student? Was it Cheminade? About that, the most total oblivion, my soul's whole attention was obviously for Gros.* (That great man died so long ago I think I can remove the *monsieur*.)

He was a young man with dark fair hair, very energetic but very fat, he may have been twenty-five or twenty-six years old; his hair was extremely curly and quite long, he was wearing a frock-coat, and said to us:

"Where shall we begin, *citoyens*? We must find out what you know already."

"But we know quadratic equations."

But being a man of good sense, he began teaching us these equations, i.e. squaring $a + b$, for example, which he made us raise to the power of two: $a^2 + 2ab + b^2$, assuming the first member of the equation to be the beginning of the square, the complement of the square etc., etc., etc.

For us, or at least for me, this was for the heavens to open. I could at last see the wherefore of things, it was no longer an apothecary's prescription falling out of the sky to resolve equations.

I felt an intense pleasure, similar to that of reading an

1. "Let it take only an instant": the words come from a tragedy by Vittorio Alfieri (1749–1803), whom Stendhal admired as a champion of political liberty.

*To be fitted in: excursions to the Grande-Chartreuse, to Sarcenas.

enthralling novel. It has to be admitted that everything that Gros told us about quadratic equations was more or less in the wretched Bezout, but there our eyes hadn't deigned to notice it. It was explained so drearily that I hadn't bothered to pay attention to it.

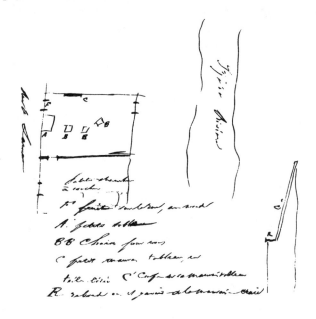

Mountain.—Rue St-Laurent.—Small bedroom.—Isère, river.
  F. Window overlooking the street, to the north.—A. Small table.—BB. Chairs for us.—C. Small cheap blackboard of oil-cloth.—C'. Section of this cheap blackboard.—R. Ledge where there was some cheap white chalk which crumbled in your fingers when you wrote on the blackboard. I've never seen anything so pitiful.

At the third or fourth lesson, we moved on to cubic equations and here Gros was entirely new. I fancy he transported us straight away to the frontiers of the science and face to face with the difficulty to be overcome, or before the veil that was to be lifted. For example, he showed us one after the other the various ways of resolving cubic equations, what

Cardano's first attempts had been like perhaps, then the progress made, and finally the current method.

We were greatly surprised when he didn't make us demonstrate the same proposition one after the other. As soon as one thing was properly understood he went on to the next.

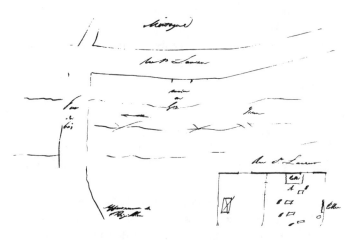

Mountain.—Rue St-Laurent.—Wooden bridge.—Gros's house.—Isère.—Bigillions' apartment.—Rue St-Laurent.—Table.—Blackboard.

Although there was nothing at all of the charlatan in Gros, he had the effect of that quality so useful in a teacher, as in a commander-in-chief: he occupied my whole soul. I revered and respected him as much perhaps as I displeased him. I have met so often with this disagreeable and surprising reaction that it is perhaps by an error of memory that I attribute it to the first of my passionate admirations. I displeased M. de Tracy and Mme Pasta by admiring them too enthusiastically.

One day* of great events we talked politics the whole

---

*29 J[anuar]y 1836. Rain and cold. Walk to *San Pietro in Montorio* where I had the idea of writing this in 1832.

lesson and at the end he wouldn't take our money. So accustomed was I to the sordid style of my Dauphinois teachers, Messrs Chabert, Durand, etc., that this very simple act renewed my admiration and enthusiasm. I fancy that on this occasion there were three of us, Cheminade perhaps, Félix Faure and I, and I fancy also that we each put a twelve-*sou* coin down on the small table A.

I remember almost nothing from the last two years, 1798 and 1799. My passion for mathematics took up so much of my time that Félix Faure has told me I then wore my hair too long, so much did I *begrudge* the half-hour I would have had to waste getting it cut.

Towards the end of the summer of 1799, my citizen's heart was wrung by our defeats in Italy, Novi and the rest, which produced intense delight in my relations mixed however with anxiety. My grandfather, more reasonable, would have wanted the Russians and Austrians not to get to Grenoble. But truth to tell, what I have to say about my family's hopes is almost entirely supposition; the hope of soon leaving them and my intense and direct love of mathematics absorbed me to the extent that I no longer paid much attention to what my relations said. I didn't tell myself so in so many words perhaps, but I felt this: "At the point I have reached, what do their maunderings matter to me?"

Soon a selfish fear came to add itself to my distress as a citizen. I was afraid that because of the approaching Russians there would be no examination in Grenoble.

Bonaparte landed in Fréjus. I accuse myself of having had this sincere desire: the young Bonaparte, whom I pictured to myself as a handsome young man like a comic-opera colonel, should make himself king of France.

The word inspired only brilliant and generous thoughts in me. This contemptible error was the fruit of my more contemptible education. My relations were like domestic servants in respect of the king. At the mere name of king or Bourbon, tears came into their eyes.

I don't know whether I had this contemptible sentiment in 1797 when I revelled in the accounts of the battles of Lodi, Arcole, etc., etc., which were the despair of my relations, who tried for a long time not to believe them, or whether I had it in 1799 at the news of the landing in Fréjus. I incline to 1797.

In the event the enemy's approach meant that M. Louis Monge, the examiner from the Ecole Polytechnique, didn't come to Grenoble. "We shall have to go to Paris," we all said. "But," I thought, "how to get permission from my relations for such a journey? To go to the modern Babylon, to the city of corruption, at sixteen and a half!" I was extremely agitated, but I have no distinct memory.

The examinations for M. Dupuy's mathematics course arrived and were a triumph for me.

I won first prize ahead of eight or nine young men, most of them older and more favoured than I was, and who all of them two months later passed into the Ecole Polytechnique.

At the blackboard I was eloquent, for the fact is I was talking about something I had been thinking passionately about for at least fifteen months and that I had been studying for three years (to be verified, from the start of M. Dupuy's course in the ground-floor classroom in the Ecole Centrale). M. Dausse, an obstinate and learned man, could see that I knew, and asked me the hardest questions, the ones most likely to trip me up. He was an alarming-looking man and never encouraged you. (He resembled Domeniconi, an excellent actor I admired at the Valle in January 1836.)

To the first prize M. Dausse, the engineer-in-chief, a friend of my grandfather's (who was present at my examination and in ecstasies), added a quarto volume of Euler. Perhaps this present was given in 1798, at the end of which year also I won first prize for mathematics. (M. Dupuy's course comprised two or even three years.)

Immediately after the examination, in the evening, or rather on the evening of the day when my name was posted up so gloriously ("But in view of the manner in which citizen B. gave his answers, of his accuracy, of his brilliant facility...," this had been M. Dupuy's final effort in his campaign: on the pretext of not harming my seven or eight classmates, the great thing had been to get them awarded the first prize, on the pretext of not imperilling their admission to the Ecole Polytechnique, but the damnably pig-headed M. Dausse had had some phrase like that above inserted into the report and consequently printed), I see myself going into the wood in the Jardin de Ville, between the statue of Hercules and the railings, with Bigillion and two or three others intoxicated by my success, because everyone thought it right and proper and it was easy to see M. Dupuy didn't like me; the report that I had gone to take lessons from that Jacobin Gros, I who had the advantage of following the course of M. Dupuy, wasn't calculated to reconcile me with him.

So as we went along, I said to Bigillion, philosophizing as was our habit:

"At such a moment, one should forgive all one's enemies."

"On the contrary," said Bigillion, "one should go up and triumph over them."

My delight had made me somewhat drunk, it's true, and I was inventing arguments in order to hide this, yet at bottom this reply typified Bigillion's profound good sense who was much more down to earth than I was, and at the same time the Spanish exaltation to which I was unfortunate enough to be subject all my life.

I can see circumstances: Bigillion, my companions and myself had just read the notice containing the sentence about me.

Underneath the archway of the Concert Hall, the report on the examinations, signed by the members of the departmental ad[ministration], had been posted up on the door of the Hall.

After this triumphant examination I went to Claix. My health had an imperious need of rest.* But I had one grave

*29 January 1836. Filippo has given me back the second volume of this work.

Archway into the gardens.—Here, on the second floor, Charvet
ap[artmen]t; on the first, M. Faure's ap[artmen]t.—On this side, 20
feet from the wall P, was my grandfather's terrace.—Place du
Département.—Public baths.—Wood, lime-trees whose branches
were cut horizontally at 30 feet.—Bronze pedestrian statue of
Hercules.—Iron railings.—Iron railings.—Sunken flowerbed three
or four feet down.

B. Bigillion.—H. Me.—A. Two others.

anxiety on which I mused in the little wood of Doyatières and among the bushes beside the road to Les Ilots, along the Drac and the 45 [degree] slope of Comboire.

(I now carried a gun only for form's sake.) "Would my father give me the money to go and be swallowed up in the new Babylon, in that centre of immorality, at the age of six-teen and a half?"

Here again the excess of passion, of emotion has destroyed all memory. I have no idea how my departure was settled on.

Comboire.—Precipices.—Drac very fast-flowing.—I was at HHH.

There was talk of a second examination by M. Dupuy. I was exhausted, worn out by hard work. To revise arithmetic, geo[metry], trigo[nometry], algebra, conic sections, statics, so that I could undergo a second examination, was an appalling labour. In fact I was at the end of my tether. This fresh effort, which I had certainly expected, but in December, would have turned me against my beloved mathematics. Fortunately, M. Dupuy's laziness, who was busy harvesting his grapes in Noyarey, came to the aid of my own. Addressing me as *tu*, which was the great sign of his favour, he told me he knew perfectly well what I knew, that a fresh examination was pointless, and adopting a dignified, priestly air he gave me a magnificent certificate certifying a falsehood, to wit that he had made me sit another examination for admission to the Ecole Polytechnique and that I had got through it splendidly.

My uncle gave me two or four *louis d'or* which I refused. My excellent grandfather and my aunt Elisabeth probably gave me presents of which I have no recollection.

My departure was arranged with a M. Rosset, an acquaintance of my father's who was returning to Paris where he had settled.

What I am about to say isn't nice. At the precise moment of my departure, waiting for the carriage, my father received my farewells in the Jardin de Ville beneath the windows of the houses facing the Rue Montorge.

He was weeping a little. The only impression his tears made on me was to find him very ugly. If my reader finds that horrifying, let him deign to remember the hundreds of enforced walks to Les Granges with my aunt Séraphie; walks I was forced to take *for my own pleasure*. This was the hypocrisy which annoyed me most and led me to execrate that vice.

Emotion has removed from me absolutely all memory of my journey with M. Rosset from Grenoble to Lyon, and from Lyon to Nemours.

It was in the early part of November 1799, because at Nemours, twenty or twenty-five leagues from Paris, we learnt of the events of the 18 Brumaire (or 9 November, 1799) which had taken place the previous day.[2]

We learnt of them in the evening; I didn't understand much about them, and I was delighted that the young General Bonaparte should have made himself king of France. My grandfather had often spoken enthusiastically about Philip Augustus and Bouvines[3]; any king of France as I saw it was a

2. The *coup d'état* by which Napoleon came to power.

3. Philip Augustus was king of France from 1180 to 1223 and a great extender of its territory; at the battle of Bouvines in 1214 he defeated a coalition mounted against him by the English King John.

Philip Augustus, a Louis XIV, or a voluptuous Louis XV, as I had met with him in Duclos's *Mémoires secrets*.

Voluptuousness in no way spoilt my imagination. My *idée fixe* on arrival in Paris, the idea to which I came back four or five times a day and especially at nightfall, the moment of rêverie, was that a pretty woman, a woman of Paris far more beautiful than Mme Kubly or my poor Victorine, would overturn in my presence or fall into some great danger from which I would save her, and go on from there to become her lover. My reasoning was that of the hunter: "So rapturously should I love her I have to find her!"

This madness, never confessed to a soul, lasted for six years perhaps. I was only cured of it in part by the desiccated ladies of the court in Brunswick among whom I made my debut in November 1806.

CHAPTER 35

PARIS

M. Rosset deposited me in a hotel on the corner of the Rue de Bourgogne and the Rue St-Dominique. It was entered from the Rue St-Dominique; they wanted to put me close to the Ecole Polytechnique which they thought I would be entering.[1]

I was greatly astonished by the sound of the bells sounding the hour. The environs of Paris had seemed to me horribly ugly: there wasn't a single mountain! This dislike increased rapidly during the days following.

I left the hotel and, for economy's sake, took a room on the quincunx of the Invalides. I received some hospitality and advice from the *mathematicians* who had entered the School the previous year. I had to go and call on them.

I had to go and call on my cousin Daru.

This was the very first visit I had ever paid in my life.

M. Daru, a man of the world, aged sixty-five, must have been thoroughly shocked by my gaucherie and this gaucherie must have been thoroughly graceless.

I had arrived in Paris with the settled intention of being a seducer of women, what today I would call a *Don Juan* (after Mozart's opera).

M. Daru had for a long time been secretary-g[eneral] to M. de St-Priest, the intendant of Languedoc, which consists today, I fancy, of seven departments. You may have read in the

1. The Ecole was at that time attached to the Palais Bourbon, now the Chambre des Députés, across the river from the Place de la Concorde.

383

histories that the famous Basville, that gloomy tyrant, had been intendant or rather king of Languedoc from 168[5] to 1710 perhaps. It was a region of States; which vestige of public debate and liberty demanded a skilful secretary-general under an intendant who was a sort of *grand seigneur* like M. de St-Priest, who was perhaps intendant from 1775 to 1786. M. Daru, a native of Grenoble, the son of a bourgeois with pretensions to nobility, but poor out of pride like all my family, had made his own way in the world and, without stealing, had amassed perhaps four or five hundred thousand francs. He had traversed the Revolution with skill, without letting himself be blinded by whatever love or hatred he might have felt for the old ideas, for the nobility or the clergy. He was a man whose one passion was for the *usefulness* of vanity or the vanity of usefulness, I saw him from too near the ground to determine which. He had bought a house in the Rue de Lille, No 505, on the corner of the Rue de Belle-chasse,* of which he modestly occupied only the small apartment above the carriage entrance.

The first floor at the far end of the courtyard was let to Mme Rebuffel, the wife of a highly reputable merchant, a man of character and warm-blooded, the complete opposite of M. Daru, M. Rebuffel, M. Daru's nephew, who got on with his uncle thanks to his accommodating, all-things-to-all-men character.

---

*I must have given the impression of being a strange creature.

To be fitted in. M. D[aru] was a tall, rather good-looking old man with a big nose, something not at all common in France, he had a bit of a cast in one eye and looked rather shifty. Mme D[aru] a little old woman, pious, rich, gentle-sounding and at bottom quite good-natured, didn't dare breathe a word in front of him. He found amusement with a pretty little girl of five, his granddaughter: Mlle Le Brun (today Mme the Marquise de Brossard). M de B[rossard] a spendthrift and a worthless general and with pretensions to the most ancient nobility. He strikes me as a fairly ignominious finagler.

Right from the start, that drawing-room nauseated me and bored me to excess. But what drawing-room could have amused me when my entire brain was taken up with a complicated romance, and the tender and sublime love *à la* Bradamante that I was then seeking? I must have been the most solemn of lunatics. What must have preoccupied them was the objection: "He's no fool though!" "What a difficult character," Mme Le Br[un] used to say; the fact is I never spoke a word in her presence.

M. Rebuffel came each day to spend quarter of an hour with his wife and his daughter Adèle, and otherwise lived in the Rue Saint-Denis at his broker's business, with his partner and mistress Mlle Barbereux, an energetic, vulgar woman of thirty or thirty-five, who looked decidedly to me as though she made scenes and cuckolded her lover and gave him plenty to think about.

I was greeted with affection and openness of heart by the excellent M. Rebuffel, whereas M. Daru senior received me with expressions of affection and devotion for my grandfather which wrung my heart and rendered me speechless.

M. Daru was a tall, rather good-looking old man with a big nose, something not at all common in the Dauphiné; he had a bit of a cast in one eye and looked rather shifty. With him he had a small wizened old woman, a complete provincial, who was his wife. He had married her in the old days for her fortune, which was considerable, and for the rest she didn't dare breathe a word in front of him.

Mme Daru was good-natured at bottom and very polite with the little dignified air appropriate to a provincial sub-prefect's wife. For the rest I have never encountered anyone more totally lacking in the celestial spark. No power on earth could have made that soul to be moved by anything noble or generous. In these sorts of souls the most cautious egotism, which they glory in, occupies the possibility, the place of the emotion of anger or generosity.

This cautious, sensible, but unattractive temperament had formed the character of her elder son, M. le Comte Daru, Napoleon's minister and Secretary of State, who had such great influence on my life; of Mlle Sophie, later Mme de Baure, who was deaf; of Mme Le Brun, now Mme la Marquise de [a blank]. Her second son, Martial Daru, had neither brains nor wit, but a kind heart; he would never have harmed a soul.

Mme Cambon, M. and Mme Daru's eldest daughter, may have had a lofty character, but I no more than glimpsed it; she died a few months after my arrival in Paris.

Do I need to warn you that I am sketching the characters of these personages such as I saw them subsequently? The final line, which seems to me the true one, has made me forget all the earlier lines (a term from drawing).

I preserve only mental pictures of my first entry into M. Daru's drawing-room.

For example, I see very clearly the little red printed calico dress worn by an attractive small girl of five, M. Daru's granddaughter with whom he used to amuse himself like the old and bored Louis XIV with Mme la Duchesse de Bourgogne. This attractive little girl, but for whom a lugubrious silence would often have reigned in the small drawing-room in the Rue de Lille, was Mlle Pulchérie Le Brun (now Mme la Marquise de Brossard, very imperious, it's said, round as a barrel and who rules the roost with her husband, M. le G[énér]al de Brossard, himself in command of the department of the Drôme).

M. de Brossard is a spendthrift who claims to be from the highest nobility, a descendant of Louis the Fat, I believe, boastful, a slippery customer none too choosy about the means by which he repairs his finances, which are in constant disarray. In sum: the character of a poor nobleman, a nasty character which usually goes with a great many misfortunes. (I call a man's *character* his habitual way of going in pursuit of happiness; or in clearer, but less meaningful terms: *the sum of his moral habits*.)

But I am digressing. I was very far from seeing things, even physical things, so clearly in December 1799. I was all emotion, and this excess of emotion has left me only a few very distinct mental pictures, without any explanation of the hows and the whys.

What I see today with great clarity, but what in 1799 I sensed very confusedly, is that on my arrival in Paris two great objects of my constant and passionate desires suddenly fell away to nothing. I had adored Paris and mathematics. Paris, without any mountains, filled me with an aversion so strong it amounted almost to homesickness. Mathematics were now nothing more to me than, as it were, the scaffolding for the previous evening's firework display (something I saw in Turin, on the day after Midsummer's Day 1802).

I was tormented by these changes of which at the age of sixteen and a half I could naturally see neither the why nor the *how*.

In reality, I had only loved Paris out of a profound dislike of Grenoble.

As for mathematics, they had been only a means. I even disliked them a little in November 1799, for I was afraid of them. I was determined not to let myself be examined in Paris, as the seven or eight pupils had been who won first prize behind me at the Ecole Centrale and who had all got in. But if my father had taken the trouble, he might have forced me to take the examination, I would have entered the School and no longer been able to go on *living in Paris writing comedies*.

Of all my passions, this one alone remained.

I can't imagine, and this thought occurs to me for the first time thirty-seven years after the event, as I write this, I can't imagine why my father didn't force me to take the examination. He trusted probably to the extreme passion he had seen in me for mathematics. My father in any case was moved only by what was close to him. Yet I was mortally afraid of being forced to enter the School, and waited for the courses to start with a terrible impatience. In the *exact sciences*, it is impossible to start a course at the third lesson.

Let me come to the mental pictures which remain with me.

I see myself taking medicine alone and forlorn in an inexpensive room I had rented on the quincunx of the Invalides at the far end, between the end (on that side of the quincunx) of the Rue de l'Université and the Rue St-Dominique, a few steps from the Emperor's Civil List mansion, where a few years later I was to play a very different role.

My profound disappointment at finding Paris so unattractive had upset my stomach. The Paris mud, the absence of mountains, the sight of so many preoccupied people going rapidly past in fine carriages beside me, who was known to nobody and had nothing to do, filled me with a profound distress. A doctor who had taken the trouble to study my condition, not very complicated for sure, would have given me an emetic and ordered me to go every three days to Versailles or St-Germain.

I fell into the hands of a notable charlatan and even more of an ignoramus; he was an army surgeon, very thin, practising in the neighbourhood of the Invalides, then a very impoverished quarter, whose business was to treat the cases of *gonorrhoea* among the students from the Ecole Polytechnique. He gave me black medicines, which I took alone and abandoned in my room, which had only one window seven or eight feet up like a prison. There I see myself sitting dejectedly next to a small iron stove, my tisane standing on the floor.

But in this state my worst affliction was the thought that kept coming back: "Great God, what a miscalculation! What then must I hope for?"

CHAPTER 36

It must be agreed that the fall was great, frightful. And it was a young man of sixteen and a half, one of the least reasonable and most passionate souls I have ever encountered, who experienced it!

I had confidence in no one.

I had heard Séraphie and my father's pr[iests] *crowing* over the ease with which they had led, i.e. deceived, such and such a person or gathering of persons.

R[eligion] seemed to me a sinister and powerful machine; I still had some belief in hell, but none in its pr[iests]. The images of h[ell] which I had seen in the octavo B[ible] bound in figured green parchment, and in my poor mother's editions of Dante, had horrified me. But where the pr[iests] were concerned, nothing. I was far from seeing what in reality it is: a powerful corporation to which it is highly advantageous to be affiliated, witness my contemporary and fellow-countryman young Genou, who often served my coffee, without stockings, at the Café Genou, on the corner of the Grande-Rue and the Rue du Département, and who for the past twenty years has been in Paris as M. de Genoude.

For support I had only my common sense and my belief in Helvétius's *Esprit*. I say *belief* deliberately, raised in a vacuum, gripped by ambition, barely emancipated by being sent to the Ecole Centrale, Helvétius could but be for me *a prediction of the things I was going to meet with*. I had confidence in this long-term prediction, because two or three small predictions had, to my not very experienced way of thinking, come true.

I wasn't *tricky*, sly, suspicious, knowing how to extricate myself from a twelve-*sou* transaction with an excess of cleverness and mistrust, like most of my companions, by counting the bits of faggot making up the bundles of kindling provided by the landlord, like my schoolfellows the Monvals, whom I had just come across again in Paris and at the Ecole where they had been for the past year. In the streets of Paris I was an impassioned dreamer, gazing at the sky and always on the point of being run over by a cabriolet.

In a word, "I was quite unskilled in the business of life"[1] and, as a consequence, I couldn't be appreciated, as one or other newspaper of 1836 said this morning, in that journalistic style that wants to replace the nullity or puerility of the thought by the unusualness of the style.

To have seen this truth about myself would have been to be skilled in the business of life.

The Monvals gave me very sensible advice, whose gist was not to let myself be robbed of two or three *sous* a day, but their ideas appalled me; they must have thought I was an imbecile en route to the madhouse. It's true that out of pride I revealed little of myself. I fancy it was the *Monvaux* or other students who had arrived at the Ecole a year earlier who found me my room and my cut-price doctor.

Was it Sinard? Had he died of consumption in Grenoble a year earlier, or did he only die there one or two years later?

In the midst of these friends, or rather these children full of sound sense and arguing over three *sous* a day with the landlord who probably made eight *sous* a day legitimately out of each one of us poor devils, and stole three, total eleven *sous*, "I was plunged into involuntary ecstasies, into inter-

1. These words are Stendhal's adaptation of Alfred de Vigny, in the preface to his tragedy of *Chatterton*, a drama based on the life and miserable death of the young Bristol poet.

minable rêveries, into infinite inventions"* (as the n[ews-pap]er so *self-importantly* says).

I had my list of the connections conflicting with my passions, for example: *priest* and *love*, *father* and *love of country*, or *Brutus*, which seemed to me to be the key to the sublime in literature. This was entirely my own invention. I had forgotten it these past twenty-six years perhaps, I must come back to it.

I was highly emotional all the time. "What must I love then if I don't like Paris?" I answered myself: "An attractive woman will overturn ten paces away, I shall pick her up and we shall adore one another, she will get to know my soul and will realize how unlike the *Monvaux* I am."

This was a deeply serious reply and I made it to myself two or three times a day, especially *at nightfall*, which often for me is still a moment of tender emotion, I am inclined to embrace my mistress with tears in my eyes (when I have one).

At that time I was a constantly emotional person with no thought, except in rare moments of anger, of stopping our landlady from stealing three *sous* a day from the *kindling*.

Do I dare to say it? But perhaps it's untrue, *I was a poet*. Not, it's true, like the amiable *abbé* Delille, whom I met two or three years later through Cheminade (Rue des Francs-Bourgeois in the Marais), but like Tasso, like a hundredth part of Tasso, forgive my presumption. I didn't have this presumption in 1799; I couldn't have written a single line. Not four years since I told myself that, in 1799, I was very close to being a poet. All I lacked was the audacity to write, a *flue* for my *genius* to escape through.

First *poet* and now *genius*, forgive my modesty.

"His sensibilities have grown too keen: what barely brushes against others, wounds him to the quick."[2]

*M. de Vigny's *Chatterton*, p. 9.

2. A further quotation, or adaptation, from *Chatterton*. As is the quotation a few lines lower down.

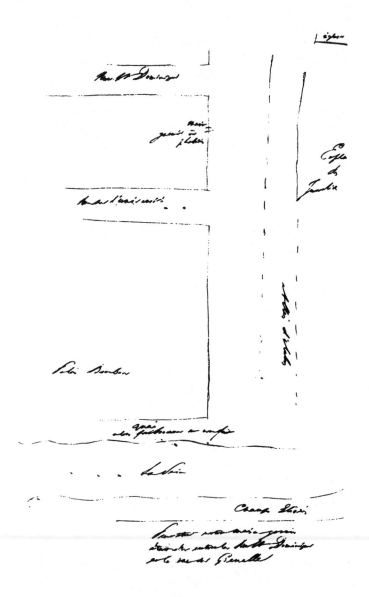

Rue St-Dominique.—Furnished lodgings where I was living.—Rue de l'Université.—Palais-Bourbon.—Tree-lined walks.—Esplanade of the Invalides.—Quay, at that time very muddy and unpaved.—The Seine.—Champs-Elysées.—Perhaps our furnished lodgings were between the Rue St-Dominique and the Rue de Grenelle.

Such I still was in 1799, such I still am in 1836, but I have learnt to hide all this beneath an irony imperceptible to the common herd, but which Fiori has quite rightly seen through.

"The affections and tendernesses of his life are crushing and disproportionate, his excessive enthusiasms lead him astray, his sympathies are too keen, those whom he pities suffer less than he does."

This is literally for me. (Its [SELF-IMPORTANCE] apart, that newspaper is right.)

The difference between me and the self-important simpletons on the newspaper "who carry their heads like the holy sacrament" is that I have never believed that society owed me the least thing. Helvétius saved me from that enormous stupidity. *Society pays for the services it sees.* Tasso's error and misfortune was to have said to himself: "What! All of Italy wealthy as it is can't pay its poet a pension of two hundred sequins (2,300 francs)?"

I read this in one of his letters.

For want of Helvétius, Tasso couldn't see that it takes the one hundred men in ten million who understand beauty, which isn't imitation or an improvement on the beautiful as already understood by the common herd, twenty or thirty years to convince the twenty thousand next most sensitive souls after their own that this new beauty is truly beautiful.

I shall remark that there is an exception when the spirit of party is involved. M. de Lamartine has perhaps written two hundred beautiful lines of poetry in his lifetime. The party of the ultras having been accused around 1818 of *stupidity* (it was known as M. de La Jobardière[3]), its wounded vanity extolled the work of a nobleman with all the irruptive force of a raging torrent bursting its banks.*

3. M. de La Jobardière was the ultraist hero of a satirical one-act comedy first performed in 1830.

*"Authority declares itself to be a stranger to the intelligence at which it takes umbrage" (*Chat*[*terton*]).

I have never had the idea then that men were treating me unfairly. The unhappiness of our so-called poets, who feed on this idea and criticize the contemporaries of Cervantes and Tasso, I find supremely ridiculous.

I fancy that at that time my father was giving me 100fr, or 150fr a month. That was riches; I never thought about being short of money, in consequence I never thought at all about money.

What I lacked was a loving heart, was a woman.

The street-girls revolted me. What could have been simpler than to do as I do nowadays, pick up a pretty girl for one *louis* in the Rue des Moulins?

I didn't lack for *louis*. My grandfather and my great-aunt Elisabeth had doubtless given me some, and I certainly hadn't spent them. But the smile of a loving heart! But the gaze of Mlle Victorine B[igillion]!

All the merry tales, exaggerating the corruption and graspingness of the street-girls, told me by the mathematicians who were then acting as friends around me, turned my stomach.

They would talk about the *pierreuses*, the cheap tarts, on the paving two hundred paces from the door of our rickety house.

A friendly heart, that was what I lacked. M. Sorel invited me to dinner sometimes, M. Daru also, I presume, but I found these men so far removed from my sublime ecstasies, my vanity made me so timid, especially with women, that I never said a word.

"A woman? A girl?" says Cherubino.[4] Good looks apart, I was Cherubino; I had very frizzy black hair and eyes of a frightening brightness.

"The man I love," or: "My lover is ugly, but no one will ever reproach him for his ugliness: he's so very clever!" That's what Mlle Victorine B[igillion] said around this time

4. In Beaumarchais's *Le Mariage de Figaro*.

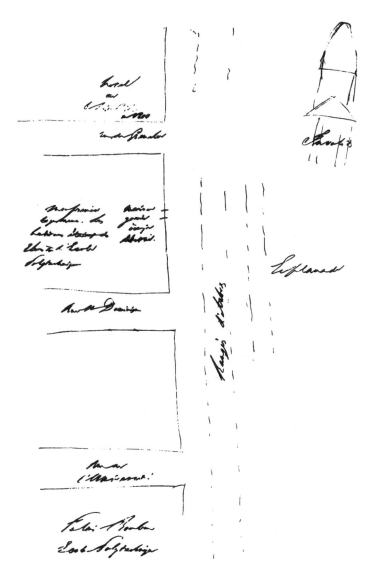

Civil List mansion in 1800.—Rue de Grenelle.—My first lodgings. The inmates were students at the Ecole Polytechnique.—Furnished lodgings where I began.—Rue St-Dominique.—Rue de l'Université.—Palais-Bourbon.—Ecole Polytechnique.—Invalides.—Rows of trees.—Esplanade.

to Félix Faure, who only found out years afterwards who she meant.

He was teasing his pretty neighbour, Mlle Victorine B[igillion], one day about her indifference. I fancy that Michel, or Frédéric Faure or he, Félix, wanted to pay court to Mlle Victorine.

F[éli]x Faure, peer of France, first president of the royal court in Grenoble, a worthless creature and *physically worn out*.

Frédéric Faure, a sly Dauphinois, devoid of all generosity, of wit, died a captain of artillery in Valence.

Michel, even slyer, even more of a Dauphinois, not very brave perhaps, captain in the imperial guard, met by me in Vienna in 1809, in charge of the workhouse in Saint-Robert near Grenoble (whom I turned into M. Valenod in the *Rouge*[5]).

Bigillion, a man of real feeling, honest, very thrifty, head clerk in the county court, killed himself around 1827, fed up, I believe, with being cuckolded, but without anger against his wife.

I don't want to portray myself as an unhappy lover on my arrival in Paris, in November 1799, or even as a lover. I was too taken up with society and with what I was going to do in that society quite unknown to me.

This problem was my mistress, hence my idea that love before you have a rank and an entry into society can't be devoted and entire as love is for someone who imagines he knows what society is like.

Often, however, I dreamt rapturously of our Dauphiné mountains; and Mlle Victorine spent several months each year at the Grande-Chartreuse, where her ancestors had received St Bruno in 1100. The Grande-Chartreuse was the one mountain I knew: I fancy I had already been there once or twice with Bigillion and Rémy.

I had fond memories of Mlle Victorine, but I never doubted for a moment that a young girl in Paris wouldn't be a hundred

5. I.e. *Le Rouge et le noir*.

times superior to her. None the less my first impression of Paris was supremely disagreeable.

This deep dissatisfaction, this disillusionment, allied to an estimable doctor, made me quite ill, I fancy. I could no longer eat.

Did M. Daru senior have me looked after during this first illness?

Passageway.—Ground floor.—Rue du Bac.—P. Door to the ground floor.—E. Staircase.

I suddenly see myself in a third-floor room, overlooking the Rue du Bac; these lodgings were entered along the Passage Ste-Marie, so much altered today and improved. My room was an attic and on the last floor of the disgraceful staircase.

I must have been very ill, because M. Daru senior brought the famous Doctor Portal to me whose face frightened me. It looked as if it were resigned to seeing a corpse. I had a nurse, which was something quite new for me.

I learnt later that there had been a risk of hydropsy of the chest. I was delirious, I believe, and a good three weeks or a month in bed.

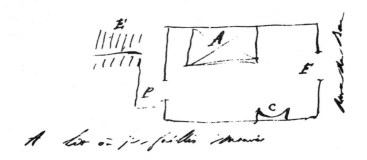

Rue de Bac.
    A. Bed where I nearly died.—P. Disgraceful staircase.—
C. Fireplace.—F. Attic window overlooking the Rue du Bac.

Félix Faure came to see me, I fancy. I believe he told me, and now I think about it I'm sure he did, that, in my delirium, I exhorted him, fine swordsman that he was, to go back to Grenoble and call out those who would be laughing at us because we hadn't entered the Ecole Polytechnique. If I ever speak again with that sentencer of the April prisoners, put questions to him about our life in 1799. That cold, timid, egotistical soul must have accurate memories; moreover he must be two years older than me and have been born around 1781.

I see two or three mental pictures of my convalescence.

My nurse used to make me my pot-au-feu near the fireplace, which seemed *vulgar* to me, and I was strongly advised not to catch cold; since I was supremely fed up with being in bed, I took heed of their advice. The physical details of life in Paris shocked me.*

*Hard work. 2 February, vile rainstorm from midday until 3. Written 26 pages and got through 50 pages of *Chatterton*. Diri and Sandre; unable to finish *Chatterton*. God, Diri is stupid! What a creature! Taking offence at everything. 3 February 1836. This evening the *Barber* at Valle and a Scribe comedy by Bett[ini].

Without any gap after my illness I see myself lodging in a second-floor room in M. Daru's house, in the Rue de Lille (or de Bourbon, when there are B[ourbons] in France), No 505. That room looked out on four gardens, it was quite vast, more or less under the roof; the [*a blank*] between the two windows sloped at an angle of forty-five degrees.

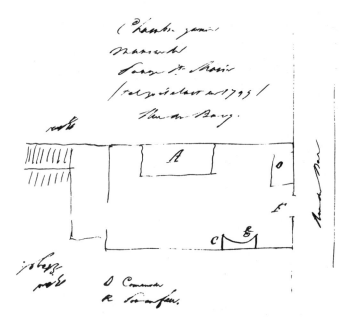

Furnished room, attic, Passage Ste-Marie (as it was in 1799), Rue du Bac.—Third floor.—Rue du Bac.—O. Chest-of-drawers. R. Pot-au-feu.

That room suited me very well. I made a notebook out of paper in order to write comedies.

It was at this time, I believe, that I dared to go and call on M. Cailhava to buy a copy of his *Art de la comédie*, which I couldn't find at any of the booksellers.[6] I ran that old Gascon

---

6. Jean-François Cailhava d'Estandoux (1730–1813), a dramatist, whose *Art de la comédie* was published in 1772.

to earth in a room in the Louvre, I believe. He told me his book was badly written, which I bravely denied. He must have taken me for a madman.

I only ever found one idea in that infernal book and even that wasn't Cailhava's but from Bacon. But is that nothing, one idea in a book? It concerned the definition of *laughter*.

My passionate cohabitation with mathematics has left me madly in love with good *definitions*, without which there are only approximations.

CHAPTER 37

But the art of comedy once on my table, I earnestly turned over the great question: should I become a composer of operas, like Grétry? or a writer of comedies?

I hardly knew the notes. M. Mention had sent me away as being unworthy of playing the violin, but I said to myself: "The notes are only the art of writing ideas down, the essential thing is to have some." And I thought I did have some. The amusing part is that I still think so today, and I am often angry I didn't leave Paris to go and be Paisiello's lackey in Naples.[1]

I have no liking for purely instrumental music; even the music of the Sistine Chapel and the choir of the chapter of St Peter's give me no pleasure (opinion confirmed on January [a blank] 1836, the day of the *Catedra di San Pietro*).

Vocal melody alone seems to me the product of genius.

A fool may be very knowledgeable, but he will never as I see it discover a beautiful melody, for example: "Se amor si gode in pace" (Act One and perhaps Scene One of the *Matrimonio segreto*).

When a man of genius takes the trouble to study melody, he achieves the lovely instrumentation of the quartet in *Bianca e Faliero* (by Rossini) or the same composer's duet in *Armida*.

In the great days of my liking for music, in Milan between

---

1. Giovanni Paisiello (1741–1816), an Italian composer more highly regarded in Stendhal's time than since.

1814 and 1821, when on the morning of a new opera I used to go to La Scala to take out my *libretto*, I couldn't help performing all the music as I read it, singing the arias and duets.

And dare I say it? Sometimes in the evenings I found my own melody *nobler* and *more affecting* than that of the *maestro*.

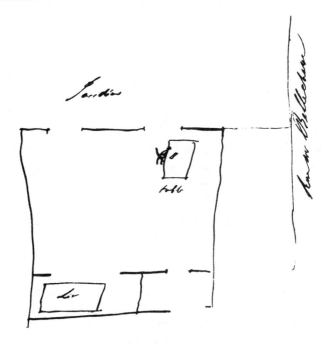

Garden.—Table.—Bed.—Rue de Bellechasse.

Since I had and have absolutely no knowledge, no way of fixing the melody on a sheet of paper so as to be able to correct it without being afraid of forgetting the original cantilena, it was like getting the original idea for a book. It's a hundred times more intelligible after being worked on.

But in fact this original idea is what you never find in the books of second-rate writers. Their strongest sentences seem to me like Priam's arrow: *sine ictu*.[2] For example, I wrote what seemed to me a delightful melody, and could see the accompaniment, for these two couplets from La Fontaine (criticized by M. Nodier for being irreligious, but around 1820 under the B[ourbon]s):

> Un mort s'en allait tristement
> S'emparer de son dernier gîte;
> Un curé s'en allait gaiement
> Enterrer ce mort au plus vite.[3]

This is perhaps the only melody I have written to French words. I have a horror of being forced to pronounce it *gi-teu, vi-teu*. The French seem to me to have the most marked untalent for music, just as the Italians have the most surprising untalent for the dance.

Sometimes, when saying stupid things to myself on purpose, to make myself laugh, or to supply jokes to the opposing camp (which I'm often very well aware of inside myself), I say to myself: "But how could I, a Frenchman, have any talent for Cimarosa's kind of music?"

I answer: "Through my mother, whom I resemble, I may perhaps have Italian blood. The Gagnoni who fled to Avignon after murdering a man in Italy perhaps got married there to the daughter of an Italian attached to the vice-legate.

"My grandfather and my aunt Elisabeth had obviously Italian faces, aquiline noses, etc."

2. A reference to the *Aeneid* and the death of Priam, whose last arrow is described as being "feeble and without weight."

3. Or literally:
A dead man went sorrowfully off
To take possession of his last resting-place;
A priest went merrily off
To bury that dead man with all haste.

"And now that five years of continuous residence in R[ome] have given me a closer acquaintance with the physical make-up of the Romans, I can see that my grandfather had exactly the Roman build, head, and nose."

"Moreover, my uncle Romain Gagnon had a head that was obviously almost Roman, except for his complexion which was very good."

I have never come across a beautiful song hit upon by a Frenchman, the best don't rise above that crudity appropriate to *popular* songs, i.e. which have to appeal to everyone, such as the captain, Rouget de Lisle's:

> Allons, enfants de la patrie . . .

a song hit upon in a single night in Strasbourg.

This song strikes me as extremely superior to anything ever made by a French head, but because of its style necessarily inferior to Mozart's:

> Là ci darem la mano,
> Là mi dirai di sì . . .

I shall admit that for me only two composers have written songs of a perfect beauty: Cimarosa and Mozart, and I'd sooner be hanged rather than have to say honestly which of the two I prefer.

Whenever my ill fate has made me acquainted with two tedious salons, it's always the one I am leaving that I find the more oppressive.

Whenever I have been hearing Mozart or Cimarosa, it's always the one I heard last who seems preferable perhaps to the other.

Paisiello I think of as quite a pleasant *piquette*,[4] which you may even hunt out and drink with pleasure at moments when you find wine too strong.

4. A drink made by diluting the *marc* or residue left by pressed grapes with water.

I would say the same of a few arias by a few composers inferior to Paisiello, for example: "Senza sposo, deh! non mi lasciate, signor governatore" (I don't remember the lines) from Fiorivante's *Cantatrici villane*. The trouble with this *piquette* is that after a moment you find it *flat*. You must only drink one glass.

Almost all authors sell out to [religion] when they write about the races of men. The very small number of men of good faith confuse proven facts with suppositions. It's when a science is beginning that someone who doesn't belong to it, like myself, may risk talking about it.

I shall say then that it's no good expecting a hound to have the intelligence of a spaniel, or a spaniel to let you know that a hare passed this way six hours ago.

There may be individual exceptions, but the general truth is that the spaniel and the hound each has its own talents.

The same probably goes for the races of men.

What is certain, as observed by myself and by Constantin,[5] is that we have met with a whole Roman circle (120, Ciabatta, met with in 1834, I believe) which is exclusively taken up with music and sings the finales from Rossini's *Semiramis* and the most difficult music extremely well, waltzing for a whole evening to the music of a country dance, in truth badly played so far as the beat was concerned. Romans, and even Italians in general, have the most marked untalent for the dance.

I have deliberately put the cart before the horse so as not to repel the Frenchman of 1880, when I shall dare to make him read that his forebears of 1830 had an untalent without equal for judging vocal music or performing it.

The French have grown knowledgeable about this kind of music since 1820, but remain barbarians at heart, for proof

5. The painter Abraham Constantin, already mentioned in Chapter 2.

of which I look no further than the success of Meyerbeer's *Robert le Diable*.

A Frenchman is less insensitive to German music, Mozart excepted.

What the Frenchman enjoys in Mozart isn't the terrible novelty of the *song* with which Leporello invites the Commander's statue to supper, but rather the accompaniment. Moreover, this before and above all else *conceited* creature has been told that this *duet* or *trio* is sublime.

A lump of iron-bearing rock, observed on the surface of the ground, makes you suppose that by digging a mine and deep galleries you will succeed in finding a satisfying quantity of metal; perhaps too you won't find anything.

That was how I was with music in 1799. Chance saw to it that I have sought to register the sounds of my soul in pages of print. Laziness and the lack of opportunities to learn physics, the stupid side of music, to wit playing the piano and recovering my ideas, played a large part in this decision which might have been altogether different had I met with a music-loving uncle or mistress. As for the passion itself, that has remained entire.

I would go six leagues on foot through the mud, the thing I loathe most in the world, to be present at a good performance of *Don Giovanni*. One word uttered in Italian from *Don Giovanni* and instantly the fond memory of the music returns and takes hold of me.

I have only one none too intelligible objection: does music appeal to me as a *sign*, as recalling the happiness of youth, or *in itself*?*

I am of the second opinion. *Don Giovanni* had attracted me before I heard Bonoldi exclaiming (at La Scala in Milan) out of his little window:

---

*M. le C[om]te Daru, died around 1830 at sixty-five perhaps, was born around 1765 (1830 – 65 = 1765). So in 1800 he was 35.

Falle passar avanti,
Di che ci fanno onor?

But this is a tricky subject, I shall return to it when I am engulfed in discussions about the arts during my very passionate stay in Milan and what in sum I might call *the flower of my life* between 1814 and 1821.

Does the aria "Tra quattro mura" as sung by Mme Festa, appeal to me as a sign, or for its intrinsic merits?

Does "Per te ogni mese un pajo" from the *Pretendenti delusi* not ravish me as a sign?

Yes, I will confess the last two are *signs*; which is why I never extolled them as masterpieces. But I don't at all believe the *Matrimonio Segreto* was a sign heard sixty or a hundred times at the Odéon by Mme Barilli; was that in 1803 or 1810?

Certainly no *opera d'inchiostro*, no work of literature gives me so keen a pleasure as *Don Giovanni*.

Nevertheless, sheet fourteen of the new edition of De Brosses, read just recently, in January 1836, came very close to it.

A great proof of my love for music, is that the comic operas of Feydeau *soured me*.

Having the use of my cousin de Longueville's box, I was only able to endure half a performance there. I go to that theatre every two or three years, overcome by curiosity, and I leave in the second act like the viscount:

Le vicomte indigné sortit au second acte

soured for the whole evening.

(French) opera soured me even more strongly up until 1830 and I still found it totally unappealing in 1833 with Nourrit and Mme Damoreau.

I have been spreading myself because we are always poor judges of the passions and tastes we have, especially when these tastes are fashionable. There isn't one affected young man in the f[aubourg] St-Germain, like M. de Blancmesnil for example, who doesn't say he's mad about music. For myself I loathe anything resembling a *sentimental French ballad. Panseron*[6] enrages me, he makes me hate what I love to distraction.

Good music sets me to dreaming delightedly about whatever is occupying my heart at the time. Hence the delightful moments I experienced at La Scala from 1814 to 1821.

6. Auguste-Mathieu Panseron (1796–1859), a composer of ballads now wholly forgotten.

CHAPTER 38

Lodging with M. Daru was nothing, I had to dine there, which bored me to death.

I disliked the cuisine of Paris almost as much as its lack of mountains and seemingly for the same reason. I didn't know what it was to be short of money. For these two reasons, I disliked nothing so much as those dinners in M. Daru's crammed apartment.

As I have said, it was situated over the carriage entrance.

It was in that drawing-room and that dining-room that I suffered cruelly as I received that education *in other people* from which my relations had very judiciously withdrawn me.

The polite, ceremonious sort, scrupulously observant of all the proprieties, still today cast a chill over me and reduce me to silence. Should they also have a religious tinge and hold forth on the great principles of morality, I'm done for.

Judge of the effect of this poison in January 1800, when it was applied to brand-new organs whose extreme attentiveness didn't let a single drop be wasted.

I used to arrive in that drawing-room at half past five, I fancy, for dinner. There I would shudder at the thought of needing to give my hand to Mlle Sophie or to Mme Cambon or to Mme Le Brun or to Mme Daru herself in order to go to the table.

(Mme Cambon succumbed gradually to an illness which even then had turned her quite yellow. In 1838, Mme Le Brun is the Marquise de [*a blank*]. The same goes for Mlle Sophie, who has become Mme de Baure. We lost Mme Daru the mother and M. Daru the father many long years ago. In

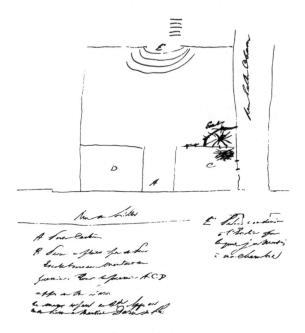

Staircase.—Rue de Bellechasse.—Rue de Lille.

A. Carriage entrance.—B. Entrance steps or rather no entrance steps. Winding staircase up to the first floor. The whole first floor ACDM. Daru's ap[artmen]t. The same area on the second floor, the ap[artmen]t of Messrs Pierre and Martial Daru, his sons.— E. Entrance steps leading to the staircase by which I went up to my room.

1836 Mlle Pulchérie Le Brun is Mme la Marquise de Brossard. Messrs Pierre and Martial Daru have died, the first around 1829, the second two or three years earlier. Mme Le B[run], Mme la Marquise de Grave (former M[inis]ter of W[ar]).)

At table, sat at point H, I didn't enjoy a single mouthful

Mme Daru.—M. Daru, I fancy.

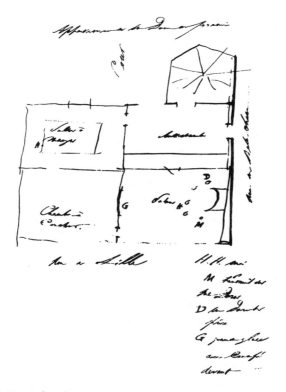

M. Daru's first-floor apartment.—Courtyard.—Dining-room.—
Anteroom.—Bedroom.—Drawing-room.—Rue de Bellechasse.—
Rue de Lille.

H, H. Me.—M. Mme Daru's armchair.—D. M. Daru senior.—
G. Large mirror with settee in front.

I ate. I had a supreme dislike of Parisian cuisine, and still
dislike it today after all these years. But this discomfort was
nothing at that age, I felt it when I was able to go out to a
restaurateur's.

It was the moral constraint which was killing me.

This wasn't the sense of injustice and hatred for my aunt
Séraphie as in Grenoble.

Would to God I had been able to settle for that kind of
unhappiness! This was far worse, it was a continual sense
of the things I wanted to do and which were out of reach.

My room.—Dining[-room].—Anteroom.—Bedroom.—Drawing-
room.—505, Rue de Lille.

Consider the full extent of my unhappiness! I who believed myself to be at once a Saint-Preux and a Valmont (in *Les Liaisons dangereuses*, an imitation of *Clarissa* which has become the breviary of the provincials), I who, believing myself to have an infinite capacity for loving and being loved, believed that the opportunity alone was lacking, I decided I was inferior and awkward in everything in a society I found sad and grumpy! What if I had been in a drawing-room I liked!

So this was the Paris I had so yearned for!

I can't conceive today how I didn't go mad between 10 November 1799, and roughly 20 April when I left for Geneva.

I don't know whether, besides dinner, I didn't also have to be present at lunch.

But how to give an idea of my foolishness? I had pictured society to myself solely and utterly in terms of the *Mémoires secrets* of Duclos, the three or seven volumes of St-Simon published at that time and novels.

I had met with society, and then only at long range, only at Mme de Montmaur's, the original of Mme de Merteuil in *Les Liaisons dangereuses*. She was by then old, rich and lame. Of that I am sure; as for morality, she objected to them giving me only half a crystallized nut when I went to see her in Le Chevallon, she always made them give me a whole one. "Children take it to heart so," she used to say.

That was all the morality I had met with. Mme de Montmaur had leased or bought the house belonging to the Drevons, young men of pleasure, close friends of my uncle R[omain] Gagnon, who had more or less ruined themselves.

This detail about Mme de Montmaur, the original of Mme de Merteuil, is out of place here perhaps, but I wanted to use the anecdote of the crystallized nut to show what I knew of society.

That isn't all, there is far worse. I imputed to myself the shame, the crime almost, of the silence that too often prevailed at the court of the bored and despotic old bourgeois that was M. Daru senior.

This was my principal sadness. As I saw it, a man should be passionately in love and at the same time bring joy and animation into every company in which he found himself.

Yet this universal joy, this art of pleasing everyone, wasn't to be based on the art of flattering everyone's tastes and weaknesses, I didn't suspect all that side of the art of pleasing which would probably have repelled me; the amiability I wanted was the pure joy of Shakespeare in his comedies, the amiability which reigns in the court of the exiled duke in the forest of the Ardennes.

That pure, ethereal amiability at the court of an old prefect, a libertine, and bored, and devout, I believe!!!

Absurdity can go no further. But my unhappiness, although founded on *absurdity*, was none the less very real.

These silences, when I was in M. Daru's drawing-room, distressed me.

What was I in that drawing-room? I didn't open my mouth there, to judge by what Mme Le Brun,* Marquise de [*a blank*] told me afterwards. Mme la Comtesse d'Oraison told me recently that Mme Le Brun feels friendship for me, ask her to elucidate on the figure I cut in M. Daru's drawing-room on my first appearance there, at the beginning of 1800.

I was dying of constraint, of disappointment, of dissatisfaction with myself. Who could have told me that the greatest joys of my life were to befall me five months later!

Befall is the right word, it fell on me out of the sky, yet nevertheless it came from my soul, it was also my one resource during the four or five months I was living in that room at M. Daru senior's.

All the sufferings of the drawing-room and dining-room vanished when, alone in my room overlooking the gardens, I said to myself: "Should I become a composer of music, or

*Foolishness of D[omini]que [*trans.* i.e. Stendhal himself].

Dates: 4 March 1818. Start of a great musical phrase *Piazza delle Galline*. This only really ended in the Rue Faubourg St-Denis, May 1824. September 1826, Saint-Omer.

else write comedies like Molière?" I sensed, very vaguely it's true, that I knew neither the world nor myself well enough to decide.

I was distracted from these lofty thoughts by another much more down-to-earth and far more urgent problem. Precise man that he was, M. Daru couldn't understand why I hadn't entered the Ecole Polytechnique or, if that year was lost, why I wasn't going on with my studies in order to take the examinations for the following session, September 1800.

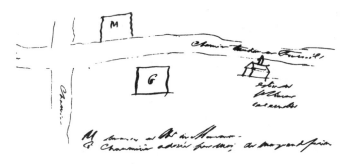

Chevallon.—Lane in the direction of Le Fontanil.—Lane.—Church of St-Vincent, I fancy.

    M. Mme de Montmaur's house.—G. My grandfather's cottage adored by me.

This stern old man gave me to understand with great politeness and restraint that this matter needed to be resolved between us. It was this very politeness and restraint, for me such a novelty, who heard myself called *Monsieur* by a relation for the first time in my life, which set my crazy timidity and imagination working overtime.

I can explain this now. I could see the question very clearly basically, but these polite and unwonted preparations made me suspect unknown and frightful depths from which I would be unable to extricate myself. I felt terrified by the diplomatic ways of this clever ex-prefect, to which at the time I was far from able to give their proper name. All of which rendered me incapable of maintaining my opinion out loud.

Not having spent one day in a college, I was a child of ten where relations with society were concerned. The mere sight of so imposing a figure, who caused everyone around him to tremble starting with his wife and elder son, speaking to me *tête à tête* and behind closed doors, made it impossible for me to say two consecutive words. I can see today that M. Daru senior's face with the slight cast in one eye was for me exactly

Lasciate ogni speranza, voi ch'entrate.[1]

Not to see it was the greatest happiness it could give me.

With me extreme agitation destroys memory. Perhaps M. Daru senior had said to me something on the lines of:

"My dear cousin, it would be right for you to come to a decision over the next seven days."

In my extreme timidity, anxiety and *disarray*, as they say in Grenoble and as I used then to say, I fancy I wrote down in advance the conversation I wanted to have with M. Daru.

I can recall only a single detail of that terrible interview. I said, though in terms less clear:

"My relations have left me more or less free to make up my own mind."

"I can see that only too well," answered M. Daru in a richly feeling tone, which struck me forcibly in a man so full of moderation and of the circumlocutory habits of the diplomat.

This remark struck me, all else is forgotten.

I was very content with my room overlooking the gardens, between the Rue de Lille and the Rue de l'Université, with a view of part of the Rue Bellechasse.

1. "Abandon hope all ye who enter here": the inscription to be found over the entrance to Dante's Inferno.

The house had belonged to Condorcet,[2] whose pretty widow was then living with M. Fauriel (today of the Institute, a true *savant* who loves knowledge for its own sake, a rare enough thing among that body).

So as not to have people pestering him, Condorcet had had a very steep, narrow wooden ladder made, by means of which he could climb up to the third floor (I was on the second) into a room above mine. How that would have impressed me three months earlier! Condorcet, the author of the *Esquisse des progrès futurs*, which I had read with enthusiasm two or three times!

But alas, my heart had changed. The moment I was alone and undisturbed and freed from my timidity, the profound feeling returned:

"Is this all there is to Paris?"

This meant: that which I so yearned after as the sovereign good, the thing to which I have been sacrificing my life for three years, bores me. It wasn't the sacrifice of three years which affected me; in spite of my fear of entering the Ecole Polytechnique the following year, I loved mathematics; the terrible question which I didn't have the wit to see clearly was this: "Where then on the earth is there happiness?" And at times I even went so far as: "*Is* there happiness on the earth?"

Not having any mountains ruined Paris absolutely in my eyes.

Having pruned trees in the gardens finished it off.

All the same, as I am pleased to discern today (in 1836), I gave the beautiful green of these trees its due.

I felt, much rather than said clearly to myself: their shape is pitiful, but what delightful greenery, forming a mass with charming labyrinths for the imagination to roam in! This last detail belongs to today. At that time I had feelings without

2. Marie Jean Antoine de Caritat, Marquis de Condorcet (1743–1794), mathematician, economist and politician, and a leading *philosophe*. He was arrested during the Terror and committed suicide in prison.

properly discerning their cause. Sagacity has never been my strong point and I lacked it completely. I was like a highly strung horse which sees not what is there but imaginary obstacles or dangers; the good thing is that I was taking courage and marching boldly on the greatest perils. I am still like that today.

The more I walked in Paris, the more I disliked it. The Daru family showed me great kindness. Mme Cambon complimented me on my artist's frock-coat, olive in colour with velvet revers.

"It suits you very well," she used to say to me.

Mme Cambon very kindly took me to the Museum with a part of the family and a M. Gorse or Gosse, a large vulgar young fellow, who was rather paying court to her. She was pining away with melancholy at having lost, a year before, an only daughter of sixteen.

We left the Museum, I was offered a seat in the fiacre; I walked back home through the mud and, flattered by Mme Cambon's kindness, had the splendid idea of going in to see her. I found her *tête à tête* with M. Gorse.

I was conscious, however, of the full extent, or part of the extent, of my stupidity.

"But why didn't you get into the carriage?" Mme Cambon said to me in astonishment.

After ten minutes I vanished. M. Gorse must have thought the strangest things about me. I must have been a singular problem in the Daru family; the answer must have varied between: *he's a madman* and *he's an imbecile.*

CHAPTER 39

Mme Le Brun, today Marquise de [*a blank*], has told me that all the inmates of that little drawing-room were astonished by my total silence. I was silent out of instinct, I felt no one would understand me; what faces to have talked to of my tender admiration for Bradamante! This silence brought on by chance was the best policy, it was the one means of preserving a little personal dignity.

If ever I meet that witty woman again, I must ply her with questions to get her to tell me what I was then like. In truth I don't know. I can only record the degree of happiness felt by this machine of mine. As I have been excavating the same ideas ever since, how to know where I had then got to? The well was ten feet deep, each year I have added another five feet, now at a hundred and ninety feet how to have the mental picture of what it was like, in February 1800, when it was only ten feet?

My cousin Mure (died as head clerk, Trade Ministry), the most prosaic creature who ever lived, was admired because after coming home around ten in the evening to M. Daru's, Rue de Lille No 505, he then went out again on foot to go and eat a certain kind of pasty at the Carrefour Gaillon.

This simplicity, this uncomplicated gluttony, which today would make me laugh in a child of sixteen, filled me with astonishment in 1800. Indeed I don't know whether I didn't myself go out again one evening, in that ghastly Paris humidity which I loathed, to go and eat some of these pasties. A gesture made a little bit for pleasure but much for glory. The pleasure was less than nothing, and the glory too, seemingly;

if anyone remarked it they must have seen it as the merest imitation. I certainly wasn't going naively to explain the reason for my gesture, I would then in my turn have been both original and naive, and my ten p.m. escapade would perhaps have given that bored family something to smile at.

The illness that led to Doctor Portal climbing up to my third-floor room in the Passage Ste-Marie (Rue du Bac) must have been serious, because I lost all my hair. I didn't fail to buy a wig, and my friend Edmond Cardon didn't fail to throw it up on to the cornice above a door one evening in his mother's drawing-room.

Cardon was very thin, very tall, very well brought up, very rich, with perfect manners, the complete tailor's dummy, the son of Mme Cardon, lady's maid to Queen Marie-Antoinette.

What a contrast between Cardon and myself! And yet we came together. We were friends at the time of the battle of Marengo; he was then aide-de-camp to Carnot, the Minister of War; we wrote to each other up until 1804 or 5. In 1815, that elegant, noble, charming creature blew his brains out when he saw them arrest Marshal Ney, his relation by marriage. He was in no way implicated himself; it was quite simply a passing madness, brought on by the extreme vanity of the courtier who finds he has a marshal and a prince for his cousin. After 1803 or 4 he took to calling himself Cardon de Montigny, he introduced me to his wife, elegant, rich, with a slight stammer, who struck me as being afraid of the ferocious energy of that Allobrogian mountain-dweller. The son of that good-natured, amiable creature calls himself M. de Montigny and is a counsellor or commissioner in the royal court in Paris.

How I would then have benefited from some good advice! How I would have benefited from the same advice in 1821! But I'll be damned if anyone ever gave me any. I got it around 1826, but that was more or less too late, and in any case went too much against my habits. I have realized clearly since that in Paris it is the *sine qua non*, but there would also have been less truth and originality in my literary ideas.

How different if M. Daru or Mme Cambon had said to me in January 1800:

"My dear cousin, if you want to have some standing in society, twenty people need to find it in their own interest to speak well of you. Consequently, choose a salon, don't fail to go there every Tuesday (if that is its day), make it your business to be amiable, or at least very polite to every one of the people who go to that salon. You'll be something in society, you can hope to appeal to an agreeable woman once you have two or three salons to carry you along. If you pick these salons from our own rank in society and attend them regularly, after ten years they will carry you anywhere. The essential thing is regularity in being one of the faithful there every Tuesday."

This is what I have forever lacked. That is the meaning of M. D's (Delécluze of the *Débats*, around 1828) exclamation:

"If only you put yourself out a bit more!"

That worthy man must have been very full of this truth, because he was furiously jealous of a remark which, much to my surprise, had created a great impression, on him for one: "Bossuet . . . is *serious claptrap*."[1]

In 1800, the Daru family used to cross the Rue de Lille and go up to the first-floor to Mme Cardon's, Marie-Antoinette's one-time lady's maid, who was very glad to have the protection of two commissioners of war as reputable as the Messrs Daru, an organizing com[missioner], and Martial Daru, a simple com[missioner]. That is how I explain the connection today and I am wrong; for want of experience I was no judge of anything in 1800. I beg the reader therefore not to pause over these explanations which I let slip in 1836: this is more or less probable fiction, it's no longer history.

So I was, or rather I fancy I was, very well received in Mme Cardon's drawing-room, in January 1800.

1. Jacques Bénigne Bossuet (1627–1704) was a prelate and author, celebrated above all for his pulpit oratory. His heavy, baroque style was not calculated to endear him to Stendhal.

They dressed up to play charades, and were always joking. Poor Mme Cambon didn't always come; such foolishness jarred on her grief from which she died a few months later.

M. Daru (later a minister) had just published *La Cléopédie*, I believe, a short poem in the jesuitical style, i.e. the style of the Latin poems written by jesuits around 1700. I find it worthless but fluent, it's a good thirty years since I read it.

M. Daru, who wasn't basically a clever man (but that is a guess made only as I write), was over-proud of being president of four literary societies at once. That sort of fatuity was rife in 1800 and wasn't as vacuous as it seems to us today. Society was being reborn after the terror of 93 and the half-fear of the years following. It was M. Daru senior who informed me with quiet delight of his elder son's fame.

As he was returning from one of these literary societies, Edmond, dressed as a street-girl, went and accosted him a few steps away from the house. This was really quite high-spirited. Mme Cardon still had the high spirits of 1788, our prudes of 1836 would find it shocking.

When he got in M. Daru found himself being followed up the staircase by the girl, who was removing her petticoats.

"I was most surprised," he told us, "to find our district had been infected."

Some time later, he took me to one of the meetings of one of the societies he presided over. This one met in a street which has been knocked down in order to enlarge the Place du Carrousel, near that part of the new gallery, to the north of the Carrousel, which adjoins the axis of the Rue Richelieu, forty paces further to the west.

It was half-past seven in the evening, the rooms were very brightly lit. The poetry appalled me, not at all like Ariosto and Voltaire! This was bourgeois and worthless (how well schooled I already was!), but I felt a longing and admiration for the bosom of Mme Constance Pipelet, who read one piece of poetry. Later on I told her this; she was then the wife of a poor devil of a hernia surgeon, and I talked with her at Mme la Comtesse Beugnot's when she was Princesse de Salm-Dyck I believe. I shall recount her marriage, preceded by a visit of two months to the Prince de Salm, together with her lover, to see whether she mightn't find the château too disagreeable, and the prince in no way taken in but knowing everything and submitting to it, and he was right.

I went to the Louvre, to Regnault's,[2] a painter, author of "The Education of Achilles," a worthless picture engraved by the excellent Bervic, and I was a pupil in his life-class. I was greatly surprised by all the gratuities you had to give for port-folios, chair-rent, etc.; I was profoundly ignorant of all these Parisian customs and, truth to tell, of all possible customs, and must have seemed miserly.

I carried my terrible disappointment with me everywhere.

"To find Paris dreary and detestable when I had imagined it as the supreme good!" I disliked everything, even including the cuisine, which wasn't that of my paternal home, that home which had seemed to me the epitome of all that was evil.

The last straw was that my fear of being forced to take an examination for the Ecole had made me dislike my beloved mathematics.

I fancy the terrible M. Daru senior said to me:

"Since, according to the certificates you're carrying, you're so much better than your seven schoolfellows who have got in, even if you got in today you could easily catch them up in the courses they're following."

M. Daru spoke to me as a man accustomed to wielding in-fluence and getting exceptions made.

Luckily for me something must have held M. Daru back from insisting that I resume the study of mathematics. My relations had no doubt proclaimed me an all-round prodigy. My excellent grandfather adored me and moreover I was

2. Jean-Baptiste Regnault (1754–1829); this particular painting is still in the Louvre.

basically his own handiwork, he had been my only mentor, mathematics aside. He had done my Latin exercises with me, he wrote my Latin verses about a fly that meets its *black* death in *white* milk almost unaided.

Such was the wit of the jesuit father, author of the poem whose verses I had rewritten. Had it not been for the authors I read in secret, I was destined to have that same wit and to admire the Comte Daru's *Ciropédie* and the wit of the (French) Academy. Was that a bad thing? I should have had successes between 1815 and 1830, a reputation, money, but my books would have been much drearier and much *better written* than they are. I believe that the affectation known as writing well in 1825–36 will seem quite ridiculous around 1860, once France has been delivered from political revolutions every fifteen years and has time to reflect on the pleasures of the mind. The strong and violent government of Napoleon (whom I liked so much personally) only lasted fifteen years, 1800–1815. The sickening government of those imbecilic Bourbons (see the songs of Béranger[3]) also lasted fifteen years, from 1815 to 1830. How long will a third one last? Will it be longer?

But I digress, our descendants will have to forgive these detours, we are holding the pen in one hand and the sword in the other (as I write this I am awaiting news of the execution of Fieschi[4] and of the new ministry of March 1836; and I've just signed three official letters addressed to m[ini]sters whose names I don't know).

Back to January or February 1800. I actually had the experience of a nine-year-old child and probably the arrogance of the devil. I had actually been the Ecole Centrale's most remarkable pupil. Moreover, what was far better, I had the

3. Pierre Jean de Béranger (1780–1857), a hugely popular writer of patriotic, Republican songs.

4. Joseph Fieschi was executed in February 1836 for his attempt on the life of King Louis-Philippe in the previous July.

right ideas on everything, I had read hugely, I adored reading. A new book, unknown to me, consoled me for everything.

But the Daru family, in spite of the success of the translator of Horace, wasn't in the least literary, it was a family of Louis XIV courtiers as described by Saint-Simon. All they liked in M. Daru the elder son was the fact of his success; any literary discussion would have been a political crime as it would tend to cast doubt on the family's reputation.

One of the misfortunes of my character is to forget success and have a deep-rooted memory of my follies. Around February 1800, I wrote to my family: "Mme Cambon holds sway over the mind and Mme Rebuffel over the senses." A fortnight later, I felt deeply ashamed of my style and of the fact.

It was a falsehood, it was far worse, it was ingratitude. If there was one place where I was less embarrassed and more natural, it was in the drawing-room of the excellent and pretty Mme Rebuffel, who lived on the first floor of the house that had given me a room on the second. My room was, I fancy, above Mme Rebuffel's drawing-room. My uncle Gagnon had recounted to me how he had possessed her in Lyon by admiring her pretty foot and inviting her to put it on a trunk so he could see it better. On one occasion, but for M. Bartelon, M. Rebuffel might have surprised my uncle in an unmistakable position. Mme Rebuffel, my cousin, had a daughter, Adèle, who gave promise of being very clever; I fancy she hasn't kept that promise. After having loved one another a little (the love of children), dislike and then indifference replaced childishness, and I have completely lost sight of her since 1804. The newspaper of 1835 informed me that her stupid husband, M. le Baron Auguste Petiet, the same who wounded me in the left foot with a sabre, had just left her a widow with a son at the Ecole Polytechnique.

Was it in 1800 that Mme Rebuffel had as lover M. Chièze, a somewhat starched gentleman from Valence in the Dauphiné, a friend of my family's in Grenoble, or was that only in 1803? Was it in 1800 or in 1803 that the excellent Rebuffel, a man of feeling and of wit, a man forever worthy of respect in my eyes, gave me dinner in the Rue St-Denis at the haulage business which he ran with a Mademoiselle Barbereux, his business partner and his mistress?

How different for me if my grandfather Gagnon had thought of recommending me to M. Rebuffel instead of M. Daru! M. Rebuffel was the nephew of M. Daru, though only seven or eight years younger, but because of his political, or rather administrative eminence, as secretary-general to the whole of Languedoc (seven departments), M. Daru aspired to tyrannize over M. Rebuffel, who, in the exchanges he reported to me, was a sublime combination of respect and firmness. I remember comparing the tone he adopted to that of J.-J. Rousseau in his "Letter to Christophe de Beaumont, Archbishop of Paris."[5]

M. Rebuffel could have made anything of me, I would have behaved more sensibly had chance put him in charge of me. But my destiny was to conquer all at the point of a sword. What an ocean of *violent sensations* I have felt in my life and at that time especially!

I felt many over the small incident I am going to relate, but in what direction? What did I desire so passionately? I no longer remember.

M. Daru the elder son (I shall call him the Comte Daru, despite the anachronism: he became a count only around 1809, I believe, but I'm in the habit of calling him that), the Comte Daru then, if you will permit me to call him that, was in 1800 secretary-general at the Ministry of War. He was working himself to death, but it must be admitted he never stopped talking about it and was always in a bad mood when he came in to dinner. At times he would keep his father and whole family waiting for an hour or two. He would finally arrive wearing the expression of an overworked ox and with bloodshot eyes. Often he went back to his office in the

5. In this Rousseau protested against the church's condemnation of his didactic novel, *Emile ou De l'éducation*.

evening; the fact was, everything had to be reorganized and the Marengo campaign was being prepared in secret.

I am about to be born, as Tristram Shandy says, and the reader is about to emerge from these childishnesses.

One fine day, M. Daru senior took me aside and made me tremble, he said to me:

"My son will take you to work with him at the War Office."

Probably, instead of thanking him, I maintained the unsociable silence of extreme timidity.

Garden.—Lime-trees.

The next morning, walking beside the Comte Daru, whom I admired, but who made me tremble, and I was never able to get used to him, nor he I fancy to me, I see myself walking along the Rue Hillerin-Bertin, at that time very narrow. But where then was the War Ministry to which we were going together?

I can only see my position at my table at H or at H'; at the one of the two desks that I didn't occupy sat M. Mazoïer, author of the tragedy of *Thésée*, a pale imitation of Racine.

CHAPTER 40

At the end of the garden were some unfortunate, heavily pruned lime-trees, behind which we used to go to pee. They were the first friends I had in Paris. Their fate saddened me: to have been pruned like that! I compared them with the beautiful lime-trees of Claix, which had the good fortune to live in the midst of the mountains.

But would I have wanted to return into those mountains?

Yes, I fancy so, if it had meant not rejoining my father there but living there with my grandfather, all well and good, but *in freedom*.

This was how far my extreme passion for Paris had sunk. And I was apt to say that the true Paris was invisible to my gaze.

The lime-trees at the War Ministry turned red from the top. M. Mazoïer no doubt reminded me of Virgil's line

Nunc erubescit ver.[1]

That isn't it, but I'm remembering it as I write, for the first time in thirty-six years; I had a horror of Virgil fundamentally, as being the protégé of [the] priests who came to say mass and talk Latin to me at my relations' house. For all the efforts of my reason, Virgil has never recovered as far as I'm concerned from the effects of that bad company.

---

1. Literally, "The Spring is beginning to turn red." The line is either not from Virgil, or else incorrectly quoted.

The lime-trees acquired buds, finally they got leaves, I was profoundly moved, I had friends then in Paris!

Each time I went to pee behind those lime-trees at the end of the garden, my soul was *refreshed* by the sight of these friends. I love them still after thirty-six years apart.

But do those good friends still exist? There has been so much building in that district! Perhaps the ministry in which I picked up the official pen for the first time is still the ministry in the Rue de l'Université, opposite the square whose name I don't know?

There M. Daru installed me at a desk and told me to copy a letter. I shall say nothing of my spidery handwriting, much worse than the present one, but he discovered that I wrote *cela* with two *l*s: *cella*.

So this was the man of letters, the brilliant *humanist* who queried the merits of Racine and had carried off all the prizes in Grenoble!!!

Today, *but only today*, I admire the kindness of the whole Daru family. What to do with so arrogant and ignorant a donkey?

Yet the fact is I attacked Racine very well in my conversations with M. Mazoïer. There were four of us clerks, and the two others, I fancy, listened to me as I skirmished with M. Mazoïer.

I had a private theory that I wanted to write up under the title of *Filosofia nova*, a title half Italian, half Latin. I had a genuine, deeply felt, passionate admiration for Shakespeare, whom I had encountered, however, only through the ponderous and bombastic phrases of M. Letourneur and his associates.

Ariosto too had a great hold over my emotions (but the Ariosto of M. de Tressan, father of the amiable captain who played the clarinet and had helped to get me taught to read, an extreme and worthless ultra and a brigadier around 1820).

I think I can see that what protected me against the bad taste of admiring the Comte Daru's *Ciropédie* and soon afterwards the *abbé* Delille was this private doctrine based on true pleasure, a deep, meditated pleasure, verging on *happiness*, that I had got from Cervantes, Shakespeare, Corneille, Ariosto, and my dislike of the puerilities of Voltaire and his school. On which subject, when I dared to speak, I was trenchant to the point of fanaticism, for I didn't doubt but that all men of sound constitution and unspoiled by a faulty literary education thought as I did. Experience has taught me that the majority allow whatever artistic sensibilities they may have to be ruled naturally by the author currently in fashion, it was Voltaire in 1788, Walter Scott in 1828. And who is it today, 1836? Happily no one.

This love for Shakespeare, Ariosto and in the second rank *La Nouvelle Héloïse*, who presided over my literary emotions on my arrival in Paris at the end of 1799, preserved me from the bad taste (*Delille minus the gracefulness*) which reigned in the Daru and Cardon drawing-rooms, which was all the more dangerous for me, all the more contagious, inasmuch as the C[om]te Daru was currently an active author whom in other connections everyone admired and whom I admired myself. He had just become *organizer* in chief, I believe, of that army in Switzerland that had just saved France at Zürich under Masséna. M. Daru senior used to repeat endlessly to us that G[enera]l Masséna had told everyone concerning M. Daru:

"There's a man I can introduce to my friends and to my enemies."

Masséna, however, whom I know well, was like a magpie, I mean an instinctive thief; they still talk about him in Rome (the Doria family *monstrance* in St-Agnès, Piazza Navona, I believe[2]) and M. Daru has never stolen a centime.

But good lord, how I do go on! I can't get round to speaking about Ariosto whose characters, stable-boys *with the physical strength of a street-porter*, bore me so nowadays.

---

2. This monstrance seems in fact to have been donated to the French occupiers of Rome, not stolen, and certainly not stolen by Masséna.

From 1796 to 1804, I didn't have *the right reaction* to Ariosto. I took his tender, romantic passages perfectly seriously. Without my knowing it, they opened up the one path by which emotion is able to reach my soul. I can only be affected deeply *after a comic passage*.

Whence my almost exclusive love of *opera buffa*, whence the gulf which divides my soul from that of M. le Baron Poitou (see at the end of the vol[ume] the preface to De Brosses which angered Colomb) and from the whole vulgar crowd of 1830, who can only see *courage when it wears a moustache*.

There alone, in *opera buffa*, can I be moved to tears. *Opera seria* aspires to move people, which puts paid instantly to the possibility of my being so. Even in real life a poor man who begs for alms with piteous cries, far from making me feel pity, makes me think with all possible philosophical severity of the usefulness of a house of correction.

A poor man who doesn't address me, who doesn't let out plaintive and *tragic* cries, as is the custom in Rome, and eats an apple as he drags himself along like the one-legged man a week ago, instantly affects me to the point almost of tears.

Hence my total antipathy for tragedy, an antipathy extending to *irony* for verse tragedy.

I make exception for that great and simple man, Pierre Corneille, in my view immeasurably superior to Racine, a courtier who was all astuteness and fine words. The rules of Aristotle, or what are claimed as such, were a handicap, as was verse for that original poet. Racine is original in the eyes of Germans, Englishmen, etc., only because they haven't yet had a witty court, like that of L[ouis] XIV, obliging all the rich and the aristocrats in the country to spend eight hours together every day in the drawing-rooms of Versailles.

In course of time the *English, Germans, Americans* and other money-grubbers and anti-logical dreamers will be brought to see the clever courtier in Racine; even the most innocent *ingénue*, Junie or Aricie, is steeped in the arts of a respectable whore; Racine was never able to create a Mme de

La Vallière,[3] but girls who are always extremely adroit and perhaps physically virtuous, though certainly not morally so. Around 1900 perhaps, the Germans, Americans and English will come to grasp just how courtier-like Racine's mind was. A century after that perhaps, they will perhaps come to sense that he was never able to create a La Vallière.

But how will those feeble eyes be able to make out a star so close to the sun? The admiration of these "polite and grasping yokels" for the civilization which lent an attractive veneer even to Marshal Boufflers (died around 1712), who was a fool, will stop them from sensing the total lack of simplicity and naturalness in Racine, and from understanding this line of Camille's:

Tout ce que je voyais me semblait Curiace.[4]

That I should be writing this at the age of fifty-three, nothing could be simpler, but that I should have felt it in 1800, that I should have felt a sort of horror for Voltaire and the gross affectation of Alzire, with my contempt bordering on hatred for religion and with such good cause, that is what astonishes me, I, the pupil of M. Gagnon who thought well of himself for having been Voltaire's guest at Ferney for three days, I, brought up at the base of that small bust of the great man mounted on an ebony stand.

Is it I or the great man who is on the ebony stand?

In fact I admire what I was, literarily speaking, in February 1800 when I was writing *cella*.

M. le Comte Daru, so immensely superior to me and to so many others as a man of industry, as a *consulting lawyer*,

3. The Duchesse de La Vallière (1644–1710) was a royal favourite at Versailles.

4. A line from Corneille's tragedy of *Horace*: "Everything I saw seemed to me to be Curiace."

didn't have the necessary wit to suspect the worth of this arrogant madman.

M. Mazoïer, the clerk, my neighbour, who was seemingly less bothered by my mixture of madness and arrogance than by the stupidity of the two other 2,500-franc clerks, had quite a good opinion of me, but I was indifferent to him. I looked on everyone who admired that *astute courtier* known as Racine as incapable of seeing and feeling *true beauty*, which to my way of thinking is Imogen's naivety as she exclaims: *"Now, peace be here, Poor house that keep'st thyself!"* *

The insults that M. Mazoïer directed at Shakespeare, and how contemptuously, in 1800!!! brought tears from me in favour of that great poet. In later years, nothing made me more adoring of Mme Dembowski than the criticisms made of her by the dullards of Milan. I can name that charming woman, who thinks of her today? Am I not the only one perhaps eleven years after she departed this earth? I apply the same reasoning to the Comtesse Alexandrine Petit. Am I not today her best friend, after twenty-two years? And when this appears (if ever a publisher isn't afraid of wasting his time and his paper!), when this appears after my own death, who will still be thinking of Métilde and Alexandrine? And despite their feminine modesty and that horror of attracting public notice that I saw in them, if they see this book being published from the place where they are now, will they not be very content?

"But who to dumb forgetfulness a prey"[5] is not content, after so many years, to find his name being uttered by a friendly mouth?

But where on earth was I? At my desk where I was writing *cella*.

---

* The lines are from *Cymbeline* Act 3, scene 6, but are spoken by Belarius, not Imogen.

5. A slight misquotation of the line from Gray's "Elegy in a Country Churchyard," which should go: "For who, to dumb forgetfulness a prey..."

Be my reader ever so slightly vulgar of soul and he will imagine that the aim of this long digression has been to conceal my shame at having written *cella*. He is mistaken: I am a different man. The errors of the man of 1800 are discoveries I am making, for the most part, as I write this. After so many years and happenings, I remember only the smile of the woman I loved. The other day I had forgotten the colour of one of the uniforms I wore. Now have you ever experienced, oh benevolent reader, what a uniform means in a victorious army that is the sole object of the nation's attention like the army of Napoleon?

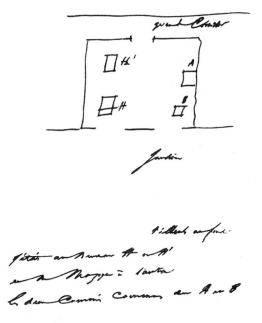

Main corridor.—Garden.—Lime-trees at the far end.—I was at the desk H or H', and M. Mazoïer at the other one. The two common clerks at A and B.

Today, thank heavens, the tribune has eclipsed the army.

It's a fact, I can't remember the street where that office was situated in which I seized hold of the administrative pen for the first time. It was at the end of the Rue Hillerin-Bertin, then lined by the walls of gardens. I can see myself walking earnestly beside the C[omte] Daru, going to his office after the gloomy, frigid lunch at the house No 505, on the corner of the Rue Bellechasse and the Rue de Lille, as the good writers of 1800 used to say.

How different for me had M. Daru said to me:

"When you have a letter to do, think carefully about what you want to say, and then about the tone of censure or command the minister who will sign your letter would want it to have. When you've made up your mind, write boldly."

Instead of which I attempted to imitate the form of M. Daru's own letters; he overdid the word *indeed* and I stuffed my letters full of *indeeds*.

What a far cry from the great letters I made up in Vienna in 1809, when I had a horrid attack of the pox, had charge of a hospital with 4,000 wounded (*l'oiseau vole*[6]), a mistress I was skewering and a mistress I adored! This whole change was brought about by my own reflections, M. Daru never gave me any advice except for his anger when he crossed my letters out.

The worthy Martial Daru was always very jovial with me. He often came to the War Office: for a commissioner of war it was the *court*. He was responsible for law and order at the Val-de-Grâce hospital, I fancy, in 1800, and M. le Comte Daru, who had the best brain in the ministry in 1800 (which isn't saying much), no doubt knew all about the Army of Reserve. The whole Corps of Commissioners of War was seething with vanity over the creation of the corps, and even more over deciding on a uniform for the *inspecteurs aux revues*. It was at that time I fancy that I saw G[ener]al Olivier with his wooden leg, recently appointed *inspecteur-en-chef*

6. An obscure punning reference to a supervisor at the hospital called Philippe Loiseau, suspected of thieving: *l'oiseau vole* can hence mean both "the bird flies" and "Loiseau steals."

aux revues. This vanity came to a head over the *braid hats* and red coats and was the staple of conversation in the Daru and Cardon households. Edmond Cardon, urged on by a clever mother who flattered the Comte Daru openly, had been promised a place as assistant to the commissioners of war.

The worthy Martial Daru soon let me glimpse the possibility that I might myself wear that fetching uniform.

I think I have discovered as I write that Cardon wore it, royal blue coat, gold braid at the collar and on the cuffs.

At this distance, where matters of vanity are concerned (a secondary passion with me), things imagined and things seen become confused.

The excellent Martial, having come to visit me at my desk, then found I had despatched a letter round the offices containing the word *information.*

"Dammit," he said to me with a laugh, "so you're already sending round letters like that!"

This was, I fancy, to usurp the privileges at least of a deputy chief clerk, I, the lowest of supernumaries.

Concerning this word *information*, the *paymaster* department, for example, gave information relating to *pay*, the *quartermaster* department information relating to *equipment*; take the case of a quartermaster officer in the 7th Light having to pay back 107 francs out of his pay, the total value of the serge he had received improperly, I had to get information from the two above-named departments so that I could write the letter which M. Daru as secretary-g[ener]al had to sign.

I am convinced very few of my letters got as far as M. Daru; M. Barthomeuf, a vulgar man but a good clerk, was then starting on his career as his private secretary (i.e. a clerk paid for by the War Office), worked in the of[fic]e where M. Daru wrote, and had to endure his strange outbursts and the excessive industry which that man, terrifying both to himself and to others, exacted from all who came near him. I had soon caught the contagion of the *terror* inspired by M. Daru and that feeling has never left me where he is concerned. I was excessively sensitive from birth and the harshness of his language went beyond all reasonable bounds.

For a long time, however, I wasn't important enough to feel the rough edge of his tongue. And now that I think sensibly about it, I can see I never really felt the rough edge of his tongue. I didn't suffer the hundredth part of what was endured by M. de Baure, a former advocate-general in the Parlement of Pau. (Was there such a parlement? I have no book in C[ivit]a-V[ecchi]a to look it up in, but so much the better, the present book is being written solely from memory and won't have been written out of other books.)

I realize that between M. Daru and myself there has always been something like a fragment of gun-carriage taken off by an enemy cannonball, but which acts as a *fender* for the body of the gun hit by the cannonball (like at Ticino in 1800).

My fender was Joinville (today the Baron Joinville, military intendant of the 1st Division, Paris), then M. de Baure. I have come to what is an entirely new idea for me: did M. Daru go easy on me? It's very possible. But the *terror* was always such that this idea has come to me only in March 1836.

Everyone in the War Office trembled as they approached M. Daru's of[fice]; as for me, I felt afraid merely staring at the door. M. Daru no doubt saw this sentiment in my eyes, and given the character I now see him as having (a *timid* character for whom the terror he inspired created a *rampart*) my fear must have been my way of flattering him.

Coarse people, as M. Barthomeuf struck me as being, must have been less susceptible to the strange words with which that *raging ox* dressed down all who came near him at times when he was overwhelmed by work.

By this *terror* he set going the seven or eight hundred clerks in the War Office, whose fifteen or twenty self-important chiefs, most of them quite devoid of talent, having been appointed as heads of departments, were given a decidedly rough time by M. Daru. Far from cutting matters short or simplifying them, these donkeys often tried to confuse them even for M. Daru (AS MAKES EVERY DAY WITH ME MY GREEK).[7] I agree that this was calculated to infuriate a man who can see twenty or thirty letters awaiting an urgent reply sitting on the left-hand side of his desk. And I often saw the letters asking for orders piled a foot high on M. Daru's desk, written moreover by people who would have been delighted to be able to say to you: "I didn't receive your Excellency's orders in time . . . ," and with the prospect of a Napoleon losing his temper at Schönbrunn and saying that there had been *negligence*, etc.

7. A reference to his Greek chancellor at Civitavecchia, whom he hated.

CHAPTER 41

My relations with M. Daru, begun in this way in February or January 1800, ended only on his death in 1828 or 1829. He was my benefactor in the sense that he employed me in preference to many others, but I spent many rainy days, with a headache from an overheated stove, writing from ten in the morning until one after midnight, and this beneath the gaze of a man enraged and constantly angry because he was *always afraid*. It was his friend Picard's *Ricochets*[1]: he was mortally afraid of Napoleon and I was mortally afraid of him.

The *nec plus ultra* of our labours will be seen at Erfurt in 1809. For seven or eight days M. Daru and I ran the entire army quartermaster's department. There wasn't even a copyist. Marvelling at what he was doing, M. Daru only lost his temper two or three times a day perhaps; it was a pleasure outing. I was angry with myself for being upset by his harsh words. This blew neither hot nor cold on my promotion, but I have never been wild for promotion anyway. Today I can see: I sought as far as possible to be separated from M. Daru, if only by a half-closed door. His harsh comments on both the present and the absent I found unbearable.

When I wrote *cela* with two *l*s at my desk in the War Ministry at the end of the Rue Hillerin-Bertin, I was still a long way from knowing the full severity of M. Daru, that volcano of abuse. I was quite taken aback, I hardly had the experience

---

1. A one-act comedy written in 1807 in which a prince's bad temper is worked off on all the many people around him.

of a nine-year-old child, yet I had just turned seventeen on 23 January 1800.

What distressed me was the worthless and incessant conversation of my fellow clerks which stopped me working or thinking. For more than six weeks, by four o'clock I was stupefied.

Félix Faure, my quite close school friend in Grenoble, didn't have mad daydreams about love or the arts as I did. This lack of madness it is that has always blunted our friendship, which has been only a lifelong companionship. Today he is a peer of France, and a first president, and feels no great remorse, I imagine, when sentencing the madmen of April to twenty years in prison—six months in prison would have been too much given the perjury OF THE K[ING]—and the wise Morey, that second Bailly,[2] to death, guillotined on 19 March 1836, guilty perhaps but not proven. Félix Faure would stand out against an injustice demanded of him at five minutes' notice, but give his vanity, the most bourgeois that I know, twenty-four hours, and if a k[ing] demands the head of an innocent man from him, he will find reasons to grant it. Egotism and the complete absence of the smallest spark of generosity, combined with the melancholy nature of an Englishman and the fear of going mad like his mother and his sister, constitute the character of this schoolfellow of mine. He is the most worthless of all my friends and the one who has made the largest fortune.

What a contrast in generosity with Louis Crozet, Bigillion! Mareste would do the same things, but without deluding himself, for the sake of advancement and *á l'italienne*. Edmond Cardon would have done the same things but complainingly and dressing them up as gracefully as possible, d'Argout with courage and reflecting on the danger to himself and overcoming that fear. L[oui]s Crozet (engineer-in-chief in Grenoble) would have risked his life heroically rather than sentence

2. For the case of the April conspirators see note on p. 67. Jean-Sylvain Bailly (1736–1793), astronomer, politician and mayor of Paris, was guillotined for ordering the National Guard to fire on republican demonstrators in Paris; Pierre Morey was the accomplice of Fieschi in his attempt on the life of King Louis-Philippe.

a generous madman like Kersausie (whom I've never met) to twenty years in prison, six months in prison would have been too great a punishment.[3] Colomb would refuse even more categorically than L[oui]s Crozet, but might be deceived.

So the most worthless of all my friends more or less is Félix Faure (peer of France), with whom I was on intimate terms in January 1800, from 1803 to 1805 and from 1810 to 1815 and 16.

L[oui]s Crozet told me that his talents barely attain to the mediocre, but his continual sadness lent him dignity when I met him *in mathematics*, I fancy, around 1797. His father, born very poor, had made a pretty fortune in the Department of Finance and had a beautiful *domaine* at Saint-Ismier (two leagues from Grenoble, road to Barreaux and Chambéry).

But it occurs to me that my severity towards this worthless peer of France will be mistaken for *envy*. Will I be believed when I add that I certainly wouldn't deign to exchange reputations with him? Ten thousand francs and to be immune from prosecution FOR MY FUTURE WRITINGS would be my *field-marshal's baton*, an ideal one it is true.

At my request, Félix Faure introduced me to Fabien, a fencing master in the Rue Montpensier, I believe, Rue des Cabriolets, near the Théâtre-Français, behind Corazza's, near the passageway facing the fountain and the house where Molière died. There I fenced not with, but in the same room as several Grenoblois.

Among others two big and dirty scoundrels (inside I mean, not in their appearance, and scoundrelly in their private, not State business), Messrs Casimir Périer, later a minister, and Duchesne, a member of the Chambre des Députés in 1836. The latter not only stole ten francs when gambling in Grenoble around 1820, but was caught in the act.

Casimir Périer was at that time perhaps the best-looking young man in Paris: he was gloomy, unsociable and madness showed in his fine eyes.

---

3. Kersausie, one of the April conspirators, was in fact sentenced to be deported.

I mean madness in the proper sense. Mme Savoye de Rollin, his sister, famously devout though not ill-natured, had been mad and had for several months passed remarks worthy of Aretino,[4] and in the clearest terms without any disguise. This was comic: where could a devout woman of the very best society have picked up a dozen words I wouldn't dare write here? What may a little explain this kind of amiability is that M. Savoye de Rollin, a man of infinite wit, a free-thinking *philosophe*, etc., etc., a friend of my uncle's, had become impotent from abuse a year or two before his marriage to the daughter of Périer *Milord*. This was the name Grenoble had given to a man of wit, a friend of my family's, who heartily despised good society and left 350,000 francs to each of his ten or twelve children, all of them more or less bombastic, stupid and crazy. Their tutor had been mine, that deep-dyed, dried-up scoundrel, M. *l'a*[*bbé*] Raillane.

M. Périer *Milord* only ever thought about money. My grandfather Gagnon, who liked him in spite of his protestantism in *good society* which greatly irritated M. Gagnon, told me how M. Périer when he arrived in a drawing-room always had to work out with his first glance the exact cost of the furnishings. Like all the orthodox, my grandfather attributed humiliating admissions to M. Périer *Milord*, who shunned good society in Grenoble like the plague (around 1780).

One evening my grandfather came upon him in the street:

"Come up to Mme de Quinsonas's with me."

"I will confess something to you, my dear Gagnon, when you have gone some length of time without mixing in good company and have grown quite accustomed to bad, you feel out of place in the good."

I presume that the good company of the wives of the presidents of the Parlement of Grenoble, Mmes de Sassenage, de Quinsonas, de Bailly, still contained a degree of alloy or of *affectation* which was too strong for so lively a nature as M.

4. A famously scabrous writer of the Italian Renaissance.

Périer *Milord*. I imagine I would have been very bored in the company in which Montesquieu shone around 1745, at Mme Geoffrin's or Mme de Mirepoix's. I discovered recently that the wit in the first twenty pages of La Bruyère (who in 1803 supplied my literary education, in accordance with the praises I had read in St-Simon in the three- and seven-volume editions) is an exact copy of what St-Simon calls having an infinite wit. But in 1836, those first twenty pages are puerile, empty, in very good taste for sure but hardly worth the trouble of being written. The style is admirable inasmuch as it doesn't spoil the thought which has the misfortune of being *sine ictu*. Those twenty pages were witty perhaps up until 1789. Wit, so *delightful* for whoever recognizes it, doesn't last. Just as a good peach goes off within a few days, so *wit* goes off within two hundred years, or much quicker if there is a revolution in the relations between one social class and another, in the distribution of power in a society.

Wit ought to be five or six degrees above the ideas that form the intelligence of an audience.

If it's eight degrees above, it gives *that audience a headache* (defect in D[omini]que's conversation when he is excited).[5]

To clarify my thought finally, I shall say that La Bruyère was five degrees above the intelligence common to the Ducs de St-Simon, de Charost, de Beauvilliers, de Chevreuse, de La Feuillade, de Villars, de Montfort, de Foix, de Lesdiguières (old Canaples), d'Harcourt, de La Rocheguyon, de La Rochefoucauld, d'Humières, of Mmes de Maintenon, de Caylus, de Berry, etc., etc., etc.

La Bruyère must have been at the level of the intelligences of around 1780, at the time of the Duc de Richelieu, Voltaire, M. de Vaudreuil, the Duc de Nivernais (supposedly Voltaire's son), when that worthless Marmontel passed for witty, in the time of Duclos, Collé, etc., etc.

In 1836, except where questions of literary art or rather *style*

5. "Dominique" here is Stendhal himself.

are concerned, and with the strict exception of his judgments on Racine, Corneille, Bossuet, etc., La Bruyère remains below the intelligence of the company that might foregather at Mme Boni de Castellane's and would be made up of Messrs Mérimée, Molé, Koreff, myself, the elder Dupin, Thiers, Béranger, the Duc de FitzJames, Saint-Aulaire, Arago, Villemain.

Wit is in short supply, I do declare; everyone reserves all his strength for his profession which gives him his position in the world. A *ready* wit, unexpected even for the speaker, Dom[ini]que's wit, alarms the proprieties. If I'm not mistaken, *wit* is going to take refuge among ladies of easy virtue, with Mme Ancelot (who has no more lovers than the first or second Mme de Talaru), but with whom you can be more daring.

What a terrible digression *for the sake of* the readers of 1880! But will they understand the allusion *for the sake of*? I doubt it, the street hawkers will have another expression then to get people to buy the king's speeches. What good is an allusion that has been *explained*? Wit of the Charles Nodier sort, boring wit.[6]

Here I want to paste in an example of the style of 1835. It is M. Gozlan[7] speaking in *Le Temps* [*a blank*].

The gentlest, most truly youthful of all the gloomy Grenoblois who fenced at the elegant Fabien's was without doubt M. César Pascal, the son of an equally amiable father and to whom Casimir Périer gave the cross when he was a minister, and the receivership-general of Auxerre to his natural brother, the amiable Turquin, and another receivership-general, that of Valence, to Casimir's nephew, M. Camille Teisseire.

But half-crooked though he may have been as a man of business, M. Casimir Périer had the Dauphinois virtue, of

6. Charles Nodier (1780–1844) was a Romantic writer specializing in the fantastic, as well as a student of folklore and of language.

7. A very minor novelist of the day.

446

knowing how to *will*. The breath of Paris, which weakens the *willing* faculty, hadn't yet reached our mountains in 1800. I am the faithful witness to that in my companions. Napoleon, Fieschi had the faculty of *willing* that is lacking in M. Villemain, M. Casimir Delavigne, in M. Pastoret (Amédée), who were brought up in Paris.

At the elegant Fabien's I convinced myself of my untalent for swordsmanship. His fencing master, the gloomy Renouvier, who killed himself, I believe, after having run his last friend through in a duel, brought me very honestly to recognize my untalent. I have been very fortunate always to fight with pistols; I couldn't foresee that good fortune in 1800, and fed up with always being too late in parrying, tiercing and quarting, I resolved, should need arise, to rush at my adversary head on. This hampered me every time in the army I found myself with my sword at my side. In Brunswick, for example, my awkwardness might have sent me *ad patres* along with the Grand Chamberlain of Münchhausen; luckily he wasn't brave that day, or rather wasn't willing to run risks.[8] I had a like untalent for the violin but, by contrast, a strange natural talent for shooting partridge or hares and, in Brunswick, a rook with a shot from a pistol at forty paces, the carriage moving at a fast trot, which earned me the respect of the aides-de-camp of General Rivaud, that very polite man (*Rivaud de La Raffinière*, loathed by the Prince de Neuchâtel [Berthier], later commander in Rouen and an ultra around 1825).

I was fortunate also to hit a *bancozeitel*[9] in Vienna, in the Prater, in the duel arranged with M. Raindre, a colonel or squadron commander in the light artillery. That three-pile hero was less than heroic!

In short, I have worn a sword all my life without knowing how to use it. I have always been fat and quick to get out of

8. This affair of 1807 was in fact settled peaceably.

9. I.e. a *bancozettel*, or "bank-note"; this other near-duel has already been referred to, in Chapter 31.

breath. My plan has always been: "Are you set?" and straight into the lunge.

In the days when I was fencing with César Pascal, Félix Faure, Duchesne, Casimir Périer and two or three other Dauphinois, I went to call on Périer *Milord* (in the Dauphiné, the Monsieur is omitted when there is a nickname). I found him in an apartment in one of his fine houses in Les Feuillants (near the present-day Rue Castiglione). He was occupying one of the ap[artment]s he was unable to let. He was the most cheerful of misers and the best of company. He came out with me, he was wearing a blue coat which had a ruddy stain eight inches in diameter on the tails.

I couldn't understand how this man, who was outwardly so amiable (roughly like my cousin Rebuffel), could allow his sons Casimir and Scipio to die of starvation.

The house of Périer took in the savings of servant girls, court ushers and small landowners at 5 per cent; these were sums of 500, 800, very occasionally 1,500 francs. When the *assignats* came in and you could get a hundred francs for one *louis d'or*, it paid all these poor devils back; several hanged or drowned themselves.

My family thought this proceeding iniquitous. It doesn't surprise me in merchants, but why, once they had made millions, did they not find an honest pretext for paying back the servant girls?

My family was beyond reproach in money matters; it had great difficulty tolerating one of our relations who paid back in *assignats* a sum of eight or ten thousand francs, lent to its authors in notes from Law's bank (1718, I believe, to 1793).[10]

I would be writing fiction were I to seek to record here the impression made on me by things in Paris, an impression so greatly modified later on.

---

10. John Law (1671–1729) was a Scottish banker who was allowed to set up a bank in his own name in France in 1716; it collapsed in a celebrated and far-reaching bankruptcy.

CHAPTER 42

I don't know whether I have said that at his father's request M. Daru took me to two or three of those literary societies whose presidency gave his father so much pleasure? There I admired the figure and especially the bosom of Mme Pipelet, wife of some poor devil of a hernia surgeon. I got to know her slightly later on, in her condition of princess.

M. Daru recited his verses with a cheeriness which seemed to me very strange on that stern, flushed face. I gazed at him in astonishment. I said to myself: "I must imitate him," but felt no inclination to do so.

I recall the profound tedium of Sundays; I went walking at random; so this was the Paris I had so longed for! The absence of mountains and woods wrung my heart. The woods were intimately linked to my rêveries of a tender and devoted love like in Ariosto. All the men seemed to me *prosaic* and worthless in the ideas they held on love and literature. I was careful not to let on about my objections to Paris. So I didn't realize that the centre of Paris is one hour distant from a beautiful forest, the residence of stags under the kings. How overjoyed would I not have been in 1800 to set eyes on the forest of Fontainebleau, where there are a few small miniature rocks, the woods of Versailles, Saint-Cloud, etc., etc.! I would probably have decided that these woods looked too much like a garden.

Deputies were due to be appointed to the commissioners of war. I gathered this from the redoubled attentiveness of Mme Cardon towards the family Daru and even towards myself. M. Daru spent a morning with the minister with the report on this objective.

My anxiety has fixed in my brain the mental picture of the office in which I awaited the outcome I had moved, my table was situated like this in a very large room.

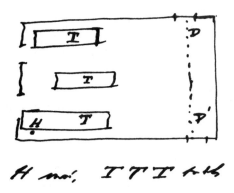

Garden, the same as in the other office.—H. Me.—T,T,T. Tables.

M. Daru followed the line DD' on returning from the minister's; I fancy he had had Cardon and M. Barthomeuf appointed. I wasn't in the least jealous of Cardon, but very much so of Barthomeuf, for whom I had always felt an aversion. While waiting for the decision I had written BAD REL- ATIVE in capital letters on my hand-rest.

Note that M. Barthomeuf was an excellent clerk, all of whose letters M. Daru signed (i.e. M. Bar[thomeuf] would present twenty letters, M. D[aru] would sign twelve, sign six or seven after correcting them and send one or two back to be redone).

Of mine he signed barely a half, and even then what letters! But M. Bartho[meuf] had the nature and face of a grocer's boy and, except for the Latin authors whom he knew as well as he knew the *Pay Regulations*, was incapable of saying a single word about the connection between literature and the nature of man, and the manner in which it affects him; I for my part understood perfectly the way in which Helvétius explains Regulus, I had made a great many applications of that sort of my own, I was far ahead of *Cailhava* in the art of comedy etc., etc., whence I went on to believe myself the superior or at least the equal of M. Barthomeuf.

M. D[aru] ought to have had me appointed and have then made me really work. But chance has guided me by the hand in five or six great circumstances of my life. I really owe *Fortune* a small statue. I was extremely lucky not to have been made a deputy with Cardon. I didn't think so at the time; I sighed a little as I gazed at his beautiful gold-braided uniform, his hat, his sword. But I didn't have the least feeling of jealousy. I suppose I realized that I didn't have a mother like Mme Cardon. I had seen her so importuning M. Daru (Pierre) as to try the patience of the most phlegmatic of men. M. Daru didn't get angry, but his wild boar's eyes were a picture. He finally said to her in my presence:

"Madame, I have the honour to promise you that, if there are to be deputies, *monsieur* your son will be one."

Mme Cardon's sister was, I fancy, Mme Auguié of the post office, whose daughters at that time were close friends of the *citoyenne* Hortense [de] Beauharnais.[1] These young ladies had been raised in the house of Mme Campan, the classmate and probably the friend of Mme Cardon.

I used to laugh and practise my 1800 charm on the Mlles Auguié, one of whom soon afterwards, I fancy, married General Ney.

I found them cheerful and attractive, I must have been a strange creature, perhaps these young ladies had sufficient wit to see that I was *strange* and not *worthless*. In short, for whatever reason, I was well received. What an admirable salon to have cultivated! That is what M. Daru senior should

---

1. Hortense de Beauharnais (1783–1837) was married against her wishes to one of Napoleon's brothers, became Queen of Holland as his wife and mother of the future emperor, Napoleon III.

have made me understand. I only glimpsed this truth, fundamental in Paris, for the first time twenty-seven years later, after the famous battle of Saint-Omer.[2] Good fortune, on which
I have so much reason to congratulate myself, introduced me
into several of the most influential salons. In 1814, I turned
down a post worth millions[3]; in 1828, I was intimately associated with Messrs Thiers (Foreign Minister, yesterday), Mignet,
Aubernon, Béranger. I was held in high regard in that salon. I
found M. Aubernon tiresome, Mignet lacking in wit, Thiers
too much of a shameless gasbag. Béranger alone I liked, but so
as not to seem to be courting power, I didn't go to visit him
in prison and allowed Mme Aubernon to take against me
as an immoral man.

And Mme la Comtesse Bertrand, in 1809 and 1810! Such
lack of ambition, or rather such laziness!

I don't much regret the wasted opportunity. Instead of ten,
I would have twenty thousand; instead of *ch[evali]er*, I would
be an *officier* of the Lég[ion] d'Honneur; but I would have
spent three or four hours a day at those platitudes of ambition
which are graced by the name of politics, I would have done
many semi-contemptible things, I would be prefect of Le Mans
(in 1814 I was about to be appointed prefect of Le Mans).

The one thing I regret is not living in Paris, but in 1836 I
would be weary of Paris, as I am weary of my solitude among
the savages of C[ivit]a-V[ecchi]a.

All told, I regret nothing except not having bought myself
an income with Napoleon's bounties around 1808 and 1809.

M. Daru senior was no less wrong in his ideas for not
saying to me:

"You ought to try and please Mme Cardon and her nieces,
the Mesdemoiselles Auguié. With their protection, you will

2. This "battle" was the rupture between Stendhal and one of his greatest loves,
Clémentine Curial.

3. Probably the post already referred to, when he would have been put in charge of
provisioning Paris.

be made a commissioner of war two years earlier. Don't breathe a word even to Daru about what I have just told you. Remember you will get advancement only through the salons. Work hard in the mornings, and in the evenings cultivate the salons; my business is to guide you. For example, earn yourself a reputation for assiduity, begin with this one. Never miss one of Mme Cardon's Tuesdays."

All of which verbiage was necessary if he was to be understood by a madman whose mind was more on *Hamlet* and *Le Misanthrope* than on real life. Whenever I was bored in a salon, I gave it the miss the following week and reappeared there only after a fortnight. What with the candour of my gaze and the extreme unhappiness and prostration of my faculties that *boredom* brings on, you can see how I must have advanced my cause by these absences! Moreover I always called a fool a fool. This mania has earned me a *host of enemies*. Since I became a wit (in 1826), the epigrams have arrived in droves and "witticisms never to be forgotten," as the kind Mme Mérimée said to me one day. I ought to have been killed ten times over, yet I have only three wounds two of which are mere *scratches* (on the left hand and foot).

My salons went from December to April 1800: Mme Cardon, Mme Rebuffel, Mme Daru, M. Rebuffel, Mme Sorel, I believe, whose husband had acted as my chaperon during the journey. These were amiable and useful people, obliging, who took a detailed interest in my affairs, who cultivated me even, because of the already very remarkable reputation of M. Daru (the Comte). They bored me, because there was nothing at all romantic or literary about them; (CUT THERE), I dropped the lot of them.

My cousins Martial and Daru (the Comte) had fought in the Vendée.[4] I have never met people more free of any sense of patriotism; yet they had run the risk of being murdered

4. This was a counter-revolutionary uprising which broke out in 1793 in the west of France and was bloodily put down by the armies of the Republic over the next two years.

twenty times over in Rennes, Nantes and all over Brittany; thus they didn't worship the Bourbons, they spoke of them with the respect that is owed to misfortune, and Mme Cardon used to tell us the truth more or less about Marie-Antoinette: good-natured, limited, extremely haughty, very promiscuous, and with no time at all for the journeyman locksmith known as Louis XVI, so unlike the amiable Comte d'Artois. For the rest, Versailles was the House of Misrule and no one, with the exception perhaps of Louis XVI and then only rarely, made a promise or took an oath to the people except with the intention of breaking it.

I think I can remember that at Mme Cardon's we read the *Memoirs* of her schoolfriend Mme Campan, very different from the simple-minded homily that was published around 1820. On several occasions we only came back down the street at two in the morning; I, who adored St-Simon, was in my element, and talked in a fashion which jarred with my usual simple-mindedness and exaltation.

I adored St-Simon in 1800 as in 1836. Spinach and St-Simon have been my only enduring tastes, at least after that of living in Paris on a hundred *louis* a year, writing books. Félix Faure reminded me in 1829 that I was talking to him in these terms in 1798.

The Daru family was entirely preoccupied first of all with the decree organizing the Corps of *inspecteurs aux revues*, a decree frequently amended, I fancy, by M. Daru (the Comte), and then by the appointment of the Comte Daru and of Martial; the first became an inspector and the second a sub-inspector, both with the braided hat and the red coat. This handsome uniform scandalized the military, far less vain even so in 1800 than two or three years later, when virtue would have been made fun of.

I fancy I have exhausted my first stay in Paris from November 1799 to April or May 1800, I've chattered on too much even, there will be erasures to make. Except for Cardon's handsome uniform (gold braid on the collar), Fabien's fencing-school and my lime-trees at the end of the War Office garden, everything else appears to me as if through a cloud. No doubt I often saw Mante, but no memory of it. Was it at this time that Grand-Dufay died in the Café de l'Europe on the Boulevard du Temple or in 1803?

I can't say. At the War Office, Messrs Barthomeuf and Cardon were deputies and I was very put out and no doubt very ridiculous in the eyes of M. Daru. For in fact I wasn't up to writing the briefest letter. Martial, that excellent creature, was always in a good humour with me and never drew my attention to the fact that as a clerk I had no common sense. He was wholly preoccupied by his love affairs with Mme Lavalette, and with Mme Petiet, over whom his sensible brother, the Comte Daru, had made himself look very ridiculous. He aspired to melt that wicked fairy's heart with poetry. I learnt all this a few months later.*

All these things, quite new for me, were a cruel distraction from my thoughts about literature or a passionate romantic love, at that time one and the same thing. On the other hand, my horror of Paris was growing less, but I was completely mad, what seemed true to me of this kind one day seemed false the next. My head was altogether the plaything of my soul. But at least I never unburdened myself to anyone.

For thirty years at least I have forgotten this very ridiculous period of my first visit to Paris; knowing that it would come wholesale at my summons I didn't let my thoughts dwell on it. Only in the past week have I been thinking about it once again; and if there is prejudice in what I write, it is against the Brulard of those days.

I don't know whether I made eyes at Mme Rebuffel and her daughter during that first visit, or whether we had the sorrow of losing Mme Cambon while I was in Paris. I remember only that Mlle Adèle R[ebuffel] recounted strange details to me about Mlle Cambon whose companion and friend she

*Fit in physical descriptions.

had been. Mlle Cambon had a dowry of twenty-five or thirty thousand francs a year, which was a vast sum at the emergence from the Republic in 1800, and suffered the fate of all those with too many advantages; she fell victim to the stupidest ideas. I presume she was to be married off at sixteen, or at least made to take a lot of exercise.[5]

I haven't the faintest recollection of my departure for Dijon and the army of reserve: the excess of joy has absorbed everything. Messrs Daru (the Comte), then *inspecteur aux revues*, and Martial Daru, sub-inspector, had left before me.

Cardon didn't come straightaway, his astute mother wanted to make him take one more step. He soon arrived in Milan, as *aide-de-camp* to the minister of war Carnot. Napoleon had employed this mighty citizen in order to *wear him out* (*id est*: to make him unpopular and ridiculous, if it were possible. Carnot soon relapsed into a noble poverty of which Napoleon only felt ashamed around 1810, when he was no longer afraid of him).

I have no mental image of my arrival in Dijon, any more than of my arrival in Geneva. The mental picture of these two towns has been erased by the more complete pictures left me by my subsequent travels. Doubtless I was wild with joy. I had with me some thirty volumes in stereotype. The idea of improvement and of a *new invention* led me to adore these volumes. I was very sensitive to smell, I spent my life washing my hands after I had been reading an old book; their smell had prejudiced me against Dante and the beautiful editions of that poet collected by my poor mother, a thought still dear and sacred to me and which around 1800 was still in the foreground.

When I arrived in Geneva, I was wild about *La Nouvelle Héloïse*. My first excursion was to the old house where J.-J. Rousseau was born in 1712, which I found in 1833 had been turned into a magnificent house, the very image of utility and commerce.

5. The girl died at the age of thirteen.

In Geneva there was a shortage of coaches. I encountered the first signs of that disorder that seemingly prevails in the army. I had been recommended to someone, seemingly to a French com[mission]er of war left behind to look after movements and transport. The Comte Daru had left a sick horse behind, I waited for it to get better.

Here finally my memories begin again. After several delays, one morning, around eight, my huge portmanteau was tied on to this young Swiss light bay, and just outside the Porte de Lausanne, I mounted.

It was for the second or third time in my life. Séraphie and my father had been consistently opposed to seeing me ride a horse, fence, etc.

This horse was only a month out of stables and after twenty paces it bolted, left the road and hurtled towards the lake in a field planted with willow-trees, I think the portmanteau had been hurting it.

CHAPTER 43

I was dying of fright, but the sacrifice had been made, the greatest dangers weren't going to stop me. I looked at the shoulders of my horse, and the three feet which separated me from the ground seemed like a bottomless precipice. The height of absurdity was that I believe I was wearing spurs.

So my frisky young horse was galloping haphazardly about among the willow-trees when I heard myself being called: it was Captain Burelvillers's sensible and cautious manservant who finally, shouting to me to pull back on the bridle and coming up, managed to stop the horse after a quarter of an hour at least galloping about in all directions. I fancy that among my innumerable fears was that of being dragged into the lake.

"What do you want with me?" I said to this servant, once he had finally been able to quieten my horse.

"My master wants a word with you."

My mind went immediately to my pistols. "It's no doubt someone who wants to arrest me." The road was covered with passers-by, but all through my life I have seen my idea and not the reality (like a *highly strung horse*, M. le Comte de Tracy said to me seventeen years later).

I came proudly back to the captain, whom I found obligingly halted along the highway.

"What do you want with me, *monsieur*?" I said to him, expecting to fire my pistol.

The cap[tain] was a tall, fair-haired man, middle-aged, thin and with a cunning, dishonest look, not at all prepossessing, quite the reverse. He explained to me that, as he passed the Porte [*a blank*], M. [*a blank*] had said to him:

"There's a young man there going off to the army on that horse, who's on a horse for the first time, and who's never seen the army. Be so charitable as to take him with you for the first few days."

Still expecting to lose my temper, and thinking of my pistols, I contemplated the straight and immensely long sabre of Ca[ptai]n Burelvillers who, I fancy, belonged to the heavy cavalry: blue coat, silver buttons and epaulettes.

The height of absurdity was that I think I had on a sabre, on reflection I'm even certain I had.

As far as I can judge, I appealed to this M. de Burelvillers, who looked like a great bird of prey and who had perhaps been expelled from one regiment and was seeking to attach himself to another. But all this is conjecture, like the physiognomies of the people I knew in Grenoble before 1800. How could I have told?

M. de Burelvillers answered my questions and taught me how to ride. We did the stage together, went together to get our billeting order, and this lasted as far as La Casa d'Adda, Porta Nova in Milan, on the left as you go towards the gate.

I was completely drunk, mad with happiness and joy. Here begins a period of enthusiasm and perfect happiness. My joy, my rapture only decreased a little when I became a dragoon in the 6th Regiment and even that was only an eclipse.

I didn't believe I was then at the peak of the happiness a human being can find here below.

Such was the truth however. And this four months after having been so unhappy in Paris, when I realized, or thought I realized that Paris was not, in itself, the peak of happiness.

How could I describe my raptures in Rolle?

I shall perhaps have to reread and emend this passage, contrary to my intentions, in case I tell artful lies like J.-J. Rousseau.

Since the sacrifice of my life to my fortune had been made

and was complete, I became excessively bold on horseback, but bold while still asking Captain Burelvillers:

"Am I going to kill myself?"

Fortunately my horse was Swiss and as pacific and reasonable as a Swiss; had it been Roman and treacherous, it would have killed me a hundred times over.

Seemingly I appealed to M. Burelvillers, but he applied himself to educating me in everything; and from Geneva to Milan, over a journey of four or five leagues a day, he was for me what an excellent tutor ought to be for a young prince. Our life was a pleasant conversation, intermixed with singular events and not without some small danger; in consequence, impossibility of the faintest appearance of boredom. I didn't dare tell of my fantasies nor talk *literature* to that bloodless roué of twenty-eight or thirty, who seemed the opposite of emotion.

As soon as we finished a day's journey, I left him, I gave his servant a gratuity to take care of my horse, I could then go off and dream in peace.

At Rolle, I fancy, having got there early, drunk with happiness from reading *La Nouvelle Héloïse* and from the idea of passing through Vevey, I may be mistaking Rolle for Vevey, I suddenly heard a majestic peal of bells ring out from a church situated on the hill a quarter of a league above Rolle or Nyon. I climbed up there. I could see the beautiful lake spread out beneath my gaze, the sound of the bell was a ravishing music which accompanied my thoughts and lent them the character of the sublime.

I fancy it was there I came closest to *a perfect happiness.*

It is worth the trouble of having lived for such a moment.

In what follows I shall speak of similar moments, where the foundation of my happiness was perhaps more real, but was the sensation as intense, the transport of happiness as complete?

What to say of such a moment without falsehood, without lapsing into fiction?

At Rolle or at Nyon, I don't know which (to be checked, the church is easy to see, surrounded by eight or ten tall trees), precisely at Rolle the happy period of my life began; it might have been the 8 or 10 of May 1800.

My heart is pounding still as I write this thirty-six years later. I abandon my paper, I wander round my room and I come back to writing. I would rather leave out some true detail than be guilty of the execrable fault of declaiming, as is customary.

In Lausanne, I believe, M. Burelvillers was pleased with me. The military policeman was a Swiss captain, who had retired young. He was some *ultra* escaped from Spain or some other court who, while performing the disagreeable task of issuing billeting orders to these rascally Frenchmen, exchanged sharp words with us and went so far as to say, when speaking of the *honour* we had of serving our country:

"If it *is* an honour . . ."

I am no doubt exaggerating the remark in my memory. I put my hand to my sabre and wanted to draw it, which proves I was wearing a sabre.

M. Burelvillers held me back.

"It's late, the town is crowded, we need to find a billet," he said, in effect, and we left the ex-captain military policeman after giving him a piece of our minds.

The next day, riding along the road to Villeneuve, M. Burelvillers questioned me as to my ability with a sword.

He was astounded when I confessed my complete ignorance. I fancy he made me take guard the first time we stopped to let our horses pee.

"So what would you have done if that cur of an aristocrat had come out with us?"

"I would have rushed him."

Obviously these words were spoken just as they came into my head.

Cap[tai]n Burelvillers held a high opinion of me after this and told me as much.

My perfect innocence and complete lack of falsehood must have been very apparent to lend value to what, in any other circumstances, would have been so much crude bravado.

During our evening halts he began to pass on to me some of the principles of swordsmanship.

"Otherwise you'll get yourself skewered like a . . ."

I've forgotten the term of comparison.

Martigny I believe, at the foot of the Great Saint-Bernard, has left me this memory: the handsome General Marmont, in his uniform of a councillor of state, royal blue trimmed with sky blue (but how is such a uniform possible?) busy getting an artillery park on the move. I don't know, but I can see him still.

Perhaps I saw G[ener]al Marmont in his general's uniform and applied the uniform of a councillor of state to him later. (He is in Rome near here, March 1836, the *treacherous* Duc de Raguse, in spite of the lie which Lieutenant-General Despans told me before my fireplace in the place where I am writing, not twelve days ago.)

G[ener]al Marmont was on the left of the road coming out of Martigny around seven o'clock in the morning, it may then have been the 12 or the 14 of May 1800.[*]

I was as cheerful and active as a young colt, I saw myself as Calderón campaigning in Italy[1]; I saw myself as a curious onlooker posted to the army in order to observe, but destined to write comedies like Molière. If I were subsequently to have a job, it would be in order to live, not being rich enough to roam the world at my own expense. I asked only to witness great events.

It was with a greater joy than usual therefore that I examined Marmont, the First Consul's handsome young favourite.

---

[*] Saint-Bernard: there I encountered danger for the first time. My Swiss horse after all was only a hack. The danger wasn't great in itself, but the accessory circumstances cut a man down to size.

1. Where the great Spanish dramatist Pedro Calderón de la Barca (1600–1681) served in the retinue of the Duke of Alba.

Because the Swiss whose houses we had lodged in in Lausanne, Villeneuve, Sion, etc., etc., had painted an infamous picture to us of the Great S[ain]t-Bernard, I was even more cheerful than usual; more cheerful isn't the word, I was happier. So intense, so intimate was my pleasure, it became thoughtful.

For some unexplained reason, I was extremely susceptible to the beauty of landscape. Because my father and Séraphie, true hypocrites that they were, had greatly extolled the beauties of nature to me, I thought I had a horror of nature. If anyone had spoken to me about the beauties of Switzerland, he would have turned my stomach; I used to skip phrases of that sort in Rousseau's *Confessions* and *Héloïse* or rather, to be exact, read them at a canter. But those beautiful phrases affected me in spite of myself.

I must have felt an extreme pleasure climbing the Saint-Bernard but I swear that, but for Captain Burelvillers's precautions, which I often found excessive and almost absurd, I would probably have been dead after the first step.

Kindly recall my very ridiculous upbringing. So that I should run no risks, my father and Séraphie had prevented me from mounting a horse and, so far as they were able to, from going out shooting. At the very most I went out walking with a gun, but never on a real hunting trip where you experience hunger, rain, an excessive fatigue.

Moreover, nature has given me the delicate nerves and sensitive skin of a woman. A few months later, I couldn't hold my sabre for two hours without my hand getting covered in blisters. At the S[ain]t-Bernard I had the physique of a fourteen-year-old girl; I was seventeen and three months, but no spoilt son of a feudal lord was ever so mollycoddled.

As my relations saw it, a soldier's courage was a Jacobin virtue, they prized only that pre-Revolutionary courage which had earned the Cross of Saint-Louis for the head of the wealthy branch of the family (M. le Capitaine Beyle of Sassenage).

My moral nature excepted, derived by me from the books

proscribed by Séraphie, I was a complete cissy, therefore, when I came to the S[ain]t-Bernard. What would have become of me had I not met with M. Burelvillers and had I been marching alone? I had money but had never even thought of taking on a servant. My head had been turned by my delightful daydreams, based on Ariosto and *La Nouvelle Héloïse*, and all warnings were lost on me; I considered them bourgeois, worthless, odious.

Whence my dislike, even in 1836, of the *comic* doings among which a low character necessarily finds himself. They make me feel a disgust verging on horror.

A droll attitude of mind for a successor to Molière!

All the sensible advice of the Swiss hotel-keepers was therefore lost on me.

At a certain altitude the cold became biting, a penetrating fog enveloped us, the road had long been covered in snow. This road, a narrow path between two dry stone walls, was covered by eight or ten inches of melting snow above slithery pebbles (like those of Claix, irregular polygons whose corners have been partly rubbed away). From time to time a dead horse caused mine to shy; soon, which was far worse, he no longer shied at all. Basically, he was a hack.

CHAPTER 44

THE SAINT-BERNARD

With each step everything got worse. I encountered danger for the first time; the danger wasn't great, it has to be admitted, but for a fifteen-year-old girl who hadn't got wet in the rain ten times in her life!

The danger wasn't great then, but it was inside me, the circumstances had cut the man down to size.

I shan't be ashamed to do myself justice, I was unfailingly cheerful. If I dreamt, it was of the phrases by which J.-J. Rousseau might have described those lowering, snow-covered mountains which rose into the skies with their points forever obscured by huge grey clouds racing past.

My horse looked like falling, the captain swore and was gloomy, his cautious manservant, who had become my friend, was very pale.

The damp went right through me; we were endlessly being impeded or even halted by groups of fifteen or twenty soldiers coming up.

Instead of the feelings of heroic friendship I assumed them to have following six years of heroic rêveries, based on the characters of Ferragus and Rinaldo, I caught a glimpse of embittered and unfriendly egotists; they often swore angrily at us, seeing us on horseback and themselves on foot. They all but stole our horses from us.

This display of the human character affronted me, but I very quickly pushed it aside in order to enjoy this thought: so I'm experiencing something difficult!

I don't remember all this, but I remember better subsequent dangers, when I was much closer to 1800, for example at the end of 1812, on the march from Moscow to Königsberg.

At last, after an enormous number of zigzags which seemed to me to constitute an infinite distance, in a chasm between two enormous pointed rocks, I caught sight to our left of a low house, almost covered by a passing cloud.

It was the hospice! There we were given, as the whole army was, half a glass of wine which seemed to me ice-cold like a *red decoction*. I have a memory only of the wine, but no doubt they added a piece of bread and cheese. I fancy we went in, or else the accounts of the interior of the hospice I was given produced a mental picture, which for the past thirty-six years *has taken the place of the reality.*

Which is where the risk of falsehood lies that I've been noticing in the three months I've had my mind on this veracious journal.

For example, I can picture the descent to myself very clearly. But I don't want to conceal the fact that five or six years later, I saw an engraving that I thought a very good likeness, and my memory is now *nothing more than* the engraving.

Which is the danger of buying engravings of the beautiful pictures you see on your travels. Soon the engraving constitutes the whole memory, and destroys the actual memory.

That's what happened to me with the *San Sisto* Madonna in Dresden. Müller's beautiful engraving has destroyed it for me, whereas I can picture to myself perfectly the nasty pastels by Mengs, in the same Dresden gallery, of which I haven't seen an engraving anywhere.

I can see very clearly the tedium of holding my horse by the bridle; the path was formed of immovable rocks set thus:

D. Precipice.—D. Precipice thus.—Frozen lake.—It may have been three or four feet from A to B.

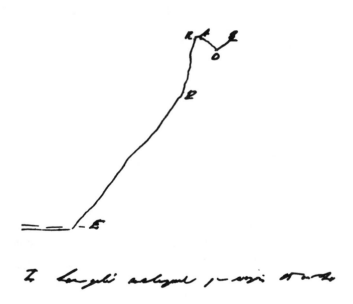

Z. Frozen lake on which I saw fifteen or twenty fallen horses or mules; from R to P the precipice seemed to me almost vertical; from P to E, it was very steep.

The curse of it was that the four feet of my horse came together in the straight line formed at point O by the meeting

of the two rocks that formed the road, and then the hack made as if to fall; to the right, there was no great harm, but to the left! What would M. Daru say if I lost his horse for him?

In any case all my effects were in the huge portmanteau, and perhaps the greater part of my money.

The cap[tai]n was swearing at his servant who was injuring his second horse, he was hitting his own horse on the head with his cane, he was a very violent man, in short he wasn't concerned about me in the slightest.

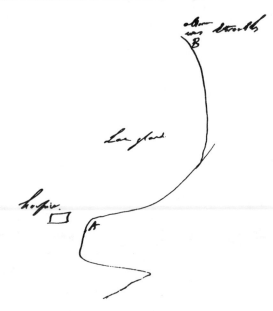

Going towards Etroubles.—Frozen lake.—Hospice.

As if this weren't misery enough, a cannon, I fancy, happened to come past; we had to jump our horses to the right-hand side of the road, but to this circumstance I wouldn't want to swear, it's in the engraving.

I recall very well the long circular descent around that infernal frozen lake.

Finally, near Etroubles or before Etroubles, near a hamlet called Saint-[*a blank*], nature started to grow less austere.

This for me was a delightful sensation.

I said to Captain Burelvillers: "Is that all there is to the Saint-Bernard?"

I fancy he lost his temper; he thought I was lying (in the terms we used to use: that I was having him on). I think I can half-see in my memories that he treated me as a conscript, which seemed to me an insult.

At Etroubles where we slept, or at Saint-[*a blank*], my happiness was extreme, but I was beginning to understand that it was only at moments when the captain was feeling cheerful that I could risk my comments.

I told myself: "I'm in Italy, i.e. in the land of the *Zulietta* that J.-J. Rousseau met in Venice, in Piedmont in the country of Mme Basile."[1]

I well understood that these thoughts were yet more contraband for the captain, who had on one occasion, I fancy, called Rousseau a writer of smut.

I should be obliged to write fiction and to try and imagine to myself what a young man of seventeen must feel, wild with happiness on escaping from the monastery, if I wanted to talk about my feelings in Etroubles at the Fort of Bard.

I've forgotten to say that I had brought my innocence with me from Paris, only in Milan was I to deliver myself of this treasure. The funny thing is, I can't clearly remember who with.

The violence of my timidity and of the sensation has completely killed the *memory*.

---

1. The reference is to two well-known episodes in Rousseau's *Confessions*.

As we went along, the cap[tai]n gave me lessons in horse-manship and to liven things up would hit his horse on the head with his cane so that it bolted strongly. Mine was a limp and cautious hack. I roused him by digging my spurs hard in. Fortunately he was very strong.

My wild imagination didn't dare share its secrets with the cap[tai]n, but it at least led me to ply him with questions about horsemanship. I was anything but discreet.

"And when a horse backs away and comes close to a deep ditch like this, what should you do?"

"Dammit, you hardly know how to stay on and you ask me about things that worry the finest horsemen!"

No doubt some robust oath accompanied this reply for it has remained engraved in my memory.

I must have bored him stiff. His sensible servant warned me that he fed to his own horses at least half the bran he had made me buy to *refresh* mine. This sensible servant offered to come over into my employ; he would have used me as he liked instead of himself being ill-used by the terrible Burelvillers.

This fine speech made no impression on me. I fancy I thought I owed an infinite gratitude to the captain.

Besides, I was so happy contemplating the beautiful coun-tryside and the triumphal arch of Aosta that I had only one wish to formulate, which was that this life might last for ever.

We believed the army to be forty leagues ahead of us.

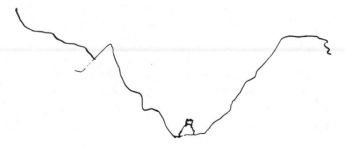

Here is a rough cross-section of the valley.

Suddenly, we found it had been held up by the Fort of Bard.

I see myself bivouacking half a league from the fort, on the left-hand side of the highway.

The next day I had twenty-two gnat bites on my face and one eye completely closed.

Here the story becomes confused with my memory.

I fancy we were held up for two or three days below Bard.

I dreaded the nights because of the bites of those ghastly gnats; I had time to be half recovered.

Was the First Consul with us?[2]

Was it, as I think, while we were on this small plain below the fort that Colonel Dufour attempted to take it by force? And that two engineers tried to sever the chains of the drawbridge? Did I see the wheels of the cannon being rimmed in straw, or is it rather the memory of the story I find in my head?

The fearsome cannonade among those high rocks, in such a narrow valley, sent me wild with excitement.

Bard.—C is the path.

The cap[tai]n finally said to me:

"We're going to go over a mountain on the left."

I have since learnt that this mountain is known as Albaredo.

After half a league, I heard this piece of advice passing from mouth to mouth:

"Only keep two fingers of your right hand on the bridles

2. I.e. Napoleon, who had in fact crossed the Saint-Bernard pass ten days before.

of your horses so that if they fall over the precipice they won't take you with them."

"Dammit, so there's danger!" I said to myself.

We halted on a small platform.

"Ah, they're taking aim at us," said the captain.

"Are we within range?" I said to the cap[tai]n.

"So the young fellow-me-lad's frightened already, is he?" he said to me gruffly. There were seven or eight people present.

R. Rampart.

This remark was like the crowing of the cock for St Peter. I see myself again: I went up to the edge of the platform so as to be the more exposed, and when he got under way again I hung back for a few minutes so as to display [my] courage. That was how I first came under fire.

It was a sort of virginity weighing as much on me as the other.

CHAPTER 45

That evening, on reflection, I couldn't get over my astonishment: "What, is that all there is to it?" I said to myself.

That rather simple-minded astonishment and that exclamation have followed me all my life. I think it stems from my imagination, I am making this discovery, along with many others in 1836, as I write this.

Parenthesis.—I often say to myself, though without regrets: "What a lot of fine opportunities I've wasted! I should be rich, at least I should be comfortably off!" But I can see in 1836 that my greatest pleasure is in *dreaming*, but dreaming of what? Often of things that bore me. The energetic steps you need to take to amass 10,000 francs a year are out of the question for me. What's more, you have to flatter, give offence to no one, etc. Such a plan is almost out of the question for me.

Oh well! M. le Comte de Canclaux was a lieutenant or second-l[ieutenant] in the 6th Dragoons at the same time as me; he passed for a schemer, clever, never losing an opportunity to curry favour with influential people etc., etc., never taking any step that didn't have an objective, etc., etc. G[ener]al Canclaux, his uncle, had pacified the Vendée, I believe, and wasn't without influence. M. de Canclaux left the regiment to enter the consular service, he probably possessed all the qualities I lack, he is consul in Nice as I am in C[ivit]a-V[ecchi]a! That ought to console me for not having been a schemer or at least astute, prudent, etc. I have had the rare pleasure of doing all my life more or less as I pleased, and I have got on as well as a man who is cold, astute, etc. M. de C[anclaux] showed me politeness when I passed through Nice in December 1833. He may score over me by having a fortune, but he probably inherited it from his uncle, and in any case has an old wife on his hands. I wouldn't swap, i.e. I wouldn't want my soul to enter his body.

I shouldn't bemoan my fate, therefore. I had an execrable lot from seven to seventeen, but since crossing Mont S[ain]t-Bernard (at an elevation of 2,491 metres above the ocean), I have never again had to bemoan my fate, but on the contrary to give thanks for it.

In 1804, I wished for a hundred *louis* and my freedom; in 1836, I wish passionately for 6,000 francs and my freedom. Anything above that would do very little for my happiness. Which isn't to say that I wouldn't like to try my hand at 25,000 francs and my freedom so that I could have a good carriage with nice flexible springs, but I would derive more annoyance from the coachman's thieving perhaps than pleasure from the carriage.

My happiness is in having nothing to administer; I should be most unhappy if I had 100,000 francs a year in land and houses. I should very soon sell the lot at a loss, or at least three-quarters of it, so as to buy an income. Happiness for me is to give orders to no one and not to be given orders, so I think I did very well not to marry Mlle Riett, or Mlle Vidau. End of parenthesis.*

I recall feeling an extreme pleasure on entering Etroubles and Aosta. "What, *that's all there is* to crossing the Saint-Bernard?" I said to myself endlessly. I even committed the sin of saying it out loud at times, and Cap[tai]n Burelvillers finally gave me the rough edge of his tongue despite my innocence, he took it

*To be fitted in elsewhere when recopied.

for showing off (*id est bravade*). My naiveties have very often had this same effect.

An absurd or merely exaggerated remark has often sufficed to mar the greatest occasions for me: at Wagram for example, next to the cannon when the grass caught fire, our friend the blustering colonel, who said: "It's a battle of the giants!" The impression of grandeur was irremediably removed for the whole day.

But good lord, who will read this? What gibberish! Can I finally get back to my story? Does the reader know now whether he's in 1800, at a madman's first entry into society, or with the sage reflections of a man of fifty-three?

I remarked before leaving my rock that the cannonade at Bard made a terrifying din; this was the *sublime*, yet a little too close to danger. Instead of pure enjoyment, the soul was still a little bit concerned with holding itself steady.

Once and for all I give warning to the brave man, the only one perhaps, who has the courage to read me, that all the fine reflections of this sort belong to 1836. I would have been greatly astonished by them in 1800; well versed though I was in Helvétius and Shakespeare, I wouldn't perhaps have understood them.

A distinct and very serious memory has remained with me of the rampart that directed this heavy fire at us. The commander of this small fort, *providentially* situated as the good writers of 1836 would put it, had thought to halt G[ener]al Bonaparte.

That evening, our billet I believe was with a *curé*, who had already been very ill-used by the twenty-five or thirty thousand men who had passed through before Cap[tain] Burelvillers and his pupil. The egotistical and unfriendly captain was abusive; I fancy I felt sorry for the *curé*, I spoke Latin to him, to make him less afraid. This was a major sin, in a small way it was the same crime as that of the vile

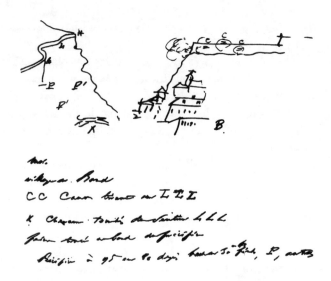

H. Me.—B. Village of Bard.—CCC. Cannon firing at LLL.—XX.
Horses fallen from the path LLL barely marked at the edge of the
precipice.—P. 95- or 80-degree precipice, 30 or 40 feet high.—P'.
Other precipices of 70 or 60 degrees, and endless undergrowth. I
can still see the bastion CCC, that is all that remains to me of my
fear. When I was at H, I saw neither corpses nor wounded, but
only the horses at X. My own which jumped about and whose bridle I was holding with only two fingers as per the order gave me a
lot of trouble.

scoundrel Bourmont at Waterloo.[1] Happily, the cap[tai]n didn't
hear me.

The grateful *curé* taught me that: *donna* meant "woman,"
cativa "bad" and that I needed to say *quanti sono miglia di
qua a Ivrea?* when I wanted to know how many miles it was
from here to Ivrea.

That was the beginning of my Italian.

I was so struck by the number of dead horses and other
military debris that I came across between Bard and Ivrea,
that no distinct memory is left. This was the first time I
experienced that sensation renewed so often later on: of find-

1. Who went over to the other side three days before the battle.

ing myself among the columns of one of Napoleon's armies. The present sensation absorbed everything, exactly like the memory of the first evening when Giu[lia] treated me as a lover. My memory is only a novel fabricated on that occasion.

I can still see Ivrea as it first appeared to me from three-quarters of a league away, a little over on the right, and to the left mountains in the distance, perhaps Monte Rosa and the mountains of Bielle, perhaps the *Rezegon de Leck*[2] which I was later to adore so.

It was becoming difficult not to find a billet among the terrified inhabitants, but to defend that billet against the bands of three or four soldiers marauding for loot. I have an impression of being sabre in hand, defending a door in our house which some mounted *chasseurs* wanted to remove to make a bivouac with.

That evening I experienced a sensation I shall never forget.

I went to the theatre in spite of the cap[tai]n who, rightly judging of my childishness and my ignorance of swordsmanship, my sabre being too heavy for me, was no doubt afraid in case I got myself killed on some street-corner. I had no uniform, which is the very worst thing among the columns of an army, etc., etc.

Anyway, I went to the theatre, they were doing Cimarosa's *Matrimonio segreto*, the actress who was playing Caroline was missing a tooth in the front. That's all that remains with me of a divine happiness.

I should be telling lies and writing fiction were I to undertake to give details.

Instantly my two great actions: 1, having crossed the S[ain]t-Bernard, 2, having come under fire, vanished. All that seemed low and uncouth. I experienced something like my enthusiasm at the church above Rolle but far purer and far more intense. The pedantry of Julie d'Etange troubled me in Rousseau, whereas everything was divine in Cimarosa.

2. This is Stendhal's phonetic version of the Italian Resegone di Lecco.

In my intervals of pleasure I said to myself: "And here I am launched on an uncouth profession instead of devoting my life to music!"

The reply was, without the least ill-humour: "One must live, I shall see the world, become a brave soldier, and after a year or two I shall come back to music, *my one love.*" I spoke these pompous words to myself.

My life was renewed and my whole disappointment with Paris buried for ever.

I had just had a clear view of where happiness lay. It seems to me today that my great unhappiness must have been: I haven't found happiness in Paris, where for so long I thought it to lie, where then is it? Mightn't it be in our Dauphiné mountains? In that case my relations would have been right, and I would do better to return.

That evening in Ivrea destroyed the Dauphiné for ever in my mind. But for the beautiful mountains I had seen that morning on my arrival, perhaps Berland, St-Ange and Taille-fer wouldn't have been vanquished for ever.[3]

To live in Italy and hear such music became the basis of all my reasoning.

The next morning, walking our horses with the cap[tai]n who was six foot tall, I was childish enough to talk of my happiness; he answered me with coarse jokes about the easy virtue of actresses. This word was dear and sacred to me, because of Mme Kubly, and that morning moreover I was in love with Carolina [*sic*] (in the *Matrimonio*). I fancy we had a serious disagreement, with some thought of a duel on my part.

I can't begin to understand my folly; it was like my provoking of the excellent Joinville (now M. le Baron Joinville, military intendant in Paris): I couldn't hold my sabre up in a horizontal line.

Peace having been made with the captain we were, I fancy,

3. These are the names of the mountains near Grenoble which Stendhal especially admired.

taken up with the battle of Ticino, in which I fancy we were involved, though not in any danger. I shan't say more, for fear of writing fiction; this battle, or engagement, was recounted to me in great detail a few months later by M. Guyardet, a b[atall]ion commander in the 6th or 9th Light Regiment, the regiment of that excellent Macon, died at Leipzig around 1809, I fancy. M. Guyardet's story, told, I fancy, to Joinville in my presence, completes my memories and I'm afraid of mistaking my impression of that story for a memory.

I don't even recall whether the engagement at Ticino counted in my mind as my second experience of coming under fire, it could in any case only have been cannon fire, perhaps we were afraid of being sabred on finding ourselves with some cavalry that had been driven back by the enemy. All I can see clearly is the smoke from the cannon or from the muskets. Everything is confused.

Except for the maddest, most intense happiness, I have in actual fact nothing to say about Ivrea to Milan. The view of the countryside was ravishing. I didn't think this was the beautiful made real, but when, after Ticino and as far as Milan, the frequency of the trees and the vigour of the vegetation, and even the stalks of maize, I fancy, stopped you seeing more than a hundred paces to right and left, I thought *this was the beautiful*.

Which was what Milan was for me for twenty years (1800 to 1820). That adored image has hardly begun to separate itself from the beautiful. My reason tells me: but the truly beautiful is Naples and Pausilippo, for example, the region around Dresden, the ruined walls of Leipzig, the Elbe below Rainville to Altona, the Lake of Geneva, etc., etc. It's my reason that says this, my heart feels only Milan and the *luxuriant* countryside that surrounds it. *

*Third volume started 20 January 1836 at page 501, finished 10 March 1836 at Civita-Vecchia, page 796.

8 April 1836. This third volume ends at my arrival in Milan. 796 pages is good, once added to by corrections and defence-works against the critics, 400 pages in octavo. Who will read 400 pages of fluctuations of the heart?

CHAPTER 46

MILAN

Entering Milan one morning, on a delightful spring morning, and what a spring! and in what a country! I saw Martial three paces away, to the left of my horse. I can see him now, it was in the *Corsia del Giardino*, just past the Rue des Bigli, at the beginning of the *Corsia di Porta Nova*.

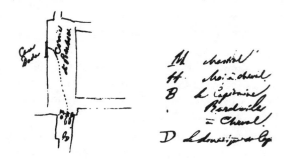

Casa d'Adda.—Corsia di Porta Nova.

    M. Martial.—M. Me, on horseback.—B. Captain Burelvillers on horseback.—D. The captain's manservant.

He was in a blue frock-coat with the braided hat of an Adjutant-General.

He was very glad to see me.

"We thought you were lost," he said to me.

"The horse fell sick in Geneva," I replied, "I only left on the [*a blank*]."

"I'll show you the house, it's only a short step away."

Martial turned about and led me to the *Casa* d'Adda at D.

I saluted Cap[tai]n Burelvillers, I've not seen him since.

The façade of the Casa d'Adda was unfinished, the greater part of it was at that time rough brick like San Lorenzo in Florence. I entered into a magnificent courtyard. I dismounted in high astonishment, admiring everything. I went up by a superb staircase. M[arti]al's servants untied my portmanteau and led away my horse.

I went upstairs with him and soon found myself in a superb drawing-room overlooking the Corsia. I was in ecstasies, this was the first time architecture had produced its effect on me. We were soon brought some excellent cutlets cooked in breadcrumbs. For several years this dish reminded me of Milan.

This town became for me the most beautiful place on earth. I am quite insensitive to the charms of my homeland, for the place where I was born I have a repugnance verging on a physical nausea (sea-sickness). Milan for me between 1800 and 1821 was the place where I wished constantly to be living.

I passed a few months there in 1800, it was the best time of my life. I returned there as often as I could in 1801 and 1802, being garrisoned in Brescia and Bergamo, and finally lived there out of choice from 1815 to 1821. My reason alone tells me, even in 1836, that Paris is better. Around 1803 or 4, in Martial's study, I used to avoid looking up at a print which showed a distant view of Milan cathedral, the memory was too tender and it pained me.

We may have been at the end of May, or the beginning of June, when I entered the Casa d'Adda (this word has remained sacred for me).

Martial behaved perfectly, indeed always behaved perfectly towards me. I am angry at not having seen that more clearly in his lifetime; because he had a surprising degree of petty vanity, I used to humour that vanity.

But what I then said to him out of a nascent worldliness, and also out of friendship, I ought to have said to him out of a passionate friendship and gratitude.

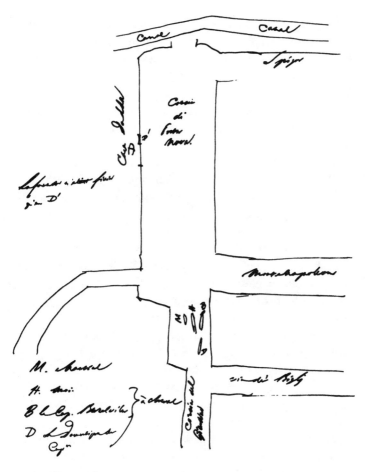

Canal.—Canal.—Spiga.—Corsia di Porta Nova.—Casa d'Adda. The façade was finished only at D'.—Monte Napoleone.—Via dei Bigli. —Corsia del Giardino. M. Martial.—H. Me.—B. Captain Burel-villers on horseback.—The cap[tai]n's manservant on horseback.

He wasn't romantic, whereas I carried that weakness to the point of madness; I saw him as a dullard for lacking such madness. Romanticism in me extended to love, to physical bravery, to everything. I dreaded the moment of tipping a porter in case I didn't give him enough and hurt his feelings.

It frequently happened that I didn't dare give a tip to a man who was too well dressed for fear of offending him, and I must have passed for a miser. This is the opposite fault from most of the subalterns I have known: their one thought was to get away without a *mancia*.

This was an interval of mad and total happiness; my mind will no doubt start wandering a little as I talk about it. Perhaps it would be better to stick to my previous line.

From the end of May up until October or November when I was commissioned as a second lieutenant in the 6th Regiment of Dragoons at Bagnolo or Romanengo, between Brescia and Cremona, I experienced five or six months of heavenly and complete happiness. *

The part of the sky too close to the sun can't be clearly seen; by a similar effect, I shall have great difficulty making a rational narrative out of my love for Angela Pietragrua. How to give a half-reasonable account of so many follies? Where to begin? How to make it even a little bit intelligible? Here I am already forgetting how to spell, as happens to me in moments of high passion, yet these are things that took place thirty-six years ago.

Deign to forgive me, oh benevolent reader! Or better than that, if you are over thirty or under thirty but of the prosaic party, close the book up!

Is it to be believed, but then everything in my story of this year of 1800 will seem absurd. This so heavenly, so passionate love, which had removed me completely from the earth and transported me into the land of fancy, but of the most heavenly, most delightful, most desirable fancy, only came to what is called fruition in September 1811.

That's all: eleven years, not of fidelity but of a sort of constancy.

*26 March 1836, at half past ten, very polite letter regarding leave of absence.

Since this great current in my thoughts, I have not been working. 1 April 1836. *Prova* [rehearsal] of 31 March, Vignaccia. *Stabat Mater*, barbaric old couplets in rhymed Latin, but at least no wit *à la* Marmontel.

The woman I loved, and by whom I believed myself in some sort loved, had other lovers, but preferred me, all things being equal, I told myself!

I had other mistresses.

(I have been walking about for a quarter of an hour before writing.)

How to recount those days rationally? I would rather put it off to another day.

If I reduced myself to rational forms I should do too great an injustice to what I wish to recount.

I don't mean what things were like.

What they were like is what I'm discovering for the first time in 1836.

But on the other hand I can't write down what they were like for me in 1800, the reader would throw the book away.

Which course to follow? How to portray a mad happiness?

Has the reader ever been madly in love? Has he ever had the good fortune to spend a night with the mistress he has loved the most in his life?

I swear I can't go on, the subject surpasses the teller.

I'm very conscious of being ridiculous or rather unbelievable. My hand can no longer write, I shall put it off to tomorrow.

Perhaps it would be better to go straight past these six months.

How to portray the excessive happiness everything gave me? It's impossible for me.

All I can do is give a summary outline so as not to interrupt the story altogether.

I am like a painter who no longer has the courage to paint one corner of his picture. So as not to ruin the centre he roughs out *a la meglio*[1] what he can't paint.

Oh unfeeling reader, forgive my memory, or rather skip fifty pages.

1. "As best he can."

Here is the summary of what, after a gap of thirty-six years, I can't recount without spoiling it horribly.

Were I to spend the five, ten, twenty or thirty years I have left to me in terrible pain I shouldn't say as I was dying: "I don't want to start again."

First of all the happiness of having Martial as a relation. A second-rate man, worse than second-rate if you like, yet good-hearted and cheerful, or rather himself happy at that time, with whom I lived.

All these are discoveries I'm making as I write. Not knowing how to describe, I am analysing what I then felt.

I'm very cold today, the weather is grey, I'm a little unwell. Nothing can prevent folly.*

As an honest man who loathes exaggeration, I don't know how to go about it.

I am writing this and have always written everything just like Rossini writing his music, I think about it, writing down each morning what I find in front of me in the *libretto*.

I read in a book I have received today: "This result is not always perceptible to contemporaries, to those who operate and experience it; but at a distance and in the perspective of history, one may observe at what point in time a people loses the originality of its character," etc., etc. (M. Villemain, preface, page x).

One spoils feelings this tender by recounting them in detail.†

---

*Work at C[ivit]a-V[ecchi]a: three or four days only from 24 Feb to 19 March 1836. The rest earning my professional bread.

†1836, 26 March: leave FOR LUTÈCE announced. The imagination flies off elsewhere: this work is broken off. Tedium dulls a mind too much tried by Rome from 1832 to 36. This work, constantly interrupted by professional duties, has no doubt suffered from this dullness of mind. Visited the Fesch gallery this morning with the prince, and the Raphael *stanze*. Pedantry; nothing in Dante or Raphael is bad; *idem* more or less for Goldoni.

8 April 1836.

Conversation with Thiers. If we give MONEY, the one rival where the jesuits are concerned.

APPENDIX A

TESTAMENTS[1]

I give and bequeath this manuscript concerning the story of my life to M. Alphonse Levavasseur; after him, to M. H[enr]y Fournier and successively to Messrs Amyot, Paulin, Wurtz, Philarète Chasles, on condition that all the women's names be carefully changed and no men's names be changed, and that it not be published, if worth the trouble, until fifteen years after my demise.

Rome, 29 November 1835.

H. BEYLE.

I bequeath and give this manuscript *Life of Henri Brulard*, etc., and all those relating to the story of my life, to M. Ab[ra-ham] Constantin, Ch[evali]er of the Légion d'Honneur, and, if he does not publish it, to M. Alphonse Levavasseur, book-seller, Place Vendôme, and, if he dies before me, I bequeath it *successively* to Messrs Ladvocat, Fournier, Amyot, Treuttel and Wurtz, Didot, on condition: 1. that before publishing this manuscript they change all the women's names: where I have put Pauline Sirot, they will put Adèle Bonnet[2]; it will be

---

1. Stendhal left no fewer than seven of these "Testaments" with the manuscript of *Henry Brulard*. The three I have omitted here merely repeat in slightly different form the conditions laid down in those translated.

2. Needless to say, these names are both equally fictitious and appear nowhere else in Stendhal's writings.

sufficient to take the names from the next list of jurymen; in short, absolutely all the women's proper names must be changed and no man's name.

Second condition: copies to be sent to the libraries of Edinburgh, Philadelphia, New York, Mexico, Madrid and Brunswick. Change all the women's names, a condition *sine qua non*.

Civita-Vecchia, 29 November 1835.

H. BEYLE.

I bequeath and give the present volume to M. le Ch[evali]er Abraham Constantin (of Geneva), painter on porcelain. If M. Constantin has not had it published within the thousand days following my demise, I bequeath and give this volume successively to Messrs Alphonse Levavasseur, bookseller, No 16 Place Vendôme, Philarète Chasles, man of letters, Henry Fournier, bookseller, Rue de Seine, Paulin, bookseller, Delaunay, bookseller; and if none of these gentlemen finds it in his own interest to have it published within the five years following my demise, I leave this volume to the oldest of the booksellers living in London whose name starts with a C.

Civita-Vecchia, 24 December 1835.

H. [BEYL]E.

I demand (*sine qua non conditio*) that all the women's names be changed before publication. I count on this precaution and on the distance in time to prevent any scandal.

Civita-Vecchia, 31 December 1835.

H. BEYLE.

APPENDIX B

THE PRIVILEGES[1]

Rome, April 10 [18]40
May G O D grant me the following letters patent:

ARTICLE 1

Never any serious physical pain until an advanced old age: then not pain, but death, from apoplexy, in bed during sleep without moral or physical pain. Each year, not more than three days of indisposition. The *corpus* and what comes out of it odourless.

ARTICLE 2

The following miracles will be neither seen nor suspected by anyone.

ARTICLE 3

The *mentula*,[2] like the index finger, in hardness and movement; this at will. Shape two inches longer than the toe, same fatness. But pleasure from the *mentula* only twice a week. Twenty times a year the privilege-holder will be able to turn himself into the person he wishes to be provided that person exists. A hundred times a year he will know for twenty-four hours whatever language he wishes.

---

1. This remarkable and revealing text was written by Stendhal in Rome in April 1840, two years before his death. It was published for the first time in 1861. It is evidence no doubt that his youthful fondness for rêverie, and for magicking into existence conditions of life far more congenial to him than those he had been forced to endure in reality, was far from dead even at the age of fifty-seven.

2. "The male member."

ARTICLE 4

Miracle. The privilege-holder having a ring on his finger and squeezing that ring when looking at a woman, she will become passionately in love with him as we believe Héloïse was with Abelard. If the ring is slightly moistened with saliva, the woman looked at will become only a tender and devoted friend. Looking at a woman and removing a ring from the finger, the sentiments inspired by virtue of the preceding privileges will cease. Dislike turns into benevolence on looking at the person disliked and rubbing a ring on the finger. These miracles will only be able to take place four times a year for an amorous passion, eight times for friendship, twenty times for a dislike to cease, and fifty times for inspiring a simple benevolence.

ARTICLE 5

Good hair, excellent teeth, good skin never grazed. Faint, pleasing smell. On 1 February and 1 June each year the privilege-holder's clothes will become as if it were the third time he has worn them.

ARTICLE 6

Miracles. In the eyes of all those who do not know me, the privilege-holder will have the form of General Debelle who died in Saint-Domingue, but no imperfections.[3] He will play whist, écarté, billiards, chess, perfectly, but will never be able to win more than a hundred francs; he will shoot with a pistol, ride and fence to perfection.

ARTICLE 7

Miracle. Four times a year he will be able to turn himself into the animal he wishes, and then turn himself back again into a man. Four times a year he will be able to turn himself into

3. This army general came from near Grenoble and was once described as "the handsomest man in France."

the man he wishes; plus, to concentrate his life in that of an animal which, in the event of the death or objection of the man No 1 into whom he has turned himself, will be able to restore him to the natural shape of the privilege-holder. Thus the privilege-holder will be able four times a year and for an unlimited period each time to occupy two bodies at once.

ARTICLE 8

Whenever the man privileged is wearing about him or on his finger for two minutes a ring he has carried for a moment in his mouth, he will become invulnerable for the period he has nominated. Ten times a year he will have the eyesight of an eagle and will be able to cover five leagues in one hour running.

ARTICLE 9

Each day at two o'clock in the morning the privilege-holder will find in his pocket a gold napoleon, plus a current coin of the country in which he finds himself to the value of forty francs. The sums that have been stolen from him will be rediscovered the following night, at two o'clock in the morning, on a table in front of him. At the moment of striking him, or giving him poison, murderers will suffer an acute attack of cholera lasting a week. The privilege-holder will be able to cut short these sufferings by saying: "I ask that the sufferings of so and so cease, or be changed into such and such a lesser affliction." Thieves will be struck down by an acute attack of cholera lasting two days, at the moment they begin to commit the theft.

ARTICLE 10

When out shooting, eight times a year, a small flag will indicate to the privilege-holder, at a distance of one league, the game that exists and its exact position. One second before the fowling-piece goes off, the small flag will be luminous; it is clearly understood that this small flag will be invisible to all but the privilege-holder.

ARTICLE 11

A similar flag will indicate to the privilege-holder statues hidden under the earth, under water and by walls; what statues they are, when and by whom they were made and the price one might get for them once discovered. The privilege-holder will be able to turn these statues into a lead ball a quarter of an ounce in weight. This miracle of the flag and the successive changes, into a ball and into a statue, can take place only eight times a year.

ARTICLE 12

The animal on which the privilege-holder is mounted, or pulling the vehicle that is carrying him, will never be sick, will never fall. The privilege-holder will be able to become one with this animal, in such a way as to inspire it with his wishes and share its sensations. Thus, the privilege-holder when riding on a horse will form one with it and inspire it with his wishes. The animal, thus made one with the privilege-holder, will have a strength and vigour three times that which it possesses in its normal state.

The privilege-holder having been turned into a fly, for example, and mounted on an eagle, will form one with that eagle.

ARTICLE 13

The privilege-holder will not be able to refuse an obstacle; should he try to do so, his organs would debar him from such an action. He will be able to kill ten human beings a year; but no human being to whom he has spoken. For the first year, he will be able to kill one human being, provided he has not addressed him on more than two different occasions.

ARTICLE 14

If the privilege-holder wished to recount or reveal one of the articles of his privilege, his mouth would be unable to form any sound, and he would suffer from toothache for twenty-four hours.

ARTICLE 15

The privilege-holder, putting a ring on his finger and saying: "I ask that harmful insects be annihilated," all insects within six metres of the ring, in every direction, will be struck dead. These insects are fleas, bedbugs, lice of all kinds, crabs, gnats, flies, rats, etc., etc.

Serpents, vipers, lions, tigers, wolves and all poisonous animals, will take flight, seized by fear, and remove themselves to a distance of one league.

ARTICLE 16

The privilege-holder, wherever he may be, having said: "I ask for my food," will find: two pounds of bread, a beefsteak well done, a leg of lamb *idem*, a bottle of Saint-Julien, a carafe of water, one item of fruit, an ice-cream and a *demi-tasse* of coffee. This request will be answered twice in twenty-four hours.

ARTICLE 17

Ten times a year, on demand, the privilege-holder will not miss the target he wishes to hit with a shot from a gun, a shot from a pistol, or a blow with any weapon whatsoever.

Ten times a year, he will wield his weapon with a strength double that of whoever he is fighting or trying his strength against; but he will be unable to inflict a wound causing death, pain or discomfort, for more than a hundred hours.

ARTICLE 18

Ten times a year, on demand, the privilege-holder will be able to reduce by three-quarters the pain of someone whom he sees, or, this person being at the point of death, will be able to prolong his life by ten days, by reducing his current pain by three-quarters. He will be able, on demand, to obtain for this sufferer a sudden and painless death.

ARTICLE 19
The privilege-holder will be able to turn a dog into a woman, beautiful or ugly; this woman will give him her arm and will have the degree of wit of Mme Ancilla and the heart of Mélanie. This miracle will be able to be renewed twenty times each year.

The privilege-holder will be able to turn a dog into a man, who will have the physical appearance of Pépin de Bellisle, and the wit of [*a blank*] (the Jewish doctor).

ARTICLE 20
The privilege-holder will never be more unhappy than he was from 1 August 1839 until 1 April 1840.

Two hundred times a year, the privilege-holder will be able to reduce his sleep to two hours, which will produce the physical effects of eight hours. He will have the eyesight of a lynx and the agility of Deburau.[4]

ARTICLE 21
Twenty times a year, the privilege-holder will be able to divine the thoughts of all the persons around him, at a distance of twenty paces. One hundred times a year, he will be able to see what whoever he wishes is currently doing; wholly excluded will be the woman he loves the most. Also excluded will be dirty and disgusting actions.

ARTICLE 22
The privilege-holder will be unable to earn any money, other than his sixty francs a day, by means of the privileges stated above. One hundred and fifty times a year, he will be able to

---

4. A celebrated mime and tightrope-walker of the day, whose part was taken by Jean-Louis Barrault in the classic French movie, *Les Enfants du paradis*.

arrange so that, on demand, such and such a person should entirely forget him, the privilege-holder.

ARTICLE 23

Ten times a year, the privilege-holder will be able to be transported to the location he wishes, at a speed of one hundred leagues per hour; while being transported he will sleep.

ABOUT THE TYPE

The text of this book has been set in Trump Mediaeval. Designed by Georg Trump for the Weber foundry in the late 1950s, this typeface is a modern rethinking of the Garalde Oldstyle types (often associated with Claude Garamond) that have long been popular with printers and book designers.

Trump Mediaeval is a trademark of
Linotype-Hell AG and/or its subsidiaries

Printed and bound by R. R. Donnelley & Sons,
Harrisonburg, Virginia

TITLES IN SERIES